GREAT

ENJOY THE WORLD AT YOUR LEISURE

ESCAPES

CONTENTS

INTRODUCTION 6

THE PERFECT GETAWAY

The shadows dance in the candlelight. Musical strains from a mariachi band float across the cemetery as the painted midnight revellers laugh and chat and dance and sing. Some people choose to perch on the graves in silent vigil. Most, however, are a little livelier in their celebration of the dead.

It's dark and eerie at the graveyard in Oaxaca, but the night is just beginning; this will party stretch on until dawn. It's the Day of the Dead, Mexico's annual festival to honour family and friends who have passed away. It's an evening spent in the company of those loved ones down at the cemetery, celebrating their lives and the things they held dear. It's ghoulish costumes and dark shapes in the night. It's tequila and mescal and the joy of friends.

It's also about as far from the world most people know as you could possibly get, a sometimes bizarre escape from the daily norm. Want to get away from the routine of home? Want to have your world so shaken, your soul so inspired that you return feeling like a different person? Then a night in a cemetery in Oaxaca during Day of the Dead is not a bad place to start.

It's not, however, everyone's idea of a great escape. And it doesn't have to be. There's a whole world of options available.

Cut to a beach in French Polynesia, one of those arcs of white sand that kiss the sapphire water of the Pacific Ocean. There's not a soul around, no one to disturb the peace of a tropical island and time to spend in the sun. This is Tikehau, an atoll that barely pokes its head above the wide expanse of the ocean, and it is home to a private resort offering seemingly unending solitude.

There are activities available on Tikehau if you want them. You can surf the breaks that crash into the coral fangs that ring the island. You can scuba dive among swirling schools of tropical fish. Or you can just wander the beaches soaking up the sun. As a brief break from the norm it's as spectacular as the revelry in the Mexican cemetery, but a completely different experience – one of solitude and relaxation rather than cultural fascination. It's an escape from reality nonetheless.

And that's what this book is all about: escape. Over the course of these pages you'll find holiday escapes of all shapes and sizes, from romantic weekends to gastronomic adventures to big-city

getaways. Whether you're holidaying as a family, a couple, a group of friends or going solo – you'll find ideas to inspire your next short break, or an interlude during a longer trip. These exciting experiences share the common thread of enjoyment and difference, a way to break up life's routine with something special, something out of the ordinary.

Some people prefer to experience that enjoyment through adventure, by kayaking across an archipelago, touring Thailand on a motorbike, or rounding up cattle at a ranch in Montana. Others want to let loose and party, bar-hopping through pulsating Tokyo, dancing on the sand in Hvar, or soaking up the music in New Orleans. And then there are times when you just want to get away from it all, from civilisation entirely, working on body and mind in a yoga retreat in Bali, or sleeping under the stars on a houseboat in Kerala, India.

These escapes can be discombobulating riots of colour if you want it, or they can be the complete absence of the things that stimulate the mind. A break to make you think, or a break to make you stop. Whatever your pleasure, whatever form it takes, an escape is a chance to reassess your life, to recharge your batteries, to so completely divorce yourself from normality that by the time you return to the nine-to-five grind you've forgotten all of your passwords. This is the chance to have an experience that will alter the way you look at the world, and perhaps even the way you look at yourself.

These journeys are not lengthy. We're talking mere days. A long weekend. Travel at its best doesn't have to be an epic adventure. It can be a perfectly planned mini-break, a couple of days to discover something different from the daily routine.

That can be enough time to soak up another culture. Spend a couple of nights in the tapas bars of Andalucia and you're starting to get an understanding of the place, of the locals' passion for flamenco dance and the heart and soul that goes into the little plates of food. Live a weekend in Berlin and you'll find enough time to be inspired by its thriving creativity, to experience a city that caters to every quirk and whim imaginable.

It's also enough time to disconnect. Whether that's achieved in a monastery in Mallorca or at Ian Fleming's Jamaican villa is up to you. It's enough time, too, to taste the flavours of the world, from the hawker food in Penang to Chile's world-class wines.

And, of course, it's enough time to take in something so completely alien that you'll be pondering the experience for months afterwards. Something like the Day of the Dead. Something like drinking tequila in a graveyard in the middle of the night while those around you pay their respects to the dead by celebrating the joy of life.

That's something different. A great escape.

BEN GROUNDWATER
Peru, May 2013

CULTURE

CHECK OUT CHICAGO'S ARCHITECTURE

CHICAGO IS AN ARCHITECTURAL MECCA, BRISTLING WITH BUILDINGS BY THE STARCHITECTS OF TODAY AND HOME TO THE WORK AND STUDIOS OF PAST MASTERS LOUIS SULLIVAN, FRANK LLOYD WRIGHT AND MIES VAN DER ROHE.

10

The panorama from Chicago's Millennium Park is of world-class architecture. Start with Frank Gehry's Jay Pritzker Pavilion, with its twisting chrome segments rippling across the lawn, then turn to the right to be greeted by a glittering plane of blades: Renzo Piano's Modern Wing of the Art Institute. Turn a little further and Adler & Sullivan's 1889 Auditorium Building on South Michigan Ave is visible in the distance, as Anish Kapoor's chrome sculpture *Cloud Gate* hovers like an alien blimp waiting to show you around the city that gave birth to the skyscraper, Chicago blues, house music, the Cubs and the *Oprah Winfrey Show*.

Chicago's pioneering skyscraper architecture, dating from the end of the 19th century is known as the Chicago School, and architect Louis Sullivan was one of its most notable practitioners. Buildings by Sullivan reveal themselves as you stroll through downtown Chicago, with intricate explosions of ornamentation cast across monumental commercial buildings. Wander in any direction and you will come across a building or two by Mies van der Rohe, whose work is attributed to the Second Chicago School of the mid-20th century – minimalistic black towers of glass and steel that inspired modernist architecture across the globe. However, it's not just the world's finest skyscrapers that entice the archi-tourist to Chicago. Frank Lloyd Wright, one of the 20th century's most famous architects and a pupil of Sullivan's, has given the region a suite of prairie-style homes that are furnished with his own designs and open to the public.

The city's appeal goes far beyond its buildings. From the 1940s to the 1970s Chicago was a hothouse for blues music, and then in the 1980s it became the crucible for house music, thanks to local radio stations, DJs and artists such as Larry Heard. Music is still at the heart of Chicago and no escape would be complete without a nocturnal adventure in sound.

ESSENTIAL EXPERIENCES

* **Immersing yourself in the Art Institute of Chicago's renowned collections of Impressionist, post-Impressionist, American and contemporary art.**

* Touring Frank Lloyd Wright's home and studio – a fascinating place filled with the details that made the architect's style distinctive.

* **Catching a Cubs baseball game at home stadium Wrigley Field.**

* Strolling the campus of the Illinois Institute of Technology's College of Architecture in Bronzeville, studded with architectural gems by the likes of Rem Koolhaas, Helmut Jahn and Mies van der Rohe.

* **Dining with a live blues act in a downtown club such as Rosa's Lounge, or tapping your toe at a blues gig on revitalised Motor Row (South Michigan Ave).**

LOCATION CHICAGO, ILLINOIS, USA | **BEST TIME OF YEAR** APRIL THROUGH OCTOBER | **IDEAL TIME COMMITMENT** A WEEKEND OR A WEEK | **ESSENTIAL TIP** DON'T MISS THE CHICAGO-STYLE BEEF SANDWICH (AND THE VIEW!) AT THE SIGNATURE LOUNGE ATOP THE JOHN HANCOCK CENTER | **BUDGET** $$ | **PACK** SOMETHING SMART TO WEAR OUT AT NIGHT: CHICAGOANS ARE VERY STYLISH

AL CAPONE, KING OF CHICAGO

Al Capone, history's most renowned mobster, may have been born in New York City, but it was after moving to Chicago that the young criminal made his mark. Exploiting the Prohibition Era of the 1920s to smuggle and bootleg alcohol, while also involved in other illegal ventures such as gambling and prostitution, Capone was able to lead the crime empire known as 'the Outfit' to great success, generating hundreds of millions of dollars in revenue annually. Capone's support of charities made him a popular figure in Chicago, but his involvement in a mob-related shooting in 1929 tarnished his image. Capone was eventually convicted on tax offences and languished in Alcatraz prison from 1931 to 1939, before dying at home in 1947.

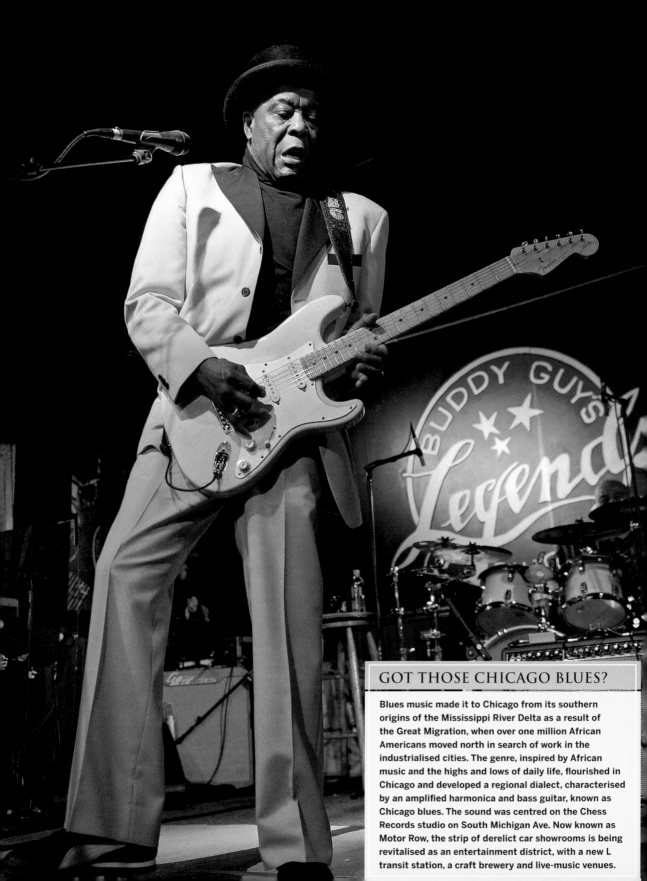

GOT THOSE CHICAGO BLUES?

Blues music made it to Chicago from its southern origins of the Mississippi River Delta as a result of the Great Migration, when over one million African Americans moved north in search of work in the industrialised cities. The genre, inspired by African music and the highs and lows of daily life, flourished in Chicago and developed a regional dialect, characterised by an amplified harmonica and bass guitar, known as Chicago blues. The sound was centred on the Chess Records studio on South Michigan Ave. Now known as Motor Row, the strip of derelict car showrooms is being revitalised as an entertainment district, with a new L transit station, a craft brewery and live-music venues.

THE PERFECT GETAWAY

Arriving at the Art Institute of Chicago on South Michigan Ave with coffee in hand, a takeaway from Così a block north, you decide to leave the Impressionists for tomorrow and focus on the most unexpected permanent collection you could imagine in a city with the largest buildings in the Midwest. The exquisite Thorne Miniature Rooms, of which there are 68, are delicately crafted interiors at 1:12 scale, covering European design from the 13th century and American design from the 17th century through until the 1930s, when the models were made.

Before heading north to one of the steakhouses by Mariano Park for lunch, you duck across the road to the Chicago Architecture Foundation. Here you will find architecture enthusiasts who can sell you Gehry fridge magnets, organise tickets for the architecture cruise on the Chicago River and answer your every Chicago question. Grab a ticket for tomorrow's bus trip to the neighbourhood where Frank Lloyd Wright lived and worked from 1889 to 1909; opt for the tour that takes in Wright's own home and studio and includes a walking tour of Oak Park – a picturesque residential area where many prairie-style homes by Wright are on show – culminating in a tour of Wright's charmingly detailed Unity Temple.

As light fades you jump on the L, the rail network elevated above the streets of Chicago's inner Loop district, and travel on the red line north to Addison station; it's only a short walk to Wrigley Field. While enjoying a Cubs baseball game you notice the scoreboard being operated by hand, the numbered plates carefully interchanged, and it becomes apparent the effort Chicagoans have invested, both today and in the many years past, in building their city and making it work.

PLAN IT

Chicago's O'Hare International Airport is 30km from downtown Chicago; catch a cab, train or bus into the city centre. Consider a B&B or homestay (booked through websites such as www.airbnb.com) in one of Chicago's elegant inner suburbs, such as Lakeview or Oak Park; good public transport allows you to expand your accommodation search beyond downtown. The Chicago Architecture Foundation is open daily until 6pm; the river cruise is offered in the warmer months. The Cubs play at Wrigley Field from April to September; book tickets well ahead.

DETOUR

Mies van der Rohe's seminal work, Farnsworth House, is considered one of modernism's masterpieces. Built in 1951, the home is a perfect expression of Mies' modernist ideal of architecture reduced to its straight-lined essence. Located near Plano, just over an hour's drive west of Chicago, Farnsworth House can be reached by car or train, or on bus tours such as those run by the Chicago Architecture Foundation.

13

OPENING SPREAD The Windy City, where the world's first skyscraper was built. **ABOVE (L)** Chicago's Museum of Contemporary Art is a design delight. **ABOVE (R)** Right back at you: Anish Kapoor's *Cloud Gate* sculpture. **LEFT** Blues legend Buddy Guy performing at his own venue on S Wabash Ave.

DECKCHAIR

* *The Blues Brothers* (1980) Seek out the film locations for this 1980s classic around the Loop district. The soundtrack is pure Chicago.

* *Ferris Bueller's Day Off* (1986) This 1980s teen flick takes it to the streets of Chicago.

* *High Fidelity* (2000) One of the most popular movies set in the Windy City is actually based on a book set in London.

* *High-Rise* (JG Ballard) This dark fiction depicts a high-rise community in social free-fall.

* *The Fountainhead* (Ayn Rand) The story of one man's modernist architectural vision pitched against the world.

* *Grand Obsessions* (Alastair McGregor) Follow the journey of two of Frank Lloyd Wright's finest protégés, Walter Burley Griffin and Marion Mahony, in this epic biography.

FLAMENCO AND TAPAS IN ANDALUCÍA

THE TRIANGLE OF LAND IN WESTERN ANDALUCÍA BETWEEN THE CITIES OF SEVILLE, JEREZ DE LA FRONTERA AND CÁDIZ IS ONE OF THE MOST CULTURALLY FERTILE REGIONS IN SPAIN, WITH MULTIPLE OFFERINGS TO SATISFY THE EARS, SOUL AND STOMACH.

14

It's Friday night in Seville. In a dark flamenco club a crowd of revellers sticks toothpicks into a tray of tapas, raises a toast with glasses of crisp, dry sherry, and turns back towards the stage. The show, which had begun rather inauspiciously 30 minutes earlier, is reaching its climax, deflecting people's attention away from plates of nutty cured ham and forcing them to lean forward in their chairs and listen. After a melancholic opening, the music has become quicker-paced and frenetic, the trio of dancer, singer and guitarist linking intuitively to create an explosive wall of sound and energy which they feed back to the hungry audience.

The drama builds with every chord, the dancer's shoes driving hard against the floorboards and the gravel-voiced singer working into an operatic crescendo. Shouts of encouragement are offered from the onlookers. The guitarist glides through a fast, mesmerising solo. Fingers blur. Feet stomp. Somebody yells óle, and then suddenly the show is over – all that is left is a pleasant ringing in the ears and the notion that an epiphany has taken place.

When wine, food and music conspire, it can be a powerful experience. In Andalucía you can experience all three on the same night – and in the same bar too, if you're lucky. Tapas were allegedly invented in Andalucía's taverns several hundred years ago, after patrons began putting small slices of food over their wine glasses to keep flies out. Sherry's origins are even older: the Phoenicians, Romans and Moors cultivated vineyards in the Jerez region, although it was the British penchant for fortified wine in the 19th century that financed the trade. Flamenco is virtually a synonym for Andalucía, a fusion of Byzantium hymns, Spanish folk songs, Jewish chants and the musical rhythms of Roma people. As with most home-grown inventions, nothing rivals experiencing them in the land of their genesis – in particular Andalucía's charismatic capital, Seville.

ESSENTIAL EXPERIENCES

* **Taking a tour of a Jerez sherry *bodega* and educating your palate with some sherry tasting.**

* Attending an Andalucian festival, such as Seville's Feria de Abril – one of the most popular celebrations in Spain – or Jerez' annual February flamenco festival.

* **Bar-hopping in Santa Cruz, Seville's medieval Jewish quarter, which hides countless packed-to-the-rafters tapas bars.**

* Circumnavigating Cádiz' romantic seawall on foot and visiting its forts and baroque cathedral.

* **Finding peace in the Eden-like gardens of the Alcázar of Seville and inhaling the scent of orange blossom.**

* Stumbling on a high-spirited flamenco show in a backstreet bar or – even better – a *peña flamenca* (private club).

LOCATION SEVILLE, SPAIN | **BEST TIME OF YEAR** MARCH THROUGH MAY | **IDEAL TIME COMMITMENT** FOUR OR FIVE DAYS | **ESSENTIAL TIP** ANDALUCIANS DINE AND GO OUT LATE (FROM 9PM); ADJUST YOUR TIME CLOCK TO ENSURE YOU'RE NOT MISSING OUT ON THE BEST NIGHTLIFE | **BUDGET** $$ | **PACK** COMFORTABLE WALKING SHOES, SUNSCREEN, CASUAL 'GOING OUT' CLOTHES

SHERRY IN JEREZ

Jerez de la Frontera, 75 minutes from Seville by bus or train, is Andalucía's beating heart. The city is the first stop on the famed 'sherry triangle' and, despite counter-claims from Cádiz and Seville, the recognised cradle of flamenco. Sherry – a very Spanish drink concocted for very English tastes – can be quaffed in one of the city's 20 illustrious sherry bodegas, or at a more down-to-earth backstreet bar with accompanying tapas. For flamenco, listen out in the historic bars of Calle Francos or enquire about venues and shows at the Centro Andaluz de Flamenco, a flamenco library and resource centre – the only one of its kind in Spain.

TAPAS IN SEVILLE

Seville's bars usually chalk up their tapa menus on a blackboard above the counter with dishes offered in three different sizes: bite-sized tapas, *media raciones* (half plates) or *raciones* (full plates). It is nearly always cheaper to eat standing at the bar than sitting down at a table. Aside from the standard Spanish fare, Seville has several local specialities, including *huevos a la flamenca* (eggs baked with chorizo and tomato sauce), *espinacas con garbanzos* (spinach with chickpeas), *gazpacho* (a cold tomato-based soup made with bread, garlic and olive oil) and *jamón ibérico* (a succulent cured ham from nearby Huelva province).

◾ THE PERFECT GETAWAY

Get comfortable in a historic hotel in Seville's Santa Cruz quarter, an ideal place from which to plan sorties. You could fill two mornings seeing Seville's weightiest sights: its gothic cathedral and the Moorish Alcázar (royal palace complex); the monuments face each other across the Plaza de Triunfo. If you're going tapas hunting in the evening, opt for a sit-down lunch around 2pm; restaurants full of swinging hams and dusty wine bottles are two-a-penny around the Plaza de la Alfalfa. Many Sevillanos enjoy a siesta between 3pm and 5pm. They wake up for a *merienda* at 5pm – a snack with coffee and cake.

Sitting pretty in medieval Santa Cruz is the Museo del Baile Flamenco, which provides an interesting prelude to a night of music. Seville's nightlife rarely kicks off before 9pm when hungry music lovers head towards a *tablao* or bar. *Tablaos* are choreographed, if touristy, flamenco shows; Tablao El Arenal in the eponymous riverside district stages some of the most authentic performances.

For greater spontaneity cruise the city's bars for tapas and live music. Some of the most fashionable places are in the Alameda de Hércules to the north. Here you can sample nouveau tapas, such as pork ribs in honey and rosemary glaze, or spicy Asian green chicken. More bars crowd the Santa Cruz quarter, home of famed flamenco venue La Carbonería, where the tapas are cheap and the music's free. Triana is another nexus: the old Roma neighbourhood on the banks of the Guadalquivir river buzzes with alfresco action until late. Close by are the city's more traditional flamenco venues, including Casa Anselma, a rambunctious bar where they don't uncork the sherry and tune up their guitars until past midnight.

◾ PLAN IT

Seville's climate is pleasant year-round. The city is at its most ebullient during its festivals in March and April. Seville International Airport is 10km northeast of the centre; airlines link it with London and other European cities. Regular buses run to the city. Seville has hotels in all categories; places fill up (and treble their prices) for festivals. Book ahead! Santa Cruz and El Arenal are the most sought-after neighbourhoods, but beware of bag snatchers.

◾ DETOUR

Sample Andalucía's food, drink and flamenco further in Cádiz, one of Europe's oldest cities, founded by Phoenicians 3000 years ago. Cádiz sits on a sinuous peninsula and is coveted for its fish restaurants, the best of which inhabit the gritty Viña quarter. Its flamenco tradition emanates from the grizzled Santa María neighbourhood, where the city's signature songs, called *alegrías,* can be heard at Peña Flamenca La Perla, perched beside the wave-lashed seawall. Cádiz also has several historic forts and a stash of raffish seafaring bars to explore.

OPENING SPREAD Flamenco in Seville isn't just about dancing; there's singing and guitar playing too. **ABOVE (L)** Very moreish: savoury *jamón ibérico* and a pale, dry sherry. **ABOVE (R)** The Hall of the Ambassadors in Seville's Alcázar. **LEFT** Drop into El Rinconcillo tapas bar, which dates from 1670.

DECKCHAIR

* ❋ ***Duende: A Journey in Search of Flamenco*** (Jason Webster) A British-American writer becomes embroiled in the intriguing, traditionally closed world of flamenco.

* ❋ ***Driving over Lemons*** (Chris Stewart) Insightful and humorous take on Andalucía through the eyes of a British expat.

* ❋ ***Collected Poems: A Bilingual Edition*** (Federico García Lorca) Spain's ultimate poet: evocative, provocative and Andalucian to his core.

* ❋ ***The Ornament of the World*** (María Rosa Menocal) The History of Moorish Al-Andalus (711–1492) in one readable volume.

* ❋ ***Dining Secrets of Andalucía*** (Jon Clarke) Definitive dining guide to the region.

* ❋ ***Camarón*** (2005) A biopic of Camarón de la Isla, the greatest modern flamenco singer.

A CULTURE SPREE IN BERLIN

WHEN BERLIN BECAME THE CAPITAL OF REUNIFIED GERMANY IN 1999, THE CITY WAS TO BE A CORPORATE SHOWCASE OF NATIONAL PRESTIGE. BUT BERLIN CHOSE THE ARTS OVER FINANCE. EDGY, EDUCATED AND ELEGIAC, IT'S NOW A CULTURAL HONEY POT, WITH MANY OF THE WORLD'S STANDOUT MUSEUMS.

As fire rendered the Reichstag a smouldering ruin in 1933, it was a sad omen of the devastation to come. But now the building is Berlin's gleaming monument to reunification, topped by a glass dome courtesy of Sir Norman Foster. With a 360-degree view over Berlin's skyline, the home of the Bundestag (Germany's parliament) is the place to come and survey the revitalised German capital.

Look out from the dome, and on one side there's the Hamburger Bahnhof, a contemporary art museum in an old railway station. To the other is Unter den Linden, Berlin's historic artery, leading down to the Unesco-listed Museumsinsel (Museum Island). Gaze across the Tiergarten, Berlin's graceful park, to spot the Kulturforum arts complex. In Berlin, culture dominates. The city hosts some 180 museums, three opera houses, 150 theatres, 130 cinemas, eight symphony orchestras and upwards of 1500 events a day. You can spend months here and not exhaust the possibilities – one of the reasons why the city is a great draw to contemporary artists, turning the city into a creative global powerhouse.

There are reasons why Berlin is so rich in culture. Partly it's because of the showboating following reunification, partly because architect-planner Karl Friedrich Schinkel wanted to turn it into a worthy capital of Prussia in the early 19th century – and partly because Berlin was divided from 1961 to 1989, giving it two of everything. But Berlin itself is a living museum. Walk the streets and you'll feel a sense of the great 20th-century battles, some of which have left bullet holes. There's plenty of public art and some of the world's most concentrated and rewarding cultural zones anywhere – most notably Museumsinsel, sitting like an artistic fortress in the Spree river. After 1990, Berlin had expected to be the commercial centre of Europe. Instead, it became the cultural centre – and mammon's loss has been the art-loving traveller's gain.

ESSENTIAL EXPERIENCES

* **Walking through six millennia of art history at Museumsinsel (Museum Island).**

* Strolling down Unter den Linden – one of Europe's richest historical boulevards.

* **Climbing wartime history at the Brandenburg Gate and the Reichstag – Berlin's triumphal gate and parliament building.**

* Remembering recent history at the Jüdisches Museum (Jewish Museum): a Daniel Libeskind–designed icon that changed the face of museums.

* **Gazing at the masters at the Gemäldegalerie, one of the world's best art collections in the world, featuring Rembrandt, Titian, Goya, Botticelli, Holbein, Rubens, Vermeer...**

* Chilling in the Tiergarten, an 18th-century hunting-ground-turned-park offering respite from a sometimes bleak city.

* **Strolling down west Berlin's great shopping strip, the Kurfürstendamm, or Ku'damm.**

LOCATION GERMANY | **BEST TIME OF YEAR** MUSEUMS ARE OPEN YEAR-ROUND BUT IT'S BITTERLY COLD IN WINTER; SUMMERS ARE LOVELY | **IDEAL TIME COMMITMENT** THREE DAYS FOR THE HIGHLIGHTS | **ESSENTIAL TIP** PURCHASE A WELCOME CARD FOR SAVINGS ON TRAVEL AND MUSEUMS | **BUDGET** $$ | **PACK** COMFORTABLE SHOES; YOU'LL DO A LOT OF HIKING IN SPREAD-OUT BERLIN

CULTURE BITES

Done Berlin's grand collections? Then try some of its smaller museums. The Brücke Museum in the suburb of Dahlem is a gem, devoted to the early 20th-century artist's group of the same name. The Bauhaus-Archiv in Tiergarten will please fans of the influential 20th-century design school. Don't forget the more absurd offerings: the Currywurst (curried sausage) museum, the football museum and the hilarious DDR Museum, a bittersweet look at life in the former East Germany. And old punks won't want to miss the Ramones museum in East Berlin, a fan's tribute to the 'Fast Four'.

OH, CABARET!

Given that many of Berlin's tourists have seen the musical *Cabaret,* Berlin has a reputation as a place of theatre and spectacle. But it took until 2009 to re-establish a theatre zone in the city's central district. Now, in the area between Friedrichstrasse, Unter den Linden and Hackescher Markt, four venues – Quatsch Comedy Club, Distel Cabaret Theatre, Friedrichstadt-Palast and the Chamäleon theatre – come together to form the nucleus of a new theatre district. The area is Berlin's own theatreland, in one of Mitte's most atmospheric neighbourhoods. Very Sally Bowles.

■ THE PERFECT GETAWAY

Start at street level – Berlin rewards the flâneur. At the Holocaust Memorial, by the Reichstag, you'll see 2711 grey stelae – great funereal slabs of concrete by New York architect Peter Eisenman. Then stroll via the Brandenburg Gate down Unter den Linden to Bebelplatz, where the Nazis burned books in 1933, and through a window in the cobbles view the underground empty library installation by Israeli artist Micha Ullman. From here it's a brisk hike to the Topographie des Terrors, an open-air exhibition atop the bulldozed Gestapo's Berlin headquarters, next to one of the few remaining parts of the Berlin Wall.

Further down Friedrichstrasse, the Jüdisches Museum (Jewish Museum) is as famous for its Daniel Libeskind design as for its content, and culminates in the Holocaust Tower: empty space surrounded by dramatic shards of concrete. Nearby, in a glass depot, is the Berlinische Galerie. With artists like Otto Dix and George Grosz, it's a heady evocation of Berlin's 1920s and '30s – the decadent Weimar years that are so captivating.

You'll need a fortifying lunch: try the bohemian areas of Kreuzberg and Hackescher Markt in Mitte (the old town). Back on Unter den Linden, go to the Spree river to find Museumsinsel: this ensemble of five treasure houses is the city's cultural highlight, with the Altes Museum (Old Museum) by Karl Friedrich Schinkel at its heart, augmented by the Neues Museum (New Museum), Alte Nationalgalerie (Old National Gallery), Bodemuseum and Pergamonmuseum – including the stupendous Pergamonaltar, taken in its entirety from Asia Minor. Here, you can run through 6000 years of world civilisation. Stupendous, but true.

■ PLAN IT

Most visitors arrive via Berlin's two international airports. Use the U-Bahn and S-Bahn underground trains to get around. Arts events happen year-round; standout festivals include the new Berlin Art Week and the Berlin International Film Festival. Berlin's Long Night of Museums takes place twice a year; venues open their doors until 2am.

■ DETOUR

Half an hour outside Berlin is Potsdam, a town renowned for its role in the post–World War II carve-up. It remains the only East German town to have experienced population growth after reunification. In the 18th-century Dutch quarter, look out for quaint shops with green shutters, and stroll around the lake – during the Cold War, these waters were patrolled by gunboats – then go to the Glienicke Bridge, the old rendezvous for spy-swaps. Cecilienhof, the mock-English villa where Churchill, Stalin and Truman met in August 1945 to finalise Europe's post-war settlement, is now a hotel with plentiful memorabilia.

OPENING SPREAD The Bode-Museum, at the head of Museum Island, houses works from the Middle Ages to the 18th century. **ABOVE** The grand and the gritty: the Bode-Museum and a street cafe in the neighbourhood of Mitte, Berlin's theatreland. **LEFT** Dressed to impress: backstage at a cabaret in Mitte.

DECKCHAIR

* ***Goodbye to Berlin*** (Christopher Isherwood) The book that gave rise to the film *Cabaret*, and a brilliant evocation of Berlin in the pulsating interwar years.

* ***Berlin Alexanderplatz*** (Alfred Döblin) Protagonist Franz Biberkopf ducks and dives on the streets of Weimar-era Berlin. Also a film.

* ***The Lives of Others*** (2006) The vicious atmosphere of Stasi-run East Berlin is nailed by director Florian Henckel von Donnersmarck.

* ***The Innocent*** (Ian McEwan) Via hero Leonard Markham, McEwan evokes the Berlin of 1955.

* ***Stasiland*** (Anna Funder) Funder's breakthrough book is a great portrait of East Germany's secret police.

* ***Funeral in Berlin*** (Len Deighton) Great Cold War potboiler that gave rise to a film, starring Michael Caine as Harry Palmer.

SALSA MAGIC IN SANTIAGO DE CUBA

GET YOUR HIPS MOVING ON A CUBAN DANCE FLOOR IF YOU REALLY WANT TO FIND OUT WHAT MAKES THIS ASTONISHING ISLAND TICK. LEARN TO DANCE AND YOU'RE GUARANTEED TO DISCOVER MORE ABOUT THE UNIQUE CULTURAL MIX THAT UNDERPINS LIFE IN THE COOLEST COMMUNIST OUTPOST.

22

You can sense Cuba's musical undercurrent from the moment your plane touches down. Baggage handlers throw suitcases around with a rhythmic flourish and customs officials shimmy in their booths to the tinny splutterings of a wall-mounted loudspeaker. Music is everywhere, and even when it's not playing, most Cuban hips seem to be twitching to a built-in metronome.

To understand the island's people and rich mix of cultures, you really need to step onto a Cuban dance floor. Under the dishevelled colonial arches of a dance school in Santiago de Cuba, you'll take your first steps into the world of salsa, guided by a trained dancer. With one-to-one tuition, moves are built up slowly over the course of a week until you're performing increasingly complex steps, learning to spin with your partner in beguiling grace. There's a dance-school work ethic as once again you 'take it from the top' to perfect each section, but the pay-off comes quickly. Within a few days, early nerves start to give way to a noticeably Latin swagger in the hips and a seductive shimmy in the shoulders. And then comes the cry of *Salsa libre!* from the instructor, the signal that it's time to improvise your moves for the next couple of bars. For some that means a creative and fluid interlude, for others a mess of limbs and helpless laughter.

Broad smiles and tired feet spill out onto the street at the end of a day's class, but your musical adventure continues. Wander the streets and live music is all around you, from the city's world-famous venue, Casa de la Trova, to a host of smaller local bars, giving you plenty of opportunity to finesse your moves. By the final night, while you certainly won't be the hottest dancer in town, you will be able to hold your own on a Cuban dance floor. You'll have a feel for the blend of Spanish *canción* and African rhythms that underpin Cuban son music, and you'll have had an experience that has taken you to the very heart of Cuban life.

ESSENTIAL EXPERIENCES

* **Discovering the rhythms and instruments that go into making son, one of Latin America's most influential forms of music.**

* Sitting in on a band's practise session or discovering musicians honing their skills in bars around town.

* **Learning to dance to traditional Cuban son and testing your skills for real on the dance floors of Santiago de Cuba.**

* Photographing classic American cars with Santiago de Cuba – Cuba's 'most Caribbean city' so they say – as your backdrop.

* **Learning Spanish in formal language lessons, then honing your new language skills in dance lessons.**

* Sampling Cuba's famous rum cocktails and getting the low-down on the history of the hard stuff at the Museo del Ron.

LOCATION SANTIAGO DE CUBA, CUBA | **BEST TIME OF YEAR** SUMMER (JUNE TO AUGUST) IS FESTIVAL SEASON; COOLER WEATHER IN SPRING OR AUTUMN IS BETTER FOR DANCE CLASSES | **IDEAL TIME COMMITMENT** ONE TO TWO WEEKS | **ESSENTIAL TIP** LEARN SOME SPANISH TO GET THE MOST FROM YOUR TRIP | **BUDGET** $$ | **PACK** DANCING SHOES

THE CUBAN BEAT

Cuban son originated in the eastern part of Cuba and is a happy combination of forceful African rhythms and poetic Spanish melody. The ethnomusicologist Fernando Ortiz called it 'a love affair between African drum and Spanish guitar'. The traditional set-up includes six musicians playing guitar, *tres* (a Cuban guitar with three sets of double strings), bass, bongos, claves and maracas. In the 1920s many bands added trumpet to the mix. Cuban son is probably the forerunner of salsa and one of the most influential forms of music in Latin America. You'll find a Casa de la Trova in most large towns – it's the best place to hear it being played live.

SANTERÍA RELIGIOUS BELIEFS

A mixture of African, Catholic and Native American traditions, Santería is a syncretic religion that focuses on building relationships between humans and powerful mortal spirits called *orishas*. Followers believe that if they carry out the right ritual, these spirits will help them fulfil their destiny. But these powerful spirits also rely on their followers. They need to be worshipped and rely on offerings of food and even animal sacrifice if they are to continue to exist. Many orishas are associated with Catholic saints, such as St Barbara, known as Changó, and St Lazarus, known as Babalú-Ayé. There is no holy text or equivalent of the Bible – the beliefs are instead passed on by word of mouth.

■ THE PERFECT GETAWAY

Learning to dance in Cuba isn't just about perfecting salsa moves or discovering the more subtle world of Cuban son. This is an escape for those who want to connect with the real Cuba, and experience as much of the island as possible. And there's no better way to do that than by staying with a Cuban family.

You'll instantly see the stark contrasts between the classic American cars and colonial architecture outside and the austere communist propaganda that forms prime-time TV. You'll see the gulf between younger Cubans, many with their sights set on Florida (a mere 150km away) and an older generation who love Fidel and blame the US trade sanctions for all of Cuba's problems. You'll be introduced to a vibrant and sociable extended family who wander in and out of each other's homes, but you'll also develop a nagging awareness of communist party members who lurk in unexpected places, keeping an eye on the island's ideology.

Cubans love to have fun and they want you to see that side of their country. Make a few friends and you'll soon find yourself being taken into bars to meet musicians or into houses to see bands practise. You'll discover the *tres* (a guitar that takes three sets of double strings), an instrument that gives Cuban music a distinctive sound, and you might even be handed a pair of claves (wooden percussion instruments) and invited to join in. Hang around for a glass of rum or two and you'll notice the African influence that delivers a more rhythmic, vibrant form of music in Santiago de Cuba than other parts of the island. It's also the source of Santería, the local religion that was brought to the island by African slaves and merged with Catholic and Native American traditions.

■ PLAN IT

Antonio Maceo Airport is 7km south of Santiago de Cuba; international flights arrive here from Paris-Orly, Madrid, Milan and Rome on Cubana airlines and from Toronto on Air Transat. There are direct flights from the Cuban capital, Havana, every day. Local families rent rooms – look for the distinctive blue insignia on the door marked 'Arrendador Divisa'. A number of Cuban dance and language specialists can organise visas, rooms and lessons, such as Caledonia Languages.

■ DETOUR

Santiago de Cuba province is home to Cuba's highest mountain, Pico Turquino (1972m). It sits at the heart of the Sierra Maestra and was the stronghold of Fidel Castro and Che Guevara's rebel forces pre-1959. Its cloud forest teems with wildlife, including the world's smallest toad and some astonishing birds. The hike up Pico Turquino starts from Las Cuevas, 130km west of Santiago de Cuba. Hit the summit and you'll find a bust of José Martí, hero of the second independence war.

OPENING SPREAD A guitar and double bass are the foundation of the local son sound. **ABOVE (L)** Pay a visit to the bar La Bodeguita del Medio in Havana. **ABOVE (R)** The rites of Afro-Cuban religions are performed at temples in Santiago de Cuba. **LEFT** Dancing girl: learn the steps at salsa school.

DECKCHAIR

* ***Buena Vista Social Club*** (1999) Documents a group of ageing musicians who take traditional Cuban music to the world.

* ***Dance with Me*** (1998) Contrasts Cuban dancing styles in the tale of a Cuban émigré who opens another world for a ballroom dancer.

* ***Our Man in Havana*** (Graham Greene) The tale of a British vacuum cleaner salesman who enlists in the British secret service and sends in bogus reports that mysteriously start to come true.

* ***Ay, Cuba!*** (Andrei Codrescu) Romanian writer Codrescu visits the 'laboratory of pre-post-communism' to compare the island with his homeland in 1989.

* ***Trading with the Enemy: A Yankee Travels Through Castro's Cuba*** (Tom Miller) Cuban lore gleaned from an eight-month tour of the island.

* ***The Reader's Companion to Cuba*** (edited by Alan Ryan) Collected works of writing on Cuba.

AN IMPRESSION OF MONET'S NORMANDY

INSPIRATIONAL – THAT'S NORMANDY. ITS CLIFFS, CATHEDRALS, GLITTERING SEAS AND GORGEOUS GARDENS HAVE MOVED MANY A MASTER TO PUT BRUSH TO CANVAS. SPEND A WEEK HERE AND YOU CAN PUT YOURSELF PROPERLY IN THEIR PICTURES.

It's like walking through a painting. The weeping fronds of willow trees sweep like long brushstrokes; pink-white waterlilies daub their liquid canvas; trailing purple wisteria forms a flowery frame. You stand on a little arching bridge and squint, causing the colours to swirl, edges to soften and shapes to blur into a vision that is discernibly a garden, yes, but one in rather lovely low-definition.

Welcome to the world of Claude Monet.

Monet was a founder of the French Impressionist movement – it was one of his paintings, an 'impression' of a sunrise, that gave the avant-garde group its name. Born in Paris in 1840, for a time he lived and worked there, gathering with fellow artists Renoir, Manet, Sisley et al at Café Guerbois to carouse and debate. But it was among his glorious gardens at Giverny, Normandy – where he made his home from 1883 until his death in 1926 – that Monet created some of his most famous works. He once said, 'Besides gardening and painting I don't know anything'. But about those two, he knew a great deal. His Giverny home, a tidy pink house with bright-green shutters, is merely a foil for what surrounds it – trellised walkways, rampant flowerbeds, fruit trees and pretty ponds arranged in disarranged fashion: tended, but not regimented or constrained. It was here that Monet, despite suffering worsening sight problems from 1908, painted his many studies of water lilies. His garden, he said, was his 'greatest expense' but also his greatest thrill: 'I am in raptures'.

However, Giverny was not the only spot in Normandy to stir Monet and his Impressionist friends. Riddled by the Seine, this seaboard province of fertile farmland, Gothic and Romanesque towns and, more latterly, moving war cemeteries, is dotted with sites that inspired their works. A week spent exploring – from gardens to riverbank to coast – is to dip into the palette of these master painters and see behind the canvas.

ESSENTIAL EXPERIENCES

* **Visiting the inspirational, lily-laden gardens of Monet's house at Giverny.**

* Attempting to paint your own picture of Rouen Cathedral 'à la Claude'; workshops are available.

* **Yomping up the coast at Étretat to admire the sea views, chalk cliffs and rock arches.**

* Strolling along the Impressionists Promenade at Sainte-Adresse; replica artworks have been placed in the exact spots on which the originals were painted.

* **Watching the sun rise over the port of Le Havre, where Monet painted *Impression, Soleil Levant*.**

* Sleeping in Room 22 of Honfleur's fancy Hôtel La Ferme Saint-Siméon, which offers an authentic Monet view.

LOCATION NORTHWEST FRANCE | **BEST TIME OF YEAR** APRIL TO OCTOBER | **IDEAL TIME COMMITMENT** SEVEN DAYS
ESSENTIAL TIP VISIT GIVERNY ON A WEEKDAY MORNING TO AVOID THE CROWDS | **BUDGET** $$ | **PACK** SKETCHBOOK, PENCILS

DOING IMPRESSIONS

Impressionism hasn't always been popular. The term, coined in 1874 to describe a group of unconventional Parisian painters including Monet, Cézanne, Renoir and Pissarro, was meant as an insult. Traditionalists just didn't get their style, which was to portray a general visual effect rather than details. They used short, rapid, often visible brushstrokes in bright, intermingling colours to convey the sense of a scene, rather than its absolute reality. They painted landscapes and urban tableaux, usually *en plein air* (outdoors) rather than in studios, to better capture changing light and spontaneity. The results? Fresh, free and – eventually – beloved worldwide.

■ THE PERFECT GETAWAY

Start in the art lover's paradise of Paris. The capital has nabbed all Monet's best works for the Orangerie and Musée d'Orsay. (And it's always nice to visit Paris.)

The Normandy trail proper starts on the next day, with Giverny. Visit in April or October to avoid the crowds, or May to June to see the rhododendrons and wisteria in flower. Nearby, Giverny's Musée des Impressionismes gives some background; it also runs painting workshops. Then trace the Seine northwest – via the castle at Les Andelys, which inspired many masterpieces – to Rouen, one of France's oldest cities. Its medieval centre is dominated by a Gothic cathedral, which Monet painted more than 30 times. On some summer evenings, Impressionist works are projected onto the facade. Also, don't miss Rouen's Musée des Beaux-Arts to see some of the paintings Paris didn't pinch.

Spend days five and six tracing the Alabaster Coast between Dieppe and Le Havre. Dieppe moved many painters: Turner loved it, and the Saint-Jacques church contains a series by Pissarro. But it was Étretat, further west, that Monet loved; he painted the rock arches here many times. Stop at pretty Sainte-Adresse, where Monet created his first Impressionist piece, before hitting Le Havre; its fine light attracted many artists and the town's museum contains the second-largest collection of Impressionist works in France. Purists should wake early for sunrise: this is where Monet painted *Impression, Soleil Levant,* the work that lent the movement its name.

Save day seven for Honfleur; painters flock here to capture its harbour full of boats a-bobbing. Monet and his chums used to climb the Côte de Grâce hill for lunch at the tavern. That simple inn is now Hôtel La Ferme Saint-Siméon; spend your last night here, in room 22 – Monet's favourite.

DECKCHAIR

* **The Private Lives Of The Impressionists** (Sue Roe) A look at the dreams, disputes, losses and loves of the avant-garde artists.
* **Monet at Giverny** (Caroline Holmes) A visual exploration of the artist's glorious gardens.
* **Katie and the Waterlily Pond: A Magical Journey Through Five Monet Masterpieces** (James Mayhew) Delightful book following the heroine's hop into a canvas – great for enthusing children about art.
* **Monet: Ready to Paint the Masters** (Noel Gregory) How-to guide on reproducing Monet paintings.
* **The Impressionists** (2006) BBC miniseries about Monet, Degas, Renoir, Cézanne and Manet, based on archive letters and records, and partly shot in Normandy.
* **Madame Bovary** (Gustave Flaubert) The author's home town of Rouen provides the backdrop to this 19th-century classic.

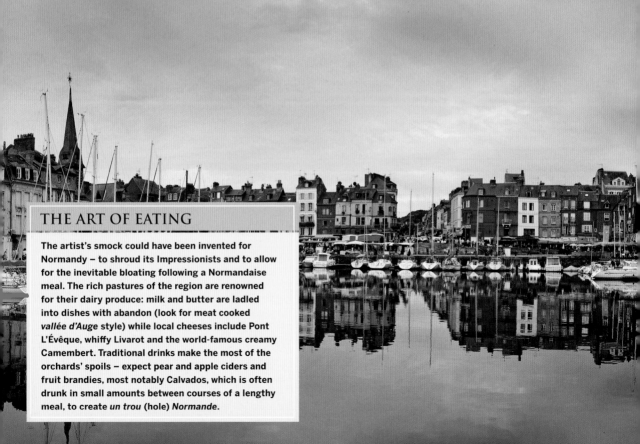

THE ART OF EATING

The artist's smock could have been invented for Normandy – to shroud its Impressionists and to allow for the inevitable bloating following a Normandaise meal. The rich pastures of the region are renowned for their dairy produce: milk and butter are ladled into dishes with abandon (look for meat cooked *vallée d'Auge* style) while local cheeses include Pont L'Évêque, whiffy Livarot and the world-famous creamy Camembert. Traditional drinks make the most of the orchards' spoils – expect pear and apple ciders and fruit brandies, most notably Calvados, which is often drunk in small amounts between courses of a lengthy meal, to create *un trou* (hole) *Normande*.

PLAN IT

Le Havre, Dieppe and Cherbourg are Normandy's key ferry ports. To reach Giverny from Paris, take the Rouen-bound train from Gare Saint-Lazare and disembark at Vernon station. Giverny is 5km from Vernon; shuttlebuses leave the station just after trains arrive. Monet's house and gardens are open daily April to October, 9.30am to 6pm; avoid queues by booking tickets online. Normandy Tourism is developing an Impressionists Cycle Trail, which will connect key sites; download a guide from the Normandy tourism board website.

DETOUR

In counterpoint to Normandy's beautiful art is its bloody horror. On 6 June 1944 thousands of Allied troops landed on an 80km stretch of coast north of Caen. The sandy beaches are still known by their D-Day codenames: Utah, Omaha, Gold, Juno and Sword. Today there's little evidence of the landings, though German bunkers are still visible in Omaha's cliffs and parts of a Mulberry harbour remain at Arromanches. There is a Memorial Museum of Peace in Caen but most moving are the war cemeteries that dot the countryside. Every nation has its own graveyards; with row upon row of headstones, each is a sobering but essential sight.

GREG ELMS | GETTY IMAGES ©

OPENING SPREAD The garden of Monet's Giverny house remains much as he depicted it. **ABOVE** For a taste of Normandy, steam mussels in cider rather than wine. **BELOW** Honfleur's harbour has been captured on canvas by amateur and world-famous artists.

INTO THE HEART OF THE MAYAN WORLD

THERE'S MORE TO SOUTHEAST MEXICO THAN THE MEGARESORTS OF CANCÚN. THE YUCATÁN OFFERS RICH MAYAN HISTORY, COLOURFUL COLONIAL CITIES, CHARMING HACIENDA HOTELS, AND PLENTY OF OPPORTUNITIES TO SWIM IN CENOTES, EAT BARBECUED PORK AND CHILL OUT IN HAMMOCKS.

OK, so the whole Mayan 'end of the world' thing didn't exactly pan out in 2012. (Never mind that that wasn't what their calendar predicted anyway.) But the Mayans, whose civilisation flourished between AD 250 and 900, knew a heck of a lot about astronomy, architecture, mathematics and civilisation-building – as sites like Chichén Itzá and Uxmal clearly attest – and their legacy in Mexico's most tropical state makes that corner of the country a compelling destination.

On top of those Mayan roots – offshoots of which are still thriving today – this region has a rich Spanish-colonial heritage. During the 19th century it was the home of plantation owners who struck it rich in the henequen trade (a plant in the agave family which was used for twine and rope). The cargo ships used to transport henequen to Europe came to Mexico laden with stone, bricks and tiles, which were used to build the plantation owners' French-style city homes in Mérida, as well as the countryside plantations themselves. When the henequen boom busted, many of these opulent haciendas were left to rot for decades. Ceilings collapsed, paint chipped and trees grew through the walls, lending them a glamorous decay. By the 1990s that crumbling grandeur began appealing to expats and wealthy Mexico City dwellers, who bought houses in Mérida and estates in the Yucatán, fixing them up and turning them into boutique hotels.

A vacation here is culturally edifying – exploring one of the most advanced pre-Columbian civilisations – and jaw-dropping: words fail when confronted with the massiveness of Chichén Itzá and the intricate detail of Uxmal. It's also relaxing, stepping out of time in a way – taking a room in a hacienda hotel, strolling the jungly grounds, imagining yourself as the owner of a 19th-century manor. And taking siestas, of course, usually in a hammock. Cap it off with a few days on the bohemian beaches of Tulum and combine history with more hedonism.

ESSENTIAL EXPERIENCES

* **Cooling off in a *cenote* (limestone sinkhole) after a hot day of sightseeing.**

* Eating *cochinita pibil*, the signature dish of the region – pork marinated in acidic juices, wrapped in banana leaves and slow-roasted, traditionally in an underground fire pit.

* **Taking an afternoon siesta in a hammock, a balmy breeze on your face.**

* Exploring Mayan culture at the Gran Museo del Mundo Maya in Mérida, a new museum inaugurated in 2012 – signifying a new beginning, not the end of the world.

* **Viewing the top-notch collection of Mexican folk art at Casa de los Venados in Valladolid.**

* Dining at Hartwood in Tulum, which not only serves great grilled fish and local meat, but perfectly encapsulates Tulum's eco-chic vibe.

LOCATION YUCATÁN, MEXICO | **BEST TIME OF YEAR** OCTOBER TO MARCH, THOUGH OCTOBER STILL CARRIES A HURRICANE RISK **IDEAL TIME COMMITMENT** ONE WEEK | **ESSENTIAL TIP** ONLY TOURISTS WEAR SHORTS, T-SHIRTS AND FLIP-FLOPS; LOCALS MAKE MORE OF AN EFFORT | **BUDGET** $$ | **PACK** A PASHMINA: THERE'S LOTS OF ALFRESCO DINING AND WINTER EVENINGS CAN BE COOL

SWIMMING IN CENOTES

Among the Yucatán's most distinctive features are cenotes, water-filled sinkholes that were formed when the limestone cratered in. Often in caves or vine-draped caverns, with craggy stalactites and small openings to the sky, an estimated 6000 of them dot the state. They were the only source of fresh water in ancient times, and sacred in Mayan cosmology because they were believed to be the entrance to the underworld. (They're also reputed to be the site of sacrificial offerings.) Now they're popular with visitors to the area, who make them the last stop on a day tour for a refreshing swim.

MAYAN HEALING PRACTICES

The Yucatán is rich with traditional wellness experiences. The yoga mecca of Tulum offers plenty of places for visitors to try *temazcal* ceremonies (chanting and offering prayers in a sweat lodge) for spiritual and physical purification. Throughout the state there are shamans who have abilities to bridge the natural and spirit worlds, bring rain and, most important for tourists, heal individuals. At Hacienda Xcanatun, guests can have massages and energy work done by lead spa therapist Carolina Martinez, the granddaughter of a famous Mayan shaman who recently attained shaman status herself.

■ THE PERFECT GETAWAY

An exploration should start in Mérida, the heart of the region. The Yucatán is Mexico's most educated and culturally rich state, and it shows in the city's grand architecture. Along with a growing handful of stylish hotels, Mérida has excellent restaurants, bars and culture, with musical performances every night and a Sunday event that turns the central plaza into a market, musical stage and party.

Stay at Hacienda Xcanatun: it's a short drive from the city centre, but isolated enough to be peaceful. The 18 suites have handmade furniture, dramatic bath-tubs (some carved from massive boulders) and – blissfully – no TVs. The sense of place is strong, with a Yucatecan chef in the kitchen and a Mayan shaman in the spa (see left). The hacienda is a superb base for excursions to archaeological sites like Chichén Itzá, a Unesco World Heritage Site, and the less-crowded Uxmal, where the central Temple of the Magician is covered in ornamentation and monster masks. Hacienda Xcanatun can set guests up with guide extraordinaire Carlos Sosa, who guides Smithsonian Institution trips.

From there, head southeast to Tulum, where Mayan culture still exists but is overlaid with stylishness now that New York fashionistas flock there and 'pop-up' hotels like the Papaya Playa Project have sprouted. For all that, it's still low-key, with a fabulous beach and appealing Mayan ruins.

Mérida to Tulum is an easy drive, but a stop midway in Valladolid is rewarding. The city is strongly Mayan and distinctly Spanish (evident in the architecture), and newly cosmopolitan. A recent influx of expat creative types has led some to call Valladolid the next Tulum. Go now, while it's still 'next'.

■ PLAN IT

Most international flights to Mérida are via Mexico City or Cancún. Hacienda Xcanatun is an hour from Mérida's airport and can arrange transfers, and excursions into the city and to Mayan sites. From Mérida it's a three-hour drive to Tulum, then a further two hours up to Cancún, from where you can fly out. Tour operators like Catherwood Travels can organise transfers and drivers for day excursions, but they aren't necessary for everyone. The Yucatán is the safest state in Mexico and its roads are good, so renting a car is an option.

■ DETOUR

The famous scuba-diving destination, Cozumel offers a more typical Mexican beach holiday, with full-service resorts and less guilt about lying on the beach, margarita in hand, instead of learning about ancient cosmology. But the island, off the coast near Playa del Carmen, is about the underwater action. Divers come to explore the Mesoamerican reef – the western hemisphere's largest and home to more than 250 species of fish, turtles, manta rays and more.

OPENING SPREAD There are thousands of cenotes in which to swim in the Yucatán. **ABOVE (L)** Traditional dress in Izamal, the 'Yellow City', close to Mérida. **ABOVE (R)** Colonial gem: the Governor's Palace in Mérida, the Yucatán's state capital. **LEFT** The Magician's Pyramid at Uxmal, a Mayan site.

DECKCHAIR

❋ *Incidents of Travel in Yucatán* (John Lloyd Stephens and Frederick Catherwood) A real-life adventure, originally published in 1841.

❋ *A Field Guide to Mexican Birds: Mexico, Guatemala, Belize, El Salvador* (Peterson Field Guides) A primer on the native birdlife.

❋ *A Forest of Kings: The Untold Story of the Ancient Maya* (David Freidel and Linda Schele) A recent interpretation of Mayan hieroglyphics.

❋ *Interpreting the Ancient Maya* (Tatiana Proskouriakoff) An overview from a mid-20th-century scholar, who produces a vision of ancient Mayan sites at the height of their grandeur.

❋ *Tales from the Yucatán Jungle: Life in a Mayan Village* (Kristine Ellingson) A memoir by an American who finds a home near Uxmal.

❋ *Outside the Hacienda Walls* (Allan Meyers) A look at the heyday and demise of the henequen plantation era.

WALTZ A WEEKEND AWAY IN VIENNA

IT'S NOT JUST AUSTRIA'S HILLS THAT ARE ALIVE WITH THE SOUND OF MUSIC – THE COUNTRY'S CAPITAL IS THE WORLD CENTRE FOR CLASSICAL TUNES, AND THE PLACE TO MEET MOZART, NIBBLE CAKE IN CAFES AND GO TO THE BALL.

34

Mozart is everywhere in Vienna. Yes, in the spiritual sense: his notes float on the breeze, his 18th-century footsteps seem to waltz on the well-heeled pavements. But he is also quite literally everywhere: in fact, you've just banged into him on the platz outside Stephansdom. So busy were you, gazing up at the Gothic cathedral's zigzag-tiled roof and latticework spire, that you bowled headlong into the man in wig and tights. Before you can apologise, he tries to sell you two tickets to tonight's *Requiem*.

Wolfgang lookalikes lurk all over Vienna's Innere Stadt – the old Imperial city – eager to tout their concerts. Ignore them. Vienna is the undisputed music capital of the world, but these offerings are the tourist tip of the iceberg – they do no justice to a city that's nurtured not only Mozart but Schubert, Johann Strauss (I and II), Haydn, Mahler and many, many more. This is the city of the Vienna State Opera, which puts on 50 different performances a year. It's the city of the Musikverein, the 19th-century Neoclassial music hall, home to the esteemed Vienna Philharmonic and reputed to have some of the world's best acoustics. Then there's the art-nouveau Konzerthaus, the eclectic Volksoper, the recently revamped Theater an der Wien and the Marionettentheater at Schönbrunn Palace, which sees puppets performing *The Magic Flute*.

Music isn't limited to traditional venues either. Vienna is a city of fine coffeehouses and many provide their patrons with live performances. Hear the ivories being tinkled at Café Schwarzenberg, the oldest cafe on the Ringstrasse, which has been serving since 1861. Or order a Mozart-torte at Café Landtmann, where piano recitals have been enjoyed by everyone from Mahler to Paul McCartney. Simply, there's no city more melodic – or, arguably, more elegant – than Vienna, whether you have the budget of a Habsburgian prince or a struggling artist.

ESSENTIAL EXPERIENCES

* **Learning about the main man at the Mozarthaus – one of Wolfgang's former apartments, now a must-see museum.**
* Catching a concert in a traditional Viennese coffeehouse – eat gooey torte while a pro plays piano in the corner.
* **Listening to music at the Musikverein or State Opera (or both), two of the world's very best classical venues.**
* Walking in Mozart's footsteps on a tour of his old Vienna haunts.
* **Being overwhelmed by art at the formidable Kunsthistorisches Museum.**
* Hearing a freebie – from organ oratories to the annual open-air Vienna Philharmonic concert in the Schönbrunn Palace gardens in June.

LOCATION AUSTRIA | **BEST TIME OF YEAR** YEAR-ROUND; WINTER FOR BALLS | **IDEAL TIME COMMITMENT** THREE TO FOUR DAYS
ESSENTIAL TIP HEAD TO THE HOFBURG CHAPEL ON SUNDAYS (9AM, SEPTEMBER TO JUNE) TO HEAR THE VIENNA BOYS CHOIR FOR FREE
BUDGET $-$$$ | **PACK** SOMETHING SMART, SO YOU CAN DRESS THE PART FOR A GRAND MUSIC HALL

THE VIENNESE WHIRL

If Rio owns the samba then Vienna owns the waltz. And as Rio marks Carnaval with bootie-shaking parades, when Vienna celebrates, it does so with grand balls – indeed, the city hosts around 450 of them, January to March. The season kicks off in sumptuous style with the Imperial Palace's Grand Bal on New Year's Eve. Anyone can buy a ticket, but you need a fancy outfit – tux or ballgown – and you need to be able to dance. Take a lesson, even if you've waltzed before: the Viennese variety is breathtakingly fast. Elmayer's Studio offers drop-in tuition sessions for tourists.

MOZART: A 60-SECOND GUIDE

Wolfgang Amadeus Mozart was born in Salzburg in 1756. He displayed huge talent almost immediately: at age four he could play piano; at five he was composing; at six he performed before royalty. From 1762 his family made several cross-continent concert tours. Following an unhappy stint as a court musician in Salzburg, Mozart moved to Vienna in 1781. It was his most brilliant and prolific period (in 1788 he wrote three symphonies in ten weeks), though his earnings were swallowed by his lavish lifestyle. In 1791 – aged just 35, but having composed 600-odd works – he died; the cause of his death remains a mystery.

THE PERFECT GETAWAY

The most harmonious Viennese getaway requires planning before you leave home. Big concerts sell out, so book in advance online. That said, don't fret if you've left it late – there's a ticket office offering 20% discounts on same-day performances near the State Opera House. Another option is joining the Opera House's 'standing tickets' queue at 6pm, to secure seatless entry for a few euros.

On your first day, get orientated. The Innere Stadt, the historic centre within the Ringstrasse (the city's main boulevard), is easily walkable. Starting at Stephansplatz, by the cathedral in which Mozart was married, embark on a Wolfgang walking tour, via the Mozarthaus Museum, Michaelerkirche (where Mozart's *Requiem* was first played) and his statue in Burggarten. The apartment in which Mozart died was in what is now the Steffl department store and there are great views from the seventh floor. It was in the Hall of Mirrors at Schönbrunn Palace that Mozart (then six years old) first played for the Empress. This Baroque complex, reached on U-Bahn line 4, is a good afternoon option; set in French-style gardens and full of Habsburgian bling; it hosts regular concerts.

Come evening, you must find some music. In April to June and September, live opera is shown on a huge screen in Herbert-von-Karajan-Platz. During July and August, when most concert halls take a break, the Summer of Music Festival fills the void. If you didn't get into the Opera House, take a tour the next day. Then commune with Strauss's *Blue Danube* and hire a rowing boat. Or laze on Danube Island, which in June hosts the free Donauinselfest, a three-day celebration of pop, rock, soul, jazz and more. Whatever would Mozart make of that...?

PLAN IT

Vienna-Schwechat Airport is 18km southeast of the city. The City Airport Train (CAT) takes minutes to reach the centre; you can also take trainline S7 or an airport express bus. The Vienna tourism website has a wealth of information; from here you can download walking tours and find links to the main music venues. Tickets for the Vienna Philharmonic New Year Concert are drawn by lot; enter the ballot in January on the orchestra's website.

DETOUR

After your fill of music, head for the hills. Vienna is the world's largest wine-growing city, with 7 sq km of vineyards nestled in its immediate vicinity. Take the bus from the centre to Kahlenberg, just north, and you're soon ambling past tidy lines of vines, the metropolis visible below. Better still, sample the fruits of this labour at the various *heurigen* – wine taverns where the current vintage is served cheap and on tap. The stove will likely be cooking a meaty speciality and the Gemütlichkeit (that Teutonic brand of cosiness) will be in abundance.

37

OPENING SPREAD Let's dance: the Vienna Opera Ball is a highlight of the city's winter season and takes place in the State Opera House. **ABOVE (L)** Admire the art in Vienna's Natural History Museum. **ABOVE (R)** Opera aside: Vienna has a cutting-edge contemporary music scene. **LEFT** Awesome opera.

DECKCHAIR

* **Mozart: A Life in Letters** (Wolfgang Mozart) This compilation of the composer's correspondence offers a window into his life.

* **The Third Man** (1949) Classic film noir written by Graham Greene, staring Orson Welles and set in atmospheric post-war Vienna.

* **The Mozart Conspiracy** (Scott Mariani) *Da Vinci Code*-ish thriller, set partly in Vienna, in which a letter by Wolfgang may be the key to unlocking a murderous mystery...

* **Last Waltz in Vienna: The Destruction of a Family 1842–1942** (George Clare) Heartbreaking account of Jewish life under the Nazis.

* **A Time of Gifts** (Patrick Leigh Fermor) Superlative travelogue, recounting the author's 1930s walk along the Danube.

* **Amadeus** (1984) This lavish Oscar-winner mixes Mozart fact and fiction to dazzling effect.

LIVE LA DOLCE VITA IN WALES

PART ITALIAN RIVIERA, PART SCI-FI TV SET, A WHOLE LOT BONKERS – THE COASTAL RESORT OF PORTMEIRION, AN ARCHITECTURAL ANOMALY SITTING BENEATH SOME OF THE NATION'S HIGHEST MOUNTAINS, IS WALES AT ITS MOST WONDERFULLY WEIRD.

Are you dreaming? You thought you were on the west coast of Wales. But it seems – from the fountain tinkling in the Piazza, the macho statue of Hercules, the pastel-toned classical architecture and campanile – that you have just walked into Italy. You are discombobulated to say the least, a feeling intensified by the disproportionate number of people walking around in polo-neck pullovers and white-trimmed blazers. What the devil is this place? And what is going on?

To answer that you must delve into the mind of Bertram Clough Williams-Ellis, the mastermind behind the surreal resort of Portmeirion. An architect with a passion for preservation, Clough Williams-Ellis (1883–1978) bought the peninsula-perched site in 1925 for less than £5,000 (about £210,000 in today's money). It was a rundown wilderness – but not for long. Combining his admiration for the Italian Riviera with a belief that well-planned development could enhance rather than destroy its surroundings, he set about creating something unique. The result of this singular vision is a beautifully bizarre bricolage of Arts and Crafts architecture, Palladian fancy and clever recycling – Clough Williams-Ellis salvaged bits and pieces marked for demolition elsewhere, calling Portmeirion a 'home for fallen buildings'. To add to the fairytale, all this eccentricity is tucked between forested hills and the peaceful estuary of the River Dwyryd.

But what about those people in polo-necks? Ah, yes, another level of weird. In the 1960s Portmeirion was used as the backdrop for surreal sci-fi/thriller TV series *The Prisoner,* which saw blazered ex-secret agent Patrick McGoohan (or 'Number Six') kept captive in 'The Village' – for unknown reasons. All the other inmates were brainwashed; Number Six was the only one with the will to escape, though his attempts were thwarted by enormous white balloons. Odd, yes. But perhaps the perfect match for Portmeirion, where nothing is quite as it seems.

ESSENTIAL EXPERIENCES

* **Riding the hill-slicing steam locos of the Ffestiniog Railway to Minffordd, from where Portmeirion is a 1.6km walk.**

* Examining the village square's Bristol Colonnade to locate the Clough Williams-Ellis gargoyle.

* **Drinking a cappuccino on the cafe terrace where Number Six drank his morning coffees and feeling truly Prisoner-cum-Italian.**

* Being pampered with a deep-sea-diving aroma massage at Battery Square's Mermaid Spa, the only spa in Snowdonia.

* **Promenading along the beach before heading up to the Grotto to watch the sun set over the Dwyryd Estuary.**

* Visiting Portmeirion's Rob Piercy Gallery to admire the works of the local artist.

LOCATION COASTAL SNOWDONIA, NORTH WALES | **BEST TIME OF YEAR** MAY–SEPTEMBER | **IDEAL TIME COMMITMENT** TWO DAYS
ESSENTIAL TIP STAY OVERNIGHT TO EXPERIENCE PORTMEIRION AFTER HOURS (AND GET FREE ENTRY) | **BUDGET** $$
PACK BLACK POLO-NECK PULLOVER AND WHITE-TRIMMED BLAZER

SNOWDONIA BY STEAM

The narrow-gauge Ffestiniog Railway runs for 21.7km from Blaenau Ffestiniog to Porthmadog; the Minffordd stop is a short stroll from Portmeirion. The railway existed long before the resort: it opened in the 1830s as a gravity-and-horse-pulled service to transport slate from quarries to the coast. In 1863 steam locomotives arrived; a year later came the first passenger cars, and tourists flocked to ride through the steep, spectacular scenery. And they still do – though the line had closed by 1946, passionate locals rebuilt the service and reopened it in 1982. Now steam-powered, heritage Pullman coaches slice though Snowdonia once more.

UNIQUE PLACE, UNIQUE PARTY

Poetry in the Piazza, rock on the Estuary Stage, big gigs on Stage No.6, intimate sets in the Jacobean Town Hall... According to its organisers, Portmeirion's Festival No.6 (named, of course, after Patrick McGoohan's Prisoner) is a gathering unlike any other, in a place unlike any other. It is 'a scene but not a herd', encouraging revellers to briefly put reality on hold. Launched in 2012, Festival No.6 takes over the resort for three days in September, packing the Italianate village with headline bands, up-and-coming acts, authors, performance artists, comics, storytellers, fire-twirlers and much more.

◼ THE PERFECT GETAWAY

The first episode of *The Prisoner* was called 'The Arrival' and saw Number Six waking up in his weird new world. Appropriately, on arriving in the village yourself – via two gatehouse arches – Six's cottage on Battery Square is one of the first buildings you find. It's now The Prisoner Shop, selling memorabilia. There's a cafe on the square, too – have a cappuccino to seal the Italian feel.

Next, explore the rest of the resort. Stroll down the cobbled path to the village green. Look closely at the Colonnade – this 18th-century edifice, rebuilt brick by brick after being salvaged from Bristol, has a more modern addition: a Clough Williams-Ellis gargoyle. Admire the pool and the Gloriette – it was from its balcony that Number Six proclaimed: 'I am not a number – I am a free man!' Carrying on through the village, you reach the quayside, where a trail leads along the beach. Further paths lead between a folly lighthouse, exotic trees and a dog cemetery; there are also ruins of the castle that stood here centuries before.

For full immersion, stay at the Hotel Portmeirion, which has hosted luminaries such as HG Wells and George Harrison; the building dates back to 1850 but has been extended and Cloughified now. Eat at the restaurant, which has windows overlooking the water. Best of all, overnighting means you can explore after the daytrippers have left. Rise early the next morning and head up to the Grotto for the best estuary view. Then do what Number Six never could: escape along the beach. Opened in May 2012, the Wales Coast Path (which skirts the country's seaboard) passes by here. Pick it up heading west and you'll reach Porthmadog, from where Criccieth Castle is 10km further on.

◼ PLAN IT

Portmeirion is 3km south of Porthmadog, signposted from the A487 road at Minffordd. A bus service runs from Porthmadog, March to October. The nearest main train stations are Llandudno Junction and Bangor. From Llandudno Junction, connect to Blaenau Ffestiniog along the Conwy Valley line, then ride the Ffestiniog Railway to Minffordd; there is a footpath to the village. Portmeirion is open every day except Christmas. The resort has two hotels and 17 cottages.

◼ DETOUR

Being so close to Mt Snowdon, Wales's biggest mountain, it would seem rude not to head up it. Ride the newly reopened West Highland Railway (a characterful narrow-gauge line) from Porthmadog to remote Rhyd Ddu station; from here, a gentle trail leads up to the 1085m summit. It's 12km there and back, and takes around six hours. Alternatively, if you're feeling more laidback-Italian than hardy-Welsh, make your way to Llanberis and take the Snowdon Mountain Railway to the top.

OPENING SPREAD Pretty in pink: Portmeirion's pastel hues brighten a Welsh day. **ABOVE (L)** From sea to sky: explore the coast and the mountains of Snowdonia National Park. **ABOVE (R)** Dancers light up Portmeirion's quirky Number Six Festival. **LEFT** Mali Llewellyn tunes her harp at the festival.

DECKCHAIR

* **Portmeirion** (Jan Morris et al) Published in 2006 to mark the 80th anniversary, this resort biography is lavishly illustrated with rare photos and drawings.

* **Blithe Spirit** (Noel Coward) The playwright penned this comedy in just five days during a stay at Portmeirion.

* **Fear in the Sunlight** (Nicola Upson) Detective fiction featuring Alfred Hitchcock and set in Portmeirion.

* **The Prisoner** (1967–68) Bonkers sci-fi/thriller TV series following a former secret agent being held captive in a mysterious coastal resort.

* **The Inn of the Sixth Happiness** (1958) Snowdonia stands in for China in this Ingrid Bergman movie; the giant gold Buddha statue used in the film now stands just off Portmeirion's piazza.

* **Portmeirion Pottery** (Steven Jenkins) Insight into the ceramic craftwork of Susan Williams-Ellis.

AUSTRALIA
VICTORIA

TASMAN
SEA

BASS
STRAIT

Launceston O

TASMANIA

SOUTHERN
OCEAN

Hobart O

FEAST ON ART IN HOBART

ESCAPE TO THE ENDS OF THE EARTH FOR ONE OF THE WORLD'S MOST REMOTE AND REMARKABLE ART EXPERIENCES. TASMANIA'S CAPITAL – NEXT STOP, ANTARCTICA – IS THE BEAUTIFUL SETTING FOR A LANDMARK MUSEUM THAT HAS TRANSFORMED THE CITY.

A pod of dolphins, ducking and diving in the bow wave, escorts your sleek motorboat from Hobart's waterfront along the Derwent River. Your destination is the Museum of Old and New Art (MONA), a privately owned gallery that opened on the outskirts of the Tasmanian capital in 2011. After disembarking, you take the glass-walled elevator into MONA's depths where, as you arrive at the base of a three-storey chasm, your first sight is of a bar, complete with a neatly dressed bartender. Your next is of New Zealand artist Julia deVille's *Cinerarium,* complete with a neatly stuffed raven watching over an urn of human ashes.

Not long ago the idea of contemplating mortality in a subterranean gallery in Hobart would have been met with incredulous laughter. Hobart, on the same latitude as Patagonia, has long been the sort of place where outdoorsy types mountain bike in the morning, kayak in the afternoon, and wind up having a Cascade or two, the city's own brew. Logging trucks still rumble through the business district, a clue to the island state's controversial source of income. But these days, Australia's poorest state prompts fewer jokes and more envious glances among mainlanders. For Hobart, at the southern tip of Tasmania is transformed.

The catalyst arrived in the shape of a millionaire gambler. David Walsh is the mathematically gifted son of a single mother from Glenorchy, Hobart's hardscrabble suburb. The art-loving entrepreneur spent his earnings on building an A$80-million museum to house his A$100-million collection. Walsh's curators describe him as omnivorous: Neolithic arrowheads and Roman, Greek and Egyptian antiquities are arranged beside provocative modern art and key pieces by Australian artists Brett Whiteley and Sidney Nolan. The result is the southern hemisphere's most exciting art experience.

ESSENTIAL EXPERIENCES

* **Arriving at MONA on the gallery's motorboat to absorb Hobart's wonderful natural setting.**

* Spending a Saturday morning at the craft and food market in Salamanca Place before devouring freshly fried seafood and chips on Constitution Dock for lunch.

* **Eating at Garagistes, a great no-reservations restaurant. Wait at Sidecar, a tiny bar nearby.**

* Hiring a mountain bike and conquering the North–South Track down Mt Wellington.

* **Tasting Tasmanian pinot noir at the Frogmore Creek cellar door, 15 minutes from the city.**

* Visiting the newly revamped Tasmanian Museum and Art Gallery.

* **Feasting on art, music and performance at MONA FOMA, the citywide summer festival.**

LOCATION TASMANIA, AUSTRALIA | **BEST TIME OF YEAR** NOVEMBER TO APRIL | **IDEAL TIME COMMITMENT** A WEEKEND
ESSENTIAL TIP HAVE A GLASS OF MOORILLA'S WINE OR A MOO BREW BEER AFTER THE ART | **BUDGET** $$ | **PACK** AN OPEN MIND

GAMBLING MAN

David Walsh, MONA's founder, made his millions
figuring out formulas for betting successfully on
racehorses in the 1980s and '90s. In 1995 he paid
A$2.5 million for Moorilla, a peninsula of land with a
vineyard between Hobart and Glenorchy, later adding
a boutique winery, a brewery and accommodation. Ten
years later Walsh began to construct the Museum of
Old and New Art. The design, by Australian architect
Nonda Katsalidis, was typically contrarian, building
down not up: some 60,000 tonnes of earth were
removed and engineers cut through 3km of rock. An
elevator sinks into a sandstone-lined shaft; visitors
begin at the bottom and make their way up three levels
to Tasmania's blinding sunlight.

■ THE PERFECT GETAWAY

Start the day at the Pigeon Hole cafe and bakery, on a hill overlooking West Hobart. The former butcher's shop, fitted out with vintage furniture, is where MONA's architects and Hobart's off-duty chefs grab a coffee and something to eat from a simple menu. Then take the boat (or bus, or bicycle) to MONA. Walsh describes his project as a 'subversive adult Disneyland'. Rather than a thread to follow through his labyrinth, visitors are handed an iPod loaded with exhibit details, idiosyncratic commentary and the option to 'love' or 'hate' pieces. Digest the day's sights (be warned: some of MONA's content can provoke forthright debate) over a glass of chilled riesling at Moorilla, Walsh's on-site winery.

The island, says Delia Nicholls, MONA's curator, has always been regarded by the rest of the country as a 'beautiful backwater' – but is now enjoying new-found cultural cachet, for which MONA is not solely responsible. The Tasmanian Museum and Art Gallery, which fascinated Walsh when he was a boy, completed a major redevelopment in 2012; the grand 19th-century waterfront building now has an impressive contemporary entrance and foyer. Go in to get to grips with the island's natural and cultural heritage.

After a day doing Hobart's museums, drop into Garagistes, a stripped-out, one-time car workshop on the edge of the CBD, for a glass of wine. Inside, all is cool, dark and airy. Trestle tables are lined up perpendicular to an open kitchen, from where chef Luke Burgess, formerly of Noma in Copenhagen, sends out platters such as veal sweetbreads spiked with sour cherry, and buckwheat, lettuce hearts and nasturtium leaves, each designed for sharing.

It's quite a jump from pulp mills and half-hewn old-growth forests to state-of-the-art museums and boutique bakeries, but Tasmania is mid-leap.

DECKCHAIR

* ***In Tasmania*** (Nicholas Shakespeare) The biographer of Bruce Chatwin takes some time out in Tassie for reflection and encounters some long-lost family members.

* ***The Fatal Shore*** (Robert Hughes) As a feat of research, it's unparalleled in Australian literature. As an account of Australia's colonial origins, it's gripping. Tasmania has a prominent place.

* ***Death of a River Guide*** (Richard Flanagan) The debut of Tasmania's star author. Flanagan went on to win awards with his third novel, *Gould's Book of Fish,* and is one of the island's most vocal protectors.

* ***The Hunter*** (2011) Willem Dafoe stars in this thriller based on a hunt for the last Tasmanian tiger.

* ***Monanism*** (David Walsh) An occasionally confronting collection of the museum's pieces and musings by the man himself.

SYMPATHY FOR THE DEVIL

The Tasman Peninsula curls towards Hobart from the south. At its tip is Port Arthur, the best-preserved example of a British convict settlement in Australia. But another important act of preservation is taking place on the Arthur Highway at the Tasmanian Devil Conservation Park. Here, the island's iconic marsupial – ferocious but elusive – is being protected from a virulent facial cancer that has been plaguing wild populations. The park, an hour from Hobart, rescues and breeds devils as the race to find a cure continues. Befitting their voracious image, the devils are fed six times daily. A piece of devil trivia: female devils give birth to around 15 young but can only suckle four. Clearly, it's a hard-knock life if you're born a Tassie devil.

PLAN IT

Most international flights to Hobart arrive via
Melbourne or Sydney. Reserve a couple of nights
at the Henry Jones Art Hotel, a former warehouse
on the harbourside, or the Islington Hotel in
South Hobart, both of which have their own art
collections on show (spot work by Matisse and
Hockney at the Islington). Boat trips to MONA can
be booked at a kiosk on the harbour, where you
can also hire a bicycle to ride out to the gallery.

DETOUR

Hobart hasn't shed its adventurous side, and the
opportunities for cycling, kayaking and hiking
within the city's boundaries are better than ever.
In 2011, a 10km purpose-built track for mountain
bikers opened on the flanks of Mt Wellington.
The North–South Track descends to Glenorchy
Mountain Bike Park; operators such as Vertigo
MTB offer rental bikes and shuttle services
back to the city. On the waterfront, Freycinet
Adventures takes first-time kayakers on tours of
Hobart's harbour or more-experienced kayakers
on multiday explorations of the spectacular
coastline. Hobart's natural setting – fringed by
hills, forest and some of the clearest water in the
world – is as uplifting as any artwork.

OPENING SPREAD *Tracing Time*, an installation by Clare Morgan featuring dandelion
seeds, leaves and a taxidermied wren; in the background, *Wall of Film* by Michel Blazy.
ABOVE Luke Burgess's curing room at Garagistes. **BELOW** David Walsh's fortress of art.

RÉUNION: A MUSICAL TREASURE ISLAND

FOR PEOPLE WHO LOVE TROPICAL ISLANDS BUT FIND BEACH HOLIDAYS BORING, RÉUNION IS THE PLACE TO HEAD. THE INDIAN OCEAN ISLAND IS HOME TO A HUGELY EXCITING MUSIC SCENE AND, FOR THOSE WHO LIKE A CHALLENGE, THE WORLD'S MOST ACTIVE VOLCANO TO CLIMB.

46

In a shanty restaurant next to the beach, youths are beating funky rhythms on what appear to be pieces of scrap metal. Women dance a sexy chicken strut while those watching salute with beer bottles and offer shouts of joy. Is this Nigeria? Haiti? Or, possibly, Salvador in Brazil? Matter of fact, this is France. To be specific, Réunion, a volcanic island in the Indian Ocean that is an 'overseas department of France'. Thus you pay with euros, get served croissants for breakfast and, even in the tropical heat, often experience a certain chic Gallic shrug.

Réunion rarely attracts international attention. The occasions for which the island, just south of Mauritius, gets noticed tend to be when Piton de la Fournaise, Réunion's very active volcano, blows its top. Otherwise Réunion is viewed as an exotic French colony (true) or, for the most part, simply overlooked. Yet anyone who has had the good fortune to encounter Réunion's vernacular music forms (maloya and sega) is aware that an exciting music scene exists here.

Where sega is light and melodic – the island's pop music – maloya, a music sung in Creole patois and reliant almost entirely on home-made percussion instruments and voice, is Réunion's equivalent of roots reggae. For aficionados of 'world' music Réunion is a treasure island. Musical tourists should try to attend the Sakifo Musik Festival: this celebration of Indian Ocean music – alongside Réunion artists there are performers from neighbouring islands Mauritius and Madagascar; acts from the French mainland add international flavour while keeping the tropical vibe – takes place in St-Pierre, a Creole town on the island's southwest coast. Stages are built along the beachfront, so the festival presents a truly lovely way to hear live music. That the temperature is balmy, the sea delicious, the food (fresh fish and spicy stews) yummy and the locals attractive all suggests that there are few finer places to experience music than at Sakifo.

ESSENTIAL EXPERIENCES

* **Watching Christine Salem, the Soul Queen of Réunion, or Danyel Waro, the godfather of maloya, in concert.**

* Climbing the active volcano Piton de la Fournaise and marvelling at its lunar landscape.

* **Falling on your knees in awe at Le Maïdo, one of the most impressive viewpoints in Réunion and a superb two-wheel destination.**

* Going heritage-hunting among the stunning Creole buildings of Hell-Bourg, a beautiful village nestled in the Cirque de Salazie mountains.

* **Driving around *le sud sauvauge* (the wild south), an exciting day trip that provides lush, tropical scenery, wild beaches, lava fields and insights into the island's large Indian community.**

LOCATION RÉUNION, THE INDIAN OCEAN | **BEST TIME OF YEAR** MAY TO OCTOBER; THE SAKIFO MUSIK FESTIVAL TAKES PLACE IN EARLY JUNE | **IDEAL TIME COMMITMENT** ONE WEEK | **ESSENTIAL TIP** TAKE GOOD WALKING BOOTS: RÉUNION IS STEEP! **BUDGET** $$ | **PACK** SUNSCREEN, HAT AND BEACH GEAR

DANYEL WARO

The godfather of maloya, Danyel Waro has been noted for his talent since the late 1970s; but for a long time he refused to record or venture beyond Réunion: a veteran activist, he distrusts the music industry. Waro has a remarkably expressive voice and his percussive music is bluesy, full of raw melody and quite beautiful. Waro is Réunion's most famous citizen and, in concert, a musician as compelling as Joe Strummer or Woody Guthrie. His concerts are exciting, celebratory affairs, while his albums are excellent – *Aou Amwin* and *Bwarouz* have both been distributed internationally.

PITON DE LA FOURNAISE

Réunion's most famous natural attraction, Piton de la Fournaise is not a dormant monster but an active geological wonder that erupts with great regularity. If it's not exploding, it is possible to trek right up to the smoking crater. This five-hour trek through lava fields and up the volcano's loose-rock sides demands a certain level of fitness, good walking boots, a hat, sunscreen and water. Climbing the volcano you may feel this is your last-ever trek – it is not a casual stroll – but once you get to the summit and look down into the smoking crater and then across to the luminescent Indian Ocean all your aches will fade.

■ A PERFECT GETAWAY

Sakifo festival is only once a year, but visitors to Réunion at other times need not worry: music is a major part of Réunion culture and you'll find it all across the island. Free weekend concerts often take place in towns and villages. The raison d'être behind Réunion's music scene is its isolation – for centuries the French government treated the island as a big sugar and vanilla plantation – and a Creole culture that blends African, European, Chinese and Indian influences to lend Réunion a unique sound. As do the sugarcane shakers and recycled steel percussion: played by musicians with a sense of rhythm and magnificent voices, this is elemental music-making and as funky as James Brown.

First, hire a car and explore le sud sauvauge (the wild south). Initially, the towns are small and the land lush; the coast is black rock and black sand. Then the landscape becomes a vast lunar park. Lava from eruptions has poured out from Piton de la Fournaise and flowed to the sea, leaving a long, black scar. With mist hanging in the atmosphere and the sea crashing below, this stretch of Réunion feels eerie, at once prehistoric and futuristic.

Don't ignore Réunion's east coast; it offers access to Hell-Bourg – a pretty Creole village – and good walking among extinct volcanoes. Réunion lacks the beaches of neighbouring Mauritius, so St Pierre and other seaside towns have built beaches and artificial lagoons. But it's best to avoid the resorts as the local musicians are not often found in them. And after a day's volcano climbing what could be better than a cold beer in a shanty bar where the locals beat out the funkiest rhythm you've ever heard while chanting in Creole?

■ PLAN IT

France is the only European country with regular direct flights to Réunion. Car hire is reasonable and there's a good bus system. Accommodation ranges from backpackers hostels to five-star hotels; homestays abound in rural areas. Sakifo Musik Festival tickets are available at the gate in St-Pierre. No trekking permits are necessary for the volcanoes. Réunion experiences a cool, dry winter from late April to October; the peak tourist season is from late June to early September.

■ DETOUR

You've climbed a volcano, now how about mountain-biking down Le Maïdo? This spectacular mountain involves an early-morning start to see the sun rise across the Cirque de Mafate, an undeveloped terrain that suggests a lost world. The Maïdo massif has 150km of marked mountain-biking trails that range from beginner's routes to those best left to experts. There are several companies offering mountain-bike services, such as group rides and guides for those who don't wish to cycle alone.

49

OPENING SPREAD A street musician plays during a festival on Réunion; note the island's French influences. **ABOVE (L)** Face-piercing at a Tamil religious ceremony on Réunion. **ABOVE (R)** Viewing the volcanic crater at Piton de la Fournaise. **LEFT** The volcanic amphitheatre of the Cirque de Mafate.

DECKCHAIR

※ **World Music: The Rough Guide** (ed Simon Broughton) Excellent section on Indian Ocean music-making.

※ **Songlines** (UK) The essential-world music magazine is a good read.

※ **Treasure Island** (Robert Louis Stevenson) A timeless yarn.

※ **Les Chants des Kayanms** (Agnès Gueneau) This lyrical tale, evoking the rhythms of maloya (traditional slave music), revolves around a love affair between a local woman and a man from the mainland.

※ **La Nuit Cyclone** (Jean-François Sam-Long) Sam-Long , a novelist and poet who helped relaunch Réunion's Creole literature in the 1970s, explores in this novel the gulf between whites and blacks in a small village, against a backdrop of black magic and superstition.

※ **Chasseurs des Noires** (Daniel Vaxelaire) An easily accessible historical tale of a slave-hunter's life-changing encounter with an escaped slave.

FEELING FADO IN LISBON

IT'S SOULFUL, PASSIONATE AND MELODIC. IT KICKS TANGO'S ASS. ITS TRADITIONS ARE PORTUGUESE. AND IT WAS RECENTLY ADDED TO UNESCO'S INTANGIBLE CULTURAL HERITAGE LIST. THIS IS FADO.

50

Hot, passionate and intimate – welcome to the intoxicating world of fado. Where a singer, silhouetted against a velvet backdrop and dim red backlighting, closes her eyes, tilts her head and sways gently. She opens her mouth and deep, wistful notes fill the room. Several people, gathered with friends around tables, know the tunes and their idiosyncrasies. Some click their fingers, others gasp in appreciation as the melody rises and falls. Some sing along, never taking their eyes off the face of the *fadista* (fado singer), as it contorts into agony, then ecstasy. Song over, applause and cheering fills the room.

A fado performance is integral to any visit to Lisbon, especially in the capital's historic neighbourhood of Alfama, a labyrinth of cobbled lanes. After midnight, Alfama casts a special spell; follow the musical notes of the mournful ballads that resonate off the stone walls. You'll soon encounter a fado club, often no more than a crowded room, where male and female singers perform for Lisboêtas who are passionate about fado and its traditions. Fado's roots are in Lisbon – and along the seafaring coast – where in the 1850s sailors and ruffians sang of life, love, fate and death. Fado's distinct bluesy tunes and lyrics are linked to the Portuguese word *saudade,* meaning longing or nostalgic yearning. Portuguese nobility eventually caught on to fado's charms, and fado performance took off more formally. In the 20th century, a 12-string Portuguese guitar and a classical guitar were added as instrumental accompaniments.

These days, new generations of stars, including Ana Moura, Carminho and Mariza, are adding their own touches to fado – contemporary fusion sounds, Cuban-style jazz and even orchestras. The best way to feel fado is in a Lisbon club. These range from touristy three-tunes-and-a-meal venues to high-quality establishments, popular among locals for their quality of fado and ambience.

ESSENTIAL EXPERIENCES

* **Getting lost in the village-like lanes of Alfama, searching for the soul of fado.**

* Jumping aboard tram 28 for a teeth-rattling, roller-coaster ride around Alfama and beyond.

* **Devouring the famous, delectable custard tarts at Antiga Confeitaria de Belém – and trying to guess the secret ingredient.**

* Absorbing the Manueline fantasy of Mosteiro dos Jerónimos in Belém – nothing compares to the moment you walk into the honey-stone cloisters.

* **Embarking on a shopping frenzy and taking in the pleasant outdoor cafes and restaurants in elegant Chiado.**

* Striding through enchanted forests to above-the-clouds palaces and castles in Sintra.

LOCATION LISBON, PORTUGAL | **BEST TIME OF YEAR** YEAR-ROUND | **IDEAL TIME COMMITMENT** THREE TO FOUR DAYS
ESSENTIAL TIP FADO IS THE DOMAIN OF NIGHT OWLS; HAVE AN AFTERNOON SIESTA TO PREPARE FOR A NIGHT OUT
BUDGET $$ | **PACK** EXTRA CASH FOR A FADO ALBUM (OR THREE)

THE FADISTAS' SONG

It's very hard to define exactly what fado is; ask the locals to explain it and you'll receive different answers. Even fadistas (fado singers) themselves struggle to define the music and songs. This may be because, as Amália Rodrigues, the Queen of Fado, famously proclaimed, 'I don't sing fado. It sings me.' Ana Moura, one of Portugal's current fado divas, thinks along the same lines: 'Fado is difficult to define. It's something you need to feel. It's a kind of music where we use the melody and words to express what's going on in our soul.' The easiest way of understanding the concept of fado and saudade – melancholic longing – is to listen to it.

LISBON'S ICONIC VIEWPOINTS

Lisbon is spread across steep hillsides that overlook the Rio Tejo. While puffing up the cobbled streets can be hard work, several steep stairways lead to *miradouros* (viewpoints) that afford mind-boggling views. The Moorish gateway of Largo das Portas do Sol gives a bird's-eye vista of Alfama's jumble of pastel houses and red rooftops. In neighbouring Graça, the pine-fringed Miradouro da Graça is the perfect place for a sundowner and sweeping vistas over central Lisbon, while Miradouro da Senhora do Monte, one of the highest points, offers the best views of the castle on the hill opposite.

THE PERFECT GETAWAY

You need a few days to get your head around Lisbon, though its magic will hit immediately. A fun way to get your bearings on your first day is to take a rattling ride on tram 28, Lisbon's vintage trolley car. It offers the ultimate spin around the city's top sights, from Basílica da Estrela to the backstreets of Baixa (downtown), via the Sé (Cathedral) and Alfama. Then, wander the streets of Baixa – Rua Augusta is delightful. Along here, pop into Museu do Design e da Moda for a superb take on contemporary Lisbon. Follow this with window-shopping and cafe-hopping in well-heeled Chiado, where some of Lisbon's top designers tout their wares, then tap into your inner-retro in Bairro Alto – an adjacent district peppered with funky boutiques. Finish your explorations by heading east of Alfama to the Museu Nacional do Azulejo (National Tile Museum), a 16th-century convent that exhibits the country's exquisite blue-and-white *azulejos*. For your evening meal, head to the pretty Santo António de Alfama.

The next morning, hop on a (modern) tram at Praça da Figueira and head to Belém, a half-hour ride from Baixa. Its must-visit experience is Antiga Confeitaria de Belém, a world-renowned patisserie that is custard-tart nirvana. This will give you energy to tackle the Manueline cloisters of Mosteiro dos Jerónimos, a Unesco World Heritage Site. Enjoy lunch while overlooking the Rio Tejo at À Margem. In the afternoon, head back to Alfama and stroll through the pretty streets. Pop into the fascinating Museu do Fado to prepare yourself for all things fado. As dusk falls and the street lanterns light up, enjoy a drink at the Wine Bar do Castelo. Then follow the soul and sounds of Portugal and head to a fado performance.

PLAN IT

As Portugal's cultural mecca, Lisbon is a great spot to catch a fado performance (reservations are necessary for some clubs). The city's tourist office can suggest fado clubs, but in order to tune into the best places, just ask the locals – a follower will know the current hot spots. Most clubs are open year-round. Most international visitors arrive at Lisbon Airport. From here, both buses and metro services run frequently to the city centre. Alfama is a handy (if cramped) base to stay; other centrally located neighbourhoods are as convenient.

DETOUR

For a stimulating experience of a different kind, the must-do day trip has to be Sintra, around 35km west of Lisbon, and accessible by train from the city. Its centre – Sintra-Vila – is Unesco World Heritage–listed for good reason. With lush gardens and forests, rippling mountains and exotic palaces, Sintra resembles a magical fairyland (but genuine – we're not talking Disneyland). If you're 'castled out', you can visit the modern art museum.

OPENING SPREAD Fado singers touch hearts in the bars and restaurants of Lisbon's Alfama neighbourhood. **ABOVE** The view from Belém Tower, guardian of Lisbon's harbour. **LEFT** Search out boutiques by day and hidden nightspots after dark in the Bairro Alto neighbourhood.

DECKCHAIR

✳ **Fados** (2007) Directed by Carlos Saura, this is one of the few movies about fado, depicting the songs, the music and dancing.

✳ **Amália** (2008) This biopic, directed by Carlos Coelho da Silva, provides an in-depth look at the life of Amália Rodrigues, the Queen of Fado.

✳ **The History of the Portuguese Fado** (Paul Vernon) This book covers the origins, history and meaning of fado.

✳ **Best of Amália Rodrigues** (Amália Rodrigues), **100 Canções, Uma Vida** (Carlos do Carmo), **Desfado** (Ana Moura), **Fado em mim** (Mariza), **Alma** (Carminho) are all albums that offer a gorgeous introduction to fado.

✳ **Tile Designs from Portugal** (Diego Hurtado De Mendoza) This book features the stunning designs and colours of Portuguese azulejos (tiles).

DIVE INTO LITERARY DUBLIN

JOYCE, SHAW, WILDE, BECKETT, STOKER: FOLLOW IN THEIR FOOTSTEPS AND DISCOVER WHAT IT IS ABOUT DUBLIN – A UNESCO CITY OF LITERATURE THAT CLAIMS FOUR NOBEL PRIZE WINNERS FOR LITERATURE – THAT INSPIRED SO MANY OF THE WORLD'S GREATEST WRITERS.

54

'Good puzzle would be cross Dublin without passing a pub,' ponders Leopold Bloom. It's not a puzzle that the central character of *Ulysses,* James Joyce's famously complex novel, is in danger of solving. At Davy Byrne's pub on Duke St, Bloom orders a gorgonzola sandwich and a glass of burgundy, which you can still devour there today.

Nearby McDaid's pulled pints for postwar playwright and novelist Brendan Behan. And one of the city's oldest pubs, Toner's, scored a first in 1922 when it hosted the abstemious poet WB Yeats. According to literary legend, Yeats was offered a glass of sherry, drank it, announced 'Now I have seen a pub,' and left.

It's hard to separate writers from pubs in the Irish capital, but they're not the only places with rich literary connections. The great novelist and playwright George Bernard Shaw spent many hours in the city's National Gallery during an unhappy childhood, its paintings easing his loneliness. He later left a share of his royalties to the institution, which has since paid for much new art. Like so many of his fellow writers, Shaw took inspiration from the city, and paid back that debt with dazzling creative works.

Dublin has long been a hotbed of writing talent, throwing up such diverse geniuses as Oscar Wilde, Samuel Beckett and Bram Stoker. But why is it so? The city is – to be frank – not one of Europe's most spectacular to look at. But maybe that's the key to escaping into Dublin's literary heart. A rainy city on an island on the western edge of Europe, with a history tinged with tragedy and a rich culture of folklore and storytelling, was destined to turn inwards – to the pubs, the libraries, the galleries, the soul – and thus produce grand stories.

Follow the example of Dublin's great writers by heading to the nearest pub; with more than a thousand of them you'll be hard-pressed to solve Bloom's puzzle. There you can sip a beer, soak up the atmosphere and put pen to paper.

ESSENTIAL EXPERIENCES

* **Peering at the beautiful detail of the *Book of Kells,* one of the oldest tomes in the world.**

* Pondering Oscar Wilde's rise and fall at his memorial in Merrion Square.

* **Seeing a new Irish play or a revival of a classic at Ireland's famous national theatre, the Abbey Theatre.**

* Poring over ancient books and other printed wonders from all around the world in the Chester Beatty Library.

* **Combining great stories and great pubs on the Dublin Literary Pub Crawl.**

* Following in Leopold Bloom's footsteps by downing a gorgonzola sandwich and a glass of burgundy at Davy Byrne's.

LOCATION DUBLIN, IRELAND | **BEST TIME OF YEAR** MAY TO OCTOBER | **IDEAL TIME COMMITMENT** A LONG WEEKEND
ESSENTIAL TIP READ ULYSSES BEFORE YOU ARRIVE | **BUDGET** $$ | **PACK** PLENTY OF IRISH LITERATURE AND AN UMBRELLA

BRAM STOKER, VAMPIRE WRITER

When it was published in 1897, no one could have guessed that *Dracula* would make Bram Stoker the most influential horror fiction novelist ever. Born in Dublin in 1847, Stoker had been a sickly child with plenty of time for reading. As an adult he became friends with Oscar Wilde and the actor Henry Irving. But it was possibly from his chance meeting with Hungarian historian and traveller Arminius Vámbéry that Stoker learned of the legend of Vlad the Impaler, aka Dracula. Vámbéry's reward? As rumour has it, he was immortalised in the novel as Abraham Van Helsing, Dracula's implacable foe.

■ THE PERFECT GETAWAY

Dublin offers many ways of exploring its literary heritage. Start at Trinity College, where the beautifully illustrated, 1200-year-old *Book of Kells* is the star attraction. Created by Celtic monks, this gospel tome contains vivid illustrations of people, animals and mythical beasts. To see it within its low-light room is a moving experience, and a reminder of the power of images when combined with words.

Also included in admission is the magnificent Long Room, an 18th-century library with oak shelves holding 200,000 books. With its vaulted ceiling and marble busts of writers and philosophers, it's like something out of Harry Potter.

East of Trinity College, Sweny's, a former pharmacy mentioned in *Ulysses,* sells books by Irish writers of all eras. Around the corner in Merrion Square you'll find a statue of Oscar Wilde lounging on a large rock. Behind St Patrick's Cathedral is Archbishop Marsh's Library. This 1701 treasure trove of rare books still has its original carved bookcases and wire 'cages', into which scholars were locked while studying valuable works: no chance of nicking a first edition here.

Another must-visit library is the Chester Beatty, in Dublin Castle's grounds. The collection of an American mining engineer, it contains a vast number of manuscripts, rare books and miniature paintings. Reaching beyond the Western world, the Beatty amassed impressive Islamic works. Seeing such a gathering of the world's creativity in one place is inspirational, and must have sparked the imagination of more than one Dublin writer. You'll quickly realise writers in Dublin are a much-valued part of the everyday landscape. Celebrate their stories, and create some of your own, too.

■ PLAN IT

Dublin is well connected by air to Europe and beyond. Combine a visit with a jaunt to the UK, as flights between the two are frequent and short. There are also ferry connections from Dublin to the UK, and from Ireland's southern ports to France. The city is small and easy to get around, offering no greater challenge than struggling to be cultural the morning after the night before.

■ DETOUR

If it's music that floats your boat, take a trip across the Emerald Isle to Galway, where pubs ring out to the sound of Celtic ballads and traditional Irish folk songs. This tiny west-coast city, two hours from Dublin by car, is a hotbed of live music venues, most of them brightly painted pubs where locals and visitors, pints of stout in hand, crowd around a band playing traditional Irish instruments such as bodhrán drums and fiddles. The Galway Arts Festival takes place over two weeks every summer; to whet your appetite for Irish music listen to songs by The Dubliners.

OPENING SPREAD The beauty of books in the Long Room of the Old Library at Trinity College. **ABOVE (L)** A Dublin bartender delivers pints of Guinness, the city's stout; it takes a couple of minutes for the head to settle. **ABOVE (R)** Crossing the River Liffey on Ha'penny Bridge, which dates from 1816.

DECKCHAIR

* *Ulysses* (James Joyce) The quintessential 'difficult book', this novel's story takes place across Dublin on a single day.

* *Gulliver's Travels* (Jonathan Swift) Dublin's satirist-in-chief created a world of giants, Lilliputians and sophisticated Houyhnhnms in his 1726 classic, which cuts government and religion down to size.

* *The Picture of Dorian Grey* (Oscar Wilde) In addition to plays like *An Ideal Husband,* Wilde wrote this entertaining novella.

* *The Deportees* (Roddy Doyle) This 2008 work explores the stories of recent immigrants to Dublin.

* *The Shelbourne* (Elizabeth Bowen) Novel featuring a landmark hotel in Dublin and its interaction with decades of Irish history.

* *Dublin Noir: The Celtic Tiger vs the Ugly American* (Ken Bruen) A collection of short crime stories set in the city.

LUXE

❦

GREAT ESCAPES

JAMES BOND'S JAMAICAN PAD

THE OLD-TIME GLAMOUR OF JAMAICA COMES ALIVE AT GOLDENEYE – A RESORT ON ORACABESSA BAY, WHERE BOND CREATOR, IAN FLEMING, USED TO WRITE HIS SPY NOVELS LOOKING OUT TO A JADE-GREEN SEA. ITS SPIRIT LIVES ON IN THE HANDS OF CHRIS BLACKWELL, FOUNDER OF ISLAND RECORDS.

It is early evening and the Caribbean waters are turning a blush pink with the falling light. The pale, glass-green water of GoldenEye's still lagoon is transformed into a jewel-like emerald now that the sun is no longer high in the sky. This is when the sun sends its shafts deep into the pool of water to light the lagoon as if from within, creating a place that's hard to beat even on Jamaica. A few stilted, candy-coloured villas have their shutters open so their occupants can better hear the surf and birdsong. Concealed by thick, glossy vegetation, the crickets provide exotic percussion to the sound of reggae emanating from the curl of white beach nearby. This is where a group of guests gather, chicly attired in Etro and flip-flops, sipping on beer and the local rum punch.

They are drinking at the bar at GoldenEye, a resort occupying 52 acres of prime real estate on the north coast of Jamaica. The salty air carries not just their voices, but the unmistakable scents of Jamaica: tangy curry and chargrilled sweetcorn cooked on the barbecue. Whether the scent emanates from the resort's restaurant or the nearby village of Oracabessa, it is hard to tell.

There is music too. But then GoldenEye's owner, Chris Blackwell, was the man who founded Island Records, launching Bob Marley and exporting reggae to the world. He also knew author Ian Fleming who, along with Noël Coward and screen legend Errol Flynn, lived on the island in its silver-screen heyday – when everyone from Liz Taylor to Sophia Loren showed up to party. GoldenEye was Fleming's former home, which Blackwell has owned since 1976. By turning it into one of the most exclusive resorts in the Caribbean, Blackwell has opened up the island's glamour to outsiders, without turning the place into a luxury cliché.

ESSENTIAL EXPERIENCES

* **Rafting Rio Grande, one of Jamaica's largest rivers, at a gentle pace.**

* Swimming in YS Falls, a seven-tiered cascading waterfall on the island's south coast. Closer to GoldenEye (30 minutes by car) is a thrilling river-tubing ride, led by experienced guides, down the White River.

* **Climbing Blue Mountain Peak (the island's highest mountain at 2236 metres), combining your trek with a stay at Blackwell's other hotel, Strawberry Hill, in these mist-wrapped, coffee-growing hills.**

* Taking a jet-ski safari from GoldenEye to Robins Bay. The sport is a favourite hobby of Blackwell's.

LOCATION: ORACABESSA BAY ON JAMAICA'S NORTH COAST | **BEST TIME OF YEAR** FEBRUARY IS THE COOLEST MONTH, JULY AND AUGUST THE WARMEST, AND CHRISTMAS AND NEW YEAR THE MOST FUN | **IDEAL TIME COMMITMENT** ONE WEEK **ESSENTIAL TIP** HEAD OUT OF THE RESORT TO EAT LOCALLY AND DANCE ON A FRIDAY OR SATURDAY NIGHT | **BUDGET** $$$ **PACK** NO TIES, JACKETS OR LOUBOUTIN HEELS – IT'S ALL ABOUT GOING BAREFOOT

HOT STREET EATS

Jamaican street food is up there with Hanoi and Bangkok for cooking infused with heat and soul. Travelling through Jamaica, a number of specialties can be picked up by just lowering your car window. The best of them include jerk chicken, yellow yam with olive oil, and slow-cooked oxtail with rice and peas (the rice infused with a hint of coconut cream). For those who can take the heat, 'go local' and lash your meal with country pepper. Bottles of the stuff, derived from the fiery Scotch Bonnet pepper grown all over Jamaica, are also a great, inexpensive gift to bring home.

■ THE PERFECT GETAWAY

Oracabessa Bay used to be a port for Jamaica's banana trade. It was also the spot that inspired author Ian Fleming, who from 1949 spent three months of every year in Jamaica, writing his famous spy novels at a rate of 2000 words a day. He wrote fourteen novels while living at GoldenEye, which Fleming first discovered for himself after British Intelligence sent him to report on U-boat activities in the Caribbean during WWII. He was easily seduced by Oracabessa's soporific pace. This led him to build his villa on the rocks, which still forms the heart of the resort that carries the GoldenEye name.

To stay in this villa, sketched by the author on his desk blotter, is expensive at $5500 a night for use of the three-bedroom main house plus two satellite villas, Sweet Spot and Pool House, all of which come with their own staff. But it is also authentic, with the villa's original footprint still overlooking a white beach below, reached by a flight of stairs. The lawn is still cut just so, and the flowers grow in tropical abundance, concealing the villa and its inhabitants from prying eyes.

To this landmark has been added clapboard and cedar, shingle-roofed villas nearby, forming a private enclave of suites and cottages that are neither too flashy nor too basic to sit ill with the glamour of Fleming's beloved home. Explore just a little further into GoldenEye's gardens, and one discovers trees planted by the likes of Johnny Depp. Go further still, up into the hills behind, and there is Noël Coward's House, Firefly, where one can enjoy the picnic hour under the shade of trees. Take a boat out for the afternoon and it is easy to see what inspired Fleming's fiction. And at the end of each day, pull out the backgammon board, best enjoyed with a martini in hand, and listen once again to the surf and the chatter of crickets.

DECKCHAIR

* ***Dr No*** (Ian Fleming) Of all the 007 books largely or partly set in Jamaica, Dr. No is one to read while staying at GoldenEye.

* ***The Long Song*** (Andrea Levy) A gripping novel from this winner of the Orange Prize. Set in Falmouth on the island's north coast, it investigates unsettling truths about slavery on Jamaica.

* ***The Italian Job*** (1969) Noël Coward, who lived on Jamaica, appeared in no film greater than this classic. You'll find him playing the role of Mr Bridger, a prison-bound criminal who bankrolls a robbery.

* ***My Wicked, Wicked Ways*** (Errol Flynn) Errol Flynn helped define the island's glamorous history after his yacht washed up here in 1942 following a storm. This is his spirited autobiography.

* ***The Harder They Come*** (1972) This Jamaican crime film, based on a 1940s real-life villain, stars reggae singer Jimmy Cliff. Its soundtrack is cited as the catalyst for reggae's breaking into the USA.

PLAN IT

GoldenEye is a magnet for celebrities who want to escape the cameras and sink into a relaxed world of like-minded souls. The resort is at its most glam over Christmas and New Year when the big names arrive from London, New York and LA. The usual way to get here is via the international airport at Montego Bay, a 90-minute drive from the resort. You can transfer to a helicopter; the 25-minute flight takes in Jamaica's dramatic coastline.

DETOUR

Firefly was the hilltop home of English playwright Noël Coward, who made Jamaica his home for 20 years. The villa's views of Jamaica's north coast were not lost on the pirate-turned-governor, Sir Henry Morgan, who used this eyrie as his lookout prior to Coward's taking up residence in 1948. Cut to the present day and Firefly's spirit remains, as if the great wit has only just walked out the door to take in the still evening air from his garden bench. Inside the house, there is an elegant salon dominated with a grand piano featuring photos of Coward's former guests, including Marlene Dietrich. By prior arrangement through GoldenEye, resort guests can enjoy a picnic in Firefly's gardens, a sunset cocktail or even a private wedding ceremony.

OPENING SPREAD The Pool House at Ian Fleming's villa, the heart of the GoldenEye resort. **ABOVE** Fishing boats moored on the White River in Ocho Rios. **BELOW** Its mists lend the Blue Mountain range its name and provide the perfect conditions for growing coffee beans.

JAMMING IN JAMAICA

For the last 50 years, Chris Blackwell has helped tell Jamaica's story through music, from the founding of Island Records in 1959 to the export of Bob Marley's 'One World, One Love' message to every corner of the earth. His passion for Jamaica is also reflected in his Island Outpost group of hotels, which includes GoldenEye, Strawberry Hill in the Blue Mountains, The Caves, and Geejam, which has its own recording studio. Thus his two worlds come together, with Blackwell's musical roots never far from his present. His love of a good rhythm is reflected in the inspired playlists available in every room at GoldenEye – created by Bruno Guez, who founded Quango Records.

OPEN DOORS IN MYSTERIOUS MARRAKESH

A RIAD FOCUSES INWARDS, CENTRED AROUND A GARDEN COURTYARD. A WORLD IN ITSELF, HIDDEN FROM THIS ROSE-TINTED CITY'S HUSTLE AND BUSTLE, IT'S A LUXURIOUS CORNER IN WHICH COUPLES WILL FIND SECLUSION.

In the oldest part of Marrakesh's medina (old walled city), things haven't changed for hundreds of years. Tiny hole-in-the-wall shops do business deep into the night; long-gowned locals chat on the corners of the tangled narrow alleys. This is a cityscape that seems to harbour enticing mysteries. Even the architecture is secretive. Great doors in ochre sandstone walls lead to sumptuous mansions that give no glimmer of what lies inside. The way through the main door is often even seemingly blocked by a wall, enhancing the privacy of the interior. It's a place where any getaway will feel secret and romantic.

Marrakesh is an exotic bird, and its streets, *souqs* (markets) and gardens tease and set your senses atingle with colour and life. It's a city of intrigue, of jewel-bright tiling, lazy pavement cafes where you can sip sweet mint tea and watch the theatre of the streets, and rooftop bars swathed in bright dyed cotton where visitors sip cocktails, away from prying eyes. You can even steam up your escape literally, by enjoying a treatment at one of the city's hammams (Turkish baths).

It's a magical experience to explore this city with a loved one, but the *riad* (traditional Moroccan house) is the pounding heart of Marrakesh's romance. These great houses are the ideal place to retreat from the whirling kaleidoscope of the city. Deep in the old town, couples can disappear into houses that have been converted into discreet hotels, such as Riad Farnatchi, a hidden palace. This sumptuous Moroccan house harbours suites of rooms with deep tiled bathtubs, secluded balconies and great arched bedrooms. Or hide away in a more modern space; somewhere such as Riad Due, where four rooms merge pared-down, funky style with artfully distressed work-of-art furniture. Here you can also lounge on shaded day beds on the roof terrace, watching the sun set over winding Marrakesh streets from the sanctuary of your romantic eyrie.

ESSENTIAL EXPERIENCES

* **Bargaining for glittering works of art in the ancient souqs of the old medina.**
* Whiling away hours over mint tea while lounging on cushions at an exquisitely tiled cafe.
* **Steaming and enjoying a relaxing, scented massage in an exotic-feeling hammam.**
* Watching the potion hawkers, musicians and acrobats on the Djemaa el-Fna.
* **Dreaming away the afternoon in the Marjorelle Garden, which once belonged to Yves St Laurent.**
* Enjoying a sundowner or a candlelit dinner on a rooftop, listening to the muezzins' calls to prayer echo across the city.

LOCATION MARRAKESH, MOROCCO | **BEST TIME OF YEAR** APRIL TO MAY, SEPTEMBER TO OCTOBER | **IDEAL TIME COMMITMENT** LONG WEEKEND TO ONE WEEK | **ESSENTIAL TIP** ALWAYS BARGAIN IN THE SOUQS BUT DON'T LOSE YOUR SENSE OF HUMOUR **BUDGET** $$$ | **PACK** SUITABLY UNREVEALING CLOTHES

ESCAPE FROM MARRAKESH

It's easy to arrange a day trip to explore Marrakesh's surrounding countryside and well worth setting aside some time to head out of the city. Around 150km northeast of the city, you can visit the thundering waterfalls of Ouzoud, which tip down over craggy ochre cliffs covered in carob and olive trees. It's refreshing to take a breather from the city's frenetic colour; this is a great place to wander and experience a taste of rural Morocco, as well as picnic under the shade of the lime trees and swim in freshwater pools that are fed by the falls.

THE HAMMAM EXPERIENCE

Turkish-style baths were established in Morocco at the time of the Ottoman Empire and are still an essential local tradition. Local hammams can be rough and ready, but there are many more luxurious versions that allow you to recline on chaise longues and sip sugared mint tea in lush surroundings between treatments. A swimming costume should be worn, and you may want to take a swimming hat to protect your hair from the oil. Once you've been washed down with hot water and have relaxed in the hot rooms, you'll be exfoliated with a rough-mitt *gommage*, before relaxing some more.

▉ The Perfect Getaway

Getting lost in the World Heritage–listed medina has to be high on your itinerary. Its souqs are lined with vividly bright arts and crafts, and the lanes peppered by workshops, mosques, hammams and shops. Whole streets are dedicated to the sale of *babouches* (leather slippers), herbs, carpets, brassware, and traditional Moroccan *djellaba* (long, hooded gowns). Part of the fun is losing your way, but eventually you'll emerge onto one of the world's greatest public spaces, the extraordinary Djemaa el-Fna, with its food stalls, musicians, performing animals, acrobats, magicians and tooth pullers. It's a quintessential Marrakesh experience to soak it in all from a pavement table at the Café de France, sipping mint tea.

Head for a drink and a snack in the French-flavoured Ville Nouvelle area at the Grand Café de la Poste, a former post office that's regained its opulent early 20th-century European style. In the afternoon, there are few places prettier than the green-, blue- and lemon-hued botanical garden designed by Jacques Majorelle and restored by Yves St Laurent and Pierre Bergé.

You'll need to have booked a few weeks ahead to get a massage and a steam bath at the city's most famous spa, Les Bains de Marrakech, but it's worth being organised to ensure you get to visit these beautiful baths. For dinner, dine under flickering candlelight reflected on great brass candelabra, with traditional music feeding the atmosphere at Le Tobsil. This restaurant is housed in a palace in the medina, and the daily set menu includes an epicurean array of salads, pigeon, fish or vegetable *b'stilla* (sweet, savoury pies) and roast lamb or chicken *tagines,* followed by fruit and rose-scented pastries for the sweetest end to an evening.

▉ Plan It

Fly to Marrakesh's Menara Airport (from where it's a 15-minute drive to the city centre) or take a boat from Spain to Tangiers and reach Marrakesh by train. As riads are small, you're advised to book ahead to get the place that you want. Be aware that during Ramadan, which takes place in the ninth month of the Islamic calendar, Muslim people fast. Your passport needs to have at least six remaining months of validity to travel here.

▉ Detour

You could turn your trip into a foodie odyssey: Moroccan food is fragrant and delicately spiced, and cooking in a riad kitchen is a fascinating way to learn something while enjoying your holiday. Riad cookery courses are very hands-on and usually encompass a trip to a local market to select produce and spices. You can learn to create traditional delicacies such as couscous, *tagines,* Moroccan salads, pastries and mint tea. Try somewhere such as Maison MK, supervised by head chef Omar El Ouahssoussi, who has taught TV chef Jamie Oliver.

65

OPENING SPREAD The ultimate bazaar; lose yourself on shopping trip in Marrakesh's souk. **ABOVE** Behind Marrakesh's closed doors is the Moroccan hospitality of the city's riads. **LEFT** The tiled courtyard of Riad Al Moussika is a haven from the hubbub outside.

DECKCHAIR

※ **The Sheltering Sky** (Paul Bowles) A quintessential Morocco read, though be warned: the romance here goes seriously awry.

※ **In Morocco** (Edith Wharton) Glimpse the colonial elite of the 1920s through eyes of novelist Edith Wharton in this travel memoir.

※ **In Arabian Nights** (Tahir Shah) Immerse yourself in the local culture through these atmospheric retellings of traditional stories.

※ **Lords of the Atlas** (Gavin Maxwell) Thrilling history following the fortunes of a prominent 20th-century Moroccan family.

※ **Casablanca** (1942) OK, it's not set in Marrakesh, but this is a great love story and essential viewing for channelling your inner Bogey or Bacall.

AN ISLAND IDYLL IN THE GREAT BEAR RAINFOREST

DESERT ISLAND DREAMS NEEDN'T NECESSARILY BE ABOUT DEPRIVATION.
NOT WHEN THAT ISLAND IS CANADA'S PRINCESS ROYAL ISLAND, ENCASED IN
WILDERNESS AND WILDLIFE AND HOME TO A FLOATING LUXURY LODGE.

66

Who doesn't love a good uninhabited island, an untouched, water-lapped bit of paradise that encapsulates those hard-to-shake fantasies about leaving the world and its worries behind? Princess Royal Island may well be that fantasy in reality.

Hard against the coast of British Columbia, south of the town of Prince Rupert, Princess Royal Island is part of the Great Bear Rainforest, one of the largest tracts of temperate rainforest in the world (covering an area about the size of Ireland). For eight months of the year the island is an untouched wilderness with not a person or human structure on it; then each June, the luxurious King Pacific Lodge is towed from Prince Rupert and anchored by the island's shores in Barnard Harbour.

The location is extraordinary, facing away from the mainland and looking out over the protected waters of the harbour to Gil Island. Bald eagles peer down from the treetops and it's not unusual to see humpback whales rising from the water just metres from the barge on which the lodge sits.

It's these sorts of wildlife encounters that are central to the lodge experience. Humpbacks and orcas cruise the straits, along with Dall's porpoises and Steller sea lions. Boat across to Campania Island and you might see black wolves right on the beach. Otters prowl beside the barge. Grizzlies, black bears and – most enticingly – spirit bears roam the islands. You can fish for salmon or trout, kayak among the whales or helicopter out to hike on a distant snow-wrapped ridge.

When you return to the lodge, no luxuries are overlooked. The large rooms feature king-size beds, slate bathrooms and deep baths with views. Dinners meld Pacific Northwest cuisine with native and traditional recipes, paired with quality wines. Later you can zone out in the lodge spa, the fireside library, or once more view the parade of wildlife through the telescope.

ESSENTIAL EXPERIENCES

* **Watching a humpback whale breach just metres from your boat.**
* Standing by the banks of a stream as spirit bears and black bears paw at a feed of salmon.
* **Sipping a wine or liqueur on the lodge deck as whales surface in the still harbour, bald eagles perching on dead branches above.**
* Searching for wolf-paw prints in the beach sands of Campania Island, across the water from Princess Royal Island.
* **Dropping a line into a crystalline stream in pursuit of trout.**
* Trading the day's wildlife sightings with other guests as you dine in view of the harbour and the dark forest.

LOCATION PRINCESS ROYAL ISLAND, BRITISH COLUMBIA, CANADA | **BEST TIME OF YEAR** THE LODGE IS OPEN JUNE THROUGH SEPTEMBER | **IDEAL TIME COMMITMENT** FOUR TO SEVEN DAYS | **ESSENTIAL TIP** STUDYING UP ON THE WILDLIFE WILL ENHANCE THE EXPERIENCE | **BUDGET** $$$ | **PACK** LODGE PACKAGES ARE ALL-INCLUSIVE; PACK LIGHT

THE GREAT BEAR RAINFOREST

Dubbed 'Canada's Amazon', the Great Bear Rainforest encompasses a wild region of mountains, islands and fjords along British Columbia's coast. One of the largest areas of intact temperate rainforest in the world, it covers an area of around 64,000 sq km from the Alaska border down to near Campbell River on Vancouver Island. Home to grizzly bears, wolves and spawning salmon, its most famous inhabitant is the emblematic spirit bear, which gives the forest its name. Remote valleys are lined with forests of old Sitka spruce, Pacific silver fir and various cedars that are up to 100m tall and 1500 years old.

HUMPBACK HIGHWAY

The star of the sea around Princess Royal Island is undoubtedly the humpback whale. Each autumn humpbacks migrate from Alaskan waters to Hawaii, a journey of around 5500km that they then make in reverse around June. It's during this return to cooler, nutrient-rich waters (the whales give birth around Hawaii but go months without eating while there) that they are observed along the British Columbia coast. Humpbacks can grow to around 16m in length, and watching them breach – propelling themselves out of the water and then slamming back down – is one of the finest wildlife sights on earth.

■ THE PERFECT GETAWAY

The sense of seclusion begins at once. The only way to reach King Pacific Lodge is by float plane, skimming over islands, looking down onto the seas that harbour the marine life you've come to see. The lodge is spectacular – native timbers, a stone fireplace and cathedral-high ceilings in the Great Hall; suites that might overlook a waterfall – but it's what's beyond the barge that will fill your days.

Intimate whale-watching is one of the prime experiences. Through June and July, resident orcas cruise past the island in pursuit of spawning salmon. As the orcas are departing, the nutrient-rich seas begin to fill with humpback whales, returning from winter seasons in warmer waters around Hawaii. Humpbacks are frequently seen in Barnard Harbour itself; in Whale Channel, the strait that separates Princess Royal and Gil islands, expect awesome breaching displays and, often, whales passing directly beneath your boat.

Wildlife viewing hits a peak in September, when bear sightings become frequent. Bears roam Princess Royal Island but the population is less concentrated than on smaller islands such as Gribbell. Here guests can wander to the edge of a stream, watching from just metres away as black bears feast on spawning salmon from the shallow water. The prize sightings are spirit, or Kermode, bears, a rare subspecies of the black bear with cream-coloured fur. They are endemic to the Great Bear Rainforest, with the population estimated at less than 1000, making them rarer than giant pandas. All this with your palatial room, the spa, a liqueur by the fire, the plunge pool – or simply a quiet hour or two in the perfect silence of the barge deck – awaiting you back in Barnard Harbour.

■ PLAN IT

King Pacific Lodge offers three-, four- and seven-night packages. Guests take a private charter flight from Vancouver to Bella Bella, connecting with a float plane to the island. The lodge has 17 rooms and suites, allowing for a maximum of 34 guests, and stays are all-inclusive. The resort is open only four months of the year (June to September), so plan well ahead; bookings can be made through the lodge website.

■ DETOUR

Spirit bears might be cute and unusual, but if you want to see the grand master of the ursine world – the grizzly bear – Knight Inlet Lodge is about the pick of Canada's stays. Set on British Columbia's longest fjord, this floating lodge, around 300km southeast of Princess Royal Island, is in prime grizzly territory – it boasts that in salmon season there can be up to 50 grizzlies within 10km of the lodge. The lodge burned down in September 2012 but is expected to be rebuilt and operational again for the 2013 season.

OPENING SPREAD Spirit bears – white-furred black bears – prowl these misty, mossy forests. **ABOVE (L)** Detour south to the hot springs of Bella Coola, also on the Central Coast. **ABOVE (R)** Humpback whales winter in Hawaii but can be seen diving all along this coast. **LEFT** King Pacific Lodge.

DECKCHAIR

* **Spirit Bear: Encounters with the White Bear of the Western Rainforest** (Charles Russell) A photographic ode to spirit bears, featuring images from Princess Royal Island. The book is part of a push to have the island declared a reserve for this bear species.

* **The Great Bear Rainforest: Canada's Forgotten Coast** (Ian McAllister, Karen McAllister and Cameron Young) Beautifully photographed book about the Great Bear Rainforest and its bears.

* **I Heard the Owl Call My Name** (Margaret Craven) Best-selling novel about a dying vicar sent to a First Nations community inside the Great Bear Rainforest.

* **Exploring the North Coast of British Columbia** (Don Douglass) Get an idea of the waters and islands from this boaties' guide to the waterways around Princess Royal Island.

SAFARI IN STYLE AMONG INDIA'S TIGERS

MAKE LIKE MOWGLI ON A TIGER-SPOTTING SAFARI IN INDIA'S PENCH NATIONAL PARK. THE REAL-LIFE SETTING FOR RUDYARD KIPLING'S JUNGLE BOOK, THIS IS HOME TO ROAMING BENGAL BEASTS, STEALTHY LEOPARDS AND A HOST OF RARE AND WONDERFUL BIRD SPECIES THAT'LL SEND TWITCHERS INTO A FLAP.

70

It paces forward slowly, muscles rippling beneath its stripes, as it sizes up its prey. This animal emanates a power that is humbling to behold; you realise you're holding your breath as you watch on from the open-top 4WD. Suddenly the dust kicks up and the tiger has struck before you can blink, while its target, the boar, barely has time to struggle before the kill is complete. Far-off thunder rumbles and a breeze blows through the teak trees – you exhale with it, having witnessed one of nature's most primal experiences...

Pench National Park offers the perfect chance to live out your Kiplingesque fantasies while camping in luxurious style. Located on the southern border of Madhya Pradesh in central India, this creature-rich retreat is home to royal Bengal tigers, majestic guar, leopards and 300-odd species of birds.

The first safari session kicks off at around 6am. After being woken with biscuits and coffee at dawn, you're bundled into the 4WD for the short drive to the park. Soon you're speeding down dirt tracks that weave through forests of mahua and teak, over grassy plateaux and along dry riverbeds. A headcount of around 25 royal Bengal tigers means you have a good chance of sighting and snapping the rare beasts in the wild.

When you've had all the animal encounters you can handle in one day, it's time to relax in style. Set right at the edge of this sprawling reserve is Baghvan (meaning 'tiger garden'), a Taj Safari Lodge that puts the glam in 'glamping'. Forget about pitching a tent or cooking over a gas stove: here, camping is of the ultra-luxe variety. Twelve bungalows each feature an elegant bedroom, alfresco bathroom and a secluded courtyard. Mosquito nets and curtains transform this open-air pavilion into a breezy bedroom where you can sleep, sip and feast among the treetops. Kipling never had it this good.

ESSENTIAL EXPERIENCES

* **Rising before dawn for an early morning safari session in Pench National Park**
* Spending the night in an elevated sleep-out *machan* (jungle pavilion)
* **Learning how to cook tandoori, curries and wholesome breads**
* Visiting nearby Pachdhar village to buy handmade pottery
* **Having dinner served under the majestic Mahua tree**
* Enjoying a sundowner at Khoka Lake, a five-minute drive from the hotel

LOCATION PENCH NATIONAL PARK, MADHYA PRADESH, INDIA | **IDEAL TIME COMMITMENT** THREE DAYS | **BEST TIME OF YEAR** BETWEEN FEBRUARY AND APRIL | **ESSENTIAL TIP** BRING A TELEPHOTO LENS FOR SNAPPING ELUSIVE TIGERS AND LEOPARDS
BUDGET $$$ | **PACK** BINOCULARS, PRACTICAL SHOES AND A WARM TOP FOR CHILLY EARLY MORNINGS

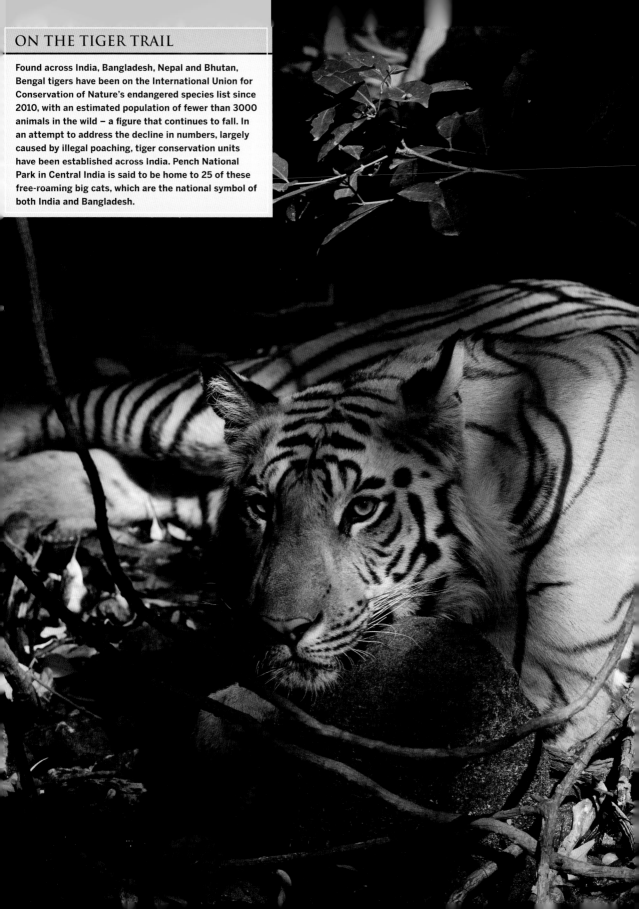

ON THE TIGER TRAIL

Found across India, Bangladesh, Nepal and Bhutan, Bengal tigers have been on the International Union for Conservation of Nature's endangered species list since 2010, with an estimated population of fewer than 3000 animals in the wild – a figure that continues to fall. In an attempt to address the decline in numbers, largely caused by illegal poaching, tiger conservation units have been established across India. Pench National Park in Central India is said to be home to 25 of these free-roaming big cats, which are the national symbol of both India and Bangladesh.

■ THE PERFECT GETAWAY

Days at Baghvan revolve around safari excursions and dining. Just after sunrise, a light breakfast is served on your verandah before you're whisked away for your first drive of the day. After a morning spent twitching (bird watching) and tiger-spotting, enjoy lunch on the wooden deck overlooking the pool. Regional cuisine – including deeply spiced goat curries, fresh-from-the-tandoor chicken and earthy flatbreads stuffed with paneer or potato – stars in the multi-course meals. Budding masterchefs can learn how to cook the dishes themselves in the interactive kitchen, mixing spice pastes and baking breads.

After your tandoori lesson, cool off with a dip in the pool, an in-suite massage treatment or a self-guided yoga session. You can also mingle with other guests in the communal lounge area, a traditional hunting lodge that's been given an Indian accent with Parsi floor tiles, rustic Rajasthani doors, hurricane lamps and antique ayurvedic massage beds that have been converted into coffee tables. Recharged, it's time for you to head back out on an afternoon safari.

While the tigers are the rulers of Pench's natural playground, this 757-sq-km reserve offers up a host of brag-worthy wildlife encounters. The forest is sparse and the ground cover far less dense than in other central Indian locales, so it's a cinch to spot sloth bears, sambar deer, wild boars and cheeky rhesus macaque monkeys. If you fancy exploring the terrain on foot, guided walks through the buffer zone surrounding the park can be arranged.

Round out your day of animal tracking with a sundowner at Khoka Lake, a five-minute drive from the hotel, or at the Junewani watering hole nearby. Here, as evening falls, hundreds of sambar deer come to sip and graze by the water's edge, and in winter the lake glows golden as the sun sets.

ARMCHAIR

* **Life of Pi** (Yann Martel) Kicking off in India, this evocative novel tells the story of Piscine 'Pi' Patel... and a tiger called Richard Parker; it was beautifully adapted for the screen by director Ang Lee.

* **Tales from the Indian Jungle** (Kenneth Anderson) Follow hunter and wildlife chronicler Anderson through the jungles of India.

* **Land of the Striped Stalker** (Rajesh Gopal) Get up close and personal with the wildlife of Madhya Pradesh.

* **The Jungle Book** (Rudyard Kipling) Kipling's classic book of tales, including that of Mowgli, the young boy raised by wolves in the Pench National Park area.

* **Vintage Madhya Pradesh** (Pankaj Rag) A coffee-table book charting the history of Madhya Pradesh.

* **Star Birds** (&Beyond) Discover the top 10 must-spy birds in Pench National Park.

◼ PLAN IT

If you're flying in from overseas, touch down in Delhi or Mumbai, then take a two-hour flight to Nagpur Airport in central India. From here, it's a 90km drive to the lodge. Hire a driver for the jaunt along National Highway 7 to the village of Turia, or ask Baghvan to arrange transfers. If time allows, stop off at neighbouring Pachdhar village to purchase handcrafted pottery. Baghvan and the park are closed from July to mid-October each year during the monsoon season – and note that the area is intensely hot from May to July.

◼ DETOUR

Baghvan is one of four luxury safari lodges in the Taj stables, all spaced four to five hours' drive apart throughout Madhya Pradesh. For a safari adventure across the region, plot a course between the retreats, visiting Mahua Kothi in lush Badhavgarh National Park, the jungle camp Banjaar Tola in Kanha National Park and Pashan Garh near the Panna reserve. Each of the resorts works a rustic-luxe aesthetic, with mudbrick abodes at Mahua Kothi, capacious canvas tents at Banjaar Tola and riverside treehouses at Pashan Garh. The safari experiences are equally diverse in each park, but all promise the possibility of spotting tigers in the wild.

OPENING SPREAD A young Bengal tiger is camouflaged on the forest floor of Badhavgarh National Park. **ABOVE** Safari lodge accommodation at Baghvan is far from basic. **BELOW** Get closer to local wildlife on the back of an Indian elephant.

A WALK ON THE WILD SIDE

While your first instinct might be to opt for the safety and comfort of an open-top 4WD for your jaunts throughout Pench National Park, an elephant safari delivers you to the best seat in the house. Not only will you be able to get closer to tigers, boars, wild dogs and more, but you'll also be able to escape the car-bound crowds. As soon as the call goes out that one of the naturalists has spotted a big cat, vehicles descend on the scene, meaning you'll have to jostle for that perfect line of sight. Atop an elephant, however, you'll feel like you have the whole park to yourself.

LIVE LIKE A STAR IN AMAZING UTAH

IN THE STARKLY BEAUTIFUL DESERT LANDSCAPES OF THE AMERICAN SOUTHWEST, AMANGIRI'S MODERN ARCHITECTURE FALLS FOR BILLION-YEAR-OLD ROCK STAR IN A MARRIAGE MADE IN SPA HEAVEN.

Sipping a sage mojito, you take your front-row seat for the light show. You're on the terrace of your suite at Amangiri, an award-winning hideaway deep in Utah's badlands, and though tickets don't come cheap, this is the show of the century. As moments pass, the sandstone formations before you, sculpted by wind and water over millions of years, begin to glow.

Landscapes don't come more dramatic – or arid – than the slot canyons and buttressed mesas of southern Utah; the rock's white, gold and orange striations betray that this land was once all under sea. Amangiri's spartan modern design, harnessing architect Rick Joy's desert aesthetics, blends into the elemental landscape with its low-profile, concrete lines. At its centre is a main pavilion, which serves as reception, dining room and living room, overlooking a free-form swimming pool that curls around an ochre escarpment. Amangiri is that rarest of things: a luxury resort that respects its natural environment.

Sidling up to the border with Arizona, and near the national parks of Bryce Canyon and Zion, this is mesa-inspired modernism on Navajo land (in fact, Amangiri required an act of Congress to allow it to be built on protected land). The resulting privacy – the nearest town, Page, is a half-hour drive away – attracts a clipboard's-worth of A-list guests. The layout of the 34 suites allows all rooms to have grandstand views of Utah from a private porch. When it does rain, which is rarely, blooming wildflowers – pink sand verbena, rose mallow and white prickly poppy – add pastel shades to the dusty colour palette. Usually, however, the breeze just ruffles the grey-green sagebrush as hawks wheel above.

Inside, the minimalist suites are kitted out with every creature comfort. But get an expert to pour you one of Amangiri's signature prickly-pear margaritas or sage mojitos at dusk, before the widescreen landscape is set aflame by the setting sun.

ESSENTIAL EXPERIENCES

* **Following an Amangiri guide along the Hoodoo Trail and exploring the sandstone towers and other geological peculiarities of Canyon Point.**
* Seeking out fossils that are millions of years old at Grand Staircase-Escalante National Monument.
* **Making like a cowboy and feasting on supersized servings of Tex-Mex staples: barbecued meat, spicy fries and zingy chillies.**
* Standing in a beam of light deep down in a slot canyon and having your photo taken there.
* **Reviving yourself in the steam room, dry sauna and cold plunge pool of Amangiri's Water Pavilion.**
* Gawping at Horseshoe Bend near Page, Arizona.

LOCATION CANYON POINT, UTAH, USA | **BEST TIME OF YEAR** SPRING (MARCH TO MAY) AND AUTUMN (SEPTEMBER TO NOVEMBER) ARE IDEAL FOR HIKING AND TOURING | **IDEAL TIME COMMITMENT** THREE NIGHTS | **ESSENTIAL TIP** A SUNSET HELICOPTER TRIP IS A MUST | **BUDGET** $$$ | **PACK** BINOCULARS AND CAMERAS, 50+ SUNSCREEN AND WALKING SHOES

SUNDANCE CINEMA

Winter brings snow and a flurry of celebs to Utah for the Sundance Film Festival. Founded by Robert Redford's production company in 1978 (almost ten years after the release of Redford's hit film *Butch Cassidy and the Sundance Kid*) it's hosted by the ski resort Park City, a snowball's throw from Salt Lake City. Sundance has grown year by year, providing big breaks to films such as *Reservoir Dogs* and *Beasts of the Southern Wild,* and documentaries including *The Cove* and *Man on Wire*. If you want to time your trip to catch a movie or two, or just hit Park City's superb slopes, be sure to book accommodation early.

SEE UTAH FROM THE SKY

Take to the cloudless skies in a hot-air balloon flight over Lake Powell for the ultimate eyeful of the Colorado Plateau's remarkable scenery. Amangiri offers an early-morning take-off from the resort, which floats you over the lake and Vermilion Cliffs. The early start is because heat (that's the balloon) rises better in cooler conditions. Or, if you'd prefer to stay on terra firma, the town of Page, Arizona, hosts an annual balloon festival (on the first weekend of November) when 50 of the colourful beauties congregate in the sky and two dozen light up in the Night Glow.

THE PERFECT GETAWAY

The headline act at this outpost of Aman, the luxury Asian hotel group, is the hiking, with walks suited to all fitness levels. Follow a guide along the resort's 4km Hoodoo Trail and see where Hopi Indians lived. The caves are a time machine, with 5000-year-old carvings of animals and traces of ancient fire pits still visible. Three *via ferrata* excursions have also been created right on Amangiri's doorstep; Italian for 'iron road', these fixed climbing routes involve ladder rungs placed on the mountain cuestas. Guests are accompanied by in-house experts who share the basics of map-reading, rope techniques and desert travel, as well as provide an insight into the local ecology and human history. Travel back into prehistoric times by booking a palaeontology tour where dinosaurs once roamed and footprints still remain at the Grand Staircase-Escalante National Monument; scour the shale for arrowheads left by the Navajos and million-year-old fossils.

After hiking through history, guests can take a journey of a metaphysical kind at the Aman Spa, where treatments are aimed at balancing *hozho*, translating from Navajo as 'beauty, harmony and health'. Each session is soundtracked by gentle chimes and chanting, and laced with local ingredients, Native American healing traditions and spiritual blessings. Journeys begin with 'smudging', the Native American ritual of burning sage or sweet grass to create a cleansing smoke that is fanned over the body to clear negative energy, and incorporate treatments such as flotation therapy, body wraps, cranial-sacral massage and more. Or simply enjoy a steam or soak in the Water Pavilion before floating into a rockside pool. A spell in this holistic complex is uplifting for mind, body and soul.

PLAN IT

The desert climate can be scorching on summer days (June through August) but balmy by night. Most appealing is spring and autumn, when it's milder and there are fewer tourists. Winter can be cold, but it's beautiful and the parks are people-free. Page Municipal Airport in Arizona is a 25-minute drive from the resort. Great Lakes Airlines links Page with Denver, Colorado, and Phoenix, Arizona. Or drive to the resort from St George, Utah; Flagstaff and Phoenix, Arizona; and Las Vegas, Nevada.

DETOUR

Grab your camera and go to Horseshoe Bend, where the Colorado River makes a 300-degree turn. Be there when the sun is at its highest and capture the corker 300m below you. Antelope Canyon is another hotspot for snap-happy visitors, who time it to have their photo taken in a spotlight as the sun seeps into this valley (usually in the morning). For a private session of the eye-popping pink, red, purple, grey and yellow illumination of sculpted sandstone, take a Hummer Adventures trip to Secret Canyon.

OPENING SPREAD Amangiri shares the natural tones of its spectacular surroundings. **ABOVE** Thrilling views from Amangiri's suites and the hot-air balloon trip that the resort can organise. **LEFT** Exploring the hoodoos of Bryce Canyon National Park in the early-morning sunlight.

DECKCHAIR

* ❋ **The Monkey Wrench Gang** (Edward Abbey) A tale of eco-warriors battling to protect the natural landscape of the Southwest before Glen Canyon Dam was built.

* ❋ **Thunderhead** (Douglas Preston and Lincoln Child) Thriller about an anthropologist's encounter with Aztec black magic in canyon country.

* ❋ **Broken Arrow** (1996) John Travolta and Christian Slater star as renegade Air Force bomber pilots in this John Woo film, shot right here – a mine-shaft shack remains on the grounds of Amangiri. But if you missed the movie, don't rush to see it.

* ❋ **Tree of Life** (2011) More atmospheric are the images in Terrence Malick's controversial, Palme d'Or–winning movie, which features lingering, soul-stirring shots of Antelope Canyon.

* ❋ **Desert Solitaire** (Edward Abbey) Abbey is drawn back to the Southwest for his tour-de-force memoir on its beauty and vulnerability.

ESCAPE TO ECUADOR'S CLOUD FOREST

SOAR UP ABOVE QUITO TO CHECK OUT THE PLANET'S GREATEST CONCENTRATION OF ENDEMIC BIRDLIFE WHILE CHECKED INTO ECUADOR'S MOST LUXURIANT ECO-EXPERIENCE: THE GROUND-BREAKING, CLOUD-TOPPING MASHPI LODGE, SITTING SERENELY IN ITS OWN BIODIVERSITY RESERVE.

When you wake up that first steamy morning and look out the window – unavoidable given that your room's walls are floor-to-ceiling glass – what Mashpi Lodge is about sinks in; along, most likely, with the sun shafting through the cloud, creating an ethereal effect as if you're still floating through a dream. Sitting amid a 1295-hectare tract of high-altitude forest, the lodge has been designed like a capsule, allowing you to feast your gaze on as much greenery as possible without troubling you with tiresome things like creepy-crawlies (for better or worse, part of the package when you're sampling one of the world's most biodiverse locales).

And you have to rub your eyes more than once. How can such a remote refuge be three hours' drive from the capital? How can you be crashing in a wilderness lodge where 300-plus (and counting) bird species reside within a hummingbird's hoot yet have access to every conceivable creature comfort? How can this huge reserve, replete with birds found nowhere else, be just for the private viewing of you, your fellow guests and a few dozen staff?

Good questions indeed. When Mashpi's creator, former Quito mayor Roque Sevilla, dreamed of establishing this paradise, he wanted to forge a reserve he could protect with his own principles yet share with nature lovers from around the globe, in a lodge that would stay at the summit of the ecolodge elect year upon year. Mashpi certainly has a rather remarkable location. Crowning the cusp of a cloud-forest ridge, it offers absolute arboreal immersion but oozes vistas, too – because of its design (all that glass) you can't look anywhere without imbibing them. Whether you're being spoiled in the spa, gorging in the restaurant or – best of all – out exploring on a forest foray, a cacophony of nature is exploding before your eyes. Mashpi is luxury, sure, but it's also a classroom in the clouds.

ESSENTIAL EXPERIENCES

* **Relaxing in the hot tub while gazing out at panoramic jungle vistas.**
* Hearing the round-the-clock chatter of thousands of insects, birds and large mammals – without even leaving your room.
* **Whooshing across a forest gorge on the Mashpi sky bike, an original way to explore the canopy.**
* Admiring the spectacular flapping hues on display during a night-time butterfly walk and witnessing how the forest transforms after dark.
* **Chilling out in a waterfall plunge pool after a sticky day bird-spotting.**
* Gliding through and above the cloud-forest canopy on the 2km gondola system.

LOCATION PICHINCHA PROVINCE, ECUADOR | **BEST TIME OF YEAR** JULY TO SEPTEMBER | **IDEAL TIME COMMITMENT** THREE DAYS | **ESSENTIAL TIP** BRING A TOP-NOTCH CAMERA AND BINOCULARS TO TRACK WILDLIFE | **BUDGET** $$$ | **PACK** BINOCULARS, CAMERA, INSECT REPELLENT, FLASHLIGHT, SWIMWEAR, SUNGLASSES, LONG-SLEEVED SHIRT AND A WATERPROOF JACKET

GREEN TO THE GILLS

Mashpi Lodge helped get protected status for a far-larger slice of forest (a further 6070-plus hectares) around its own reserve: one of many pioneering projects that's been implemented to preserve this biome. Staying here, you're savouring and saving a place that would have been left to loggers and gold prospectors had Sevilla & Co not intervened. Then there's the team of resident biologists, conducting critical ongoing research into wildlife hereabouts. The building itself got transported here mainly by hand to minimise pollution. And there's the little things: locally made furniture, subdued LED lighting to avoid enticing insects, and a work commitment with local communities to supply produce and have a staff that's 80% comprised of villagers from the vicinity.

THE PERFECT GETAWAY

Appetite for adventure whetted? Then Mashpi has achieved something: inspiring you to sally forth to see, feel and think about the forest. But staying here comes with responsibilities: you'll need to blend into your environment to minimise disturbance to wildlife, much like the lodge building does.

Mashpi's most common package is the three-day/two-night stay (you can linger longer), so time-planning is of paramount importance. Some people favour a lodge-based break, and why not? The 22 rooms and suites are large and light, and the hot tub has panoramic views. The restaurant (all meals are included), bubbling with Ecuadorian coastal-mountain fusion cuisine, has two floors and views as alluring as the dining and Ecuadorian chocolate tastings.

But why would you want to waive the 2km canopy gondola ride? Glide up into the dense forest and down again, gawking at the birdlife and the preposterously varied plants. Or amble back on one of the hiking trails where, masterminded by naturalist guides, you'll likely garner your most memorable wildlife sightings. Hikes aren't just dense foliage and fleeting glimpses of fauna. They take in *leks* (locales where birds, like the vibrant red Andean cocks-of-the-rock, gather to mate); they wind to viewpoints, where the reserve's 22 hummingbird species can be observed; and they lead to waterfalls, to cool off in after the day's action.

And the highlight? A stay here is a vault into the unknown. New species are constantly being discovered, and just when you set your sights on the birds you could get sidetracked by night-time treks and butterfly flocks fanning out in luminous hues, or the nocturnal rustle of a puma or *tigrillo* (mini-tiger).

PLAN IT

Quito's Mariscal Sucre International Airport has direct flights to Central America, North America, Europe and other South American transit hubs like Lima and Bogota. Arrange with the lodge in advance which Quito hotel you want picking up from. Pick-up from other points in Ecuador needs to be arranged several weeks prior. Book well in advance, too: Mashpi is designed to get guests up close and personal to the forest, so it doesn't have that many rooms.

DETOUR

More jungle? Ecuador can slake your appetite. Its forested wildernesses are all the more interesting for being so accessible. Off the Quito–Mashpi road there's a bunch of them: like the Pululahua Geobotanical Reserve, which features a cloud forest with a volcano (it last erupted 2500 years ago, but the soil's resultantly rich with endemic plants), and the Mindo-Nambillo Forest Reserve, another cloud-forest birding mecca fanning out from the tiny town of Mindo.

OPENING SPREAD A collared inca hummingbird siphons nectar from flowers in cloudforest local to Mashpi Lodge. **ABOVE (L)** A view of Mashpi Lodge, surrounded by waves of forest. **ABOVE (R)** Floor-to-ceiling glass walls mean that even a drink at the bar is a wildlife-spotting opportunity.

DECKCHAIR

* *The Birds of Ecuador* (Robert S Ridgely and Paul J Greenfield) This bird-watcher's bible covers the feathered members of the entire country in two outstanding volumes.

* *Cumandá* (Juan León Mera) Considered to be the first novel (1879) by an Ecuadorian writer, this is a tragic tale of love set in Ecuador's steamy jungle.

* *A la Costa* (To the Coast; Luis A Martinez) Another seminal Ecuadorian work: the first to deal literarily with Ecuador's two regions of *selva* (forest) and *costa* (coast) and the protagonist's journey between the two to find meaning in life.

* *El Ultimo Rio* (Pastrana's Last River; Nelson Estupiñan Bass) About the only work translated into English by one of the most important exponents of Afro-Latino writing.

FOOD & DRINK

GREAT ESCAPES

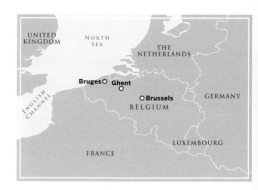

THE BELGIAN BEER ODYSSEY

LITTLE BELGIUM MAY BE THE BUTT OF JOKES – FEW FAMOUS PEOPLE, LOTS OF EU BUREAUCRATS – BUT IT IS THE BORDEAUX OF BEER. THE COUNTRY'S 125-PLUS BREWERIES MAKE WELL OVER A THOUSAND BEERS, DRUNK WITH SACRAMENTAL ZEAL. NO MERE DRINK, BEER IS A SHORTCUT TO BELGIUM'S SOUL.

82

Flanders, Belgium's northern province, is an idyllic agricultural landscape where cows graze by lazy rivers as church bells chime in the background. It's also the beer centre of the world, where beer lovers pilgrimage to St Sixtus Abbey. Here, silent monks of the Trappist order brew Westvleteren 12: a revered beer available only at the abbey itself and in the nearby In De Vrede cafe.

But St Sixtus Abbey is merely the tip of the beer iceberg. For Belgium is the world's most beer-friendly country, where connoisseurship meets camaraderie over goblets of rich, strong ale. Ghent, Antwerp, Brussels, Leuven – each town and city has bars offering hundreds of styles where you'll learn how to assess a beer's aroma before taking a sip. As the late beer writer Michael Jackson put it, Belgium has 'the greatest variety of styles, the most gastronomically interesting specialties, and the most unusual beers in the world'. And, he might have added, the most exacting beer rituals – every good bartender knows how to serve each beer properly, with its own glass and beer mat.

In Belgium too, beer is part of gastronomy: not just for quaffing, but a connoisseurs' experience. If Belgian food is 'French food in German portions', as the phrase has it, then Belgian beer is treated like wine: paired with food, poured carefully, bouquets savoured.

Belgium's singular beer culture is due to its northern European location. Above the wine belt, and blessed with good-quality water, its position at the confluence of German and Latin cultures has been conducive to beer – as has its Catholic monastic culture, which from the Middle Ages onwards developed brewing as a revenue-raiser. Which is why Belgium's six Trappist breweries, including St Sixtus Abbey, are still silently making some of the world's best beers – and why each year, the world comes to drink them.

ESSENTIAL EXPERIENCES

* **Learning all about your tipple at Brasserie Cantillon Brouwerij in Brussels – a museum of beer history.**

* Driving or cycling through Flanders, stopping at small towns and breweries.

* **Eating *moules et frites* on Brussels' Grand Place, before heading into the city's bars.**

* Walking along the canals of Bruges, stopping awhile for a beer.

* **Admiring the Ghent Altarpiece, a medieval masterpiece painted by the Van Eyck brothers in 1432 in St Bavo Cathedral, Ghent.**

* Gazing at the guild halls on Grote Markt, Antwerp's grand market square, surrounded by great beer bars.

* **Seeking solace in Bruges' Bequinage, a group of whitewashed homes for lay orders.**

LOCATION BELGIUM | **BEST TIME OF YEAR** YEAR-ROUND | **IDEAL TIME COMMITMENT** FOUR DAYS | **ESSENTIAL TIP** DON'T DRINK AND DRIVE; STRICT DRINK DRIVING LAWS ALLOW ONLY UP TO 0.05MG OF ALCOHOL PER 100ML OF BLOOD | **BUDGET** $$ **PACK** BEER MONEY, A RAINCOAT FOR UNEXPECTED SHOWERS AND SHOES THAT CAN COPE WITH COBBLES

TASTING NOTES

On a beer odyssey, know your Belgian beer styles.
Pilsners are golden, served cold: think Stella Artois,
Jupiler. Lambic is the Champagne of beers, naturally
fermented by the Belgian air. Gueuze is a blend of
young and old ferments. Kriek is a cherry beer, one of
several Belgian beers brewed with fruit. Then there are
white beers, brown ales and red 'sour' beers. Trappist
means that the beer is brewed by Trappist monks; it
comes in various styles, including Dubbel (like a brown
ale) and Tripel (a pale ale of significant punch). Watch
out for notes of coriander, liquorice and spices – and
don't be afraid to wax lyrical. Belgians do.

■ THE PERFECT GETAWAY

Come from northern France into the pastures of Flanders – the Flemish part of northern Belgium – and you'll soon be drinking beer in medieval towns, where old guild houses and canals prove a perfect backdrop. Detour to Westvleteren, near the French border, where monks at St Sixtus Abbey make the pungent Westvleteren 12. If you're driving, arrange stays at places like the Brouwershuis in Watou, a B&B owned by the St Bernardus Brewery.

In Bruges, a canal toytown of impossible quaintness, you'll find a host of pubs, including owner Daisy Claeys' famous Brugs Beertje, which serves over 300 brews – including the eccentric Kwak, served in a surreal glass supported by a wooden frame. In Ghent, the traditional De Dulle Griet stocks over 400 brews, while Antwerp's Kulminator pips it with over 500. But it's Leuven that claims the 'beer city' crown, both as the home of Stella Artois and what it calls the 'longest bar in the world': the combined forces of 40 pubs in the Oude Markt. Of course, the capital Brussels puts up a good shout. Here, you'll eat *moules et frites* (mussels and chips) at an open-air restaurant before drinking at bars that include La Mort Subite (Sudden Death), where prices are chalked up on huge mirrors, and the historic gem De Ultieme Hallucinatie, where even the piano is art nouveau.

Some breweries open for visits, like De Dolle Brouwers in Esen, while brewpubs make unique offerings like Ghent's Gruut, specialising in herby medieval recipes. With such a cornucopia, it's odd to think that Belgium almost lost its beer culture to drink corporations in the 1970s. Thankfully, old traditions have been revived, and from Flanders down to French-speaking Wallonia, you'll find many new beers to try. Just remember the words for 'cheers': *proost* in Flemish and *santé* in French.

DECKCHAIR

* ❋ *Great Beers of Belgium* (Michael Jackson) The most authoritative beer guide .
* ❋ *Magritte* (David Sylvester) The great Belgian artist went to his studio every day and painted trains coming out of fireplaces. Plenty have argued that beer and Belgian surrealism are linked…
* ❋ *Maigret and Monsieur Charles* (Georges Simenon) Or any other book featuring Jules Maigret, one of Belgium's great detectives.
* ❋ *Food Culture in Belgium* (Peter Scholliers) More than waffles, chocolate and chips, Belgian food is now feted – try mussels, eels, tarts and Gentse Waterzooi.
* ❋ *Tintin* (Hergé) Belgium is the world capital of *bandes dessinées* – comic books for all ages. The greatest of them all is Tintin.
* ❋ *The Poisonwood Bible* (Barbara Kingsolver) Evangelical Baptist Nathan Price takes his family to the Belgian Congo in 1959.

■ PLAN IT

You can reach Belgium by Eurostar from London and Paris. Airlines from around the world fly into Brussels, and Charleroi Airport hosts low-cost carriers. The best towns are Bruges, Ghent and the capital, Brussels, which hosts the Belgian Beer Weekend in the first weekend of September; the Bruges Beer Festival is held in February, and the Zythos Bierfestival – Europe's largest beer-tasting festival – takes place in Leuven at the end of April.

■ DETOUR

Scars and souvenirs of WWI remain poignant attractions in the Flanders countryside, and no more so than in Ypres – or 'Wipers' as the British and Australian 'Tommies' called it – which is all the more extraordinary for having been meticulously rebuilt following the war.

Here, the Menin Gate and its Memorial to the Missing bears the names of the 54,896 fallen from British and Commonwealth troops whose bodies were never found. 'To the British Armies of the Empire who stood here from 1914 to 1918', the inscription reads, 'and to those of their dead who have known no grave'. Each evening, the Last Post is sounded.

CHRISTIAN HÜRETTN | CORBIS ©

OPENING SPREAD Belgium's charismatic beers – funky, fruity and packing a punch – are produced by almost 200 breweries. **ABOVE** The tastiest beer in the world? Visit the Westvleteren monastery to decide. **BELOW** Merchants' houses line the canals of Bruges.

BIKES, BEER AND FRITES

What would entice you to stand for hours beside a muddy roadside in icy April rain? In Belgium, it's to watch a bunch of grimacing cyclists pound past. Bike racing is Belgium's national obsession. Early-season one-day races, such as the Tour of Flanders (you can't miss the flags of a black lion on yellow background), La Flèche Wallonne and Liège-Bastogne-Liège are known as the Spring Classics. The raucous spectators are fortified by beer, of course, and frites. No ordinary chips, these: they're double-fried, crispy, and served in a cone with mayonnaise. You'll need every calorie to keep warm waiting for the racers.

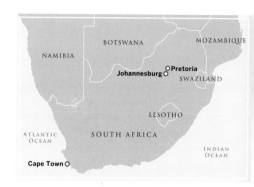

A CRAFTY TASTE OF CAPE TOWN

CULINARY CAPITAL OF SOUTH AFRICA, CAPE TOWN IS SHOWING OFF ITS
BOUNTIFUL PRODUCE WITH A RETURN TO ARTISANAL PRODUCTS. EXPLORE
THE WHOLE PENINSULA, FROM THE CITY BOWL TO CAPE POINT, TO DISCOVER
FINE-FOOD MARKETS, EXQUISITE WINERIES AND INNOVATIVE RESTAURANTS.

86

It's Bree St in central Cape Town on a warm summer's afternoon, and time for
an urban picnic at Jason Bakery. Here the picnic baskets are full of surprises
like spicy *soujouk* or chorizo sausages, beer bread and farm butter, homemade
pickles and chutneys, rillettes, prosciutto and chocolate crackle-top biscuits.
Order a jug of gin and tonic garnished with cucumber, mint and lime to wash
it down, and engage in some serious people-watching.

Jason himself is the new breed (or is it old breed?) of baker, firing up his ovens
in the early hours to produce his famous bacon croissants and a wide array
of breads, and fashioning other specialist foods by hand, like buffalo bresaola
and pork pies. This is the trend. Local farmers, purveyors of fine foods, organic
merchants, bakers, grocers, fishmongers, butchers and artisan producers of wines
and craft beers are celebrated at markets, shops, restaurants and bars all over the
peninsula. Capetonians love nothing better than a quick trip to the market on a
week night, or a longer browse with lots of tastings on Saturday morning.

Dutch settlers arrived in 1659 to establish a garden so that sailors rounding
the Cape wouldn't die of scurvy, which probably makes the then governor Simon
van der Stel the first *garagiste* winemaker in Cape Town! The peninsula is home
to a handful of wineries, including the oldest of them all, Groot Constantia
(established by Van der Stel). Others in the Constantia Valley offer tastings,
restaurants and picnics. Just to prove that the Cape is not just about wine, tasty
craft beers are also being produced in the area; suddenly, supping the amber
nectar everywhere from fancy hotels to specialist bars is all the rage.

Dubbed the Tavern of the Seas, Cape Town offers a feast of culinary adventures.
With a tradition that embraces African, Indian, European and Malay influences,
South African cuisine is a fascinating mixture that's waiting to be explored.

ESSENTIAL EXPERIENCES

* **Browsing Neighbourgoods Market in Woodstock for artisanal foods.**

* Popping into Escape Caffe in Bree St for serious coffee and cheesecake.

* **Tasting the fish fresh off the boats at Kalk Bay harbour.**

* Spreading a blanket on the grass, pouring local wine and tucking into a picnic hamper at one of the peninsula's exquisite wine farms.

* **Sharing a Bucket o' Love at &Union (that's craft beer bottles in a bucket!) while listening to live music on a Wednesday night.**

* Sampling at least one of the cuisines from further north in Africa – Ethiopian, Nigerian or Cameroonian are all on offer.

LOCATION CAPE TOWN AND THE CAPE PENINSULA, SOUTH AFRICA | **BEST TIME OF YEAR** OCTOBER TO MARCH | **IDEAL TIME**
COMMITMENT TWO DAYS TO ONE WEEK | **ESSENTIAL TIP** DON'T DRIVE OVER THE LIMIT (0.05MG OF ALCOHOL PER 100ML OF
BLOOD); DRINK DRIVING LAWS ARE STRICTLY ENFORCED | **BUDGET** $$ | **PACK** A HEALTHY APPETITE

GREAT GRAPES

The Constantia Valley is home to the very first wine farm in South Africa: Groot Constantia. The elegant farmhouse is nestled under the Table Mountain range with views down to the sea. The museum, cellar tours, restaurant and tasting room will keep you busy. Klein Constantia, Buitenverwachting and High Constantia are a few of the other valley wineries, as well as Constantia Uitsig and Steenberg in Tokai. Some have superb restaurants and offer picnics on the lawns. Further south and on the Atlantic side of the peninsula is Cape Point Vineyards in Noordhoek. Taste the wines, then indulge in a picnic hamper.

GRAIN POWER

Beer was brewed at the Cape one year before the first wine was produced, so it's only right that locally brewed craft beer is now gaining a huge increase in fans. It's even got its own language, just like wine: think 'chewy malt backbone' or 'hoppy with nutty overtones'. Banana Jam Cafe in Kenilworth has 10 craft beers on tap, including their own Cream Ale. If you can't decide, then try the tasting platter of six samples. Boston Breweries Tasting Room in the Cape Quarter offers six brews, from a light Johnny Weiss Gold to their Black River Coffee Stout, via a 'Naked Mexican'.

■ THE PERFECT GETAWAY

Saturday morning sees you at the award-winning Neighbourgoods Market in Woodstock's Old Biscuit Mill. Breakfast is a mango-and-orange smoothie followed by a Thai scramble, or salmon hollandaise rosti and coffee. Taste as much as possible for free, too, like the *biltong* (dried strips of salted meat), olives, pesto, cheeses, breads and ice cream. Everything here is made by food artisans, using organic raw materials from local farmers.

Now you're heading down the peninsula to the Constantia Valley, where you'll find modern wineries housed in gracious Cape Dutch buildings. Stop off at Klein Constantia, where your tasting might include Jane Austen's favourite tipple, the dessert wine Vin de Constance. Ready for lunch, you drive over the Table Mountain range to Noordhoek, where Cape Point Vineyards produces 'cold climate' wines kissed by sea breezes. Choosing one of their sauvignon blancs, you laze on the lawns with a picnic hamper, enjoying the sea views. Dinner time and you're back in Woodstock, where the Test Kitchen transforms fresh market produce into an imaginative menu, and every dish is paired with a wine.

Another day, another breakfast, this time at the Loading Bay in De Waterkant, where the homemade breads are baked in a wood-fired oven. Just down the road, the colourful Bo-Kaap area is home to descendants of Malay slaves. Here you join a cooking safari, exploring the spice shops before concocting a Malay lunch. Or you could sample another strand of the cuisine scene: African food offered by migrants from further north, including Mali, Nigeria, Malawi and the Congo. Bebe's Restaurant in Long St dishes up Cameroonian and Ethiopian soul food.

■ PLAN IT

Fly into Cape Town International Airport and head for your hotel in the City Bowl, Waterfront or Green Point. Cape Town Tourism can help you find accommodation. The Wine Desk at the Victoria & Alfred Waterfront helps plans tours around wine. You'll need reservations if you'd like to picnic at a winery, but not for tastings (often subject to a small fee). Look out for the Craft Beer Project in February and the Fresh Wine Festival in March.

■ DETOUR

Follow your nose to the spices of the Bo-Kaap by trying Andulela's Cape Malay Cooking Safari. Enjoy a meander around this area, a visit to the museum and shopping for spices, then whip up a traditional Malay lunch. If you are intrigued by Xhosa culture, Andulela also offers an African Cooking Safari in vibrant Gugulethu. For an insight into township life, start with a local tour, then sit down to some serious cooking in a family home. Coffeebeans Routes offers the Cape Town Cuisine Route, visiting home kitchens as well as easy-to-miss markets.

OPENING SPREAD The Groot Constantia vineyard stands near the neck of the Cape peninsula. **ABOVE** Chefs in Cape Town's restaurants use local ingredients. **LEFT** Sample beer from local craft microbreweries such as Triggerfish and Jack Black in the bars around Victoria and Alfred harbour.

DECKCHAIR

* ***Grape: Stories of the Vineyards in South Africa*** (Jeanne Viall et al)
  A readable, thought-provoking historical account of the development of South Africa's wine industry.

* ***Ukutya Kwasekhaya: Tastes from Nelson Mandela's Kitchen***
  (Xoliswa Ndoyiya) Includes recipes for the *umqusho* (maize and beans) and *umsila wenkomo* (oxtail stew) enjoyed by Madiba.

* ***John Platter Wine Guide*** (John Platter) Quintessential guide to South African wine. It includes information on the wine routes, too.

* ***Philida*** (André Brink) Based on the true story of a slave on the Stellenbosch estate, which became the prestigious Solms-Delta winery of today.

* ***Reuben Cooks Local*** (Reuben Riffel) Cape Town's own celebrity chef tells stories around the recipes that celebrate local produce.

TASTY ADVENTURES IN HOI AN

IF YOU'RE THE SORT OF TRAVELLER WHO BELIEVES THAT EATING LOCALLY IS ONE OF THE BEST WAYS TO IMMERSE YOURSELF IN A CULTURE, PREPARE TO BE AMAZED BY HOI AN, VIETNAM'S CULINARY CAPITAL.

Eating is a round-the-clock pastime in Hoi An. Dawn breaks, and chefs promptly set up stalls on the town's streets, dishing up breakfasts of porridge, spicy broths and smoothies to hungry passers-by. By mid-morning, markets fill with customers and local chefs piling high their baskets with fistfuls of aromatic herbs, pungent spices, bundles of vegetables and flapping fish freshly plucked from the surrounding seas.

A sleepy town of boho boutiques and bicycle-clogged thoroughfares, Hoi An has a long and distinguished foodie heritage. In centuries past, merchants from across Asia journeyed to this thriving port to trade in spices, coffee, tea and sugar. They've long since set sail, but the recipes they left behind linger on in Hoi An's cosmopolitan culinary repertoire, which deftly blends Japanese, Chinese and European influences. Furthermore, Hoi An is situated right in the middle of Vietnam – perfectly poised to pick from both the subtler flavours of the north and the fierier cooking traditions of the south.

There's no better way of getting to grips with Hoi An's food culture than by taking a cooking lesson here. A number of restaurants offer masterclasses in preparing Vietnamese dishes – think crunchy spring rolls, fragrant curries and steaming *pho* (noodle soup) – but don't leave without mastering local stalwarts, too. Look out for *cao lau* (a Japanese-style noodle dish that tradition dictates must be made using water from a particular well in Hoi An) and *banh bao* (aka 'white rose'; fluffy flower-shaped dumplings).

Evening draws in over Hoi An, and belts are loosened a notch or three as diners gorge themselves at restaurants lining the lantern-lit quays. Eventually, diners depart to sip on *bia hoi* (Vietnamese beer) at roadside stalls, while chefs retire to their kitchens, preparing for another day of serious eating ahead.

ESSENTIAL EXPERIENCES

❋ **Watching paper lanterns floating on the water at dusk from the Japanese Covered Bridge.**

❋ Learning to roll chunky noodles for cao lau – Hoi An's favourite dish – at a cooking school.

❋ **Testing your two-wheel prowess on a motorbike tour around the idyllic back roads of central Vietnam.**

❋ Getting under the skin of Hoi An's maritime history in the Chinese assembly halls.

❋ **Gobbling down chillies before breakfast on a street-food tour and haggling over freshly caught fish at the morning market.**

❋ Being measured at one of Hoi An's famous tailor shops (the city has long been known for fabric production).

LOCATION HOI AN, VIETNAM | **BEST TIME OF YEAR** FEBRUARY TO MAY | **IDEAL TIME COMMITMENT** TWO DAYS
ESSENTIAL TIP PLACE FOOD IN YOUR OWN BOWL BEFORE EATING AT MEALS: LIFTING IT STRAIGHT FROM THE COMMUNAL BOWL TO YOUR MOUTH ISN'T SOCIALLY ACCEPTABLE | **BUDGET** $ | **PACK** IMODIUM; NOT ALL STREET FOOD IS 100% TRUSTWORTHY!

A TASTE OF VIETNAM'S CUISINE

Moulded by influences from across Asia and Europe, Vietnamese food is as bafflingly diverse as it is delicious. Hoi An's most famous dish is cao lau – thick noodles (similar to Japanese soba noodles) paired with pork and greens. Venture north of Hoi An and you'll soon encounter Vietnam's most exported dish: *pho bo* (beef noodle soup). Go south, and you might happen across *canh chua ca,* a sour fish soup from the Mekong Delta with generous quantities of vegetables and herbs. Also in the south, Ho Chi Minh City (Saigon) has a wide variety of *banh mi* – a short baguette sandwich inherited from French colonial rule, potentially containing anything from sausages to sardines.

TAMING THE DRAGON

According to legend, Hoi An's 16th-century Japanese Covered Bridge wasn't just built for crossing from one side of the water to the other. The Japanese community in Hoi An believed in a gigantic subterranean dragon who caused earthquakes and other unfortunate events every time he shifted his body weight about. Reasoning that his head was in India and his tail in Japan, they decided the bulk of the dragon must be located in Vietnam, and resolved to pin him down and prevent further tragedies by constructing this bridge. A small temple on the north side of the bridge was built by sympathetic locals to pray for the unfortunate dragon's soul.

THE PERFECT GETAWAY

On top of its foodie pedigree, Hoi An can claim to be Vietnam's most beautiful city, with leafy streets of mustard-yellow townhouses and mahogany-shuttered shopfronts and a sublime riverside setting. Begin your culinary adventure by rising early to join a street-food tour and see the Old Town ahead of the crowds. The Original Taste of Hoi An offers encyclopedic tours of stalls, where you'll meet vendors serving banh mi and Hoi An–style wonton pancakes before signing off with a comprehensive tasting session at lunchtime.

Afterwards, walk off your lunch with a tour of the town's magnificent assembly halls – originally built by Chinese merchants who sailed to Hoi An in its 17th-century heyday. The most elaborate is the marshmallow-pink Fujian assembly hall, containing model boats and murals of Chinese sailors journeying homeward through stormy seas. Spend the rest of the afternoon on a motorcycle tour exploring the patchwork of rice paddies and meandering canals around Hoi An.

Back in Hoi An, book a table for dinner at Lantern Town, a restaurant in a breezy colonial-era building, where seafood figures prominently, or for something more contemporary opt for Green Mango's French-accented dishes. On an evening stroll along the waterfront you'll pass fishing boats creaking at their moorings and paper lanterns drifting serenely in the current, before arriving at the 16th-century Japanese Covered Bridge – Hoi An's famous landmark.

The next morning, pay a visit to Gioan, which runs the liveliest cooking courses in town. After buying materials at a market and sizzling them down to size, you'll leave with a cookbook to add a pinch of Hoi An pizazz to your own kitchen.

PLAN IT

The easiest way to get to Hoi An is via the seaside resort of Danang, 30km to the north; buses take an hour. A few airlines operate direct flights to Danang from major Asian cities. Vietnam Airlines offers flights from hubs in Europe and elsewhere in Asia, changing at Ho Chi Minh City or Hanoi. Danang is also a stop on Vietnam's North–South Railway, with trains running from Ho Chi Minh and Hanoi.

DETOUR

An hour or so to the north, Hue is Hoi An's main contender for Vietnam's culinary crown. A stately city of palaces and pagodas, Hue became the capital of Vietnam under the Nguyen dynasty, with royals recruiting an army of chefs from across the country to prepare extravagant banquets in their honour. Fast-forward a century or two, and restaurants keep the spirit of the imperial banquets alive, serving dishes sculpted into weird and wonderful shapes. If you'd prefer something a bit more humble, however, head to the city's Dong Ba Market to pick up Hue's signature pancakes – *banh khoai*.

93

OPENING SPREAD Hoi An's morning market sees locals select fresh fish straight from the boat. **ABOVE** Whether you sit down at a restaurant in an old colonial building or graze from street-food stalls, Hoi An will thrill your tastebuds. **LEFT** Hoi An was built on the banks of the Thu Bon river.

DECKCHAIR

* *The Quiet American* (2002) Despite being set in Saigon (Ho Chi Minh City), the most recent adaptation of Graham Greene's novel was partly filmed in Hoi An.

* *Vietnamese Street Food* (Tracey Lister and Andreas Pohl) A street-food photo odyssey of Vietnam, with easy-to-follow recipes.

* *The Songs of Sapa* (Luke Nguyen) Australian-Vietnamese chef Luke Nguyen does justice to the diversity of Vietnamese cooking.

* *Vietnam: Rising Dragon* (Bill Hayton) BBC correspondent Bill Hayton's take on the economic and political challenges facing modern Vietnam.

* *Dispatches* (Michael Herr) A visceral first-hand account of the Vietnam War by *Esquire* reporter Michael Herr.

* *A Dragon Apparent: Travels in Cambodia, Laos and Vietnam* (Norman Lewis) A classic of travel writing from the 1950s.

PUGLIA ON A PLATE: INSIDERS' ITALY

EVER WONDERED WHAT'S IN THE HEEL OF ITALY'S BOOT, OR WHERE ITALIANS HOLIDAY IN THE SUMMER? ON BOTH COUNTS IT'S PUGLIA, WITH ITS SILK-WHITE BEACHES, ANCIENT TOWNS AND FRESH PRODUCE AND FINE WINES.

94

Come July and August, Italian families from all over the country pack up their bags and start for the south. It's time to celebrate the glorious, long Italian summer. August is so reliably sun-baked that many restaurants and businesses around the country simply shut up shop, with signs on the doors reading: 'gone to the beach, back in September'.

Whatever Italy's economic and political ups and downs, there's always the south, with its forget-your-cares beaches, a fierce sun in a cloudless sky, and delicious food fished fresh from the sparkling sea or grown and sun-ripened and brought from the field to your table. It was only recently that the rich and varied region of Puglia came to the attention of foreign tourists, and it still feels undiscovered. It's difficult to say what it was that first grabbed people's attention. Was it the white town of Ostuni, which shimmers on its hilltop, visible for miles? Was it honey-hued Lecce, a historic university city, with its baroque style?

No, it must have been the beaches, which can feel closer to the Caribbean than the Mediterranean, such is the clarity of the water and the softness of the white sand. They get full to bursting in July and August, but there is an advantage to coming here in peak time: it's festival season. Every night at least a few towns kick up their heels with free music festivals playing the traditional music of the *pizzica*, the Pugliese folk dance.

July and August may be when everyone in Italy heads to Puglia, but you don't have to come here then. In May, June and September, the sea is warm, prices are lower, businesses are still open, and the beaches are almost deserted. Come out of season, but when the weather's still balmy, and you'll have an entirely different kind of holiday: a tranquil meander around the towns and countryside, and all those white-sand expanses almost entirely to yourself.

ESSENTIAL EXPERIENCES

* **Floating in the warm, translucent sea beside a glimmering white beach.**

* Attending a *sagra* (food festival) paying tribute to a local foodstuff, such as snails, sea urchins or bread.

* **Dancing to the pizzica music in a small-town piazza, the band playing on a bandstand blazing with light bulbs.**

* Eating the traditional pasta of the region, orecchiette (meaning 'little ears'), washed down with local wine, and followed by a glass of homemade *limoncello* (lemon liqueur).

* **Taking a *passeggiata* (early-evening stroll) along the promenade in any of Puglia's seafront towns.**

* Enjoying the rustic, sun-bleached setting and the curious architecture of the local trulli farmhouses.

LOCATION PUGLIA, ITALY | **BEST TIME OF YEAR** MAY TO SEPTEMBER | **IDEAL TIME COMMITMENT** ONE TO THREE WEEKS
ESSENTIAL TIP ITALIANS TAKE THEIR HOLIDAYS IN JULY AND AUGUST, SO IT'S BUSIER, PRICIER AND HOTTER IN THESE MONTHS
BUDGET $$ | **PACK** AN APPETITE: PUGLIA IS FAMOUS FOR ITS FOOD

CASTLES

Facing the Adriatic and Ionian Seas, Puglia had an essential strategic position as the stepping stone to the eastern Mediterranean. Greeks, Romans, Saracens, Aragons, Normans and Swabians have all made their mark here, and the coastline and landscape is marked by impressive fortifications and walled townscapes. Most extraordinary is the geometric perfection of the middle-of-nowhere octagonal Castel del Monte, built in 1240 by Holy Roman Emperor Frederick II. Frederick left the most significant fortresses in the region, building and rebuilding castles at Oria, Trani and Bari, among others – great squared-off edifices that speak of the region's embattled past.

PUGLIESE CUISINE

Pugliese cuisine is born out of *cucina povera* ('cooking of the poor'; peasant food), with unique dishes that merge bountiful local fresh vegetables and straight-from-the-sea fish. Specialities include the glorious comfort food *riso, patate e cozze* (rice, potatoes and mussels), *taralli* (a kind of hard Italian pretzel) and *friselle* (dried bread rolls softened with olive oil and served topped with tomatoes, which were once the easy-to-carry food of farm workers). The iconic pasta is orecchiette, small ear-shaped pasta hand-made without the addition of egg, while one of the most divine local concoctions is *burrata* – a kind of mozzarella that, when you cut into it, oozes fresh cream: the food of the gods.

■ THE PERFECT GETAWAY

In one of Puglia's prettiest regions, the rolling Valle d'Itria, you'll spot curious, circular stone houses dotting the countryside, their white-tipped roofs tapering up to a stubby point. These are *trulli*, Puglia's unique rural architecture. Many of the trulli today have been converted into remarkably serene boutique hotels and villas. The rustic architecture is often merged with a contemporary aesthetic, while the surrounding grounds are shaded by a tangle of olive, orange, lemon, walnut and hazelnut trees, and overgrown cacti laden with prickly pears. Seek out a place with a swimming pool, as you'll need somewhere to escape the heat.

Any of the hilltop towns in the Valle d'Itria are worthy of a visit, including Ostuni, Cisternino and Martina Franca, which are also gaining fame for their wine. Farther south, in the charismatic, Greek-flavoured region of Salento, the most beautiful towns are Lecce, with its impressive churches and cathedral, and the seaside, fortress-dominated escapes of Otranto and Gallipoli. Beaches in this region include the brilliant-blue-meets-white Baia dei Turchi and Melendugno.

If you head south to Santa Maria di Leuca, a heart-in-your-mouth drive along an epic rocky coast, you'll spy deserted towers where locals once kept a watch to warn of the regular invasions from the east. Alternatively, head north along the coast to the elegant coastal town of Trani, whose waterfront cathedral has the sea lapping at its foundations. Beyond here is Puglia's Gargano Peninsula, which feels closer in spirit to the rocky, vegetation-covered Croatian coast (to which it was once joined) than to elsewhere in Puglia. It's a greener coastline, with more long sandy beaches: a magnet for Italians in summer and dotted by pretty towns.

■ PLAN IT

The airports at Bari and Brindisi have domestic connections, plus flights from European cities. Once in Puglia, car hire is advisable, though there are train and bus connections. If travelling in July and August book ahead for accommodation. For families and groups of friends, self-catering villas and *agriturismi* (farmstays) are the best bet, but for couples there's an excellent choice of boutique hotels too, particularly around Fasano.

■ DETOUR

If you enjoyed your Puglian sojourn, try nipping next door to Basilicata. Francis Ford Coppola's family originates from this out-of-the-way region, where the film director owns an exquisite hotel, Palazzo Margherita, in the village of Bernalda. Rivalling the Amalfi, a stretch of coast by Maratea has a roller-coaster road that passes turquoise sea and volcanic-sand beaches. But Basilicata's most alluring place is the extraordinary town of Matera, built across a network of caves. Integrated into townhouses, the caves now house some of Italy's most unique hotels.

97

OPENING SPREAD A trio of trulli: once dry-stone-built shelters or storehouses, Puglia's unique dwellings are fast becoming boutique hotels. **ABOVE** The town of Vieste stands on the Promontorio del Gargano. **LEFT** Fresh seafood, handmade pasta and a dash of local olive oil: good food is simple in Puglia.

DECKCHAIR

* **Reasonable Doubts** (Gianrico Carofiglio) Written by an anti-Mafia prosecutor, this thriller follows Guido Guerrieri, a defence counsel, who takes on the case of a Pugliese drug smuggler.

* **The Past is a Foreign Country** (Gianrico Carofiglio) Winner of the Premio Bancarella award; another tense psychological thriller by Carofiglio, based in Bari.

* **Puglia: A Culinary Memoir** (Maria Pignatelli Ferrante) Recipes, anecdotes and history combine in this evocation of the local cuisine.

* **The Castle of Otranto** (Horace Walpole) Generally regarded as the first-ever Gothic novel, this 1764 novel is set against an Otranto backdrop.

* **Christ Stopped at Eboli** (Carlo Levi) Set in Basilicata, this tale of Levi's time in exile (imprisoned by the Fascists) is a classic account of southern Italian small-town life.

HAWKER-FOOD HEAVEN IN PENANG

ARRIVE ON AN EMPTY STOMACH AND GRAZE AT WILL: BETWEEN
OUTRAGEOUSLY GOOD HAWKER FOOD AND A BURGEONING HANDFUL OF
MODERN RESTAURANTS, PENANG IS ONE OF THE PLANET'S BEST ESCAPES
FOR FOOD-OBSESSED TRAVELLERS.

98

People come to the Malaysian island of Penang just to eat. Even if you thought
you came here for another reason, your priorities might change dramatically
once you start digging into the Indian, Chinese, Malay and various hybrid
treats available. Days revolve around where and what to eat, and three meals
a day starts to sounds depressingly scant. It's the same for locals, for whom
eating out is a daily event.

In the island's compact capital of George Town, centuries of immigration
and trade interact to create culinary shifts within a few minutes' walk. Sleepy
Chinatown laneways are resurrected at dawn as busy dim sum eateries,
crammed in the diffuse tropical light with loyal regulars. Head a few blocks
southeast to Little India for breakfast, and the tropical humidity is alleviated
by softly spinning ceiling fans and refreshing glasses of *teh tarik* (pulled tea).

Penang's famed hawker centres become the focus later in the day, with legions
of long-established stalls turning out dishes imbued with culinary clues from
India, the Malay peninsula and many Chinese provinces. When Hokkien settlers
from Fujian province took local wives several centuries ago, Peranakan food
(also known as Nyonya food) evolved through the marriage of Chinese and local
flavours. One of the planet's first fusion cuisines, it combines Chinese staples
like soy sauce and tofu with tropical ingredients like lemon grass, coconut and
galangal; the tamarind-heavy *asam laksa* is an essential Penang hawkers' dish.

An almost perverse obsession with food among the locals means that visitors
are often smothered in culinary companionship; the traveller who makes the
effort to partake in the region's edible delights will undoubtedly make a few
makan kaki (food friends) along the way. Simply put, in this part of the world
it's not 'How are you?' but *Sudah makan?* (Have you eaten yet?)

ESSENTIAL EXPERIENCES

* **Negotiating a tasty path around Penang's hawker centres – ask locals for their recommendations on the best char kway teow or asam laksa in town.**

* Sampling regional dishes – Chinese, Indian, Malay and Nyonya – in the compact and bustling cafes of Chinatown and Little India, and around Gurney Drive and Jalan Burmah.

* **Exploring George Town's compelling overlap of different ethnic groups and cultures.**

* Finding relief from Penang's tropical heat amid the ornate interiors of the former mansions of Chinese millionaires and Peranakan merchants.

* **Staying in one of the boutique hotels housed in Penang's restored colonial buildings, such Muntri Mews or Mango Tree Place.**

LOCATION PENANG, MALAYSIA | **BEST TIME OF YEAR** DURING JULY'S GEORGE TOWN FESTIVAL OR FOR ONE OF PENANG'S
CULTURAL FESTIVALS | **IDEAL TIME COMMITMENT** AT LEAST THREE DAYS TO SAMPLE THE CULINARY DIVERSITY
ESSENTIAL TIP VEGETARIAN OPTIONS ABOUND | **BUDGET** $$ | **PACK** A CULINARY SENSE OF CURIOSITY

HERITAGE HOTELS

Architecturally, Penang's cultural and historic DNA has left much for modern travellers to explore. Most famous is Cheong Fatt Tze Mansion, the 38-room former residence of a penniless Chinese immigrant who rose to become one of Asia's most wealthy men. Combining a rich cobalt exterior and an eclectic and elegant interior, the 1880s mansion is almost luminous. Other ornate buildings reflecting Penang's history of wealth and influence include the Khoo Kongsi clanhouse and the Pinang Peranakan Mansion; the British colonial era is reflected by the stately Eastern & Oriental Hotel. Following George Town's inscription as a Unesco World Heritage Site in 2008, the city's celebrated townscape is now protected, and boutique hotels are opening in restored colonial shophouses and mansions.

CLASSIC PENANG DISHES

Penang's riot of hawker centres can create havoc for the indecisive visitor. Order the following to make tasty sense of the island's culinary collage: *char kway teow* (flat rice noodles with shrimp, bean sprouts, egg and sweet Chinese sausage), *Hokkien mee* (egg noodles in a pork broth with prawns, egg, bean sprouts and water spinach), *asam laksa* (thick white noodles in a spicy fish broth punctuated with tangy *asam*, a sour tamarind paste), *cendol* (shaved ice with mung-bean noodles, coconut milk and palm sugar) and *lau hao* (a refreshing nutmeg juice sweetened with Chinese sour plum).

■ THE PERFECT GETAWAY

Begin your culinary adventures in George Town by heading to Little India on your first morning and breakfasting on super-flaky *roti canai* (layered flatbread) at Special Famous Roti Canai on Jalan Transfer. After getting agreeably lost amid Little India's colourful labyrinth, continue to the art galleries and restored shophouses on nearby Lebuh Armenian. Recharge with lunch and a lassi or fresh juice at the tiny Amelie before entering the dramatic Khoo Kongsi, an elaborate clanhouse for the Chinese Hokkien community. For dinner, visit the sprawling Esplanade Food Centre, where hawker food favourites and Penang's cheapest and coldest beer combine with a seafront location. Finish with a George Town nightcap in the colonial ambience of Farquar's, at the Eastern & Oriental Hotel.

The next morning breakfast on dim sum at Tho Yuen on Lebuh Campbell in Chinatown. Try the *lo mai gai* (sticky rice with chicken, mushroom and Chinese sausage). After breakfast, spend your morning exploring Chinatown, stopping for refreshment at hole-in-the-wall tea shops and taking a guided tour of Cheong Fatt Tze Mansion. Then arrive at noon to secure a table for lunch at the popular Teik Sen on Lebuh Carnarvon. A few interesting streets to the east, negotiate a path around Penang's colonial district, stopping at Fort Cornwallis, the Pinang Peranakan Mansion and the Penang Museum. Dinner is your chance to sample some of Penang's best Nyonya food at Nyonya Breeze on Lorong Abu Siti. Order a glass of *lau hao* (nutmeg juice) to soothe dishes like *kari kapitam* (chicken curry). Spend your third morning at a cooking class with Nazlina's Spice Kitchen: here's your chance to recreate Penang's spicy culinary blend for yourself.

■ PLAN IT

Penang is reached by flights from Kuala Lumpur, Singapore and Bangkok. Ferries make the hop from Penang's capital of George Town to Butterworth, which has road links to Singapore and Kuala Lumpur, and the 13.5km-long Penang Bridge, which links the island to peninsular Malaysia. For a full immersion into Penang's culinary melting pot, book early to visit during one of the festivals: the Tamil celebration of Thaipusam, the Chinese Hungry Ghost Festival or the Hindu festival of Deepavali.

■ DETOUR

Divert northeast to Hanoi for Asia's other great street food destination. Vietnamese, Chinese and colonial French culinary influences underpin the rustic dining experiences dotted throughout the city's labyrinthine Old Quarter. The Vietnamese capital's best food is dished up by vendors crowding the sidewalks with smoking charcoal burners, tiny plastic stools and queues of expectant locals. Many stalls have been operating for decades, and offer just one perfectly-executed dish.

101

OPENING SPREAD Pinang Peranakan Mansion has been restored to show how wealthy Chinese emigrants lived in 19th-century Penang. **ABOVE (L)** Making *nasi lemak*, rice steamed in coconut milk and served with a hot sambal. **ABOVE (R) AND LEFT** Sampling street food, such as char kway teow.

DECKCHAIR

* ❋ *Cradle of Flavor: Home Cooking from the Spice Islands of Indonesia, Singapore, and Malaysia* (James Oseland) A beautiful tome covering the foods of Malaysia and its neighbours.

* ❋ *The E&O Hotel: Pearl of Penang* (Isla Sharp) The illustrated history of Penang's most famous colonial hotel.

* ❋ *Penang: Through Gilded Doors* (Julie de Bierre) More stunning photographic evidence of Penang's architectural heritage.

* ❋ *Leaving the Heart Behind* (Joan Foo Mahoney) Two families and two cities – Penang and Tokyo – are showcased in this novel spanning four decades from 1936.

* ❋ *The Gift of Rain* (Tan Twan Eng) A tale of loyalty set in Penang, leading up to the Japanese occupation in late 1941.

* ❋ *Indochine* (1992) Catherine Deneuve swans around colonial Vietnam, but Cheong Fatt Tze Mansion is used for many interior scenes.

CHILE'S GRAPE ESCAPES

YOU'VE HAD A NIP IN THE NAPA VALLEY AND YOU'VE IMBIBED IN BORDEAUX –
BUT HAVE YOU EVER SIPPED SOME OF THE WORLD'S BEST RED WINES IN THE
SHADOW OF THE ANDES?

'God was bringing the devil in his luggage.'

So says Pablo, the tour guide at Vina Santa Cruz, as he strolls through the vines clinging to the rolling hills. He's referring to an old saying in Chile, used to describe how wine ended up in these parts. It was brought here by missionaries, Pablo says, to be used during mass as they sought to convert the locals. However, those locals showed just as much passion for the wine as they did the religion. And so here we are today, surrounded by hectare after hectare of grapes, with the Andes soaring high above on the horizon. Wine isn't the devil anymore – instead, it's a booming industry, and one Chileans are justifiably proud of.

This is the Colchagua Valley, one of Chile's premier wine-producing areas and a short drive south of Santiago. The area is famous for its cabernet sauvignon, which explains the fat bunches of ruby-red grapes hanging from the rows of vines that stretch as far as the eye can see. People come to Colchagua to try the wine – though it's mostly local Chilean tourists, as the area isn't widely visited by international travellers. But there are other reasons to come here. For example, how many vineyards have you been to that have both a DeLorean and a llama?

This is Vina Santa Cruz, home to 180 hectares of vines, and the aforementioned car and animal. The car – a replica of Marty McFly's time machine from the *Back to the Future* films – is in the display room and it's as popular with kids as the wine is with their parents. The llama is up on top of a hill. When the tour of the winery concludes, Pablo points up to that summit. 'We've seen the heart of our wine,' he says. 'Now let's go and see its soul.' Up top are three pavilions, each dedicated to an ancient culture that left its mark on Chile: the Mapuche, the Aymara and the Easter Islanders. It's a nice tribute to the land's former owners – the ones who were here before the devil arrived in God's luggage.

ESSENTIAL EXPERIENCES

* **Wandering through the Museo Colchagua and taking in thousands of years of ancient history.**

* Sampling wine, wine and more wine in some of the region's 26 vineyards.

* **Trying the local Chilean cuisine at a restaurant in Santa Cruz, one of the area's more charming towns.**

* Riding the gondola at Vina Santa Cruz and walking through the pavilions dedicated to three of the area's ancient cultures.

* **Star-gazing at Vina Santa Cruz, or just marvelling at the winery's meteorite collection.**

LOCATION COLCHAGUA VALLEY, CHILE | **BEST TIME OF YEAR** HARVEST (MID-MARCH UNTIL THE END OF APRIL); WINERIES ARE OPEN YEAR-ROUND | **IDEAL TIME COMMITMENT** THREE DAYS | **ESSENTIAL TIP** ORGANISE A WAY BACK TO YOUR HOTEL BEFORE GOING TO THE WINERY: TAXIS ARE SCARCE IN SANTA CRUZ | **BUDGET** $ | **PACK** A JUMPER; TEMPERATURES DROP QUICKLY AT NIGHT

HOW WINE CAME TO CHILE

Blame the missionaries. When Spanish conquistadores decided to have their way with Chile, it opened the door for missionaries to begin preaching the good word. In order to conduct Mass the missionaries needed wine, which prompted Diego García de Cáceres to plant the first vines in Santiago in 1554. By the 1800s the vineyards had grown from supplying merely the local Sunday Mass to exporting their product to Europe, and production peaked just before WWII. These days the industry has been scaled back slightly, but the country is still well known for its top-quality cabernet sauvignons.

PISCO INFERNO

While Chile is known around the world for its wine, local residents are even more passionate about another grape-based tipple: *pisco*. Produced in the vine-growing regions north of Santiago, pisco is a type of grape-based brandy whose native origins are fiercely fought over by Chile and neighbouring Peru. Regardless of where it started, Chileans consume plenty of pisco, particularly in the famous cocktail the pisco sour – a mix of pisco, egg whites, sugar syrup, lime juice and bitters. If you want to try the very best, keep your eye out for Gran Pisco, the most sought-after (and most alcoholic) version of the spirit.

THE PERFECT GETAWAY

Wine is undoubtedly the winner here. From the cabernet sauvignons to carménères, merlots and syrahs, there's something to suit almost every taste in reds. It's worth planning to visit at least four or five wineries during a trip to the Colchagua Valley, all of which can be reached from a base in the Spanish colonial town of Santa Cruz. The Vina Santa Cruz winery is an undoubted attraction, with its gondola, cultural exhibits and observatory, which houses the largest private meteorite collection in Latin America.

For pure liquid enjoyment, however, cast your net further afield. Most wineries in Colchagua are family-owned, including Viu Manent and Neyen de Apalta, and Vina Montes is a definite highlight of the area. Once the tasting is over, or maybe before it begins, there's plenty to keep visitors occupied in the town of Santa Cruz. The city's main square is the perfect spot to wander around for an hour or so, and the streets are filled with traveller-friendly shops.

Perhaps the town's centrepiece, however, is Museo Colchagua, named the best private collection in South America. The museum houses a dazzling array of artefacts, from million-year-old fossils and Incan pottery, and Spanish colonial carriages to steam locomotives and a curious collection of Nazi memorabilia. One of the newer sections is dedicated to the 2010 Chilean mining disaster (when 33 miners were trapped underground for 69 days), with a recreation of events housed in a full-scale model of the chamber in which the men were trapped.

You could easily spend a whole day here taking it all in. Except, of course, you'd be missing out on all that wine tasting.

PLAN IT

It's possible to visit Colchagua Valley as a day trip from Santiago, and plenty of companies offer that service. A more enjoyable way to see the valley, however, would be an overnight tour, giving you the chance to sample some of the region's cuisine over dinner. Those looking for a more independent experience can take a bus from Santiago down to Santa Cruz and hire a car to make their own way through the vineyards. Although an organised tour will allow you to enjoy more of the product on offer.

DETOUR

There's no need to go all the way to the source to sample Chilean wines – Santiago boasts an appealing array of restaurants and wine bars that stock the local drop. The suburb of Bellavista, the city's creative hub, is home to its best dining. Try Restaurante La Pescadería, a seafood joint with a long wine list. In Santiago's old centre, Bocanariz has more than 300 Chilean wines on offer, with 35 by the glass. Over in upmarket Providencia Baco's modern cuisine is a local favourite.

OPENING SPREAD Haras de Pirque vineyard is in the Maipo Valley, the wine-growing region closest to Santiago. **ABOVE** The city stands in the foothills of the Andes at an ideal altitude for ripening grapes. **LEFT** Aging gracefully: barrels of wine in the cellar of Los Robles winery in the Curicó Valley.

DECKCHAIR

* **By Night in Chile** (Roberto Bolaño) A dying priest's rantings form a chilling indictment on Chile's brutal Pinochet regime in this novel by one of the country's foremost writers.

* **After-Dinner Declarations** (Nicanor Parra) Chileans are famously passionate about poetry, and Parra is the country's latest darling.

* **La Buena Vida** (The Good Life; 2008) Chilean filmmaker Andres Wood's story of four characters struggling through life in Santiago.

* **Sideways** (2004) It's not about Chile, but this American cult classic will put you in the mood for wine tasting.

* **Se Arrienda** (For Rent; 2005) Alberto Fuguet's acclaimed movie follows the life of a fictional composer in Santiago.

* **The Motorcycle Diaries** (Ernesto 'Che' Guevara) Che Guevara's tale of adventure and transformation will be enough to stir anyone's passion for life on the road in South America.

TAKING TEA IN SRI LANKA

MIST-SHROUDED MOUNTAINS AND EMERALD-GREEN TEA FIELDS FORM THE BACKDROP FOR SRI LANKA'S HILL COUNTRY, WHERE THE HEDONISTIC DAYS OF BRITISH COLONIALISM CAN STILL BE GLIMPSED IN ELEGANT BUNGALOWS, PANDERING BUTLERS, AND GIN AND TONICS AT SUNDOWN.

106

Taking tea is an art form in the Hill Country of Sri Lanka, a verdant, high-altitude region in the heart of the nation. Home to mist-covered mountains and mirror-flat lakes, this lofty location has long been a favourite destination for Sri Lankan high society. In the past, expat tea-planters made their homes here, and each summer Colombo's leading families fled the city's humidity for these cool climes. Today, the days of the Raj seem to linger on, with polo grounds, golf clubs and lavish bungalows set in English-style gardens. Terraced hillsides are covered in a carpet of emerald-green camellia bushes, punctuated by the colour-pop of sari-clad women who move through the waist-high shrubs with a peaceful rhythm. For hours each morning, they pluck the tender, top-most leaves and buds, tossing them into a basket slung over their backs.

From these hand-picking methods to the colonial-era factories dotted among the Brit-named towns (think Aberdeen, Norwood and Hatton), much remains unchanged since tea was introduced in the mid-1800s. A tour of the 1830s-era Norwood factory brings the history of Sri Lanka's tea production to life, as Andrew Taylor, the grandson of James Taylor – the man credited with bringing tea to Sri Lanka – waxes lyrical on the wonders of tea. After touring the roasting and rolling rooms, groups are guided upstairs to the drying area, an open-sided space where tonnes of freshly picked tea leaves have been fanned across tables. As warm air circulates through the greenery, the space is filled with one of the most divine scents you're ever likely to sniff. Elizabeth Arden, eat your heart out.

At a tea-tasting session, guests smell, swirl and sip their way through different brews sourced from the region, noting citrus flavours, golden hues, smoky characteristics and those astringent tannins that cause your mouth to pucker. After Taylor's tutorial, your afternoon cuppa will never taste the same again.

ESSENTIAL EXPERIENCES

* **Tea tasting and a guided tour at the historic Norwood factory.**
* Sipping a gin and tonic on the verandah while dusk falls over the mountain landscape.
* **Cycling between Ceylon Tea Trails' four colonial-era planters' bungalows.**
* Dining on tea-inspired cuisine at the villa's communal table.
* **Soaking in a green-tea bath – it's good for the skin as well as the tastebuds.**
* Climbing Sri Pada during pilgrimage season, timing your ascent to arrive at sunrise.

LOCATION BOGAWANTALAWA VALLEY, HILL COUNTRY, SRI LANKA | **BEST TIME OF YEAR** DRY SEASON (JANUARY TO APRIL) FOR SRI PADA PILGRIMAGES | **IDEAL TIME COMMITMENT** THREE DAYS | **ESSENTIAL TIP** APPLY FOR A VISA PRIOR TO ARRIVAL **BUDGET** $$ | **PACK** BRING BOOTS AND HIKING KIT FOR SRI PADA, AND A PASHMINA TO KEEP OUT THE MOUNTAIN CHILL

COFFEE OR TEA?

In the early 1800s, the Hill Country's colonial settlers cleared the jungles and planted coffee trees, only to have the crop wiped out some 40 years later after a fungus infection spread across the countryside. Faced with a huge loss of revenue, a few brave planters, including James Taylor, heard about tea-growing in similar conditions in India. Taylor embarked on a trip to Assam in northern India, returning with seeds for the tea bushes that now proliferate throughout the region. The Taylor family is credited with bringing tea to Ceylon, igniting one of Sri Lanka's main industries.

ASCENDING ADAM'S PEAK

Tea-fiends aren't the only ones to journey to the Hill
Country. From January to April, travellers descend on
the region to climb Sri Pada, Sri Lanka's most sacred
mountain. Also known as Adam's Peak, depending on
your religious persuasion the mountain is said to have
the footprint of Buddha, Shiva or Adam at its summit.
Lantern-lit trails lead the way up the 2243m-high
mount, with most ascents taking place overnight.
Climbers rush to arrive before sunrise in order to see
the spectacle known as Shadow of the Peak, as the
mountain's majestic shadow seems to rush headlong
towards the summit.

■ THE PERFECT GETAWAY

For an ultra-luxurious Hill Country foray, book a stay at Ceylon Tea Trails, four colonial-era planters' bungalows set around mirror-like Castlereagh Lake. Misty mornings kick off with a pot of tea and a full English fry-up – particularly necessary if you've tapped into the bar's supply of *arrack* (palm-toddy whisky) the night before. You can spend your days lounging on deckchairs beside stream-fed swimming pools, playing games of croquet, or cycling through tea fields. Should you fancy a cucumber sandwich, your *domo* (house boy) is never far away. Yes, the 1800s are alive and well in Sri Lanka's High Country.

The butlers have a knack for knowing when to swap the Earl Grey and scones for a G&T and canapés, which are served on the breezy verandah as the evening storm rolls in over the lake. Tea makes another appearance at dinner, served at a communal table in the dining room, followed by glasses of locally brewed *arrack*. For a more virtuous end to the evening, run a tea-scented bath back in your suite.

From January to April, the lodges are the base camp for nearby Sri Pada, the mystical mountain said to feature a holy footprint at its summit. For a fee, the hoteliers can arrange guides for the climb, who'll steer you up the lantern-lit path in time for the sunrise. The rest of the year, tea is at the top of visitors' to-do list. Tours of the Hill Country's tea factories offer a snapshot of times gone by. Lined with louvred windows to let the breeze waft through, these warehouses are filled with museum-worthy machinery, manned by barefoot workers wearing a light dusting of dried tea leaves. In one concession to modern times, the stacks of canvas bags are now stamped with words such as 'single-origin' and 'FairTrade'.

■ PLAN IT

If Castlereagh Lake's water levels are at their peak, make a grand entrance to Ceylon Tea Trails by seaplane from Colombo, a 30-minute chartered flight away. If the water's down, take a seaplane to Kandy, a three-hour drive away, or make the five-hour drive from Colombo, weaving through mountain passes and villages. You can also catch the train from Kandy to Hatton. Guests at Ceylon Tea Trails receive a tour of the Norwood factory.

■ DETOUR

Sri Lanka's cultural heartland, Kandy, is located in the northern Hill Country. Kandy's most revered site is the gilded Temple of the Tooth Relic, said to house one of Buddha's teeth. Pay your respects here at the morning service, a high-energy event with singing, dancing and drumming, before strolling around the lake. After soaking up the heritage sights of the old capital, spend the night at the Kandy House, a boutique hotel set in an ancestral manor on the outskirts of town, where *arrack* sours are poured as evening falls.

OPENING SPREAD A hard job: tea pickers working in the plantations of Nuwara Eliya. **ABOVE (L)** Several factories offer tea-tasting tours. **ABOVE (R)** Colonial accommodation in tea planters' bunglows at Ceylon Tea Trails. **LEFT** Elephants parade in the Buddhist festival of Esala Perahera in Kandy.

DECKCHAIR

* ***Cinnamon Gardens*** (Shyam Selvadurai) Delve into the hedonistic world of 1920s Ceylon in this Sri Lankan–Canadian novel.

* ***A Year in Green Tea and Tuk-Tuks*** (Rory Spowers) Follow journalist Spowers as he relocates with his family from London to an abandoned Sri Lankan tea estate.

* ***Elephant Walk*** (1954) Starring Elizabeth Taylor, this film explores the opulent lifestyle of British planters in Ceylon.

* ***Woolf in Ceylon*** (Christopher Ondaatje) Learn about Leonard Woolf's years in Ceylon, before he met Virginia.

* ***Running in the Family*** (Michael Ondaatje) A vivid account of Ondaatje's family life in Colombo and the Hill Country.

* ***The Fountains of Paradise*** (Sir Arthur C Clark) This sci-fi story features a futuristic elevator that climbs to the top of Adam's Peak.

CHASING CHEESE AND CIDER IN ASTURIAS

DONE THE TAPAS THING? DRUNK THE CERVEZA? HOW ABOUT A PIECE OF
SPAIN WITH UNIQUE FLAVOURS AND INTIMATE GASTRONOMIC EXPERIENCES,
RIGHT BESIDE SOME OF THE COUNTRY'S MOST SPECTACULAR MOUNTAIN
SCENERY? WELCOME TO THE CABRALES REGION OF ASTURIAS.

The cider pours like a waterfall from the waiter's hand, tipped from on high, in the Asturian custom, to generate the required fizz. As the cider hits the glass it foams and bubbles like a sorcerer's potion, though the sound can only just be heard over the hubbub of a weekend evening on the cobblestones of Arenas de Cabrales' main square.

All around the square, similar apple waterfalls pour into glasses as *culin* – the ritual of cider tasting – continues. It's a time-honoured tradition in this region that produces around 80% of Spanish cider – anything up to 30 million litres a year, depending on the apple harvest.

Toasts – *salud!* – are cried, and then the cider is quickly poured long and strong down thirsty throats. A few drinkers slug it back in a single shot, for everyone here knows that to leave the cider for more than few seconds is to lose its fizz. On each table around the square, plates are arrayed in a sea of tapas. There are black puddings, brochettes and, naturally, Cabrales' other star culinary attraction: its wonderful cheese, veined with natural blue-green moulds (similar in style to the famed Roquefort cheeses of France) from the caves that puncture the limestone Picos de Europa, the lumpy mountain range that's now falling into shadow behind the town.

Looking about at this scene, it's clear that time has moved on in Asturias and Cabrales. Once considered an epicurean black hole between the famed *pintxos* (tapas) of San Sebastian and the *pulperias* (octopus restaurants) of Galicia, it was a place of peasantry, where the food – *fabada* (bean stew), sausage, chorizo – was typically as solid and unadulterated as its mountains. In this square tonight, however, you can see that this land of cheese and cider is now as enticing as the metaphoric land of milk and honey. It's an experience to drink to. Salud!

ESSENTIAL EXPERIENCES

* **Being assaulted by the scent of maturing cheese as you step down into one of the Picos de Europa's cheese caves.**
* Saluting the good life as you enter into the culin spirit in one of Asturias' many bars or *sidrerias*.
* **Mingling with the cheese's source as you wander through the cows around the grassy Col Pandebano in the Picos de Europa.**
* Paying homage at the Museo de la Sidra (Cider Museum) in Nava, Asturias' biggest cider production centre; come in July for the Festival de la Sidra Natural.
* **Finding the perfect blend of cheese and cider on the Ruta'l Quesu y la Sidra.**

LOCATION ASTURIAS, SPAIN | BEST TIME OF YEAR SPRING AND AUTUMN | IDEAL TIME COMMITMENT THREE TO FIVE DAYS
ESSENTIAL TIP IF VISITING THE REGION IN SUMMER, BOOK AHEAD - IT'S A POPULAR DOMESTIC HOLIDAY DESTINATION
BUDGET $ | PACK A HEAD TORCH - FOR VISITING THE CHEESE CAVES

GARGANTA DEL CARES

If you want to walk off all that cheese and cider, you've come to the right mountains. The rugged Picos de Europa is laced with trails, including the spectacular Ruta del Cares, one of the most popular walking trails in Spain. This 11km path cuts through the Garganta del Cares, a limestone gorge almost as deep as the Grand Canyon. Splitting the Picos like a fracture, the gorge and trail begin in the village of Poncebos, near Arenas de Cabrales, following a path blasted through the high cliffs to the town of Cain, at the gorge's head.

■ THE PERFECT GETAWAY

In Cabrales it's said that the higher the village, the better the cheese. And there's no higher village than Sotres. At the edge of the village, with its steep, winding lanes and stone houses, you'll find Quesería Maín, where computer-programmer-turned-cheesemaker Jessica López Fernandez produces some of the finest cheese around – in 2011 her cheese won the top prize at the Certamen del Queso contest.

The operation is low-key and simple, but welcoming of visitors – in 2012, Quesería Maín began construction of visitor facilities that will include cheese-making courses. Until then, drop-in visitors are welcome; ask at the Hotel Sotres.

Inside the *quesería,* Jessica prepares the curds, drying them for two to three weeks in a refrigerated room before moving them into the Picos de Europa's caves – natural caves that are still used for cheese making. The highest cave is at 1600m – requiring a two-hour walk – where the temperature lingers at around 6°C, and the air is thick with humidity and the pungency of cheese.

Across the valley, in hilltop Asiego, you'll find an equally personal gastronomic experience on the Ruta'l Quesu y la Sidra (Cheese and Cider Route). Cider maker Javier Niembro leads guests on a two-hour walk into a cheese cave and through his 20 hectares of apple orchards, from where 10 varieties of apple are blended to create ciders at the small Sidreria Niembro. It's at the sidreria, among the narrow squeeze of Asiego's medieval streets, that you'll finish your stroll. Depending on the season, there may be apples being pressed or bottled around you (the fruit is collected in October and November), while at any time of year there'll be a mouthwatering tapas meal over which to linger.

■ PLAN IT

Asturias Airport at Santiago del Monte is the most convenient airport for Cabrales. It's about 150km away by road, so consider hiring a car, which also makes it easier to reach places such as Sotres and Asiego. Otherwise, Alsa buses connect via Oviedo (50km from the airport) to Arenas de Cabrales. In summer the Picos de Europa crawls with visitors, so come on the cusp of the season or book ahead. Arenas de Cabrales is the most convenient base.

■ DETOUR

Deviate east to San Sebastian, the Basque city with a reputation as one of the planet's premier dining tables. Said to have more Michelin stars per capita than anywhere else on earth, it's a destination that chef Ferran Adriá (of elBulli fame) has described as the finest place to eat in the world. *Pintxo* – the Basque version of tapa – is San Sebastian's star. It's a bite-sized culinary art form, with some of the finest found in pintxo bars such as La Cuchara de San Telmo and Astelena. Wash 'em down with a glass of *txakoli,* the young Basque white wine.

OPENING SPREAD Sotres is the highest town in the Picos de Europa National Park; *queso de Cabrales* is ripened in its cool, limestone caves. The town is a good base for exploring local walking trails. **ABOVE** You can buy sausage in the markets of Asturias with which to make the regional speciality fabada.

DECKCHAIR

* *A Food Lover's Pilgrimage to the Camino de Santiago* (Dee Nolan) A personal account of the famed walk across northern Spain incorporating local food traditions.

* *La Regenta* (Leopoldo Alas y Ureña) A 19th-century tangled love circle in fictional Vetusta, a thinly veiled version of the Asturian city Oviedo.

* *The Cuisines of Spain: Exploring Regional Home Cooking* (Teresa Barrenechea) An appetising book on Spanish food.

* *Walks and Climbs in the Picos de Europa* (Robin Walker) An après-cheese guide to the mountains that dominate the view wherever you are in Cabrales.

* *Vicki Cristina Barcelona* (2008) Asturias takes centre stage in this Woody Allen movie, much of it set in Oviedo; the locals loved it so much that they've erected a statue of Allen.

ROMANCE

GREAT ESCAPES

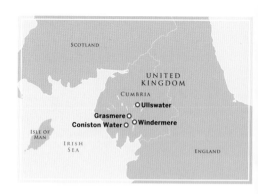

GET POETIC IN THE LAKE DISTRICT

IF IT'S ROMANCE YOU WANT, TRY THE ENGLISH LAKE DISTRICT. ITS FELLS, LAKES AND WOODS UNLEASHED 'THE SPONTANEOUS OVERFLOW OF POWERFUL FEELINGS' THAT STARTED THE ROMANTIC MOVEMENT. VISIT TODAY AND SEE WHAT EMOTIONS IT KINDLES IN YOU.

114

Wandering along the lake shore, you look up. A lonely cloud floats along, its shadow passing from vale to hill. You look down again and – whaddyaknow? – beneath the budding trees ahead is a host of golden daffodils. And, yep, they are fluttering and dancing in the breeze.

You're on the shores of Ullswater, where Wordsworth and his sister Dorothy walked on 15 April 1802, inspiring his most famous verse.

If you can see the daffodils, it's probably that same time of year now, but no matter if it isn't – this is one of the most scenic spots in the Lake District. You're sure to see something sublime, whether it's the autumnal colours of heather and leaves, or the shafts of sunlight as a shower moves across the head of the valley.

It might seem strange that such big feelings could have been caused by such little hills and lakes. But it wasn't the scale of the place that made it such fertile ground for Wordsworth and Coleridge or for visitors today.

Despite its low height, the terrain is steep, so the compact national park packs in hundreds of peaks, many bristling with crags. People have lived in these valleys for thousands of years – there are Roman forts, medieval castles and Victorian villas all cheek-by-jowl. But it's the unpredictable, annoying weather that actually made this place Wordsworth's muse: it provides an endless play of light and dark on the hillsides, views half-glimpsed then snatched away. It's a place to fire the imagination, to feel the elements and think about humanity's place in nature; to consider what – and who – is most important to you.

So do as Wordsworth did: go out for a stroll and soak in the magic of the landscape. You'll find you see the world a bit more clearly and appreciate the simple things like human relationships a little bit more.

ESSENTIAL EXPERIENCES

* **Getting spray-soaked at the bottom of Aira Force before heading down to the Ullswater lakeshore for a bit of daffodil-spotting.**

* Stopping in at Sarah Nelson's Gingerbread Shop in Grasmere for six slabs made from her secret recipe while you're waiting for your tour of Dove Cottage.

* **Trying onion ash, Alexander seed or wood sorrel for the first time at the second-best restaurant in Britain, L'Enclume.**

* Stumbling upon Claife Station as you walk alongside Windermere and imagining what holidays were like before cameras.

* **Driving over the highest pass in the Lake District and reaching the ominously named road 'the Struggle'.**

LOCATION LAKE DISTRICT NATIONAL PARK, NORTHWEST ENGLAND | **BEST TIME OF YEAR** APRIL FOR DAFFODILS, MAY TO JUNE FOR BETTER WEATHER | **IDEAL TIME COMMITMENT** A TWO-DAY TOUR OR A WEEK'S STAY | **ESSENTIAL TIP** THIS IS THE HOME OF STICKY TOFFEE PUDDING – DON'T MISS IT | **BUDGET** $$$ | **PACK** WALKING BOOTS, WATERPROOF JACKET, WATERPROOF TROUSERS AND PLENTY OF LAYERS

THE FIRST ROCK CLIMB

Samuel Taylor Coleridge wasn't just a brilliant poet, tortured soul and opium addict. He was also England's first recreational rock-climber. On 5 August 1802, he went out for a walk in the Lakeland hills but ended up descending a series of ledges that grew ever steeper. Eventually he had to drop down a 3m cliff onto a tiny sloping ledge, before squeezing through a narrow cleft and onto safer ground. The route is today called Broad Stand – a 'Difficult'-graded rock-climb. Somehow, Coleridge managed to survive it. His reaction? 'I lay in a state of almost prophetic Trance and Delight'.

◼ THE PERFECT GETAWAY

The daffodils got one Wordsworth poem; Aira Force, the waterfall right next to them, three – and it has the advantage of looking better in the rain. Start your Romantic tour here with a stroll along Ullswater's shore, then up to the falls.

Drive south to Grasmere and you'll discover that Wordsworth wasn't just the father of Romantic Poetry, he was also the father of Lake District tourism. He was none too pleased about this, but you should be – after 200 years of visitors, the area has food and lodgings to suit everyone. So after you've visited his houses (three of which are open to the public)and been for a stroll along Loughrigg Terrace for the best views of his precious Vale of Grasmere, you'll have earned a night at the Drunken Duck. This middle-of-nowhere pub wasn't around when Wordsworth wrote the lines 'a genial hearth, a hospitable board, and a refined rusticity', but that's still a pretty good description of a place that manages to combine brewery, gastropub and boutique inn in a rural setting.

Stay as many nights as you can then head for Ambleside and buy a Walker's Ticket on the Windermere Lake Cruises. This gets you onto a boat to Wray Castle, a Victorian Gothic lump. From there, it's a 90-minute stroll through woodland along the quiet west shore of Windermere to Ferry House, from which you can cross the lake to the teashops of Bowness, before taking a third boat back to your car.

If you've the appetite for one more treat, drive along Windermere to the village of Cartmel. This is home to L'Enclume, reckoned by foodies to be the second-best restaurant in Britain. The ingredients are all local, most of them foraged. With meadowsweet, borage flower, pink fir and mugwort on the menu you'll find pretty much every local bloom except the daffodil.

DECKCHAIR

* **The Golden Store** (William Wordsworth and Nancy Martin) Illustrated introduction to Wordsworth's work and life for first-timers.

* **Swallows and Amazons** (Arthur Ransome) Children's adventure classic set on a fictional lake that is half Windermere, half Coniston Water.

* **The Immortal Dinner** (Penelope Hughes-Hallett) Lively account of an infamous 1817 dinner party attended by Wordsworth, John Keats and Charles Lamb.

* **Footsteps** (Richard Holmes) Holmes mixes travel and memoir to draw parallels between his own experiences and those of the Romantics in this genre-changing biography.

* **The Maid of Buttermere** (Melvyn Bragg) Historical novel based on 19th-century bigamy scandal in a Lakeland valley.

* **The Tale of Peter Rabbit** (Beatrix Potter) Catch up on the area's other famous writer before visiting the Windermere area.

PLAN IT

If arriving by train, Penrith is on the main London–Glasgow line. With military planning, it is possible to do this trip on public transport from Penrith, but a car makes things a whole lot more flexible. Try rental companies Practical or Enterprise. Avoid school holidays, as the Lake District receives 16 million visitors a year, and book the Drunken Duck and L'Enclume a couple of months ahead. Entry to Dove Cottage (Wordsworth's first house) is by timed guided tour only, so buy your ticket with a couple of hours to spare.

DETOUR

If you've had enough of the great outdoors and want a bit of indoor beauty, the Lake District is also an important area for the Arts & Crafts movement, inspired by William Morris and John Ruskin. You can visit Brantwood, Ruskin's Coniston Water house, which he designed as an embodiment of his ideals of craftsmanship, natural light and organic form. Even more impressive is Windermere's Blackwell House, with its elegant White Drawing Room and oak-panelled Great Hall, every piece of which was hand-carved by local craftsmen. Check the Blackwell House website for details of upcoming exhibitions and lectures.

ASHLEY COOPER / CORBIS ©

OPENING SPREAD Hire a rowing boat made for two and scull across Derwentwater. **ABOVE** Daffodils turn to the sun at Troutbeck, near Windermere. **BELOW** Looking out over Keswick and Derwentwater from Latrigg fell, the landscape that inspired Romantic poetry.

THE REAL WORDSWORTH

People think of Wordsworth as serious, Victorian and establishment. By the time of his death at the age of 80, he was. But as a young man he was a rebel. He failed his Cambridge exams to spite his family, walked to Italy without telling anyone, then got involved in revolutionary politics in France. He had a secret French love-child, and his own government spied on him and Coleridge because they were so reactionary. A generation later, Byron may have been 'mad, bad and dangerous to know', but he was only following in the footsteps of William 'Wildchild'.

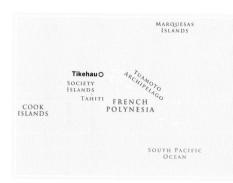

LIVE THE TROPICAL DREAM ON TIKEHAU

BE CAPTIVATED BY THE SILENCE, INTENSELY STARRY SKIES, EMPTY PINK-SAND BEACHES, BLUE LAGOONS AND LANGUID PACE OF LIFE ON THE FRENCH POLYNESIAN ISLAND OF TIKEHAU, WHERE YOU CAN COMMUNE WITH EACH OTHER IN LUXURIOUS ISOLATION.

118

The soles of your feet are kneaded by soft pink sands while warm water swishes gently around your body and your hair is tousled by a light trade wind. Together you swim into a lagoon so clear you can see a school of peacock-coloured parrotfish several metres away. There's no one else in sight – it's just you, your honey and an abundance of swaying palms.

Much of the Tikehau experience is visceral, but Jacques Cousteau backed the paradisiacal atmosphere with fact in 1987 when he declared that Tikehau has the greatest variety of fish species in French Polynesia. Don a mask to swim in the lagoon with colourful fish, manta rays and reef sharks inhabiting dramatic coral seascapes. Kayak empty turquoise coves, kitesurf prevailing winds, and surf, snorkel or dive the ingoing current of the Tuheiava Pass: in or on the water everything feels like a rush of bright blue streaked with rays of sun.

Then there's the land. Think of a postcard photo of a tiny, flat deserted island encircled by a white-sand beach with nothing but a cluster of coconut trees in the middle. Now imagine a few dozen of these, some several kilometres long and others only big enough for a single palm, all strung in a circle around a giant turquoise lagoon. This is an atoll. Now erode those islets into sweeping, twisting little bays lined with pink and white sand. This unique erosion is what makes Tikehau stand out as one of the prettiest atolls in the country.

Nature is everywhere but Tikehau doesn't make you rough it. Environmentally friendly, stylish luxury awaits in the grand, over-the-water style of Tikehau Pearl Beach Resort or the naturalistic manner of Ninamu Resort. Both are on private islands whose palm-fringed beauty rival anything on Bora Bora and whose privacy is unparalleled. Dine on fine French-Polynesian fusion cuisine, sleep under butter-soft sheets and commune with the stars, the ocean and each other.

ESSENTIAL EXPERIENCES

* **Swimming in clear, warm-water bliss with dancing manta rays.**
* Watching the sun quickly dip below the orange horizon to the strum of a ukulele.
* **Luxuriating in your very private natural-wood bungalow or over-the-water villa while listening to the soft swish of the surf.**
* Paddling a kayak through turquoise waters to a deliciously deserted pink-sand beach.
* **Hearing the squawk of hundreds of seabirds on their forested islet nesting grounds.**
* Smiling at village kids playing football on the dried-grass local pitch.
* **Drinking French wine or a fresh tropical-fruit-juice cocktail whenever you want.**

LOCATION TIKEHAU, FRENCH POLYNESIA | **BEST TIME OF YEAR** APRIL, MAY, OCTOBER AND NOVEMBER | **IDEAL TIME COMMITMENT** THREE TO FIVE DAYS | **ESSENTIAL TIP** THE BEST ATOLL FOOTWEAR ARE CHEAP, PLASTIC REEF SANDALS, AVAILABLE AT THE VILLAGE SHOP | **BUDGET** $$$ | **PACK** SUNSCREEN AND BUG SPRAY (EXPENSIVE IN FRENCH POLYNESIA)

GOING LOCAL

Luxury not your style or budget? There are several small pensions on the atoll that range from simple family-run affairs to chic boutique operations. All are located in or near Tuherahera Village. The best include Relais Royal Tikehau, on a gorgeous private islet with plain yet comfortable rooms; Pension Hotu, which has tiny, artistic, fan-cooled bungalows on a stretch of beach near the village; Tikehau Village, which is almost a resort, with one of Tuherahera's best restaurants and a huge white-sand beach; and Fare Hanariki, a basic but isolated set-up on a private islet with four bungalows.

SURFING THE PASS

Tuheiava Pass is home to semi-secret yet fantastic left- and right-breaking waves on a relatively shallow reef. The right is the easier of the two and is rideable by intermediate surfers and up, while the left can get hollow with faces of up to 10ft. Ninamu Resort offers shuttles to the waves and in normal conditions this takes about 15 minutes, through the clear blue pass to the anchorage. Spectators can look for beach shells and stroll the outer reef while they watch from the shore. Surf season runs from November to April.

THE PERFECT GETAWAY

As you approach Ninamu Resort from Tuherahera Village by motorboat, it feels like you're hallucinating. The water is a patchwork of blues ranging from translucent aqua to a profound indigo and the islet you're headed for is a swirl of greens and bright white sand. Your bungalow is one of only six – it's a luxurious thatched masterpiece of gnarled wood, plush cushions and gauzy white fabrics.

The first thing you do is get in the water and the light waves instantly lull you to an island rhythm. The night is spent under the stars at the Crusoe-with-style bar, perhaps to the sound of ukuleles or just the breeze through the palms and waves lapping the shore. In the morning you go snorkelling to watch, in awe, several manta rays as they congregate around a lagoon site called La Ferme aux Mantas, where schools of wrasses eat the parasites off their wings.

The next day see the rest of the atoll on a lagoon tour. You visit Motu Puarua, an island in the centre of the atoll's lagoon where seabirds come en masse to nest in the low trees. Then boat to Île d'Eden, an islet where the Church of the New Testament has grown superb organic gardens and built fish parks where you can view shimmery blue, silver and gold jacks and ulua (giant trevally).

From here, your guide takes you to one of the atoll's finest pink-sand beaches, where they barbecue fresh fish and serve prepared dishes of *poisson cru* (raw fish salad in coconut milk), coconut bread, rice and fruit. Meanwhile, you're free to swim, snorkel and explore the area on your own. Lastly, you get a glimpse of traditional Polynesian life on a stroll through flower-filled Tuherahera Village. Stay as many days as you like for more water sports or just exploring the atoll.

PLAN IT

Fly to Papeete in Tahiti, then take Air Tahiti direct to Tikehau. Your resort or pension will meet you, and you'll either walk, get driven or boat to your destination. When you arrive at your lodging you'll be given your activity options. Ninamu Resort has their activities included in the price, while Tikehau Pearl Beach Resort offers a slew of activities that you can mix and match. Book accommodation well in advance during summer and winter holidays.

DETOUR

While you're in the Tuamotu Archipelago, why not visit another atoll? Several flights per week head to Rangiroa, one of the world's largest atolls. More famous for diving (think lots of sharks) than romance, the main town, Avatoru, will feel like the big smoke after a few days on Tikehau. Bike around, watch dolphins frolic in Tiputa Pass at sunset and dine at any of several fine restaurants. Day lagoon excursions take in the Île aux Récifs, a bizarre, raised, dead-coral reef, and the intensely azure Lagon Bleu (Blue Lagoon).

121

OPENING SPREAD Stay in thatched huts at Pearl Beach resort on Tikehau. **ABOVE** The only hazard on Tikehau might be falling coconuts.
LEFT With warm, shallow water around Tikehau you're guaranteed to see tropical fish while snorkelling.

DECKCHAIR

* **Blue Latitudes: Boldly Going Where Captain Cook Has Gone Before** (Tony Horwitz) Follow in the footsteps of Captain Cook.
* **Mutiny on the Bounty** (1935, 1962, 1984) The story of the famous uprising aboard the *Bounty* has been embellished by big-budget film-makers three times in 50 years.
* **Breadfruit** (Célestine Hitiura Vaite) Novel series set in a very realistic Tahitian community.

* **Piracy in the Pacific: The Story of the Notorious Rorique Brothers** (Henri Jacquier) The true story of mother-of-pearl pirates in the Tuamotus.
* **The Sex Lives of Cannibals** (J Maarten Troost) Hysterical read about life on Tarawa Atoll.
* **Couples Retreat** (2009) Romantic comedy mostly filmed at the St Regis Resort on Bora Bora.

ROMANCING THE RIVIERA

OFTEN REFERRED TO AS LES TROIS CORNICHES AFTER THE THREE SCENIC ROADS THAT RUN FROM NICE TO MONACO AT DIFFERENT ALTITUDES, THIS CORNER OF THE FRENCH RIVIERA IS FAMED FOR ITS STUPENDOUS BEAUTY AND HIGHBROW HISTORY.

122

One of the most enduring images of Alfred Hitchcock's classic film *To Catch a Thief* is of Grace Kelly speeding along the French Riviera in a blue cabriolet, an unflappable Cary Grant next to her in the passenger seat. Kelly, with her perfect blonde perm, candy-pink twinset and scarf flowing in the breeze, looks every bit the poster girl of 1950s glamour. Grant and Kelly end up kissing on a viewpoint above Monaco at the end of the scene; it was in Monaco that Kelly herself found her Prince Charming – Prince Rainier of Monaco, whom she married in 1956 in what the media dubbed 'the wedding of the century'.

Today, the shimmering blue sea, languorous curves of the shores, sheer drop of the coastal cliffs and exquisite sunlight look just as captivating as they did in Grace Kelly's era. The Grande Corniche, the highest of the three coastal roads, and backdrop of that famous car chase, was officially built by Napoleon in the early 19th century but first used by the Romans to link Rome with modern-day Provence. It's a succession of superlative views and the ultimate scenic drive.

Below is the Moyenne Corniche. Built in the 1920s to alleviate congestion on the coast road (already!), it snakes through maquis-covered slopes and culminates at the medieval village of Èze. Built on a rocky promontory 427m above the sea, Èze lives up to its 'eagle's nest' moniker. Inside, the village is all higgledy-piggledy pebbled lanes and phenomenal views. Visit off-season or stay in the village overnight and you'll be won over by the magic of the place.

And finally there is the Basse Corniche, which skims the Mediterranean's shore, passing through postcard Villefranche-sur-Mer and *belle-époque* beauty Beaulieu-sur-Mer. It was here that wealthy Americans wintered in the late 19th and early 20th centuries; many also took a punt at the casino. Little did they know that a Hollywood star would one day marry Monaco's sovereign.

ESSENTIAL EXPERIENCES

* **Spending a day in Nice, the belle of the Côte d'Azur.**

* Sampling the high life in the hedonistic principality of Monaco and tempting your luck at Monte Carlo's fabulous casino.

* **Driving along the scenic corniches and revelling in the beauty of the Mediterranean coastline.**

* Treating yourself to a night or a meal at Château Eza and discovering the medieval village of Èze.

* **Immersing yourself in the Riviera's glorious Roman past in La Turbie and its *belle-époque* heyday in Beaulieu-sur-Mer.**

* Spending an afternoon swimming off Villefranche-sur-Mer's glorious beaches.

LOCATION CÔTE D'AZUR, FRANCE | **BEST TIME OF YEAR** MAY TO OCTOBER | **IDEAL TIME COMMITMENT** TWO DAYS TO TWO WEEKS | **ESSENTIAL TIP** PLAN AHEAD (FOR BOTH TICKETS AND ACCOMMODATION) DURING ANY OF THE FESTIVALS AND EVENTS **BUDGET** $$ | **PACK** EVENING WEAR

MONTE CARLO'S CASINO

Anyone who is anyone, it seems, has taken a gamble at Monte Carlo's casino, from James Bond to European royalty and celebrities; the glamour appeal of this neoclassical confection is undeniable. Designed by Paris opera-house architect Charles Garnier, the casino is a sumptuous building, with gilded chandeliers, stuccoed ceilings, oak-panelled walls and the rarefied atmosphere of unbridled wealth. Spending an evening here needn't cost the earth, however: entry to the main gaming room (Salon Europe) costs just €10 and the minimum bet is €5. Jackets are compulsory for men after 8pm; as for women, dressing up is *de rigueur* and impossible to overdo.

FESTIVALS GALORE

The French Riviera plays host to very high-profile events, each reason enough to plan your holiday around. Sports enthusiasts should look out for Monaco's Monte Carlo Masters tennis series in April and the glitzy Monaco Grand Prix on the last weekend of May. Another highlight on the principality's calendar is its International Circus Festival, which features gravity-defying acrobatics. In Nice, don't miss the Carnival in February – one of the oldest and biggest in the world, complete with street parades and floats. Finally, summer visitors will revel in Nice's world-famous jazz festival and its overspill (and free) Fringe Festival on the seafront and in Vieux Nice.

THE PERFECT GETAWAY

There can be no more magical place to stay in the area than Château Eza, Èze's 400-year-old castle and former home of Prince William of Sweden. Not only do you get the village to yourself once the tour groups have gone, the hotel's 10 rooms are the last word in luxury, with bags of charm and those incredible views in the most exclusive rooms. At least come for drinks on the panoramic terrace or have lunch and feast on Michelin-starred Mediterranean gastronomy.

From Èze it's easy to explore the area. The Basse Corniche trio of Beaulieu-sur-Mer, St-Jean-Cap-Ferrat and Villefranche-sur-Mer make an ideal day trip: visit the curious Villa Kerylos in Beaulieu and the over-the-top Villa Ephrussi de Rothschild on Cap-Ferrat, and wind down in the azure waters of Villefranche.

The next day, hit the glitz of Monaco, visiting the prince's palace, exploring the world-class aquarium and ogling at the yachts and sports cars. Come night-time, there is only one place to go: the legendary Casino de Monte-Carlo. In the other direction, Nice is a concentrate of Mediterranean delight. Spend the morning shopping at the market on Cours Saleya and savour your lunch on the beach. Once you've had enough sun, mooch around Vieux Nice, the city's atmospheric Old Town, and finish your day in one of Nice's numerous bars and restaurants.

And finally, make sure you rent a car to motor along the Grande Corniche, which runs 600m above the coast. Don't try and stop for pictures – opt instead for Le Trophée des Alpes, a Roman monument in La Turbie, or the Parc Naturel Départemental de la Grande Corniche, a nature reserve where the views stretch so far in every direction you can start to make out the curvature of the earth.

PLAN IT

You can travel to the Riviera year-round; avoid the wetter months of March, April and November if you can. It's only warm enough to swim from May to October. The nearest international airport is Nice Côte d'Azur Airport, from where you'll find plenty of buses to Nice and Monaco and connections to Èze (one hour in total). Book ahead to stay or eat at Château Eza.

DETOUR

If you've had enough glamour and itch to don your walking boots, you're in luck: hundreds of kilometres of trail line the Riviera, all with mesmerising panoramas. Given the setting, there are some very steep walks, but plenty of easier routes, too: the Sentier du Littoral (coastal path) runs from Cap-d'Ail to Menton with a hiatus in Monaco (easily covered by bus). Another easy option is the loop around millionaires' lair Cap-Ferrat. More challenging are walks in the hills around La Turbie and Èze. For a full list, consult the excellent *Guide RandOxygène Pays Côtier*.

OPENING SPREAD Villefranche-sur-Mer, a popular port for cruise ships, featured in *To Catch a Thief*. **ABOVE (L)** The ultimate honeymoon hotel? Chateau Eza in Èze. **ABOVE (R)** Cary Grant and Grace Kelly in a clinch in *To Catch a Thief*. **LEFT** Eye-catching plumage at the Nice Carnival.

DECKCHAIR

* ***To Catch a Thief*** (1955) This Alfred Hitchcock classic, starring Cary Grant and Grace Kelly, tells the story of a retired jewel thief fighting to clear his name after he is wrongly accused of committing robberies on the French Riviera.

* ***Tender Is the Night*** (F Scott Fitzgerald) A vivid account of life on the Riviera during the decadent 1920s Jazz Age.

* ***GoldenEye*** (1995) One of several Bond films taking in Monaco and the Riviera, with spectacular car chases, the Monte Carlo Casino, and a helicopter stolen from a military ship moored in the port of Monaco.

* ***The French Riviera: A Cultural History*** (Julian Hale) A fantastic history of the Côte d'Azur that delves into its vibrant past, with panache and (Champagne) buckets of anecdotes.

SLEEP UNDER THE STARS IN KERALA

EVEN IN A COUNTRY THAT DAZZLES AS MUCH AS INDIA, THE KERALAN BACKWATERS STAND OUT AS SPECIAL. THESE WATERWAYS, AMONG THE SUBCONTINENT'S MOST STARTLINGLY BEAUTIFUL AND TRANQUIL PLACES, ARE WHERE LOVERS CAN ESCAPE INTO AN INTIMATE WORLD OF THEIR OWN.

126

The mirroring waters reflect a thick fringe of arched, nodding palms framing a brilliant central ribbon of blue sky. Coconut trees shade the water on either side of you as you glide along the canals on your narrow houseboat-made-for-two, constructed from wood and woven coconut leaves.

Kerala's floodlike network of limpid lagoons is linked by kilometre upon kilometre of canals and channels, both constructed and natural, which stretch almost the entire length of Kerala state. Known as the backwaters, they are a place where people live almost on the water: on either side of you there are strung-out villages, temples hung with bright prayer flags, people doing their washing and children on their way to school. This is one of India's most peaceful places, but it's also vibrantly, thrillingly alive.

Your graceful, homespun craft is a *kettuvallam,* a long type of traditional barge that was once used for cargo. These days, they have been converted into tourist houseboats of all degrees of comfort and size. For the utmost privacy, you can hire a one-bedroom boat and chug gracefully around the waters, mooring up under the firmament of stars overnight. The crew cooks you meals on the boat, so you can choose what you'd most like to eat, then enjoy candlelit dinners watching the night's reflections dance across the water. For a boutique experience, try *Discovery,* the Malabar House houseboat, which combines contemporary design with the curves of the traditional boat and is decorated in white linens with blazing bright silks. The boat is narrower than most, so it can slip down channels that are inaccessible to larger craft. Not only does it have ecofriendly electric engines, but they are silent, so you can float quietly through the reeds.

Drifting along the vast, tendril-like waterways is one of India's most romantic experiences – you could stay here for days, exploring the countryside and being lulled to sleep under the stars.

ESSENTIAL EXPERIENCES

* **Eating a Keralan curry, made from fresh fish and spiced coconut milk, on your houseboat underneath the stars.**

* Taking an open canoe boat to glide around the narrower waterways.

* **Witnessing daily life around the waterways: coir-making, toddy-tapping and bird-watching.**

* Getting slippery with oil via a traditional four-handed Ayurvedic massage.

* **Visiting the historic spice port of Kochi (Cochin); and watching the cantilevered Chinese fishing nets at work as the light turns pink at dawn or dusk.**

* Exploring a jungle-like, luxuriant spice plantation and stocking up on fresh spices such as cardamom, black pepper, nutmeg and ginger to take home.

LOCATION KERALA, SOUTHERN INDIA | **BEST TIME OF YEAR** OCTOBER, NOVEMBER, MARCH | **IDEAL TIME COMMITMENT** TWO DAYS TO ONE WEEK | **ESSENTIAL TIP** AVOID CHRISTMAS AND NEW YEAR | **BUDGET** $-$$ | **PACK** MOSQUITO REPELLENT

COCONUTS, SPICES & THE COAST

What will you eat on the boat? You're in for a treat.
Keralan cuisine is fragrant and delicate, using the
natural resources of India's lushest state. The region
is rich in plantations; cardamom, ginger, black pepper,
curry leaves, thyme, basil, mint, bay leaf, coriander
and sage grow profusely, scenting the regional cuisine.
Other major crops are coffee, tea and cashews. With
such a long coastline, fresh fish is a staple of the
diet. Coconut milk mellows the flavours, and almost
everything is cooked in coconut oil, making the cuisine
much lighter than the ghee-based dishes of the north.

ALL ABOUT AYURVEDA

The term *ayurveda* comes from the Sanskrit *ayu* (life) and *veda* (knowledge), and it's an ancient form of medicine. Its philosophy sees us as having three *doshas* (elemental humours): *vata* (air), *pitta* (fire) and *kapha* (water/earth). Treatments aim to bring these three into balance, helping to avoid illness. Such treatments include massage, diet, steam baths and purification medications. Some of these, such the internal purification and intense detox of *panchkarma*, are not for the faint-hearted, but the traditional ayurvedic massage, which leaves you slithery with oil and is often performed by two masseurs, is a unique and eventually relaxing experience.

THE PERFECT GETAWAY

It's time to slow right down. Allow time so that you can enjoy this blissed-out journey. You can simply drift along the coconut-palm-lined waterways, reading, relaxing and watching life on the river slide past. Take books, games and things to doodle on; this is a romantic respite from modern life, where you'll be surrounded by more shades of green than you could believe were possible.

To add to the experience, you could also arrange a trip on which you explore the surrounding watery countryside via village tours. On such a tour you'll be able to experience some of the local villages that you'd otherwise just float past. You can see traditional artisans making coir, the tough material created from coconut palms that's used for everything from boats to rope. Small shipyards on the way are where local people construct the kettuvallams by hand from wood, a craft that doesn't appear to have changed for hundreds of years. Likewise 'toddy tapping' – the art of extracting palm beer from the trees.

It's also worth visiting the small Catholic churches that dot the waterways and making a trip to the edge of the rice paddies to gaze out over their green expanse. Between the towns of Kollam (Quilon) and Alappuzha (Alleppey), both launching places for the backwaters, there's the Mata Amrithanandamayi Mission, a huge ashram run by one of India's few female gurus, Amma, who often conducts all-night *darshans* (communions), hugging thousands of her devoted followers. But the essential romance of the backwaters trips is in the passing details: the glimpses of life on the riverbank; the chance to be lulled to sleep on a gently rocking boat; dining under an inky sky smeared with stars.

PLAN IT

Fly to the airports at Thiruvananthapuram (Trivandrum) or Kochi (Cochin) to reach southern Kerala. From the airports you can take a bus or taxi to the hubs of backwater tourism: Alappuzha (Alleppey), Kollam (Quilon) and Kottayam. At any of these you can hire the houseboat of your dreams but check the boat out before you agree to anything as they vary greatly in quality.

DETOUR

If you'd like to experience some less-explored waterways, head to Kerala's Northern Backwaters, which lie close to Payyanur, 50km north of Kannur. The huge body of water is fed by five rivers and there are very few houseboat operators, so the area has a completely different, untouristed feel to it compared with the more extensive southern backwaters. You'll have a very narrow choice of boats, but it feels much more remote and off the beaten track. You're also well placed for seeing some of Kerala's incredible Theyyam rituals – traditional, masked temple theatre.

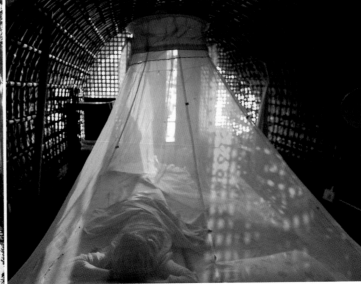

OPENING SPREAD Start your sojourn on Kerala's backwaters at Alappuzha (Alleppey). **ABOVE (L)** You'll be part of daily life on the waterways. **ABOVE (R)** Mosquito nets keep out the pests. **LEFT** In the shirodhara ayurvedic treatment warm oil is slowly poured onto your forehead.

DECKCHAIR

* ❋ *The God of Small Things* (Arundhati Roy) Poetic, evocative Man Booker Prize–winning masterpiece set in Kerala.

* ❋ *The Moor's Last Sigh* (Salman Rushdie) This great novel evokes the area's spice-laden past and is partly set in Cochin.

* ❋ *Where the Rain is Born: Writings About Kerala* (ed Anita Nair) A short-story collection that brings alive Kerala's traditions.

* ❋ *The Better Man* (Anita Nair) The lyrical, colourful tale of a man who returns to his village in northern Kerala and transforms his life.

* ❋ *Midnight's Children* (2012) Deepa Mehta's film of Salman Rushdie's epic novel about India's partition in 1947.

* ❋ *Before the Rains* (2007) This Merchant Ivory cinematic epic – the story of a British spice planter's affair with his servant – is set in 1930s Kerala.

IT'S A PIRATE'S LIFE IN NASSAU

ONCE A RUM-SOAKED BOLT-HOLE FOR BUCCANEERS, NASSAU IS NOW A GETAWAY FOR LOVERS, WHERE COUPLES GET ROMANTIC IN THE FRAGRANT BACK GARDENS AND LABYRINTHINE WINE CELLARS OF AN 18TH-CENTURY PIRATE'S MANSION, NOW KNOWN AS THE GRAYCLIFF HOTEL.

130

A warm wind is blowing off the Caribbean Sea, the hibiscus is in bloom, and you and your beloved are sitting with your feet kicked up on your private balcony high in the hills overlooking the cobblestoned Old Town of Nassau. Add a glass of golden rum in hand and you've got a pretty good idea of what it was like to be a gentleman pirate surveying his bounty in the mid-1700s.

This is the Graycliff Hotel, built in 1740 by the fearsome pirate Captain John Howard Graysmith, who plundered Spanish galleons throughout the Caribbean with his schooner, *Graywolf*. Graysmith built the Georgian-style mansion atop a hill looking down over the gin-clear water so he could spot any incoming ships. Later, the house became a garrison for the US Navy, Nassau's first inn, and a playpen for Jazz Age Americans looking to party during the years of Prohibition.

Today, you're free to roam about the hushed hotel, whose creaky antiques and mismatched Oriental rugs suggest an era of long-ago – and possibly ill-begotten – opulence. Swim in the Spanish-tiled pool, crack open a musty tome in the leather-lined library or puff a Cohiba straight from the hotel's own cigar factory. The hotel restaurant is famous for its French-Caribbean cuisine, and the wine cellar, with more than 250,000 bottles from 400 vintners, including such precious rarities as an 1865 Château Lafite and a 1727 Rüdesheimer Apostelwein (one of the most expensive bottles in the world), is world-renowned. In between naps, swims and wine-soaked feasts, you and your love can stroll down the hill into Nassau town for all manner of 21st-century amusements. Continue the pirate theme at the interactive Pirates of Nassau museum, climb the hand-hewn limestone steps to 18th-century Fort Fincastle, or snorkel the Technicolour reef surrounding the island. Perhaps you'll even find a chest of lost pirate treasure!

ESSENTIAL EXPERIENCES

* **Puffing a hand-rolled Cuban cigar made on-site at the Graycliff's Cuban-staffed cigar factory.**

* Sipping a mellow, vanilla-inflected cognac from the hotel's Cognateque, with some 9000 bottles of cognac and port.

* **Gawking at psychedelically coloured fish along the reefs of New Providence.**

* Shopping for duty-free gemstones, batik fabric tablecloths, sticky rum cakes and local straw baskets along downtown Nassau's West Bay St.

* **Shaking your booty to local goombay music at Arawak Cay, downtown Nassau's beloved outdoor food centre – a must-try for its conch fritters.**

LOCATION NASSAU, NEW PROVIDENCE, THE BAHAMAS | **BEST TIME OF YEAR** MID-DECEMBER TO MID-APRIL | **IDEAL TIME COMMITMENT** THREE TO FOUR DAYS | **ESSENTIAL TIP** AVOID THE CROWDS BY HEADING SLIGHTLY WEST OF CABLE BEACH: THE SANDS ARE JUST AS BEAUTIFUL BUT MUCH QUIETER | **BUDGET** $$$ | **PACK** FORMAL DINNER ATTIRE, SUNSCREEN AND AN EXTRA SUITCASE FOR BRINGING BACK LOCAL RUM

PARADISE ISLAND

You can't spend any time in Nassau without noticing what looks like a pink Disney castle across the harbour. This is the Atlantis resort at Paradise Island, a jaw-droppingly huge resort–meets–amusement park with a Disney-esque Lost City of Atlantis theme. You don't have to be a resort guest to gawk at the lobby's indoor shark tanks, brave the twisting slides at the 57-hectare on-site waterpark, or try your luck at the blackjack tables in the massive Atlantis casino. The complex is home to some of the area's best see-and-be-seen restaurants, including an outpost of the Nobu sushi empire and a Southwestern American joint from TV grill guru Bobby Flay.

SHAKE IT AT JUNKANOO

Masked dancers whirl, cowbells clang, drums beat a ceaseless tattoo. This is Junkanoo, the Bahamas' national festival and the equivalent of New Orleans' Mardi Gras or Brazil's Carnaval, which starts every year in the early morning hours of Boxing Day (26 December). With origins in West African secret societies, Junkanoo grew as a tradition among slaves on the British plantations, who hid their faces with masks to obscure their identities. Today, the festival is an integral part of Bahamian identity, with dancers and teams competing for the most elaborate costumes and dances. If you're not around then, head over to Nassau's Arawak Cay to watch dancers practise on weekend evenings.

■ THE PERFECT GETAWAY

A long weekend is an ideal amount of time for a romantic Nassau getaway. Plan on spending your first day hitting the beaches. Cable Beach is the island's main sandbox. Paddle in the turquoise surf, rent a boogie board, or just lie on a lounge chair and relax under the white-hot Caribbean sun. Afterwards, chow down on cracked conch (fried conch, a type of sea snail) and Bahamian-style mac 'n' cheese at Arawak Cay, aka 'the fish fry', a collection of crayon-coloured shacks just west of downtown Nassau. Wash everything down with a glass of 'sky juice', a high-octane blend of gin and coconut water, the local speciality.

On your second day, take advantage of the Graycliff's grounds and swimming pool. Stroll among the hibiscus and bougainvillea in the walled garden, float in the tiled pool, visit the on-site cigar factory and chat (*en español*, of course) with the Cuban cigar rollers who work here. In the afternoon, hit up West Bay St, Nassau's main shopping district. Duty-free gems are a major draw, but if you don't fancy an emerald the size of your fist, there are plenty of fun souvenirs to choose from – look for local woodcarvings (bonefish are popular subjects). In the evening, dine at the Graycliff Restaurant, where French-style dishes have a Caribbean influence – think crispy duck with Bahamian citrus sauce.

On your third day, follow a pirate-themed itinerary through Nassau's historic sites – Fort Fincastle, the Pirates of Nassau museum, Blackbeard's Tower – before catching your flight home. If you've got extra time, hop a fast ferry to the pink-sand shores of Eleuthera. Either way, don't forget your souvenir bottle of local firewater Ron Ricardo.

■ PLAN IT

Fly into Nassau's Lynden Pindling International Airport and catch a taxi to the Graycliff Hotel, about 20 minutes away. Book well in advance at the Graycliff, especially during the winter high season. If you're planning on scuba diving or taking a snorkelling excursion, arrange this in advance. The Bahamas Ministry of Tourism website has helpful information about transport and tour operators.

■ DETOUR

With more than a few days, hop the two-hour fast ferry to Eleuthera, the skinny island east of New Providence. Eleuthera's 'mainland' is a quiet place of pineapple plantations, empty pink-sand beaches and crumbling lighthouses. Rent a car and drive to Lighthouse Beach, a stretch of coral-coloured sand at the island's southern tip. Off the northeast coast, Harbour Island, known locally as 'Briland', is a car-free village of pastel cottages, boutiques and the kind of bistros where you can eat a US$50 lobster in your bare feet. It's popular with celebrities; if you see Mick Jagger, just nod and smile.

133

OPENING SPREAD Leave your footprints on a pink-sand beach at Harbour Island. **ABOVE (L)** Look out for a Nassau grouper, the national fish, when diving or snorkelling. **ABOVE (R)** The mosaic'd swimming pool at the Graycliff awaits. **LEFT** The Bahamian version of Carnaval is just as colourful.

DECKCHAIR

✻ **Pirates of the Caribbean** The Graycliff's builder John Howard Graysmith may not have been as glamorous as Johnny Depp, but these fun Disney films will get you in the *aarghh* spirit.

✻ **Under the Black Flag: The Romance and the Reality of Life Among the Pirates** (David Cordingly) The former head of exhibitions at England's National Maritime Museum explores the golden age of piracy in the Caribbean.

✻ **Never Say Never Again** (1983) Underwater scenes from this James Bond flick were filmed around New Providence.

✻ **Islands in the Stream** (Ernest Hemingway) This posthumously published Hemingway novel was partially set on the nearby islands of Bimini.

✻ **Bahamian Anthology** (College of the Bahamas) This collection features stories, plays and poetry by Bahamian writers.

CRUNCH THROUGH KRAKÓW IN WINTER

KRAKÓW OLD TOWN COMES INTO ITS OWN IN WINTER. THE CROWDS HAVE GONE, THE STREETS ARE SNOWY AND THE WHOLE PLACE SEEMS TO SPARKLE IN THE COLD NIGHT AIR – PERFECT FOR AN UNHURRIED FEW DAYS OF EXPLORATION AND INDULGENCE...

134

Your noses are red as Rudolph's even before the horses start moving, but at least the driver has given you a pile of blankets to wrap over your huddled knees. A flick of the reins and you're off, the big wheels of your open carriage rolling easily over the cobbles. Leaving the big square, you enter the grid of little streets that forms Kraków Old Town. The snow everywhere draws your eyes upwards, away from the blank ground to the colourful buildings, where it outlines the Gothic towers and domes of churches, and the curly tops of baroque townhouses. Your noses are tingling in the cold air, but the ride doesn't take long – the Old Town is barely a kilometre from one end to the other.

The farthest you can go is Wawel Castle, up on the hill. This was the political centre of power in Poland for over 500 years and the Old Town below it was the intellectual and cultural capital of the country for a lot longer. Its tiny centre is ringed on three sides by parkland (where the ancient city walls once stood) and on one by river. In between, it is stuffed full of ancient houses, a thousand years' worth of churches, and the biggest medieval town square in Europe. No wonder it's packed in summer.

But come in winter and it's a different story: less busy, and on a crisp day more beautiful – the kind of place best explored with your loved one. You can take in the sights, sure, but you'll need to leave plenty of time for warming your hands on a cup of hot chocolate, or slurping a hot *grzaniec* (mulled wine) as you browse the arcades full of knick-knacks under Cloth Hall. Days are short, so dinner may as well be long. The churches are full of music in the evenings and the Christmas trees stay up until the end of January, making the city feel strangely festive right through the darkest months.

Don't go with friends. You won't need them. Kraków in winter is perfect for two.

ESSENTIAL EXPERIENCES

* **Trying to find a love potion at the Museum of Pharmacy, a historic townhouse stuffed full of more potions and elixirs than Hogwarts.**

* An afternoon of mulled wine, *pierogi* (dumplings) and cake spent next to a fire or stove; try Cafe Camelot, Nostalgia or Cherubino.

* **Descending under the largest medieval square in Europe to Rynek Underground, where you can see medieval street stalls and other long-forgotten chambers.**

* Catching a concert at any of the Old Town's numerous churches.

* **Viewing the 15th-century altarpiece in St Mary's – a gilt masterpiece and the biggest of its kind in the world.**

LOCATION KRAKÓW, POLAND | **BEST TIME OF YEAR** DECEMBER TO FEBRUARY | **IDEAL TIME COMMITMENT** A LONG WEEKEND | **ESSENTIAL TIP** SENSIBLE FOOTWEAR IS BEST FOR SNOWY CITY STREETS - WEAR BOOTS | **BUDGET** $$ **PACK** EVERY WARM PIECE OF CLOTHING YOU'VE GOT

KRAKÓW'S STREET SNACKS

They're for sale on every street corner, but *obwarzanki* are not bagels — explicitly not, since the EU gave them protected status in 2009. The *obwarzanek krakowski* (its full name) is, it must be said, strikingly similar to a bagel: it is white bread that has been rolled into a ring, parboiled and then baked. Buy one covered in poppy-seed, salt or sesame. The difference? Two strands of dough are twisted together to form the ring. Locals will tell you that the obwarzanek predates the bagel (also, they claim, a Kraków invention). Whatever the truth, buy a hot one – you'll love it.

◼ THE PERFECT GETAWAY

Kraków isn't a city where you need much of a plan. A few minutes in an open carriage will give you a whistle-stop drive-by of pretty much everything, after which you can retreat to one of the cafes to warm up. Cracow Chocolate Factory is a good place – there's a cafe upstairs. Then just pick a direction and start walking. Everywhere is beautiful. Hit the park, and you know you've reached the edge of the Old Town – time to turn around. You won't miss Wawel Castle on the south side. You could while away an hour or a day here strolling round the state rooms of the palace or the chapels of the cathedral. When you've finished, take the cheesy way out: follow the signs for the Dragon's Den cave. You descend into the underworld and emerge blinking on the banks of the river Vistula.

Spend the next day wandering the streets. There's the square to see, its arcades full of market stalls and pretzel stands. There's one of the most amazing medieval church interiors you'll ever see: St Mary's is a blaze of blues and golds. Or there's the Collegium Maius, Poland's oldest university building, with its collection of alchemical devices and astronomical instruments used by Copernicus. But the itinerary isn't the point. It's not about seeing things; it's about being there together. Wrap up warm, crunch about until your toes are starting to go numb, then duck into the nearest cafe or bar until you're glowing again. Then repeat.

And when the sun goes down – as it does early at this time of year – the best place to head is underground, to one of the city's cellar jazz bars like Piano Rouge. Find yourself a sofa, order something vodka-based and see if you can't get yourself a red nose of a different kind.

◼ PLAN IT

December is a busy time to visit Kraków, so book ahead or wait until January for bargain prices. RyanAir and EasyJet both service Kraków from the UK and Paris. Kraków has accommodation for all budgets, but in winter location is everything, so splash out on Hotel Copernicus, underneath the castle and opposite the 14th-century townhouse where Pope John Paul II lived in the '60s.

◼ DETOUR

To escape the cold, head 14km out of town to Wieliczka Salt Mine (pronounced *vyeh-leech-kah*). As you descend the stairs, the temperature rises to a year-round 14°C (57°F). The mine has been in operation for 700 years and is vast. But what makes it special is the art. As you explore the tunnels, sculpture after sculpture pops out from the rock, the translucent salt often glowing from within thanks to clever lighting. The tour culminates with a visit to the Chapel of St Kinga, a 12m-high chamber where the altar, the crucifix, the chandeliers – everything – is carved from salt.

OPENING SPREAD Looking towards St Mary's church from the Cloth Hall. **ABOVE (L)** Dining at Camelot Cafe in Kraków. **ABOVE (R)** In winter, a snowy Kraków is a romantic city to explore; you can view Gothic Wawel Castle from the Vistula river cruises, or head up the hill to see inside.

DECKCHAIR

* **Winter Under Water** (James Hopkin) Atmospheric novel about an Englishman struggling to understand his Polish lover and her home town.

* **The Polish Officer** (Alan Furst) A ripping yarn of spies and derring-do set on the eve of WWII.

* **Schindler's Ark** (Thomas Keneally) Man Booker Prize-winning novel on which the Oscar-winning film *Schindler's List* was based – both harrowing and both set in Kraków.

* **Dragon of Krakow and Other Polish Stories** (Richard Monte and Paul Hess) Collection of traditional folk tales.

* **Solaris** (Stanisław Lem) Sci-fi classic from the best-selling Polish writer, still as fresh and relevant as it was in 1961.

* **Knife in the Water** (1962) The first film from Kraków-raised Roman Polanski is a tale of rivalry and sexual tension set in Poland's northeast.

CITIES

GREAT ESCAPES

LAID-BACK IN LJUBLJANA

ONE OF EUROPE'S SMALLEST CAPITALS, LJUBLJANA FEELS LIKE A PLEASANT, SELF-CONTENTED TOWN BUT ITS PETITE SIZE CONCEALS A WEALTH OF CULTURE, SIGHTS, ACTIVITIES AND GOOD OLD-FASHIONED FUN THAT WOULD BE THE ENVY OF A CITY TWICE AS BIG, MAKING IT PERFECT FOR A WEEKEND GETAWAY.

138

As Slovenia's largest city and its political, economic and cultural capital, Ljubljana is where virtually everything of national importance begins, ends or is taking place. Of course that might not be immediately apparent in spring and summer, when cafe tables spill into the narrow streets of the Old Town and street musicians and actors entertain passers-by in Prešeren Square and on the little bridges spanning the Ljubljanica River.

Since independence from Yugoslavia in 1991 after a 10-day war, Slovenia has revelled in its position at the heart of Europe. The town of Maribor was the 2012 European Capital of Culture, and Ljubljana's cultural scene is thriving, with fashion designers such as the city's own Marjeta Grošelj, open-air gigs and performances, and galleries including the pioneering Equrna (named after the goddess of the Ljubljanica River) all finding a place among the city's baroque boulevards and backstreets.

The city itself is a living museum of the work of renowned architect Jože Plečnik (1872–1957). Stroll the embankments of the Ljubljanica to explore his finely detailed, temple-like market halls and the vibrant Central Market plaza. Plečnik's redesign of Ljubljana's largest park, the 510-hectare Tivoli, created a long promenade through this eclectic cultural garden. The centrepiece of Plečnik's Ljubljana is the National and University Library of Slovenia, a short walk south of Prešeren Square. The monumental form is a deftly woven mass of brick and reclaimed stone modelled on an Italian palazzo. Inside, a colonnaded black-marble staircase rises up to the light of the main reading room.

All the while Ljubljana Castle hovers quietly above. Established in the 12th century, this hilltop fortification is part of Roman and Habsburg history. Take the daring steel-and-glass funicular railway up for an overview of the city.

ESSENTIAL EXPERIENCES

* **Cruising the Ljubljanica River – a picturesque and inexpensive way to see the city.**

* Joining a walking tour of Jože Plečnik's work in the Old Town and taking a guided tour of his house in the suburb of Trnovo, a museum of the architect's life and work.

* **Wandering through the open-air Central Market and the market halls, observing the theatre of daily life in the city.**

* Travelling by foot or funicular to Ljubljana Castle, to climb the soaring spiral stairs in the Viewing Tower and look out over the city and its surrounds.

LOCATION LJUBLJANA, SLOVENIA | **BEST TIME OF YEAR** MARCH TO OCTOBER; SPRING, TO HAVE THE CITY TO YOURSELF, SUMMER, FOR AN ESCAPE TO THE COUNTRYSIDE | **IDEAL TIME COMMITMENT** A LONG WEEKEND | **ESSENTIAL TIP** THERE'S NO RUSH: YOU WON'T NEED A CHECKLIST OF SIGHTS TO TICK OFF | **BUDGET** $$ | **PACK** WALKING SHOES; YOU'LL DO ALL YOUR EXPLORING ON FOOT

JOŽE PLEČNIK

After working in Vienna, Belgrade and Prague, the Slovenian-born architect Jože Plečnik returned to his homeland in the early 1920s to take up a post at the University of Ljubljana. The gentle urban character of the city is the legacy of this important but largely unknown pioneer of modern architecture. In the mid-20th century Plečnik determinedly transformed this compact European capital, modelling it on ancient Athens. His deft hand carefully stitched a suite of classically inspired buildings, streets, bridges, plazas and parks into the fabric of the medieval city. Plečnik's house in Trnovo is dedicated to his life and work.

BOATING ON LAKE BLED

Pick up the pace with a side trip to Bled, one of Slovenia's most popular tourist resorts. This beautiful medieval town in the Julian Alps is just 55km from the centre of Ljubljana and serviced by good transport links with the capital. The picturesque escape is best known for its sparkling glacial lake, the medieval castle on its edge and the 15th-century church that sits on an island in the middle of it. After a relaxed weekend meandering the streets of Ljubljana, Lake Bled and the streams and rivers that run into it are the ideal destination for swimming, rafting, canoeing, cliff-diving – and more peaceful walking.

■ THE PERFECT GETAWAY

Take a seat on the steps that circle the statue of poet France Prešeren – composer of the Slovenian national anthem – in the main square to begin your encounter with Ljubljana. A collection of handsome art-nouveau buildings from the early 20th century provides a colourful backdrop to the theatre of the square, with the 17th-century salmon-pink Franciscan Church of the Annunciation as a centrepiece. For actual drama and music, head 10 minutes west to the Slovenian National Opera and Ballet Theatre; a recent restoration of the neo-Renaissance building brought fresh colour to its pink facade and the cheeks of its cherubs.

Head south from Prešeren Square, across the intriguing Triple Bridge, to find the Old Town. Between the Triple Bridge and the Dragon Bridge the market halls, created by architect Jože Plečnik in the 1940s, curve along the eastern side of the riverbank. Strolling in the opposite direction from the square you will find one of the city's most famous buildings, the Cooperative Bank. Architect Ivan Vurnik designed this strikingly decorative example of the Slovenian national style in the 1920s. The city's army barracks, a 15-minute walk northeast, are now an exciting museum quarter, housing the white-clad Museum of Contemporary Art Metelkova since 2011. As the country straddles East and West, so the museum reaches out to avant-garde Eastern European art in a West-leaning nation.

Famished flâneurs should end the day by taking the funicular up to Ljubljana Castle – not only to drink in the views over the city, but also to savour a fresh take on traditional Slovenian cuisine by three of the city's top chefs at Gostilna na Gradu, where they bring harmony to Slovenia's varied ingredients.

■ PLAN IT

By air you will arrive at Ljubljana's Jože Pučnik Airport, 26km from the city centre. Bus services and taxis connect the airport to the city. From Venice or Vienna a scenic train journey will bring you to Ljubljana railway station, walking distance from the city's cobbled centre. Stay in a hotel on one of the city's pedestrian-friendly streets. The Vander Urbani Resort in the Old Town has serious design credentials. Book early: Ljubljana is a small capital.

■ DETOUR

For 10 days every September, the town of Maribor, 130km northeast of Ljubljana on the Austrian border and the heartland of Slovenian winemaking, celebrates the birthday of the single oldest grape-growing vine in the world. Now more than 400 years old, the Zametovka vine has survived war and disease to be rewarded with its own Old Vine Festival, marking the annual grape harvest. Fancy a taste of its fruit? Unless you're a visiting dignitary, you're out of luck. Console yourself with sampling wines from local vineyards at the festival.

OPENING SPREAD A double-spiral staircase leads to the top of the watchtower in Ljubljana Castle. **ABOVE (L)** Dragons guard a bridge over the Ljubljanica river. **ABOVE (R)** The spires, domes and rooftops of Ljubljana's compact city centre. **LEFT** Gondolas on picturesque Lake Bled.

DECKCHAIR

* ***Architectural Guide to Ljubljana*** (Janez Koželj and Andrej Hrausky) An illustrated guide to more than 100 buildings in the capital, with much emphasis on architect extraordinaire Jože Plečnik.

* ***Ulysses*** (James Joyce) Joyce spent a night in Ljubljana railway station in 1904 on his way to Trieste; look for the monument by the sculptor Jakov Brdar. Joyce's stream-of-consciousness style is ideal for an unplanned weekend in Ljubljana.

* ***The Story of Post-Modernism: Five Decades of the Ironic, Iconic and Critical in Architecture*** (Charles Jencks) The rediscovery of Jože Plečnik's classical architecture in the 1980s was simultaneous with the emergence of the postmodern architectural movement.

* ***The 8.55 to Baghdad*** (Andrew Eames) Inspired by Agatha Christie's trip from London to Baghdad in the 1920s, Eames sets off on a cross-continental adventure, with an intriguing sojourn in Ljubljana.

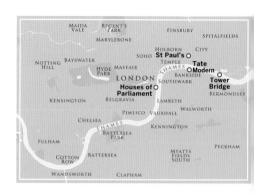

TREAD THE BANKS OF THE THAMES

GO WITH THE FLOW IN LONDON, WALKING A SECTION OF THE THAMES PATH
AS IT MEANDERS THROUGH THE CITY'S WILDS, THE MIGHTY RIVER BORDERED
BY INFAMOUS TOWERS BOTH OLD AND NEW.

142

In a field in rural Gloucestershire, a dribble of water gurgles up from the ground. By the time it flows through London, almost 300 kilometres later, this water has become the most famous river in Britain: the Thames, the lifeblood and raison d'être of a city. Along the river's banks, the Thames Path is like a guidebook in motion for walkers. If a place in London is worth seeing, chances are that it's on these banks. To walk this path is to join the dots not only between the city's star attractions, but also between its history and its future.

On the ever-bustling Southbank, it's invariably as though the whole world has come to visit, and there's a curious disconnect between your activity – hiking – and the scenery. The peaks here aren't rock or ice, they're glass and concrete: the Matterhorn-sharp tip of the Shard, the bulging Yosemite-like dome of St Paul's Cathedral, the spiralling escarpment of the Gherkin. The 'forest' is in planted rows, the canyons are Tudor-lined and the wildlife calls come in a babel of languages.

It's this self-created sense of removal that makes this Thames Path through London so appealing. Outside the Tate Modern, as other people slurp at ice creams and watch buskers, you're scanning the roofline for the pair of peregrine falcons, Misty and Houdini, that nest here.

Beside you, the river looks almost static, unmoving, as though painted into the cityscape. On foot, however, you've been here long enough to notice the river ebbing and flowing with the tide, sucking out to sea and refilling again. Nobody else seems to even notice the river, lost among the spectacle of the London Eye, the galleries and the cafes, but you're drawn to it. It's your contour, your guiding line across the map of London. It's the reason the city is here, and thus ultimately your reason for being here also. You wander on, merging into the throng of people.

ESSENTIAL EXPERIENCES

* **Wandering across the Teddington weir and lock, the defining line between the tidal and non-tidal Thames.**

* Finding peace at the riverside Peace Pagoda in Battersea Park.

* **Watching rowers glide past, their oars stirring the river in unison.**

* Savouring an aerial view of your walk from the London Eye, Europe's tallest Ferris wheel.

* **Filling the empty spaces of your bag or backpack with literary treasures from the South Bank book market beneath Waterloo Bridge.**

* Stepping through time as you stride across the Greenwich Meridian.

LOCATION LONDON, ENGLAND, UK | **BEST TIME OF YEAR** MAY TO OCTOBER | **IDEAL TIME COMMITMENT** ONE DAY
ESSENTIAL TIP MAKE USE OF PUBLIC TRANSPORT TO PINPOINT FAVOURITE SECTIONS | **BUDGET** $ | **PACK** WALKING SHOES, WATER

THE BOAT RACE

The Thames is all things to all people, including being
the setting for one of the world's most famous sporting
contests. Each March or April, rowing eights from
Oxford and Cambridge universities power upstream
from Putney Bridge, as they've done since 1829, in the
Boat Race. If you're walking on race day, don't expect
to make it along the banks between Chiswick Bridge
and Putney, as it's estimated that around 250,000
people line the river to watch the race. If you're walking
on any other day, look for a stone marker, inscribed
with 'UBR', just downstream from Chiswick Bridge. This
is the race finish post. From here, it's 6.8km along the
race course to Putney Bridge.

A LONG WALK

If the Thames' London journey has you primed for more, consider walking the entire Thames Path. At its source near Kemble in Gloucestershire, the river trickles unspectacularly from beneath a field, and it's here that the Thames Path begins. Over the next 12 or 14 days, you'll walk 294km, passing through classic English rural scenes and the likes of the Cotswolds, Oxford and Henley-on-Thames before entering more urban areas around Reading and into London. It may be one of the flattest long-distance walks you ever undertake, with the river's source only 107m above sea level.

■ THE PERFECT GETAWAY

It's worth starting out at Putney Bridge or Wandsworth. For the next couple of hours you'll view aspects of London you may never have seen, no matter how much time you've spent here. Between Putney Bridge and Vauxhall Bridge, the Thames Path doesn't always adhere to the banks of the river. At various times the trail swivels inland, wandering through moneyed residential streets, industrial areas, around part of the perimeter of Battersea Park, along the edge of a waste transfer station, and right by the famous doors of the Battersea Dogs and Cats Home. There'll be times when you may see nobody, which you may once have thought almost impossible in a city of eight million people.

Beyond Vauxhall, a more familiar London presents itself, first the Houses of Parliament and then, seemingly, the entire London playbook of emblems: Big Ben, the London Eye, the Tate Modern, Shakespeare's Globe, the Millennium Bridge. Take it slow; there's enough here to fill days of your time.

But South Bank needn't be all about city icons. A book market under Waterloo Bridge could distract you for an hour. Every few steps there's something new to see as South Bank weaves its practised charms, which you feel more intensely for the contrast to the falling leaves and kiddie football matches you passed a couple of hours ago in Wandsworth Park. Grab some lunch by the river, and then rejoin the path as it squeezes its way through the dark warren of Bankside. Here, in just a few steps, you'll pass the replica of Sir Francis Drake's *Golden Hinde* warship and Southwark Cathedral, London's oldest cathedral building. From here it's a short stroll to Tower Bridge, a fitting icon at which to end a Thames trek.

■ PLAN IT

Planning for the Thames Path is simplicity itself. Pick a starting point near a train or tube station and stride off downstream towards the city or your chosen end point. If you plan to walk sections of the path distant from the city centre, such as from Kingston upon Thames or Teddington, there are good pubs and restaurants along the river at Richmond and slightly inland at Barnes. Planning information, including walking distances, are available on the official Thames Path website.

■ DETOUR

By Tower Bridge, most of London's finest sights will be behind you and Greenwich may begin to feel rather distant – you still have 8km to walk to reach the Greenwich foot tunnel, with the barrier 9.5km beyond that. Instead, hop aboard a Thames Clipper at Tower Millennium Pier. Disembark at Sir Christopher Wren's masterful Old Royal Naval College buildings in Greenwich, slip inside the Old Brewery and toast your feat with a restorative Greenwich-brewed beer from the Meantime Brewery.

145

OPENING SPREAD History meets modernity: the Palace of Westminster and the London Eye. **ABOVE (L)** Edifice of art: London's leading contemporary art gallery, Tate Modern, is undergoing expansion. **ABOVE (R)** Refuel in Borough Market. **LEFT** The Millennium Bridge links Tate Modern to St Paul's.

DECKCHAIR

* **Three Men in a Boat** (Jerome K Jerome) Classic 19th-century account of a two-week boating holiday on the Thames.

* **Thames: The Biography** (Peter Ackroyd) Companion book to Ackroyd's famous London 'biography', recounting the history of the river.

* **Thames** (Stephan Kaluza) German artist Kaluza spent four months photographing the Thames; this book is the culmination of his 30,000 images.

* **I Never Knew That About the River Thames** (Christopher Winn) Facts, trivia and legends about the river.

* **Wind in the Willows** (Kenneth Grahame) Famed kids' tale set along the Thames – you may never look at those riverside rats and moles the same way again.

* **The Thames Path** (Leigh Hatts) Useful guidebook if you plan to walk sections of the path outside of London.

A FRESH TAKE ON THE BIG APPLE

New York: so familiar from a million movies – you've seen it all before, right? Wrong. Paddle a kayak, wander a revamped trainline or hail a next-generation cab for a new take on this iconic metropolis.

The Big Apple looks really big. Towering. Gargantuan. Titanic, even. Of course, it always does: Lower Manhattan contains one of the densest concentrations of skyscrapers in the world; here, legion shards of shiny metal-and-glass rise like a supersized Giant's Causeway. But still, right now, it looks bigger than ever.

And that's because your own perspective has taken a dive. You are viewing this mighty metropolis not from the back of a yellow cab or on foot along the avenues, but from water level, from the seat of a kayak.

It's really quite surreal, gliding along the Hudson in this way, the splish of water on paddles mixing with the muted rumble of traffic and sirens. Being on the river feels serene: back to nature. Yet a glance to the side reveals not treetops but tower-blocks, the art-deco masterpieces of the Empire State and Chrysler peeking out like roses between the thorns.

So, it's pretty special down here with the ducks, but doing battle with the Hudson is no walk in Central Park. The tidal river has quite a current; an out-and-back trip from one of the West Side piers – with a midway stop for a cold one – likely means rowing against the flow in one direction. There are also a frightening number of enormous ships to avoid, which make you feel very small indeed.

But this is something even novices can try, with a good guide and a little tuition. And the effort is worth it for the chance to get a view and a sensation few NYC visitors ever do. From your lowly, bobbing vantage, you can gaze over to Lady Liberty (rendered strangely small by perspective), float beneath the great grey hulk of the USS *Intrepid*, remind yourself that this glorious Gotham is an island – and earn that enormous, post-paddle slice of New York cheesecake to boot.

ESSENTIAL EXPERIENCES

* **Gazing up at the behemoth-like skyscrapers from a water-level perspective – and feeling really, really small.**

* Refuelling after your exertions at a proper NYC deli – double pastrami on rye, anyone?

* **Rowing on the lake in Central Park – a little bit cheesy, a little bit brilliant.**

* Ascending the Empire State Building for the ultimate overview.

* **Taking Manhattan Kayak Company's sushi tour – a vigorous paddle over to New Jersey's Mitsuwa Market, to break for its finest raw fish before heading back.**

* Exploring New York's green spaces – stroll along the elevated High Line and buy artisanal cakes from Union Square's farmers market.

LOCATION NEW YORK, USA | **BEST TIME OF YEAR** MAY–SEPTEMBER | **IDEAL TIME COMMITMENT** FOUR DAYS
ESSENTIAL TIP CHECK THE TIDES: BEGINNERS SHOULD SIGN UP FOR A TRIP THAT GOES WITH THE FLOW | **BUDGET** $$
PACK SUN BLOCK, SUN HAT, SWIMMING COSTUME/TRUNKS

A RIVER RUNS THROUGH IT

The Hudson River flows for 500km through New York State, from Lake Tear of the Clouds to the Atlantic Ocean, passing the Adirondacks, state capital Albany and the Catskill Mountains. The Lenape called it Muhheakantuck (the 'river that flows two ways'); today it's named after British explorer Henry Hudson, who navigated it in 1609, trying to find the Pacific. The Hudson isn't the USA's longest waterway but it's one of its most important. Nearby, trade between Native Americans and settlers flourished, influential families (Roosevelts, Rockefellers) laid roots, America's first art movement began and writers such as Wharton and Irving set their tales.

CIRCUMNAVIGATE THE CITY

Manhattan Island has a perimeter of 45km – and there are several ways to make a circumnavigation. Experienced, fit kayakers should be able to paddle all the way round, from the Gotham-esque south to the trees and tidal pools of the north, in about eight hours; Manhattan Kayak Company runs guided trips. Too tough? Board the Circle Line's Full Island Cruise, which takes the effort out of waterbound sightseeing and only takes three hours. Landlubbers might prefer the Great Saunter – every May the Shorewalkers preservation group organises a mass hike around Manhattan.

THE PERFECT GETAWAY

New York, new schmork. More 'a perfect weekend in...' features have been written about the Big Apple than the city has yellow cabs. So this isn't another, but rather suggestions on how to see this old favourite in a new way. A kayak trip is a great start, best done in the warmer months, in light wind. For something a bit more Batman, paddle after dark. Your headtorch will pale next to all that city glitter; watch as the lights of the Empire State change colour, dependent on occasion – red/pink for Valentine's Day, green for Earth Day...

Of course, ascending this art-deco icon remains one of the best ways to overlook the city. Not an original suggestion, maybe. But did you know it's open until 2am? Ride the elevator late at night to prove that, indeed, the city doesn't sleep; Thursdays to Saturdays, 10pm to 1am, there's live music on the observation deck. For an even loftier perspective, take a helicopter flight. Trips zip over the sights – the Statue of Liberty, the skyscrapers, the river you've just navigated.

Back on the ground, start at the High Line, a 1.6km-long park built on an old elevated freight rail line. Its first section opened in 2009; the final stretch is to be confirmed, but the quirky park is flourishing and hosts regular exhibitions.

Another new development is the Citi Bike scheme, launched in 2013. This fleet of 10,000 cycles at 600 stations in Manhattan, Brooklyn and Queens makes short journeys greener – and more fun. You need gumption to tackle NYC's roads this way, but the buzz is hard to beat. More traditional is to hail a cab, which, from October 2013, will be gradually replaced by boxier Nissans, complete with glass roofs – so when stuck in traffic, you can still admire the city.

PLAN IT

New York City has two main international airports. JFK is in Queens; the AirTrain links it with the A-train subway line to Manhattan. Newark is in New Jersey; airport express buses to Manhattan take 45 to 60 minutes. Manhattan Kayak Company offers a range of kayak options. Guided trips start from 75-minute sessions. Citi Bike passes are available for 24-hour and seven-day periods.

DETOUR

For alternative ways to go wild-ish in Manhattan, visit its green spaces. First, Central Park: hire a boat to row on the lake or try a spot of birdwatching – 230 species have been recorded here. Hudson River Park is a waterfront recreation area with bike trails, sports fields and, in summer, RiverFlicks – a series of free movie screenings. Bryant Park is an oasis off Times Square; not big but packed with facilities, from pétanque and ping pong spaces to a free Reading Room. Union Square Park is home to the city's biggest Greenmarket, where local family farmers, butchers and bakers sell their produce.

149

OPENING SPREAD A bird's eye view of the bristling skyscrapers of the Big Apple. **ABOVE (L)** The mighty span of Manhattan Bridge links Lower Manhattan with Brooklyn. **ABOVE (R)** Rowing on the lake in Central Park. **LEFT** New York state of mind: dining out in the West Village.

DECKCHAIR

* *Canoeing and Kayaking New York* (Kevin Stiegelmaier) The top 50 paddles across the state.

* *Inside the Apple: A Streetwise History of New York City* (Michelle and James Nevius) A lively rundown of NYC's biggest moments.

* *Manhattan* (1979) Many films have been made here, but Woody Allen's classic is the biggest silver-screen love letter to NYC.

* *Miracle on the Hudson: The Extraordinary Real-Life Story Behind Flight 1549* (Various authors) Perspectives from the survivors of the 2009 Hudson River plane crash.

* *The Age of Innocence* (Edith Wharton) This Pulitzer-winning novel skewers the East Coast high society of the 1870s.

* *The Bonfire of the Vanities* (Tom Wolfe) A novel of greed and corruption, set in 1980s New York.

EMBRACE QUÉBEC CITY IN WINTER

YEAH, IT'S COLD. BUT WINTER IN HISTORIC FRENCH CANADA IS ALSO COMPLETELY COOL: WHERE ELSE CAN YOU HUG A GIANT SNOWMAN, REFUEL ON CRÊPES AND HAUTE CUISINE, SKI RIGHT IN THE CITY AND SLEEP ON A BED OF ICE?

150

Ahead: glittering grooves sliced into virgin snow; naked trees, shivering in an icy breeze; a sky so blue it should be X-rated. As for you, you're wrapped in as many layers as a pass-the-parcel, with skinny skis on your feet and poles clasped in your mittens. You could be gliding through a winter wilderness, were it not for the thrum of Québec City just a hockey-puck's throw away.

Québec City is a North American anomaly. The continent, north of Mexico at least, doesn't really do old towns. But the capital of Canada's Francophone province is the exception, founded in 1608 and bequeathed a comely, European-style mish-mash of stone walls and cobbled alleys. To be here is almost to be in Carcassonne, sipping café au lait on terraces amid French voices, lorded over by a château. Yes, just like France – except for the in-city cross-country skiing...

For that is peculiarly Canadian. When most would cower in the nearest heated bar, the Québécois embrace winter. And the best place to do so is the Plains of Abraham. In 1759, this is where General Wolfe's army defeated that of French General Montcalm to claim the place for Britain; now it's the city's premier park, an urban lung of meadows, woodland and – in season – cross-country ski trails.

Fortunately, it's an easy (if energetic) sport to pick up: only the toes of your boots are snapped into skis, so you can step-glide with the help of your poles. The main issue is concentrating on technique when there's so much to look at: the ice-littered St Lawrence River to one side, the city skyline (including iconic Château Frontenac) to the other. As you schwoop along, you'll near-yelp at the novelty of practising a back-country pastime in a city of 500,000 people.

Better, when you've finished on the Plains, the city's pleasures await you right there: the boutique hotels, the French-accented eateries and the stands selling stodgy *poutine* (chips, cheese and gravy) – calorific, yes, but you've earned it.

ESSENTIAL EXPERIENCES

❉ **Tucking into a comforting plate of *poutine* – the refined, Frenchified version of chips, cheese and gravy.**

❉ Hugging Bonhomme, the big, jolly mascot of the Québec Winter Carnival.

❉ **Gliding around the Plains of Abraham on skis, looking out over canons, treetops and the St Lawrence River.**

❉ Wrapping up warm for a night in an ice room at the sparkling Hôtel de Glace.

❉ **Riding the ferry over to Lévis, for fine, inexpensive views back to the old city.**

❉ Boarding the gastro-train to Le Massif, for gourmet cuisine, panoramic views and a day on the piste.

LOCATION QUÉBEC, CANADA | **BEST TIME OF YEAR** DECEMBER TO MARCH | **IDEAL TIME COMMITMENT** FOUR DAYS
ESSENTIAL TIP SKI IN THE RIGHT DIRECTION: THE PLAINS OF ABRAHAM'S SKI TRAILS ARE ONE-WAY
BUDGET $$ | **PACK** THERMALS, GOOD GLOVES, LOTS OF LAYERS

THE CARNAVAL DE QUÉBEC

To truly embrace Québec's Winter Carnival, know some basics. First, don a *ceinture fléchée* – this traditional arrow-weave sash should be tied around the waist. Next, carry a stick – special plastic canes (topped with a bust of Bonhomme) have hollowed-out middles in which to store your favourite tipple. And talking of booze, make it Caribou: when the first settlers here found First Nations people drinking caribou blood, they added wine to make it less icky; now the drink has morphed into a potent mix of wine, liquor, port, maple syrup and spices – guaranteed to warm your cockles on a cold night.

THE PAPA OF THE PISTE

Herman Smith-Johannsen was born in Norway in 1875 but settled in Canada in 1932. He was a passionate skier and quickly earned the nickname 'Jackrabbit' for his remarkable ability to hop around easily in deep snow. Instrumental in popularising skiing across North America, he cut some of the first cross-country ski trails, organised races and taught lessons. In 1972 he was awarded the Order of Canada and in 1982 was inducted into the Canadian Sports Hall of Fame. He died in 1987, aged 111 – legend has it he was skiing round his nursing home till the end.

THE PERFECT GETAWAY

No matter the season, your first stop in Québec City must be the hill-tumbling Old Town, still encircled by stone ramparts. This cluster of 17th- and 18th-century houses is where you'll find twisty streets, massive murals and cafes a-plenty. Follow the marked, 5km VivaCité walking route for an overview and board the ferry across the St Lawrence to Lévis, just for the joy of looking back.

For the most romantic sleep, book into Auberge St-Antoine, a hotel part-housed in the port's original wharf buildings. For something more chilled, the Hôtel de Glace (Ice Hotel) is ten minutes from the city: its artful snowy suites, sculpted afresh each winter, have Arctic sleeping bags to keep you toasty.

Once oriented, it's time to hit the Plains. This green space (magically white come winter) is the Québécois equivalent of Central Park, an urban playground with abandoned canons, a Joan of Arc garden and a 28-species arboretum. From December to April, 12.6km of cross-country trails – suitable for beginners – are cut. Hire some kit, read the rules (keep left when overtaking...) and off you go. There are no huge hills, but ascending any slope on cross-country skis takes effort: try the splayed herring-bone technique and hope you can beat gravity.

After a few hours you'll be exhausted – but exhilarated. Time to refuel. As cute as Vieux-Québec is, head for the less touristy neighbourhoods of Faubourg St-Jean or Nouvo St-Roch; try Le Billig (526 Rue St-Jean), a crêperie par excellence. If you've timed it right, your visit will coincide with Winter Carnival. Ice sculptures, parades, skating rinks, snow slides...the city is overcome with glacial gaiety. It's wonderful, kitschy fun – raise of glass of Caribou liquor and join in.

PLAN IT

Québec City's Jean Lesage International Airport is 16km southwest of the centre. Bus 78 runs from the airport to Les Saules bus terminal, Monday to Friday. The Québec Winter Carnival is held for 17 days every January/February; accommodation must be booked well in advance. The ferry to Lévis runs regularly, daily. Skis, boots and poles can be hired from the Plains of Abraham's Discovery Pavilion.

DETOUR

If you must leave Québec City, do so aboard Le Train du Massif de Charlevoix. This gastro rail-trip launched in 2011 following the renovation of a 19th-century track between the city and La Malbaie, 140km east. Now plush rolling stock, kitted out with mood lights and picture windows, completes this day-long return 'rail-cruise' – so called because it hugs the north shore of the St Lawrence; when the tide's in it feels like you're afloat. The focus is on scenery and gourmet cuisine but the train can get you from A to B: winter itineraries stop at arty Baie-St-Paul or Le Massif de Charlevoix's ski slopes.

OPENING SPREAD The charm and ambience of Québec City, one of north America's oldest old towns, replete with chateau. **ABOVE** Olde-world charm in Basse Ville, dusted with snow for extra sparkle. **LEFT** Slip-slidin' away: fun for all at the Winter Carnival.

DECKCHAIR

* ***Winter Wonderland*** (Belinda Jones) Heart-warming chick lit, played out at the fairytale Québec Carnival.

* ***I Confess*** (1953) Hitchcock used Québec City as the setting for this noir-ish suspense thriller.

* ***To Quebec and the Stars*** (HP Lovecraft) The fantasy and 'weird fiction' writer loved Québec City – his novels evoke a sense of the place, while this essay collection includes musings on the province.

* ***Shadows on the Rock*** (Willa Cather) American novel about Québec, set in the early days of New France.

* ***Where the River Narrows*** (Aimée Laberge) This family saga spans from the early days of settlement to the 1970s – a thoughtful look at modern Québec.

* ***Quebec: The Story of Three Sieges*** (Stephen Manning) Military history at its most readable.

FIND BANGKOK'S INNER CALM

HUMID, FRANTIC, NOISY: ADJECTIVES FOR BANGKOK RARELY INCLUDE PEACEFUL OR QUIET. BUT YOU CAN LEAVE THE CHAOS BEHIND ON AN EXPLORATION OF THE CALMER SIDE OF THAILAND'S INTENSE CAPITAL CITY.

154

The longtail boat drops you off at a dock on the river, then chugs away, leaving you to walk the raised cement path through the mangrove forest. You emerge at a small collection of buildings that nearly blends into the background; climbing the stairs, you join the branches in the treetops in your open-air 'nest', a room at the Bangkok Tree House. Yes, you're still in Bangkok.

The fierce growl of túk-túks and the thick scent of diesel fumes disappear behind you as you duck into the calm of a Buddhist temple. Bangkok's pollution is sloughed off your skin as you indulge in a renowned Thai massage and body treatment. You wake up to the city at dawn, watching groups of Thais performing a slow t'ai chi in Lumphini Park. You sip a sunset cocktail in one of the city's famous sky bars, leaving the chaos far below you.

Bangkok can overstimulate even the most Zen traveller, but pockets of calm do exist in this steamy city. A quiet canal, a shady park or a meditative hour in a temple: these are all experiences that beckon the frazzled visitor. They need to be sought out, however; Bangkok does not immediately present its quieter side to the undiscerning tourist. Time of day can be just as important as location when seeking silence, with dawn being the best time to appreciate the tranquillity that Bangkok often keeps hidden. Then, the only sounds that greet you will be the swish of brooms on sidewalks and the barefoot padding of Buddhist monks in saffron robes receiving alms in the streets.

Make your trip to Bangkok a restorative one by visiting sights that offer downtime. Thailand's Buddhist culture is a natural diversion from go-go bars and traffic, and so are its spas. The city's surrounds, with mangrove forests and hidden canals, are also great for escaping the pandemonium. Those who make the effort to seek out Bangkok's peaceful side will be richly rewarded.

ESSENTIAL EXPERIENCES

* **Removing your shoes and padding quietly through the calm of one of Bangkok's many Buddhist temples.**

* Watching Thais perform fluid t'ai chi in unison like schools of fish at dawn in Lumphini Park.

* **Receiving a traditional Thai massage in the hushed surrounds of a high-end spa.**

* Listening to and watching the city awake, especially monks receiving alms in the streets.

* **Winding down with a cocktail at a swank five-star hotel or sky bar.**

* Escaping the city's bustle on one of the Chao Phraya River's islands.

* **Surrounding yourself with modern and traditional art at one of Bangkok's many fine galleries.**

LOCATION BANGKOK, THAILAND | **BEST TIME OF YEAR** NOVEMBER TO MARCH | **IDEAL TIME COMMITMENT** FIVE DAYS
ESSENTIAL TIP AVOID TÚK-TÚKS AND INSIST THAT TAXIS DRIVERS TURN THEIR METERS ON | **BUDGET** $$
PACK TEMPLE-APPROPRIATE CLOTHING, INSECT REPELLENT, EAR PLUGS

A WALK IN THE PARK

Step off the hot streets and into the shade of the massive trees that define Lumphini Park, Bangkok's largest and most central public space. Created in the 1920s by King Rama VI, the park – named after Buddha's birthplace in Nepal – is home to Bangkok's first public library. Lumphini is easy to reach via Metro (subway) or Skytrain, and pleasant to visit at any time of day. Large water monitors sun themselves near the artificial lake; in the evening joggers take advantage of the paved paths. You'll see picnicking families, beautiful gardens and cheerful paddle-boaters churning the lake's waters.

■ THE PERFECT GETAWAY

Set the tone for your Bangkok escape by sleeping at the Bangkok Tree House. An ecofriendly resort, the Tree House sits on an island in the Chao Phraya River, with rooms ('nests') perching above the mangrove forest. You will leave the city behind as you disembark from the boat. Choose your level of comfort – a room with air-conditioning, an open-air platform, or a mattress floating on the river.

As you choose sites to explore in Bangkok, remember to make reservations at a few of the quieter ones. A Thai massage and spa treatment is a quintessential Thailand experience, and Bangkok is a wonderful place to indulge. The Health Land Spa offers serenity from the moment you enter the facility, where you are greeted by the trickle of running water and the scent of lemon grass. Spa treatments range from an hour-long Thai massage to a three-hour package that includes a body polish and milk bath.

When you are touring Bangkok, include a few of the more peaceful spots in your itinerary. The Jim Thompson House is a soothing museum surrounded by jungle, an odd oasis in this busy city. The complex of teak structures was the home of Jim Thompson, an American entrepreneur who founded the Thai Silk Company. After touring the museum, pause at the pond-side cafe for a nibble.

End your day with a cocktail at one of Bangkok's sky bars. You will be storeys above the hubbub, with the city view and warm night air to calm your nerves. Sirocco Sky Bar was made famous in *The Hangover Part II*, but there are plenty to explore; the Sofitel's Park Society offers an unparalleled view of Lumphini Park and the city skyline, while the Nest lures the weary traveller with daybeds.

■ PLAN IT

Bangkok's main airport, Suvarnabhumi, is an international hub servicing flights from all over the world. Plan a couple of months in advance if you are visiting during high season, which is November through March. The Bangkok Tree House has a very limited number of rooms and needs to be booked well in advance. You do not need to book spa services more than a day ahead.

■ DETOUR

Step off the temple treadmill with a tour of Bangkok's modern art scene. Airy, cool galleries give you insight into the modern psyche of Bangkok's art world. The website www.bangkokartmap.com is updated regularly with openings and shows. The Bangkok Art and Culture Centre, in the city centre, is a good introduction to the city's art and culture scene. Kathmandu Photo Gallery is located in a renovated pre-war shophouse and is Bangkok's only dedicated photo gallery. Also check out the minimalist 338 OIDA Gallery, Bangkok's artiest new addition.

OPENING SPREAD Temple time out: checking out the *chedis* (stupas) of Wat Pho, a Buddhist temple in Rattanakosin district. **ABOVE (L)** The Buddha reclines at the temple of Wat Pho. **ABOVE (R)** Bangkok's canals, lilyponds and greenery offer pockets of calm in the frenetic city.

DECKCHAIR

* **The Beach** (Alex Garland) A backpacker's quintessential novel, the story begins in Bangkok and travels to a fictional island in the Gulf of Thailand. The 2000 movie of the same name stars Leonardo DiCaprio.

* **Bangkok 8** (John Burdett) The first in a series of police thrillers centred on Bangkok's prostitution scene.

* **The Hangover Part II** (2011) Escapism at its best: three friends trace their night after waking up in Bangkok with no memory of the previous evening's antics.

* **Brokedown Palace** (1999) Two American high-school graduates are thrown into Bangkok's prison system when they unknowingly transport drugs in their luggage.

* **Four Reigns** (Kukrit Pramoj) One woman's life both in and outside the monarchy, spanning the reigns of four Chakri kings.

CHILL-OUT

--- ❧ ---

GREAT ESCAPES

CRUISE THE TURKISH COAST

FOR SHEER ESCAPISM, NOTHING BEATS HOLIDAYING ON A TURKISH GULET. THESE STURDY, WOODEN MOTOR-SAILERS – UPWARDS OF 50FT LONG – CRUISE ALONG THE COAST, EXPLORING ANCIENT SITES, ANCHORING IN QUIET BAYS AND SERVING UP DELICIOUS MEALS.

Imagine the scene. You are sitting under the sun canopy that shades the deck at the high stern of the gulet. The boat tugs gently at the anchor chain, and the waves lap lazily against the side. A warm wind wafts the scent of pine needles from the pristine woods fringing the sandy beach just across the water, and the only other sounds are the distant rasp of cicadas and the occasional clink from the galley where lunch is being prepared. Another gulet is anchored a hundred yards away, but otherwise there is no sign of civilisation.

You have spent the morning reading and swimming straight off the side of the boat, and now a starched white cloth has been spread on the table and is being steadily loaded with a sumptuous lunch: salads of ripe red tomatoes; dishes of beans and okra in olive oil; savoury pastries; burghul and kebabs; cherries, melons, peaches and kiwifruits. For the next hour or so, you will gorge yourself, and then probably fall asleep for a while as the captain casts off and motors gently along the coast to your next anchorage.

Or you might lie back and enjoy the unspoilt scenery passing slowly before you: steep limestone mountains that plunge directly into the deep blue water, the occasional headland, a sheltered bay or a perfect natural harbour. In the distance you might spot a sand bar crowded with tourists – but they won't affect your world. They are trapped ashore, while you are free to cruise to a quieter spot. As the heat of the day subsides a little, perhaps you will call in at one of the quieter anchorages and explore some local ruins – the remnants of Roman occupation or the powerful Lycian civilisation that once ruled these shores.

This is daily life aboard a Turkish gulet. Deeply relaxing, yet never boring – it's the ideal way to combine sightseeing with a thoroughly stress-free holiday.

ESSENTIAL EXPERIENCES

* **Grazing on meze, the best way to sample Turkish food: lots of small portions of salads, pastries, kebabs, seafood and fish served all at the same time.**

* Snorkelling in a gin-clear sea and enjoying the fabulous underwater views (bring your own kit).

* **Sleeping on deck and enjoying the cool breeze, dark skies and diamond-bright stars.**

* Seeing the endangered loggerhead sea turtle: nesting sites are protected, but you may see them in the water or, with special permission, when they come up the beach at night.

* **Exploring ruins – even if you are turned off by ancient history, you'll love the atmosphere of the sites.**

LOCATION TURQUOISE COAST, TURKEY | **BEST TIME OF YEAR** MAY, JUNE AND SEPTEMBER | **IDEAL TIME COMMITMENT** ONE OR TWO WEEKS | **ESSENTIAL TIP** PLAN YOUR ITINERARY CAREFULLY AND AGREE ON IT WITH THE GULET OPERATOR BEFORE YOU BOOK AND PAY | **BUDGET** $$ | **PACK** SUNHAT AND SNORKELLING GEAR

WHO WERE THE LYCIANS?

Many of the ancient sites you see in this part of Turkey
look like Greek or Roman ruins, but they are more likely
to be ancient Lycian remains. Lycia was made up of a
string of prosperous and powerful cities, which first
became established on the Anatolian seaboard in the
6th century BC and profited from the trade of the busy
sea route that skirted the coast. Though wealthy, the
Lycians suffered from the constant battles between the
Persians and Greeks, finally succumbing to the Romans
and becoming part of the empire.

XANTHOS

Xanthos was one of the great Lycian trading ports. It was made famous in ancient times for the mass suicide of its inhabitants when they were attacked by Brutus in 42 BC. Then in the 1840s, the British archaeologist and explorer Sir Charles Fellows rediscovered and excavated the site. He removed a series of impressive sculptural reliefs – the battle friezes from the Nereid Monument – and shipped them back to the British Museum. You can still see them there today. However, 20th-century excavations have revealed more of the city, and there is lots to see at the site still, including an excellent Roman-style theatre.

■ THE PERFECT GETAWAY

There are dozens of possible itineraries for a cruise along Turkey's southwestern Turquoise Coast, from the sheltered bays around Bodrum to the more exposed coast towards Antalya. But an ideal itinerary – for six or seven nights – would begin at Göcek, a picturesque harbour in a quiet bay on the Gulf of Fethiye, near Dalaman. Spend the night on board, and the next morning motor out into the bay to see half-submerged Roman ruins (dubbed Cleopatra's Baths), before sailing on to the opposite coast for a night or two at Fethiye. This is a lively resort where you can book a day trip to see the ruined Lycian city of Pınara, lost among the mountain pine forests; Xanthos, with its superb views; and Letoon, a charming 'sanctuary precinct', before finishing at the hill fort at Tlos.

From Fethiye, it's a pleasant sail around the headland to Gemiler Island, a good anchorage for swimming and snorkelling. Heading west along the coast, the best overnight shelter is in the pine-fringed bay at Ekincik. From here take a water-taxi through the reed beds and waterways of the Dalyan delta to the riverside town of Dalyan itself, famous for the Lycian temple tombs carved into its rock faces. Make sure you explore the Roman ruins of Kaunos further downriver.

The next overnight stop should be Loryma, a sheltered bay opposite the Greek islands of Rhodes and Symi, which has remained completely undeveloped since the Athenian fleet once sheltered here during the Peloponnesian War more than 2000 years ago. Finish your cruise at Marmaris, a busy city with a bazaar and a beach resort attached. The port is on the quieter side of town and is a good place to spend your last night on board slowly readapting to everyday life.

■ PLAN IT

Fly to Bodrum, Antalya or, for the itinerary outlined in this getaway, Dalaman, about half an hour from Göcek by taxi. From outside Europe, you'll need to change planes in İstanbul or Ankara. Lots of travel companies offer gulet holidays, and the degree of flexibility offered varies. DayDreams Travel and Blue Cruise, both UK-based, offer among the most flexible, tailor-made arrangements. For lower prices, and less intense heat, travel in June or September (when the sea is at its warmest), rather than high summer (July and August).

■ DETOUR

If you don't like the thought of being at sea, but want to see the best of the coastal sights, consider a walking holiday along part of the Lycian Way, which runs along the coast from Fethiye to Antalya. You need to be fit and prepared for some rough ground, but the route is well marked and the views are wonderful. Plan it via www.cultureroutesinturkey.com, which includes details of accommodation and how to reach the start from Dalaman or Antalya.

OPENING SPREAD Turkish gulets are still made from wood but a diesel engine is preferred to sail for most. **ABOVE** Life on the ocean wave, the easy way. **LEFT** The ruins of the amphitheatre at Xanthos; the Xanthosians twice committed mass suicide rather than submit to invaders.

DECKCHAIR

❋ **The Odyssey** (Homer) The classic account of Odysseus' voyage home from Troy, on the Turkish coast, to Ithaca.

❋ **A Fez of the Heart** (Jeremy Seal) Highly insightful and entertaining story of a journey through modern Turkey.

❋ **Birds Without Wings** (Louis de Bernières) Gripping novel of the struggle between Christians and Muslims in a small Anatolian town a century ago.

❋ **My Name is Red** (Orhan Pamuk) Revolves around the murder of a 16th-century miniaturist painter, by Turkey's great Nobel Prize–winning novelist.

❋ **Lords of the Horizons** (Jason Goodwin) One of the most recent and readable histories of the Ottoman Empire.

❋ **The Daughters of Mars** (Thomas Keneally) The story of two Australian nurses at Gallipoli.

SPA BLISS IN BALI

BALI MAY BE BEST KNOWN FOR BACKPACKER BARS AND SURF BEACHES, BUT BEHIND THE ISLAND'S BEGUILING SURFACE BEATS A HOLISTIC BOUTIQUE HEART. LUXE SPA RETREATS OFFER SERIOUS PAMPERING WITH A LITTLE SPIRITUAL WELLBEING ON THE SIDE, WHILE VILLA-STYLE STAYS ARE IN VOGUE...

162

There's always a moment in every spa treatment when you think, 'Phew! This is going to be a good one.' Perhaps you're enjoying aromatherapy in a treehouse treatment room in Fiji or getting pummeled by a powerful hammam lady in Turkey. Maybe it's a four-hand massage in Sardinia or a feet-first manipulation on a beach in Thailand.

Bali is a case in point, with a plethora of spa treatments on offer, from budget to bling. No visit to this island is complete without being massaged, scrubbed, cleansed, bathed and blissed out to within an inch of your life. Indonesian massages are all long strokes and much stretching, skin-rolling and palm-and-thumb pressure, with pampering taking place in your villa, relaxation *sala* (open pavilion), on the beach or in tropical gardens. Sometimes it seems as though there's a salon at every street corner (especially in chichi Seminyak and Ubud, of *Eat, Pray, Love* fame), while upscale hotels here offer some of the world's best spas, invariably open to non-guests, too. Throw in great-value prices and calm, tuned-in practitioners and you'd be crazy not to indulge in a little detox (even if you plan to retox again right afterwards).

Bali's best spa breaks don't involve hair shirts and worthy-but-dull lentil dishes, though. Cue Alila Villas Uluwatu, an eco-glam getaway clinging to the coast on Bali's southern Bukit Peninsula. The 61 indoor-outdoor pool villas, designed by Singaporean architects WOHA, are wow-worthy. The infinity pool gazes towards the Indian Ocean and a cabana lounge bar cantilevers over the cliff (cocktails, anyone?). Spa Alila's 'Journey to You' includes a full day's pampering, from dawn yoga to a massage under the stars – or shake off that jet-lag at some of the island's surf breaks nearby. Who knows, maybe you'll find enlightenment sitting on your board watching the sunset at Uluwatu Beach.

ESSENTIAL EXPERIENCES

* **Catching a magical gamelan performance on a sultry Ubud evening.**
* Indulging in a Balinese spa treatment, such as a rhythmic massage, cleansing body wrap or romantic bathing ritual.
* **Sampling local specialities such as** *babi guling,* **spit-roasted suckling pig marinated for hours.**
* Hitting the beach (or, better still, surfing) at Seminyak, Canggu or the Bukit Peninsula.
* **Swinging by a sea temple: at clifftop Pura Luhur Uluwatu at sunset, Kecak dance shows come with mischievous monkeys; Pura Tanah Lot offers shoreside strolls.**
* Bar-hopping in Seminyak, from La Lucciola to Potato Head Beach Club and Ku De Ta.

LOCATION EAST OF JAVA IN THE INDONESIAN ARCHIPELAGO | **BEST TIME OF YEAR** THE DRY SEASON (APRIL TO SEPTEMBER) | **IDEAL TIME COMMITMENT** 10 DAYS | **ESSENTIAL TIP** BEWARE OF MONKEYS: THEY'LL GRAB YOUR SUNGLASSES, CAMERA AND SNACKS | **BUDGET** $$$ | **PACK** MOSQUITO REPELLENT, MASK AND SNORKEL, PRELOADED IPOD; SURFBOARD IF YOU'RE A WAVE-RIDER

SPIRITUALISED

You won't just leave Bali with a well-kneaded neck; chances are you'll feel spiritually revived, too. It's hard not to be inspired by this deeply devout island, with its enchanting mix of Hindu and animist rituals. Devotion is a part of daily life and you'll see offerings of fruit, food and flowers everywhere, from the sea shores to the village streets. Temples are a-buzz with ceremonies and there's almost always a religious blessing or procession going on (even cremations are a theatrical affair). Seek out yoga sessions, traditional healers or enlightening mind/body/spirit workshops, especially those found in Ubud.

CULTURE CLUB

There's more to Bali than beaches and bars, so take in some of the dazzling arts that make this island tick. Experience an evening performance of the Kecak, Barong or Legong dance in Ubud, the island's cultural centre, or at sea temple Pura Luhur Uluwatu. Clad in vibrant silk and ikat patterns, the sensuous dancers use minutely choreographed eye, hand and body movements. The hypnotic sound of the gamelan orchestra will also draw you in, and try to catch a *wayang kulit* (shadow-puppet) show, based on Indian epics the *Mahabharata* and *Ramayana*. Art galleries and crafts boutiques complete the picture.

■ THE PERFECT GETAWAY

To make the most of Bali's charms, treat yourself to a trip combining coast and country, seduction and soulful serenity. For coastal thrills, kick off in sybaritic Seminyak, home to Bali's most stylish bars, restaurants and boutiques. The buzzy beach here, and at chic neighbour Legian, is better for posing or surfing than swimming, as the rips can be risky. Naughty little sister Kuta to the south is beloved of backpackers, with a sandy strip full of jogging expats, kids flying kites and hawkers selling sunglasses.

For the perfect Indo house party, book into Luna2 Private Hotel on Seminyak Beach. This pad boasts five retro-modern rooms and a pool flaunting an image of Marilyn Monroe. If you prefer laid-back lounging, make for sleepy Canggu Beach, where Bali meets Ibiza at tropical-modern Oazia Spa Villas. Its seven suites are spread over three villas, each sporting a frangipani-fringed saltwater pool.

Next head inland, where lime-green rice paddies and vertiginous valleys make for a soothing change. Go trekking, mountain-biking or rafting, or delve within, care of yoga and meditation sessions. Base yourself at country town Ubud, home to alternative therapies, dance, music and galleries. For the ultimate wellbeing sanctuary, check into Ubud's Como Shambhala Estate. Or for a group getaway escape to three-suite Villa Sungai, a rural retreat in Cepaka village that is a serene blend of traditional Balinese romance and sleek modern style.

Finally, chill out on the Bukit Peninsula, famous for its dry landscape, coastal cliffs, beaches and surf breaks. Karma Kandara stars a cliff-top spa with an inclinator to whisk you down to its boho beach club. Talk about taking it easy!

■ PLAN IT

Fly into Bali's Ngurah Rai International Airport, south of capital Denpasar, served by many regional carriers. If required, you can buy a 'Visa on Arrival', payable in cash. From here it's a 30-minute drive to Seminyak, or 90 minutes to inland Ubud. Many hotels offer free transfers and chauffeur-drivers are plentiful. Traffic in Bali is hectic, but if you'd rather self-drive, bring an International Driving Permit.

■ DETOUR

Bali may be a Hindu heartland, but why not make a detour to Borobudur, Indonesia's most famous Buddhist temple, on neighbouring Java? About 40km northwest of culture-rich Yogyakarta, it was built during the 9th century, but abandoned around the 14th century as the influence of Islam increased. With 500 serene stone Buddha statues set atop nine platforms, this striking shrine was rediscovered in the 19th century and now enjoys Unesco World Heritage status. Visit at dawn to soak up the sunrise before the tourist hordes. The views of volcanoes from the stupa summit are stupendous.

165

OPENING SPREAD Tirta Empul Hindu temple in central Bali. **ABOVE (L)** Prayer offerings at Balinese temples include food and incense. **ABOVE (R)** Enjoy a sea view during your massage. **LEFT** Puru Ulun Danu Bratan is one of Bali's most important temples; it's surrounded by water.

DECKCHAIR

* ❋ **Bali: The Food of My Island Home** (Janet de Neefe) Bali's spicy, fragrant cuisine, extolled by the famous Ubud-based chef.
* ❋ **Eat Pray Love** (Elizabeth Gilbert) The best-selling memoir-turned-movie of one woman's search for fulfillment in Italy, India and Bali.
* ❋ **A House in Bali** (Colin McPhee) A Canadian composer's love affair with gamelan music.
* ❋ **The Year of Living Dangerously** (Christopher Koch) A thriller capturing political turmoil in 1960s Jakarta, as seen through the eyes of a foreign correspondent.
* ❋ **Creating Sacred Space with Feng Shui** (Karen Kingston) Decluttering tips, inspired by Balinese (rather than Chinese) customs.
* ❋ **Bali: Sekala & Niskala** (Fred Eiseman) The island's religion and rituals revealed.

WAKE UP IN THE WILDS OF CALEDONIA

THE SLEEPER TRAIN FROM LONDON TO SCOTLAND'S HIGHLANDS IS BRITAIN'S MOST ROMANTIC RAIL RIDE. WHAT'S MORE, IT DEPOSITS YOU IN A WORLD OF GREAT GLENS, STEAM LOCOMOTIVES AND CASTLE STAYS, FOR A TASTE OF THE CALEDONIA YOU LONG TO FIND.

166

Initially: disorientation – why on earth are you rocking like a baby in a cot? Ah, you're on a train. Remembrance sneaks through the first fog of waking; you open your eyes to see cabin walls and the base of the bunk above. Not Orient Express wood-panel grand, maybe, but cosy nonetheless.

When you pulled down the blind the night before, it was to shut out city suburbs, commuter towns and clogged roads. As you draw it up now, you can't help but yelp. There's a loch – a loch! – glittering in the early morning sun. The office blocks are gone, replaced by hills clad in heather. You're now transfixed by what's outside – so much so you almost ignore the knock at the door: the attendant delivering your wake-up cuppa. But back to the window. You watch as the train makes a wide horseshoe curve through a glen, crosses the bleakest of moors and passes a sign: 'Corrour Summit: 1350ft (411m) above sea level' – the railway's highest point. Loch Treig, Tulloch and Monessie Gorge all roll by. Then, at 9.54am, you finally clicketty-clack into Fort William station – the self-proclaimed Outdoor Capital of the UK.

Ah, the outdoors – inhale that Highland air! Because, although the rails that delivered you to this point were part of the thrill, this is where the escape proper begins. You're at the heart of ancient Caledonia now, a landscape that – despite the odd gift shop full of tartan tat and ginger-bearded kitsch – effortlessly conjures bright-eyed romance out of the bracing air.

The options from Fort William are manifold: Ben Nevis lairds over the town, beckoning Munro-baggers; the rift of the Great Glen stretches north; tear-jerkingly gorgeous Glen Coe (the 'Valley of Weeping') is just south. But you're going to ignore all that to get back on the train, ride it to the sea and then sail to a pauper's castle and a community so tight-knit they bought their own island...

ESSENTIAL EXPERIENCES

* **Tucking into a plate of haggis, neeps and tatties in the Caledonian Sleeper's lounge car – a fine supper before bedding down in your berth.**

* Waking up to see beautiful-but-bleak Rannoch Moor outside your train cabin's window.

* **Feeling like Harry Potter aboard the Jacobite Steam Train, which runs (in summer only) from Fort William to Mallaig.**

* Raising a dram of liquid gold at Skye's Talisker Whisky distillery.

* **Booking the four-poster Oak Suite at Rum's grand Kinloch Castle hostel – a right royal bargain.**

* Mixing with the friendly locals at a ceilidh dance on the vibrant isle of Eigg.

LOCATION CENTRAL SCOTLAND | **BEST TIME OF YEAR** LATE SPRING TO EARLY AUTUMN | **IDEAL TIME COMMITMENT** FIVE TO SEVEN DAYS | **ESSENTIAL TIP** SLEEPER-CAR RESERVATIONS ARE RELEASED 12 WEEKS IN ADVANCE OF TRAVEL – BOOK EARLY FOR BEST FARES | **BUDGET** $–$$ | **PACK** EAR PLUGS

OVER THE SEA TO SKYE

In 1745, the 25-year-old 'Bonnie' Prince Charlie – exiled claimant to the British throne – landed on the Outer Hebridean isle of Eriskay. From here, he raised a Highland army and fought to restore his Jacobite dynasty to power. It didn't work. After a disastrous defeat at Culloden in 1746, he went into hiding, aided by a raft of loyal followers including, most famously, Flora MacDonald. It was Flora who smuggled young Charlie (disguised as a servant girl) over the sea to Skye; she is buried in a cemetery behind the Museum of Island Life on Skye's Trotternish Peninsula.

■ THE PERFECT GETAWAY

The Caledonia Sleeper deposits you in Fort William. But from there, continue to Mallaig on a sublime 90-minute stretch of the West Highland Line, which wends below mountains, past lochs and over the graceful Glenfinnan Viaduct (sit on the left for the best views). In summer a steam-hauled service runs this route, for added old-fashioned appeal.

Mallaig is a working port: ferries bound for Skye and the Small Isles depart year round. Depending on how much time you have, visit just one or scan the CalMac timetable to plan a multi-island hop. Sizeable Skye is a 30-minute sail from Mallaig. Long popular with tourists (but big enough to allow escape from the crowds), this Gaelic isle is Scotland in microcosm. There are shops selling hand-spun Aran jumpers (which are *so* back in fashion) and a resurgent population of golden eagles. The jagged Skye Cuillin peaks satisfy walkers, while the Talisker Distillery offers intoxicating tours.

After Skye, backtrack to Mallaig to sail to Rum, the biggest of the Small Isles – and the place to sleep like a king, for less. Turreted Kinloch Castle, a former Edwardian hunting lodge, is now a hostel where £55 secures the Oak Suite, complete with four-poster bed.

Some Mallaig–Rum ferries run via tiny Eigg, where you'll find the warmest Scottish welcome: people have time for people here. Eigg is owned by its 70-odd residents who, fed up with being at the mercy of landlords, clubbed together and bought the island in 1997; the buy-out anniversary is celebrated each June with an all-night ceilidh. Hire a bike to cycle to Singing Sands beach or access the trail up An Sugrr. Then do what the locals do: drink beer on a bench outside the village shop (there's no pub) and discuss another unspoilt Eigg day.

DECKCHAIR

❋ **The Waverley Novels** (Sir Walter Scott) Published anonymously in the early 19th century, Scott's tales evoke romantic Caledonia.

❋ **Harry Potter franchise** (from 2001) In the film adaptations of JK Rowling's wizarding works, the steam train from Fort William to Mallaig stands in for the Hogwarts Express.

❋ **Adrift in Caledonia** (Nick Thorpe) Entertaining travelogue about hitchhiking through Scotland on a variety of vessels.

❋ **Raw Spirit** (Iain Banks) The Scottish novelist goes on a rip-roaring mission to find the perfect single-malt whisky.

❋ **Consider the Lilies** (Iain Crichton Smith) Elegiac novel about the tragic Highland Clearances.

❋ **The Penguin Book of Scottish Folk Tales** (ed Neil Philip) A compendium of myths and legends, set amid the Highlands and islands.

RAILWAY RUMPUS

The residents of Fort William, fed up with having to travel 80km to the railhead of Kingussie to board a train, demanded a railway of their own – so the building of the West Highland Line began in 1889. Its construction was a challenge: there were mountains to negotiate and bogs to cross; lack of cash also forced the use of tight curves and steep gradients rather than more direct, but pricier, cuttings and viaducts. The first trains left Glasgow for Fort William in 1894; the Mallaig extension opened in 1901, connecting the west-coast fishing town to the rest of Scotland.

■ PLAN IT

The Caledonian Sleeper is run by ScotRail. Its Highland service leaves London Euston nightly (excluding Saturdays), splitting into three sections in Edinburgh: one bound for Perth, Aviemore and Inverness; one for Dundee and Aberdeen; and one for the West Highlands and Fort William. Book early to get the best fares for a two-bed sleeper compartment for London–Fort William. Four trains a day (one on Sundays) link Fort William and Mallaig; journey time is 90 minutes. Caledonian MacBrayne runs ferries from Mallaig to Skye and the Small Isles year round. Services are not daily and are less frequent October–March.

■ DETOUR

Ignore the big CalMac ferries at Mallaig. Instead, hop aboard the wee MV *Western Isles* for Knoydart. This misty peninsula, a 45-minute sail north, is often considered the mainland's last true wilderness: its bulging peaks and wildlife-stalked moorland are only reachable by boat or on foot. The Western Isles ferry runs twice daily and docks at Inverie, the area's hamlet-size hub, squeezed between hills on the peninsula's south side. It has a tiny post office, a small shop and the Old Forge – Britain's remotest, and possibly most convivial, pub.

OPENING SPREAD Raw and rugged: Trotternish peninsula at the north of the Isle of Skye.
ABOVE Baronial style in Kinloch Castle on the Isle of Rum in the Inner Hebrides.
BELOW The Caledonian sleeper train rattles through the Highland's glens.

TRANQUILLITY IN HONG KONG

WANT TO ESCAPE ONE OF THE WORLD'S MOST DENSELY POPULATED CITIES? TAI O, ONE OF HONG KONG'S LAST REMAINING FISHING VILLAGES, IS A RARE WINDOW INTO AGE-OLD CHINESE TRADITIONS, INTRIGUING COLONIAL HISTORY AND A UNIQUE NATURAL ENVIRONMENT.

170

An outdoors person might describe Hong Kong as pure urban jungle: a nitty-gritty, over-populated city where high-rises crowd the skyline and pollution spoils the waterways and the air. Not so. On the far-flung western corner of Lantau Island a respite from the urban chaos exists in the form of Tai O, a fishing village built on stilts over the waterways that run into a pretty bay at the mouth of the Pearl River Delta. Such is its remoteness, Tai O has escaped the rapid urban development that Hong Kong is known for, ensuring the traditional aspects of this ancient settlement have remained intact.

During the 1960s and '70s, Tai O was at its peak, home to 30,000 people who were riding the wave of thriving fishing and salt industries on the Pearl River Delta trade route. When the fish were all but depleted, the people left for the big smoke. Today, about 2000 residents – mostly elderly folk – ply a small trade in the scaled-down fishing industry, allowing visitors an intriguing look into an age-old culture. On streets crowded with skewed red shop awnings, old women sell dried squid and *haam yue,* the popular and pungent salted fish. Jars of shrimp paste are sold from umbrella-shaded street carts, and barbecues smoke with the smell of the day's catch – grilled prawns, oysters and abalone.

A meander through the labyrinthine backstreets, across rickety bridges and past stilt houses, reveals salted fish hanging like washing on a line and baskets brimming with sea critters. The clickety-clack of mah-jong tiles is as familiar a sound as the lapping of tidal water coursing through the stick-thin house stumps. In the temple, huge whale vertebrae are still venerated with incense, a nod to the trade that made this place tick for centuries. The opening of a teeny hotel in the village's former marine police station has heightened the getaway potential. Take a trip to Tai O: it's the most tranquil place in Hong Kong.

ESSENTIAL EXPERIENCES

* **Getting the low-down on Tai O's history on a cultural boat tour along the village waterways.**

* Taking a sunset boat tour for a chance to see the rare Chinese white dolphin.

* **Taste-testing some local street morsels, such as chargrilled abalone and squid.**

* Hiking in the surrounding hills.

* **Meandering around the village's old streets and stopping in at the Tai O Cultural Workshop on Wing On St, a folk museum on the ground floor of a century-old building.**

* Paying respects at one of four local temples, where incense still burns and whale bones from a bygone era gather dust.

LOCATION TAI O, LANTAU ISLAND, HONG KONG | **BEST TIME OF YEAR** SEPTEMBER TO NOVEMBER AND MARCH TO MAY | **IDEAL TIME COMMITMENT** THREE DAYS | **ESSENTIAL TIP** SUNSET AND SUNRISE ARE BEST FOR DOLPHIN-SPOTTING | **BUDGET** $$ **PACK** BINOCULARS, WALKING SHOES, CANTONESE PHRASEBOOK

LEGENDARY STAR FERRY

You can't say you've 'done' Hong Kong until you've taken a ride on the Star Ferry. For a mere HK$2.50 (HK$3.40 on weekends) you can board the upper deck of one of the boats in this small fleet, first launched in 1888. With names like Morning Star, Celestial Star and Twinkling Star, the ferries are most romantic at night, when they are festively strung with lights and the towering skyscrapers on both sides of Victoria Harbour bathe the water in a neon glow. If possible, take the trip on a clear night from Kowloon to Central; it's not half as dramatic in the other direction. If you time your run for 8pm you'll see the nightly laser light show, an unmissable HK spectacle.

CHINESE WHITE DOLPHINS

Stories about Chinese white dolphins living in
Hong Kong waters are almost apocryphal, perhaps
unsurprisingly given the overfished local waterways
and poor water quality. But visitors to Tai O have a
chance to see these wondrous albino-white (adults)
and pink (young) cetaceans slinking through their
natural habitat in Tai O Bay, just 200m from shore.
Sunset is the perfect time to see their dorsal fins
ducking and diving in the water as they feast on fish,
an opportunity most day-tripping tourists will miss
(which might account for the rare sightings). But
overnighters can join the hotel's sunset tour for a
chance to spot them. It's also an opportunity to size up
the unique natural environment from the water.

■ THE PERFECT GETAWAY

It's a 20-minute walk from the village to Tai O Heritage Hotel, or you can take a short boat ride for the best view of the white building peeking through the overgrown trees, a vision from a bygone era. At the end of the 19th century this stretch of water, the line of demarcation between British and Chinese power in the South China Sea, was rife with pirates. The marine police station, built in 1902, became the eyes and ears of the coast, and was the first line of defence for Hong Kong's Victoria Harbour. Once a modest complex with no running water, it has been transformed into a restaurant and nine luxury suites (with feather pillows and fluffy duvets), while preserving the character of the original building.

Hints of the past are everywhere. Spotlights that once beamed across the water have been resurrected. Two 100kg cannons have been dusted off, repainted and restored to their rightful position. In reception, two holding cells with big, clunky iron doors tell the stories of suspect characters and occasional drunks who spent the night under lock and key. Guard towers at each end of the building are a nod to the station's strategic location on the most southern corner of the colony.

Visitors can get the low-down on a hotel tour or a boat trip through the Tai O waterways. Both are run by the Hong Kong Heritage Conservation Foundation, which oversaw the redevelopment project. A sunset boat tour is the best chance to spot endangered Chinese white dolphins, which live in the surrounding waters. With mountains on three sides, this is also ideal hiking territory. If more leisurely pursuits take your fancy, the hotel's rooftop restaurant, with lovely water views, has an Asian fusion menu and chilled white wine.

■ PLAN IT

From Hong Kong International Airport, take bus S to Tung Chung (15 minutes), then bus 11 to Tai O (40 minutes). From Central, catch the ferry from Pier 6 to Mui Wo (35 to 55 minutes) and take bus 1 to Tai O (50 minutes). Arriving at Tai O, take a two-minute ride on the boat shuttle near the Tai O bus terminus or follow the signs for a 20-minute walk to the Tai O Heritage Hotel around the water's edge. It's essential to book months in advance, particularly for weekend stays.

■ DETOUR

Two attractions are a short bus ride from Tai O. Po Lin Monastery, founded in 1906, with its gardens, prayer flags and Buddha statues, is a pleasant place to meander midweek (avoid weekends and public holidays). Nearby, Tian Tan Buddha is a massive (34m) bronze Buddha seated on a lofty hilltop. The best views of it are from Ngong Ping 360 scenic cable car, which departs from above Tung Chung MTR station. An ideal Tai O itinerary would include these stops en route to the village.

173

OPENING SPREAD Hong Kong city and Victoria Harbour. **ABOVE (L)** Hung out to dry: this fishing village on Lantau island continues to bring in the catch. **ABOVE (R)** Mending nets. **LEFT** The white-washed and colonnaded frontage of the Tai O Heritage Hotel, now restored by local enterprise.

DECKCHAIR

* ***Old Tai O Police Station: The Evolution of a Centenary Monument*** (Hong Kong Heritage Conservation Foundation) A detailed account of the revival of this historical building, and its links to Tai O.

* ***The Last Governor*** (Jonathan Dimbleby) Chris Patten's last days as governor and the handover from British sovereignty to Chinese rule.

* ***A Modern History of Hong Kong*** (Steve Tsang) Get to grips with the city's topsy-turvy past.

* ***Travelers' Tales Guides: Hong Kong*** (James O'Reilly) Armchair reading for travellers in situ.

* ***Kowloon Tong: A Novel of Hong Kong*** (Paul Theroux) See the city through a travel guru's imagination.

* ***Gweilo: Memories of a Hong Kong Childhood*** (Martin Booth) This love affair with the city is set during one of its most interesting colonial periods.

CRETE: TO THE BEACHES & BEYOND

SAMPLE CRETE IN ALL ITS HISTORICAL, CULTURAL AND CULINARY COMPLEXITY. EXPLORE THE REGION OF RETHYMNO AND ENCOUNTER BLISSFUL TRANQUILLITY ON PALM-STUDDED PREVELI BEACH ON THE ISLAND'S CORRUGATED SOUTHERN COAST, RIGHT ON THE DEEP BLUE LIBYAN SEA.

174

Scene 1: You, at your desk, on the phone, at the computer, in a meeting, stuck in traffic, at the supermarket, in the kitchen... Cut!

Scene 2: You, dozing in the warm sand, with palm fronds swaying in the breeze and a sonic cocktail of birdsong and surging waves washing over you.

In Crete, there's no shortage of places where you can be the star of your own escapist movie. One of them is Preveli Beach – a sandy sliver of Eden basking in splendid isolation on Crete's south coast. Far from the hubbub of the big resorts in the north, its stunning setting makes it one of the island's most celebrated strands – remote, yet accessible. Also known as Palm Beach, Preveli Beach is like an exclamation mark idling at the mouth of the Megalopotamos River at the end of its meander through the ruggedly dramatic Kourtaliotiko Gorge. Where the canyon meets the beach, the stream's chilly water tumbles through a jungle of oleander, eucalyptus and endemic palm trees into a lagoon hemmed in by soft sand and the shimmering Mediterranean.

Coming from Rethymno, your journey to Preveli follows the river through the gorge, which starts south of Koxare. Caves honeycomb the steep, ochre-reddish walls of this crack in the mountains where hippies lived in the 1960s and '70s. Just a few years ago, archaeologists stumbled upon 130,000-year-old stone hand-axes here, fuelling speculation that Crete may well have been a stepping stone in the migration of African hominids to Europe.

You'll first spot Preveli Beach from a parking lot near the 17th-century Preveli Monastery, high above the Libyan Sea. From here, a footpath zigzags down the cliffs, each bend revealing swoon-worthy vistas. It takes 20 minutes to reach the beach, but any exertion fades into bliss as the day unwinds – soaking up the rays, hitting the waves or dipping into the freshwater pools on the river banks.

ESSENTIAL EXPERIENCES

* **Kicking back beneath a palm tree on Preveli Beach, breaking only for cooling dips in the Mediterranean or the freshwater pools formed by the Megalopotamos River.**

* Coming face to face with Crete's rebellious past on a tour of 17th-century Preveli Monastery.

* **Getting lost wandering the labyrinth of lanes that is Rethymno's charming Venetian-Ottoman historic centre, then heading to the harbour for an alfresco fish dinner.**

* Sampling the rich tapestry of flavours and textures of authentic Cretan country cooking over lunch at Iliomanolis in Kanevos.

* **Rubbing shoulders with the ghosts of the Minoans on a tour of the restored Knossos palace ruins, which opens up a fascinating window onto this ancient civilisation.**

LOCATION CRETE, GREECE | **BEST TIME OF YEAR** MAY, JUNE, SEPTEMBER AND OCTOBER | **IDEAL TIME COMMITMENT** ONE WEEK
ESSENTIAL TIP AVOID PREVELI BEACH IN JULY AND AUGUST WHEN THE WINDS CAN BE FIERCE AND CROWDS LARGE
BUDGET $$ | **PACK** TOWEL, BATHING SUIT, SUNGLASSES, HAT AND STURDY SHOES FOR HIKING DOWN TO THE BEACH

BEAUTY, BLOOD & BRAVERY

Cutting an imposing silhouette high above Preveli
Beach and the glistening Mediterranean, Moni Preveli
(Preveli Monastery) encapsulates the core values of
the Cretan spirit: bravery, defiance and independence.
A centre of resistance during the Turkish occupations
in the 18th and 19th centuries, it also played a key role
in WWII, hiding trapped Allied soldiers from the Nazis
until they could be rescued in a daring submarine
escape. A memorial showing a gun-toting abbot flanked
by an Allied soldier commemorates this heroic act.
The Germans retaliated by partly devastating the
monastery, confiscating its livestock and arresting the
monks, although they were later released.

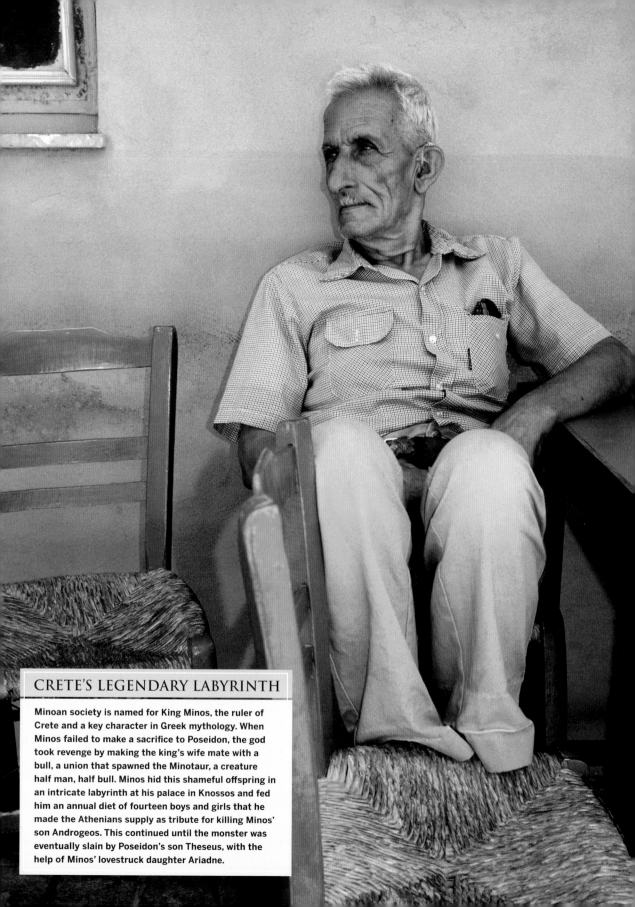

CRETE'S LEGENDARY LABYRINTH

Minoan society is named for King Minos, the ruler of Crete and a key character in Greek mythology. When Minos failed to make a sacrifice to Poseidon, the god took revenge by making the king's wife mate with a bull, a union that spawned the Minotaur, a creature half man, half bull. Minos hid this shameful offspring in an intricate labyrinth at his palace in Knossos and fed him an annual diet of fourteen boys and girls that he made the Athenians supply as tribute for killing Minos' son Androgeos. This continued until the monster was eventually slain by Poseidon's son Theseus, with the help of Minos' lovestruck daughter Ariadne.

THE PERFECT GETAWAY

Preveli is one of the star attractions in the region of Rethymno, an intriguing quilt of bubbly seaside resorts, tranquil hamlets steeped in timeless tradition, velvety hills blanketed in wildflowers and olive trees, and ancient monasteries whose monks stood firm against the Turks. Above it all thrones Mt Psiloritis (2456m), Crete's highest mountain and the mythological birthplace of Zeus.

Spend a couple of days exploring the region's eponymous capital, Rethymno, one of Crete's most charismatic towns. Wander the tangle of pedestrianised lanes in the historic quarter, lorded over by the Venetian fortress with its mosque-turned-cathedral and outdoor amphitheatre, to spot more vestiges of Venetian rule, which lasted from the 13th to the 17th centuries. One of the loveliest is the Rimondi Fountain, with its trio of lion heads spouting water into basins.

Quite a few of Rethymno's Venetian-era stone mansions have been converted into boutique hotels. One of the best known is Avli Lounge Apartments, which has also spawned a respected restaurant. Pick a table in the bougainvillea-shaded courtyard and settle down for a meal of farm-fresh Cretan fare: menu stars include cheese-stuffed lamb and sea bass drizzled with lemon-saffron sauce.

The region is also famed for its rustic mountain tavernas. Among those enjoying cult status with gourmets is Iliomanolis in tiny Kanevos, where owner-chef Maria lets you into the kitchen to let you choose from whatever local specialities she's whipped up. It's on the road from Rethymno to Plakias, a popular southern seaside resort. En route you'll also pass through the pretty village of Myrthios, its whitewashed buildings draped across a hillside with grand views of the Med.

PLAN IT

Most visitors travel to Crete by air; the majority of flights land at Iraklio, 80km east of Rethymno. Rethymno itself has a wide variety of lodging options. There are lots of quieter getaways in the surrounding countryside and big luxury resorts along the coast. If you don't have a car, tour operators run trips through the gorge to Preveli Beach, about 35km south of Rethymno, but it's just as easy to get there by public bus.

DETOUR

Crete is scattered with vestiges of the Minoans, a mysterious Bronze Age people that dominated much of southern Europe 4000 years ago. Their capital was in Knossos, a palace complex whose ruins were partially reconstructed in the early 20th century and now offer an engaging introduction to Minoan society. Stand in the Throne Room where the ruler once held court, picture robed ladies sashaying down the Grand Staircase to the royal apartments, or marvel at the drainage system. Colourful frescoes attest to the Minoans' artistry.

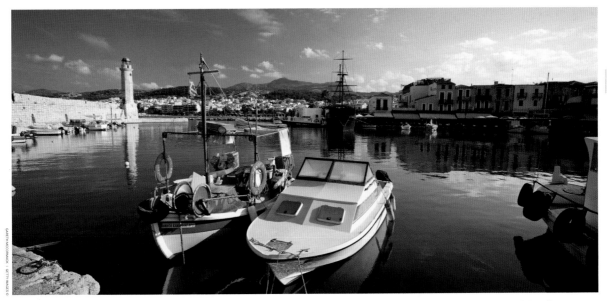

OPENING SPREAD Remote Balos Bay in northwest Crete. **ABOVE** Rethymno's placid harbour was built by Venetians to accommodate their galleys. **LEFT** Watching the world go by from a Cretan taverna.

DECKCHAIR

* ***Zorba the Greek*** (Nikos Kazantzakis) This Crete-born author's most famous book is about the art of embracing life to the fullest.

* ***The Cretan Runner*** (George Psychoundakis) The gripping story of a shepherd boy turned messenger for the Cretan resistance during the Nazi occupation.

* ***The Dark Labyrinth*** (Lawrence Durrell) A philosophical tale of a group of English travellers exploring a dangerous labyrinth on Crete.

* ***The Island*** (Victoria Hislop) Moving tale about a British woman's discovery of her family's connection to Crete's former leper colony on Spinalonga.

* ***Night Ambush*** (1957) This movie grippingly retells the kidnapping of Nazi general Heinrich Kreipe by British forces in 1944.

* ***Moon Maiden*** (SV Peddle) Minoan life at the Palace of Knossos is recreated in this fantasy tale of love, ambition and betrayal.

MEDITATING IN MALLORCA

SWAP RINGTONES FOR GOAT BELLS ATOP MALLORCA'S PUIG DE MARIA (MARY'S MOUNTAIN), WHERE A MEDIEVAL HERMITAGE PERCHED AMONG CYPRESS AND PINE TREES ABOVE POLLENÇA INVITES RESPITE AND ISLAND-GAZING.

178

Whether you make the hour-long climb on foot like a true pilgrim or brave the road, it's a long way up to Santuari de la Mare de Déu des Puig, a former nunnery straddling a hump-backed hill in northern Mallorca. Your pilgrimage begins in the town of Pollença, where a narrow, potholed road swings precariously up to the 333m-high convent. The road is so tortuous that taxi drivers refuse to come here, and even locals familiar with its twists and turns say three Hail Marys before cranking into first gear. The road ends abruptly and a rocky footpath takes over, making a steady – if slippery – ascent past woods of holm oak, pine, olive and cypress trees where goats scamper.

Though modest in height, this fist of rock commands one of Mallorca's finest outlooks: to the west the hauntingly beautiful peaks of the Tramuntana range, to the east the gently curving bays of Alcúdia and Pollença and the jagged Formentor peninsula, flicking out into the Mediterranean like a dragon's tail.

Appreciate these celestial views from the 14th-century hermitage, and find time to reflect in the silence of its courtyards and dimly lit corridors, where the stone floors have been polished smooth by pilgrims over centuries. The nuns upped and left for Palma in 1576, but the atmosphere is still one of contemplation in the gothic chapel, where incense fills your nostrils, and in the beamed refectory where grace was said before meals. Your room for the night is a cell turned guest room – fittingly spartan, with icons hanging on lime-washed walls and heavy wooden furniture. There is no air-con in summer, no heating in winter, no TV or wi-fi, and bathrooms are communal – but such simplicity feels in keeping with the humble life of the hermitage, inviting you to relax, meditate, find serenity in austerity. This is a Mallorcan escape immune to time and trends – just 70km from the party-mad crowds of Magaluf, but a million miles away in spirit.

ESSENTIAL EXPERIENCES

* **Rising at an ungodly hour at the hermitage to see the sun rise over the Bay of Alcúdia.**
* Eating paella on the convent's sea-facing terrace, as the cicadas strike up their dusk chorus.
* **Striking out on foot into the olive groves and citrus orchards of the Tramuntana from the villages of Fornalutx, Sóller and Deià.**
* Drawing breath on the hair-raising clifftop drive from Pollença to Formentor, a curving bay washed by the bluest of seas.
* **Enjoying street life and cafe culture in Pollença, after a sweaty 365-step trek up the Calvari.**
* Lingering at Sa Foradada as sunset silhouettes the coastline's weird rock formations.

LOCATION MALLORCA, SPAIN | **BEST TIME OF YEAR** SPRING THROUGH AUTUMN (APRIL THROUGH NOVEMBER) | *IDEAL TIME* **COMMITMENT** ONE WEEK | **ESSENTIAL TIP** AVOID HIKING IN THE MIDDAY HEAT | **BUDGET** $ | **PACK** STURDY SHOES FOR THE HIKE TO THE TOP OF THE CONVENT

THE SERRA DE TRAMUNTANA

From Puig de Maria you are within easy striking distance of the eerily beautiful and remote Serra de Tramuntana, a spine of jagged, pockmarked limestone peaks that forms the backbone of northwestern Mallorca. Awarded Unesco World Heritage status in 2011, this spectacularly buckled mountain range thrusts above olive groves, citrus orchards and ochre villages pasted onto the hillsides. In the north, where the mountains collide with the sapphire-blue Mediterranean, its cave-riddled heights drop suddenly to a coastline indented with coves. Tour buses trundle up the mountains occasionally, but you'll need your own wheels to reach the remotest corners. Or explore its web of trails on foot or by mountain bike – these mountains offer some of the best hiking and cycling in Spain.

■ THE PERFECT GETAWAY

After taking time out at the convent, meander downhill to Pollença. This honey-coloured town in the foothills of the Tramuntana is ideal for an amble, its back-streets hiding bohemian bars, family-run bistros and artisan workshops. For a slice of Mallorcan life, pull up a chair at a cafe on Plaça Major, where teenagers flirt and old men in flat caps meet to sip coffee, chat and put the world to rights. Then be lured east by the sea to the cliff-hugging, stomach-flipping road that snakes 18km from Port de Pollença to Cap de Formentor: few roads in Mallorca elicit such gasps. Break at Formentor beach for a splash in crystal-clear water.

When you're ready to move on from Pollença, head west into the Tramuntana, following the road that slithers up to Santuari de Lluc. Cupped in a valley and fringed by walking trails, this 13th-century monastery attracts day trippers en masse; arrive early in the morning before crowds interrupt the monastic calm, or hole up in one of the cells overnight. The hermitage is a hairpin-riddled drive from Sa Calobra, a bay gouged out of the cliffs, where the sea is deep and cold.

Meandering west along the Ma10 mountain road brings you to Fornalutx, at the foot of Mallorca's highest peak, Puig Major (1445m). This village is a terrific spot to drop off the map and hike through terraces planted with citrus trees to Sóller, where daily life is woven around a cafe-rimmed plaza dominated by a modernist church designed by Joan Rubió i Bellver, one of Gaudí's protégés.

Further on is Deià, a higgledy-piggledy village favoured by artists and writers. For coastal drama, nearby Son Marroig, the one-time mansion of Hapsburg Archduke Luis Salvador, offers sea views from its colonnade. From here, a 3km trail winds down to the elephant-shaped outcrop of Sa Foradada, one of Mallorca's most beautiful sights.

DECKCHAIR

* ❋ ***A Winter in Mallorca*** (George Sand) An account of Sand's winter sojourn in Valldemossa from 1838 to 1839.
* ❋ ***Trekking through Mallorca: GR221 – The Drystone Route*** (Paddy Dillon) Details the Ruta de Pedra en Sec through the Serra de Tramuntana, including a detour to Puig de Maria.
* ❋ ***Snowball Oranges*** (Peter Kerr) Fun page-turner about a winter spent in Mallorca.
* ❋ ***A Bull on the Beach*** (Anna Nicholas) Entertaining holiday yarn about British expats learning to farm in Mallorca's mountains.
* ❋ ***Mallorca: Car Tours and Walks*** (Valerie Crespi-Green) Ideal companion for seeing the hinterland on foot or by car.
* ❋ ***Wild Olives: Life in Majorca with Robert Graves*** (William Graves) Insightful portrayal of the life and work of English poet Robert Graves, written by his son.

RURAL HIDEAWAYS

Want to tiptoe off the beaten track? Northern Mallorca is honeycombed with rural *agroturismos* (farmstays), *fincas* (rural properties) and hermitages. A solace-seeking favourite at the foot of the Serra de Tramuntana is Finca es Castell in Binibona – rimmed by mountains and olive groves, this farmhouse turned boutique hotel has been in family hands since the 15th century. Kate Moss and Sting are fans of La Residencia, Deià's five-star A-list retreat, with oak-beamed lounges, a spa, tennis courts and every other imaginable luxury. For 600 years of history and coastal walks on your doorstep, choose between the hilltop Sant Salvador Hotel, in Felanitx, and Ermita de la Victòria, on a pine-cloaked peninsula near Alcúdia.

◼ PLAN IT

Pollença is a 40-minute drive northeast of Palma de Mallorca, the island's major city. Flights operate year-round to Palma airport, served by budget airlines such as Ryanair, Jet2 and easyJet. All of the major car hire companies are represented. For inexpensive transfers, try Resort Hoppa or Shuttle Direct. Every season has its own appeal in northern Mallorca, but bear in mind that Santuari de la Mare de Déu des Puig's unheated cells get chilly in winter. Book at least a couple of months ahead if you plan to stay in the peak summer months of July and August. Call +34 (0)971 184 132 for reservations. The convent is off the Ma2200 Palma–Pollença road.

◼ DETOUR

Take the lead from pilgrims who for centuries have also flocked to Pollença to clamber up the 365 steps of the Calvari (Calvary) – occasionally on their blistered hands and knees. Breathe in the scent of the cypress trees and flower-draped stone houses as you ascend the stairway that leads steadily up to a tiny 18th-century chapel. From this 330m-high vantage point, the views reach across the town to Santuari de la Mare de Déu des Puig on the hill opposite, and beyond to the Serra de Tramuntana.

OPENING SPREAD Looking west from Son Marroig. **ABOVE** The scent of citrus fruits fills the air of the Sóller valley. **BELOW** In the foothills of the Serra de Tramuntana farms and estates have become boutique hotels.

GOOD VIBRATIONS IN BYRON BAY

BYRON BAY IS THE PERFECT PLACE TO CATCH UP WITH YOURSELF. IT'S A CONDITION OF ENTRY THAT YOU LEAVE YOUR BAD KARMA AT THE DOOR. THUS UNENCUMBERED, YOU CAN RECONNECT WITH YOUR INNER SELF AND REALIGN YOUR CHAKRAS BEFORE RETURNING TO NORMAL LIFE.

182

First there's the sound of a chuckle from the gumtree outside your window. Then come gales of full-blown laughter. Byron Bay's locals boast that they are the first people the sun kisses as it rises in the morning; the town sits on the tip of the easternmost point of the Australian mainland, making it the place to pay your salutations to the sun. But you don't need an alarm call to watch the sunrise when you've got raucous kookaburras to shoo away your slumber.

Now wide awake, you make your way to Palm Valley (just a short walk if you are staying in town). From here, you climb the uphill track to the lighthouse. No lingering along the way – you can enjoy the views on the trip back down. At the top, you find a glistening white lighthouse standing sentry over the bay below. Built in 1901 and lovingly maintained, it's an icon of the region. But this place has a deeper, richer past. A sacred spot for the indigenous Arakwal people, this circle of land was a site of Aboriginal initiation rituals for eons, time that casts a long shadow over the present moment. You choose your place on the circle from which to watch the sun rise over the Pacific, absorbing the intense and still energy of this place as you welcome the new dawn. Even the most hardened cynic feels the spirits of the land here.

To the Arakwal people, Byron Bay is known as Cavanbah, the 'meeting place'. To its dreadlocked and tie-dyed younger residents, it's known as Chill-Out Central, where surf and sunshine meet. And to its bendy baby-boomers, it's known as a healing place, where mind and body meet in cosmic alignment at its many yoga or therapeutic retreats. Positive energy flows here, from the top of the hills and valleys formed by volcanic eruptions, down through creeks and estuaries to the rocky bays and sweeping beaches below. Whatever your age or inclination, Byron Bay is an escape from everyone else – and a retreat back to yourself.

ESSENTIAL EXPERIENCES

* **Kayaking with pods of dolphins playing in the waves beside you.**
* Watching the humpback whales' annual migration from the Lighthouse.
* **Visiting a yoga ashram, or simply attending classes at the renowned Byron Yoga Centre.**
* Letting it all out with a twilight drumming session on Main Beach.
* **Taking your pick from massage, acupuncture, reiki or reflexology at Osho's House.**
* Sampling the beautiful produce of the region and meeting its colourful characters at the Byron Bay Farmers Market every Thursday morning.
* **Taking the multicoloured day-trip bus to hippie central, 'magic' Nimbin.**

LOCATION NORTHERN NEW SOUTH WALES, AUSTRALIA | **BEST TIME OF YEAR** MARCH TO APRIL; JUNE TO NOVEMBER FOR WHALE SPOTTING | **IDEAL TIME COMMITMENT** FOREVER (OR AT LEAST A WEEK) | **ESSENTIAL TIP** AVOID PEAK SEASON (DECEMBER TO FEBRUARY) | **BUDGET** $-$$$ | **PACK** SWIMSUITS, WALKING SHOES AND AN OPEN MIND

DEEP RETREAT

For an even deeper reconnection with self, consider
a trip to neighbouring Mullumbimby to attend the
annual Spirit Festival (February/March), where
transformation, healing and even sexual magic are on
the agenda in the form of tantra, yoga, meditation,
dance and other healing workshops. This revolutionary
event has a global line-up of presenters catering to all
tastes. If the timing doesn't work, you can attend one
of the many meditation and yoga retreats throughout
the town or dotted around the beautiful hinterland.

THE PERFECT GETAWAY

There is stretching happening on every corner in Byron, but if it's yoga you're after there is no better choice than the Byron Yoga Centre, the longest-running school in town. Drop-in classes are held throughout the day, starting at 6am. Each teacher has their own style, but the philosophy of the school is 'Purna', meaning integration or completeness. Although the practice is alignment-based, the focus here is on yogic values, which include truthfulness, simplicity and a burning effort to achieve a goal ('burning' being the operative word). The values of the centre seem to flow through its teachers and into the practise.

Yogic values teach that you only keep what you have by giving it away, so time to splash some cash in the direction of the Cape Byron Kayaks crew in exchange for a chance to say hello to one of the bay's 300 resident bottlenose dolphins or, if you're lucky, to see humpback whales – from June to November, these magnificent mammals make their annual migration. Curious by nature, the humpbacks swim close to the coast and are not shy of paying you a visit while you kayak – and at up to 15m long, you can't miss them. If the whales are curious, then the dolphins are positively intrusive, ducking and diving and splashing in the waves around you. A short stop at Wategos Beach for a drink and a Tim Tam (Australia's iconic chocolate biscuit) does little to still the beating heart from the exhilaration of being so close to these animals. Hold onto your paddles as you surf the waves back to shore at Clarkes Beach.

From your early-morning meeting with the sun and yogic meeting of body with mind to your communion with the bay's mammals, you'll start to feel your crown chakra melting into your heart chakra right about...now.

PLAN IT

There are three airports to choose from: Ballina, Gold Coast or Lismore. Ballina is the closest, but there are cheaper, more frequent flights to Gold Coast, and catching the bus to Byron is a breeze. The only golden rule of a spiritual escape in Byron is to avoid high season (summer), or peak periods such as Easter, end-of-school week and the music festivals, when accommodation is hard to find.

DETOUR

Kick your spiritual side to the kerb for the day and go shopping. If it's Thursday, start with a trip to the Byron Bay Farmers' Market, where you can sample the area's finest produce. On the first Sunday of the month, local crafters display their wares at the Byron Community Market at Butler Street Reserve – it's feathers, candles and tie-dyed T-shirts galore, complemented by a sizzling array of food carts and the distant strumming of a ukulele or thumping of a *djembe* drum. On any other day, head to the Byron Arts & Industry Estate, where, with a bit of hunting around, you can find local artisans at work and buy their goods for a fraction of the price in town.

184

OPENING SPREAD Byron Bay from on high. **ABOVE** Surf's up at Clarkes beach. Most of Byron's many surfing instructors take beginners to the gentle waves near The Pass, where there is plenty of tentative tumbling going on; the more advanced head to Cosy Corner on wilder Tallow Beach.

DECKCHAIR

* ***Byron Bay: The History, Beauty and Spirit*** (Peter Duke) Byron comes alive in pictures and anecdotes in this book by a local author.

* ***After the Party*** (Jesse Blackadder) A novelised journey into alternative Byron lifestyles (and a dinner party best avoided).

* ***Death of a Whaler*** (Nerida Newton) This poignant tale of healing and renewal after a tragic whaling accident is set in Byron in the 1960s.

* ***Byron Bay Summer Days*** (2012) A filmic homage to the youth of Byron and their spiritual pursuits: music, surfing and hanging out.

* ***The Battle for Byron*** (1996) Classic documentary about eco-minded Byronshire residents and their resistance to large-scale development in the area.

SHOESTRING

GREAT ESCAPES

SLEEP OUT ON THE KENYAN SAVANNAH

WHY PUT THE WALLS OF A HOTEL ROOM BETWEEN YOU AND AFRICA'S WILDLIFE? ON A SHOESTRING TENTED SAFARI, YOU CAN SLEEP SURROUNDED BY THE SOUNDS OF THE SAVANNAH, WITH JUST A THIN PIECE OF CANVAS SEPARATING YOU FROM THE NEAREST HERD OF WILDEBEEST.

186

Night falls slowly in the savannah. Shadows creep across the grassland like stalking leopards as the glare of afternoon fades to the crimson glow of evening. Just before the fat sun slips behind the horizon, a cut-out parade of African animals appears, silhouetted against the sunset – zebras, wildebeest, hartebeest, elephants, jackals. Now where would you rather be? Here, looking out through the doorway of your tent, or inside, queuing for the hotel buffet?

For our money, tented safaris are the only way to experience the African wilderness. To take in the pulse of Africa and the natural rhythms that drive two million ungulates to migrate across the plains from Tanzania to Kenya, you have to feel the grassland under your feet, not sit in a swanky hotel room surrounded by home-like comforts. Your bed should be inches above the African soil. The view from your pillow should be one of unfamiliar constellations, framed by a triangle of canvas. Nights should be full of strange sounds, and mornings should start with a mug of coffee in a folding chair, in front of a vista of gambolling gazelles.

Fortunately, bush camping in Africa is no longer the exclusive preserve of millionaire bushwhackers and Discovery Channel filmmakers. Kenya offers tented safaris for all sizes of wallet, and even the cheapest come with creature comforts – toilets and showers, hot meals cooked in the camp kitchen and cold bottles of Tusker beer at sundown. Even better, getting up close and personal with Africa's fauna is simply a case of stepping outside your tent. By day you can look forward to foot safaris into the bush, led by local guides who are well versed in getting close to the wildlife you want to see, and keeping a safe distance from predatory types. And by night, don't be entirely surprised if you hear baboons and other wildlife making daring dashes through your camp.

ESSENTIAL EXPERIENCES

* **Eating alfresco safari suppers – on many safaris, dinner is served on trestle-tables in front of a breathtaking natural vista.**

* Witnessing your first kill – the full cycle of life unfolds on safari; seeing a predator at work is one of the most sought-after safari experiences.

* **Sipping a spectacular sun-downer – the perfect end to a perfect day: a cold Tusker beer in hand, a herd of wildebeest filling the skyline.**

* Sleeping in the wild – even bedtime is an adventure under canvas; strange sounds fill the night and stars shine brilliantly in the absence of light pollution.

LOCATION MAASAI MARA, KENYA | **BEST TIME OF YEAR** JULY TO OCTOBER | **IDEAL TIME COMMITMENT** ONE WEEK
ESSENTIAL TIP BRING SPARE CAMERA BATTERIES – LIONS WON'T WAIT FOR YOU TO RUSH BACK TO CAMP FOR ANOTHER SET
BUDGET $–$$ | **PACK** A WILDLIFE-SPOTTING GUIDEBOOK TO HELP YOU SORT YOUR ELANDS FROM YOUR IMPALAS

THE SKY'S THE LIMIT

Having saved your pennies by joining a budget tented safari, you might have a little left over for one of Kenya's most spectacular experiences. Balloon rides over the Maasai Mara don't come cheap – prices start at US$300 – but you'll get a view of the wildlife normally reserved for soaring vultures in search of fresh kills. As the ground drifts away beneath your feet, the African terrain is suddenly revealed: waterholes ringed by circles of herbivores, clusters of acacia trees sheltering families of elephants, rocky outcrops stalked by leopards and languid pools full of lumbering hippos.

THE TERROR OF TSAVO

Before you zip up the flap of your tent for the night, spare a thought for the workers who drove the Kenya–Uganda Railway through the grasslands of East Africa. During one perilous summer in 1898, an audacious pair of lions consumed more than 35 railway workers, creeping silently into camp at night, then vanishing into the night with hapless victims. The killing spree was finally ended by Lieutenant-Colonel John Henry Patterson, who recorded his slaying of the lions in his epic memoir, *The Man-Eaters of Tsavo*.

■ THE PERFECT GETAWAY

The first consideration when choosing a tented safari is deciding where to set up camp. As a rule, the more remote and inaccessible the location, the more impressive the wildlife. Many of Kenya's most spectacular tented camps are only accessible by light aircraft; if a main road runs past your tent, skittish gazelles will keep a wide berth. The good news is that you can find proper wilderness even at the budget end of the spectrum. Seek out a camp away from the park boundaries, with trees for cover and nearby waterholes. Endure a longer ride to camp if it gets you away from human activity and closer to the 'Big Five' must-see animals – lions, elephants, buffalo, leopards and rhinos.

The epicentre for budget tented safaris is the Maasai Mara, on the Kenya–Tanzania border. From July to October, millions of wildebeest, gazelles and zebras undertake the epic migration here from Tanzania's Serengeti National Park, trailed by predators who call them lunch. Migration season is also peak season for prices. If watching the pennies is the priority, choose the dry months or the even-cheaper rainy seasons. The animals are still out there, but with plenty of water to drink there's less incentive to come out into the open.

Or cast the net wider and seek out less-visited reserves, such as Amboseli National Park. Wherever you stay, days are focused on game drives and nature walks in hot pursuit of African wildlife, and evenings are filled with conversations about the best lion's kill and how to tell the difference between a kudu and a hartebeest. Keep a bird-life guide handy to identify Africa's most colourful residents flitting from tree to tree on the edge of your camp.

■ PLAN IT

Choose your optimum season (July to October for mass migrations; March to June and October to December for minimum prices). Start by flying to Nairobi, which has hundreds of safari operators. Standards vary from the spectacular to the shoddy; look for members of the Kenya Association of Tour Operators (KATO). For no-frills, bring your own tent to the Maasai-run Riverside Camp near Masaai Mara's Talek gate; more cash buys more comfort at the German-run Aruba Mara Camp nearby.

■ DETOUR

If a balloon safari is outside your price range, consider the epic views from the top of Mt Kilimanjaro. At 5895m, Africa's tallest mountain is one hell of a vantage point. A short hop across the Tanzanian border from the Maasai Mara, Kilimanjaro can be summited in seven days, with seven routes offering varying degrees of challenge. You don't need ropes and ice-axes, but this is a gruelling ascent, with an impressive reward – the chance to stand on a snow-covered summit, nearly 6km high, just 330km south of the equator.

OPENING SPREAD In Kenya's wet season most wildlife is harder to spot but you can't miss the elephants – or Mt Kilimanjaro. **ABOVE** Changing roles: Maasai tribesmen are now becoming safari guides and protectors of the park's endangered wildlife. **LEFT** A contemplative lion in the Maasai Mara.

DECKCHAIR

* ***Out of Africa*** (Isak Dinesen/Karen Blixen) Probably the definitive account of the colonial experience in East Africa; also adapted into an Oscar-winning film starring Meryl Streep.

* ***The Flame Trees of Thika*** (Elspeth Huxley) An essential memoir of a childhood on Kenya's coffee plantations.

* ***Whatever You Do, Don't Run*** (Peter Allison) Cautionary tales about African wildlife from a game-warden who has seen everything.

* ***Field Guide to African Wildlife*** (National Audubon Society) An excellent country-by-country guide to the wildlife of Africa.

* ***The Lunatic Express*** (Charles Miller) A history of the railway line that formed the lifeline of British-era Kenya.

* ***The Constant Gardener*** (John le Carré) Tragedy and corporate corruption unfold against an epic Kenyan backdrop in this literary thriller from the doyen of espionage writers.

CHIC AND CHEAP: ON A TUSCAN BUDGET

YOU DON'T NEED TO BREAK THE BANK TO ENJOY 'LA BELLA VITA' IN TUSCANY.
FROM SUN-DAPPLED HILLS AND SOME OF THE WORLD'S GREATEST ART TO
FRESH, RUSTIC FOOD AND WINE, HERE THE BEST THINGS IN LIFE CAN BE,
WELL, ALMOST FREE.

190

Saturday morning in Siena and the sunlight sweeps the contours of Il
Campo's old brick pavement. Here, Italians in designer shades sip their third
cappuccino of the day and flick through the newspapers, seemingly oblivious
to the medieval Palazzo Publico and its 14th-century bell tower, the Torre del
Mangia. Although breakfast was only two hours ago, you devour a tiramisu
ice-cream cone from a nearby gelateria as the Duomo's church bells chime.

Tuscany is all about indulgence. This celebrated region in the northwest
of Italy has a reputation for offering some of the best pasta, pizza, steak and
wine in Europe. It's a feast for the eyes too: cypresses line country roads
like Roman pillars and old farmhouses overlook valleys of sloping vineyards
that unfold towards the horizon. Florence, the region's capital and home to
Michelangelo's *David*, is itself a work of art. Red-roofed houses, Renaissance
statues and cathedral spires adorn both sides of the glistening River Arno.
Ancient cities like Siena, Arezzo and Lucca rise above the morning mist, each
one a mysterious world of its own.

An easy and affordable way to explore a city like Lucca is on two wheels. Hire
a bicycle for a day from the Puntobici bike shop near the Piazza Verdi and cycle
Lucca's 5km city walls that encircle the Old Town, now a parkland trail with
grass lawns, picnic tables and various species of trees. While riding along the
ramparts, soak in the sights of the Apuan Alps and the rooftops of basilica-form
churches, without pausing too long to notice there are no railings separating
you from a 12m drop to the ground. After working up an appetite, you'll enjoy a
pranzo di lavaro (a cheap 'working lunch') at a local cafe such as Trattoria Gigi,
followed by a shot of espresso. Tuscany is only as expensive as you make it –
and enjoying its ancient cities and romantic landscapes won't cost the earth.

ESSENTIAL EXPERIENCES

* ✳ **Sampling wines along the 'vineyard-hopping' S222 Route in Chianti.**
* ✳ Cycling the city walls of Lucca, complete with lush parklands and vantage points.
* ✳ **Staring in awe at the sheer perfection of Michelangelo's *David* at the Galleria della Accademia in Florence – it makes other sculptures look like, well, stone.**
* ✳ Tucking into a juicy *bistecca alla fiorentina* in the peaceful village of Panzano.
* ✳ **Climbing up the Duomo in Florence to gaze at the rooftops of this majestic Renaissance city.**
* ✳ Eating tiramisu icecream overlooking the bowl-shaped Il Campo Piazza in Siena.

LOCATION NORTHWEST ITALY | **BEST TIME OF YEAR** MAY TO SEPTEMBER | **IDEAL TIME COMMITMENT** ONE TO TWO WEEKS
ESSENTIAL TIP SHOP AT LOCAL MARKETS FOR BEST-PRICED BREADS, CHEESE, HAM AND WINES | **BUDGET** $ | **PACK** A GOOD BOOK,
MAP AND CAMERA, BUT LEAVE SPACE FOR BOTTLES OF OLIVE OIL AND CHIANTI

PIAZZA OF PASSION

Thousands of Sienese cheer in unison, roars ricocheting off the Campo's walls, as a tornado of dust and colours flies past. Welcome to the Palio di Siena – annual horse races held on July 2 and August 16. Lasting just three laps (or 90 seconds), the Palio has the intense atmosphere of a Roman chariot race. Passions run high as the *contrades* (city districts) compete for the coveted Drappellone, a large painted canvas. If not fazed by crowds or the sight of horses falling, head to the Campo early, with the locals in their historical costumes, and watch the race for free.

■ THE PERFECT GETAWAY

Nothing prepares you for seeing Michelangelo's *David* 'in the flesh'. Walking slowly around the statue, the centrepiece of Florence's Galleria della Accademia, it's easy to become mesmerized by its detail...but this is just the beginning of your Tuscan love affair. In the Piazza della Signoria, Cellini's gruesome sculpture of Perseus holding Medusa's severed head seems to come to life. Nearby, you can spend many cheap hours wandering the galleries of the Uffizi Museum, a universe of art that includes Botticelli's dream-like *Birth of Venus*.

When your stomach tells you it's time to eat, stroll down the Via de' Macci to the farmers market and grab some bread and prosciutto before browsing the Mercato Centrale. South of here is the Duomo, a gothic domed cathedral: climb its 463 steps for a bird's-eye view of the city. Stay at a family-run B&B for a more intimate Florentine experience; the Relais del Duomo is one such gem.

After Florence, head down Route S222 to Siena and soak up the best of the Chianti wine district. Stop midway and rent a mountain bike in Greve to discover the area; ride up the hill to Verrazzano Castle and take a wine-tasting tour of its famous cellars.

In Siena, check into the Hotel Alma Domus. Part of an old monastery, its renovated rooms overlook the San Domenico Basilica. For dinner, tuck into spicy Sienese spaghetti or some wild boar at the Trattoria Papei behind the Palazzo Pubblico. While you're here, head to the Campo, one of Italy's great squares, then grab a combo museum ticket from the Museo Civico. South of Siena, end your Tuscan odyssey with a dip in the Petriolo Baths, natural hot springs in a woodland setting. Part of the Farma River, they're free to use and the soothing sulphuric water bubbles away at a pleasant 42°C. Who needs a fortune to live the good life?

DECKCHAIR

* ❋ ***Under the Tuscan Sun*** (Frances Mayes) The most popular Tuscany memoir, in which an American divorcee renovates a dilapidated old house in Cortona.

* ❋ ***Too Much Tuscan Sun*** (Dario Castagno) A light-hearted take on Tuscan tourism by a local guide – an antidote to all those expat titles.

* ❋ ***A Room with a View*** (1985) Merchant Ivory adaptation of Forster's novel partly set in Florence, starring Helena Bonham Carter.

* ❋ ***War in Val D'Orcia*** (Iris Origo) Intimate diary by a woman who protected child refugees in her villa during WWII.

* ❋ ***A Thousand Days in Tuscany*** (Marlena de Blasi) A Venetian baker and an American chef move to Tuscany in this recipe-filled novel.

* ❋ ***Tea with Mussolini*** (1999) Zeffirelli's charming Florentine biopic stars Judi Dench and Maggie Smith.

■ PLAN IT

Florence is Tuscany's transport hub, with its airport offering connections to European capitals, and Santa Maria Novella railway station, linked to Rome (90 minutes) or Milan (1¾ hours) by high-speed, low-cost trains. Reasonably priced B&Bs are found on the outskirts of Florence and Siena; more remote towns such as Castellina in Chianti offer cheaper accommodation. Most of the large towns have tourist offices and are easy to explore on foot, but for the rest of Tuscany, the only way to get around is by hire car or riding a bicycle.

■ DETOUR

Tuscany doesn't usually conjure up images of sandy beaches, moored fishing boats and clear blue waters, but that's a description of Isola d'Elba, the largest island in the Tuscan Archipelago. Overrun with day-trippers in the summer, out-of-season Elba is a hiker's heaven. Trails cover the whole island, passing Etruscan forts and tiny Catholic churches, plus scuba divers can check out a German aircraft wreck in the Tyrrhenian Sea. Napoleon was exiled here in 1814: both of his homes are open to visitors. Ferries leave from Piombino on the mainland and arrive at Portoferraio, a bustling ancient town full of charm outside of August, the peak tourist month.

OPENING SPREAD Stand in Siena's Piazza del Campo for the best view of the Palio. **ABOVE** The reconstructed Michelangelo room in Florence's Uffizi gallery opened in 2013; his *Doni Tondo* painting survives in its original round frame. **BELOW** Florence's skyline.

MEAT THE BUTCHER

Billed as the best meat outside of Argentina, the *bistecca alla fiorentina* (Florentine steak) is a T-bone or porterhouse steak, grilled over a charcoal fire. But one of the best places to sample this mighty meat is not in Florence but further south in the small village of Panzano, Chianti, home to eccentric butcher Dario Cecchini. Aside from the signature steak, from Monday to Saturday Dario also serves his take on fast food, a half-pound beef burger with sides. Diners at Antica Macelleria Cecchini are free to bring their own wine and chat to other guests sitting at the long communal table.

HAWAII ON A DIME

AMERICA'S ISLAND GETAWAY DOESN'T HAVE TO BE EXPENSIVE – FROM SHRIMP TRUCK LUNCHES TO HOURS OF BEACHSIDE IDYLL AND ENCOUNTERS WITH THE LOCALS ON 'THE BUS', IT'S POSSIBLE TO DO O'AHU ON LITTLE MORE THAN SPARE CHANGE.

194

The guy across the aisle looks like Nick Nolte. Not the polished Nick Nolte from films, but the Nick Nolte from that infamous drunken mug shot – the one with the Hawaiian shirt and the leathery, sun-creased skin, the electric-shock hair and the dazed expression. His lookalike glances up now, locks eyes and breaks into a lopsided smile: 'What's happenin', man?'

You meet your fair share of characters – friendly ones, too – on 'The Bus', O'ahu's sole form of public transport and the saviour of budget travellers. It's also popular with the occasional frazzled local, which is why Nick Nolte's doppelgänger is sitting red-eyed across the way. He's on his way to the North Shore, the same as everyone else on board.

O'ahu might conjure up images of fancy hotels and overpriced mai tais, but Hawaii's main island doesn't have to be an expensive destination. Start with transport. Most visitors with cash to splash hire a car if they want to get around, but a mere US$25 buys you four days of sights, sounds and local characters on The Bus. Surfing Nick Nolte is just one of them.

It's people like him that you'll remember after taking a budget tour of O'ahu, more so than the beaches and the palm trees and the cheap drinks. There are plenty of characters, for instance, down at Ono Hawaiian Food, one of Honolulu's most authentic restaurants. The establishment's name, if you added a comma, would be a summation of most visitors' feelings towards the local cuisine, but this is good stuff. The chef eats his dinner in the dining room with the rest of the punters, and with dishes like *laulau, haupia, pipikaula* and *naau puaa*, you know you're eating Hawaiian food unadulterated for tourist taste buds. It's different and delicious. Wipe your plate clean, pay the bill, and jump back on The Bus with its whacked-out celebrity lookalikes. It's time for another adventure.

ESSENTIAL EXPERIENCES

* **Eating fried seafood while sitting in the sun at one of the North Shore's famous shrimp trucks.**

* Drinking rum cocktails at La Mariana Sailing Club, one of Hawaii's last authentic tiki bars.

* **Going Hawaiian-shirt shopping at Bailey's Antiques, which has thousands upon thousands of colourful garments, ranging from US$5 to US$5000.**

* Sampling true local cuisine at Ono Hawaiian Food in Waikiki.

* **Learning to play the ukulele for free at Ukulele Puapua, a shop that's part of the Sheraton in Waikiki.**

* Getting a 'shave ice' from Matsumoto – it's just crushed ice and sugary syrup, but it's worth queuing up for.

LOCATION O'AHU, HAWAII, USA | **BEST TIME OF YEAR** YEAR-ROUND | **IDEAL TIME COMMITMENT** ONE WEEK
ESSENTIAL TIP DON'T EXPECT TO SEE THE FAMED BIG WAVES IN SUMMER; EVEN WAIMEA BAY IS LIKELY TO BE DEAD FLAT
BUDGET $ | **PACK** BOARDSHORTS AND SUNSCREEN – THAT'S IT

ALOHA, GOOD-LOOKING!

It's not just a tourist thing – Hawaiians really do love their brightly coloured, patterned shirts, referred to as 'aloha shirts'. The gaudy garments were popularised in the 1930s by a local called Ellery Chun, who turned his Chinese grocery store into a producer of ridiculously colourful tops and coined the popular term. Pretty soon the local surfers started buying aloha shirts, and then the tourists, and before Chun knew it he had a full-scale craze on his hands. That craze has lasted some 80-odd years – vintage aloha shirts now sell for as much as US$5000, and there's a thriving trade in new and secondhand numbers.

HOLLYWOOD IN HAWAII

It's the question so often asked in Hawaii: where did
they shoot *Lost*? And what about *Jurassic Park*? Good
news is the filming locations are easy to scout out if
you know where you're looking. The initial plane crash
in *Lost* and much of the first season of the hit TV show
were filmed at Mokuleʻia Beach on the North Shore
of Oʻahu. Nearby is Police Beach, where the bulk of
season two was shot. The Kaʻaʻawa Valley, meanwhile,
has been in more movies than Tom Cruise. OK, not
quite. But a large amount of *Jurassic Park* was shot
there, as well as scenes from *50 First Dates, Pearl
Harbor, Mighty Joe Young,* and plenty from *Lost*.

■ THE PERFECT GETAWAY

The cliché that the best things in life are free rings true in O'ahu. Take ukulele lessons: a tutorial in the quintessential Hawaiian instrument costs nothing at Ukulele Puapua, a store in Waikiki. There you can spend an hour learning the basics – how to hold, how to strum – with no pressure to buy. Of course, once you realise your own awesomeness you might not need any more encouragement.

Another free activity is a trip to Bailey's Antiques, which is ostensibly a shop, but feels more like a museum dedicated to 'aloha shirts' and kitsch souvenirs. The store bulges with vintage and new shirts and knick-knacks. It's in a great position, too – across the street you'll find Ono Hawaiian Food, the perfect lunch stop for traditional island cuisine.

For a day away from the touristy buzz of Waikiki, jump on The Bus to the old town of Hale'iwa on the North Shore. This is where the famous shrimp trucks such as Macky's, dish up huge plates of fried shrimp for about US$12. It's all pretty rough-and-ready – collect your plastic plate and then take a seat at a wooden bench. Want dessert? Just down the road you'll find Matsumoto's, where locals queue down the street for the island's best shave ice (crushed ice with syrup). The North Shore's best attraction, of course, is at Waimea Bay. There you won't pay a cent to just lie on the sand and watch the world go by.

There is one final stop on your shoestring tour of Hawaii: the Hideaway Bar in Waikiki. One of Honolulu's few 'dive' bars, what the Hideaway lacks in fancy decor it certainly makes up for in drinks prices, with beers during 'power hour' going for a buck each. It mightn't be beachy or kitsch, but it sure is affordable.

■ PLAN IT

Winter (November to April) is the perfect time to visit O'ahu for big-wave viewing. If lying on the sand is more your thing, Hawaii is a year-round destination. Los Angeles and Sydney provide the easiest access but flights also operate from Japan and Korea. Honolulu Airport is a short bus transfer from Waikiki, where most hostels and hotels are located, or a two-hour bus ride to the less touristy North Shore, where accommodation is harder to come by in November or December.

■ DETOUR

Hawaii doesn't have to be done on a strict budget. Start with lunch at Alan Wong's for Hawaiian haute cuisine, where traditional dishes are reinterpreted with serious skill. Next, pick up your rented convertible and go for a lap around the island before parking it at Halekulani Resort, one of Waikiki's finest and therefore most expensive beachfront hotels. To finish things off, grab a cocktail and a bite to eat at Nobu, every celebrity's favourite Honolulu watering hole.

OPENING SPREAD The ukulele is thought to date back to the work of Portuguese cabinet-makers who had settled on Hawaii in the 19th century. **ABOVE** Surfing Waimea Bay: only for the brave. **LEFT** Spot a velociraptor? The area of O'ahu where *Jurassic Park* was shot.

DECKCHAIR

* **The Descendants** (2011) The scenery in this George Clooney film will have you booking the next flight over.

* **Big Wednesday** (1978) Granted, it's set in California, but this cult film's most important scenes – the ones in the huge surf – were shot in Hawaii, mostly around Waimea Bay.

* **Point Break** (1991) Another cult surf classic, featuring Keanu Reeves in all his Johnny Utah glory.

* **Honolulu** (Alan Brennert) This 20th-century tale of a Korean immigrant in Hawaii's capital provides a window into a surprisingly complex culture.

* **Diamond Head** (Charles Knief) This murder mystery set among the palm trees of the Aloha State makes perfect airplane reading.

* **Hawaii** (James Michener) Michener's novel tackles Hawaiian history, from the volcanic formation of the islands onwards. Epic.

CAMEL CARAVANS IN RAJASTHAN

PEACE AND QUIET IS IN SHORT SUPPLY IN FRENETIC INDIA. TO ESCAPE THE CACOPHONY, LOOK NO FURTHER THAN JAISALMER, THE LEAPING-OFF POINT FOR THE STILL SERENITY OF THE THAR DESERT.

198

At first light, the fortress city of Jaisalmer is a timeless tableau straight out of Arabian Nights. Atop the city walls, devout Brahmins tip offerings of water and petals from polished brass jugs. Women in crimson saris create sudden flashes of colour as they dart through the winding alleyways that weave a cats' cradle through the old city.

But the fort is just the prelude to the greater adventure of roaming onto the bone-dry plain that sprawls west towards Pakistan. Rolling from thorny scrub to scalloped dunes, the Thar Desert is punctuated by villages, rocky outcrops and ruins. On a camel safari through this rugged terrain, the main sounds to break the silence are the stomach rumbles of your single-humped beast of burden, and the jangle of the ankle bells worn by children in the villages you pass.

Led by guides with moustaches almost as wide as their turbans, a safari can last as long as you choose to pay for. The rate-determining factor for most is the discomfort of camel-back riding; getting seasick on a ship of the desert is not unheard of. Nevertheless, it pays to persevere – with three days or more, you can roam beyond the tourist haunts to forgotten outposts and ghost villages, abandoned centuries ago by villagers who could no longer tolerate the excesses of the local maharajas. If djinns ever existed, this is where they would be found.

India is better known for honking horns than peace and tranquillity, but camping beneath the stars – with soft sand for a mattress and the fireside songs of camel drivers as a lullaby – will whisk you back to the centuries before the internal-combustion engine bought cacophony to the subcontinent. As darkness falls, constellations radiate in the sky and shooting stars trace brief trails across the wash of the Milky Way. Wind, sand and stars: who could ask for more?

ESSENTIAL EXPERIENCES

* **Sleeping beneath the stars:** with skies this clear and light-pollution-free, the constellations are as clear as neon signs.

* Listening to desert melodies: evenings often end with impromptu after-dinner concerts, complete with beating tablas and wailing *shennai* horns.

* **Enjoying sand-dune sunsets:** while your guides unsaddle the camels and set up camp, you'll be treated to a free light show on the horizon.

* Tucking into campfire curries: relive the days of the great spice caravans as you sit down to a desert dinner with your guides.

LOCATION JAISALMER, RAJASTHAN, INDIA | **BEST TIME OF YEAR** SEPTEMBER TO MARCH | **IDEAL TIME COMMITMENT** THREE DAYS TO A WEEK | **ESSENTIAL TIP** DRESS FOR CAMEL RIDING – WEAR LOOSE-FITTING COTTON CLOTHING, SUPPORTIVE UNDERWEAR AND A WIDE BRIMMED HAT OR FLOWING SCARF TO KEEP OFF THE SUN | **BUDGET** $–$$ | **PACK** SUNSCREEN, A WATER BOTTLE, MOSQUITO REPELLENT AND A TORCH FOR NIGHT-TIME TOILET TRIPS

IF YOU LIKE CAMELS...

Jaisalmer isn't the only place in India where you can get the hump. In the high-altitude deserts of Ladakh, the two-humped Bactrian camel is king. With the decline of the Silk Route, cargos of salt, silk and spices have been replaced by adventurous travellers, exploring the rugged valleys north of Leh. Board your even-toed ungulate at Hunder (Hundur) and follow the glacier-carved Nubra Valley past villages of mud-brick houses and towering Buddhist monasteries to the hot springs at Panamik – the perfect end-point after days rolling in the saddle.

■ THE PERFECT GETAWAY

Choosing a camel safari is a little like choosing a camel. It pays to investigate several, finding out exactly what each has to offer, before handing over your rupees. Hordes of travellers make the overnight hop to the Sam sand dunes, but this is more a packaged 'desert experience' than a proper desert immersion. To feel the flow of the desert sands, you need to leave civilisation behind.

Luckily, this is a bespoke trip, so it's easy to assemble an itinerary that fulfils the Arabian Nights fantasy. While parched, the Thar Desert is far from empty. Tiny mud-brick villages are scattered across the countryside, and dotted here and there are the ruins of vanished civilisations. To the southwest, the ancient village of Kuldhara was abandoned to the winds in the 18th century, after a bitter falling out between the Paliwal Brahmins and the Rajput rulers of Jaisalmer. Nearby the toppled fort of Khaba keeps guard over time-worn stones. To the northwest, beneath a surreal backdrop of wind turbines, the graceful cenotaphs of the rulers of Jaisalmer at Bada Bagh provide a home for scuttling lizards and dust devils.

To experience the peace of the desert, you'll have to forego certain creature comforts. Sleeping arrangements are bedrolls and blankets, and meals on safari are camping classics cooked on an open fire. Simple, pure-veg curries and hot-from-the-fire chapattis dominate the evening menu; the lavish breakfast buffet is likely to consist of eggs and sweet milky cups of chai tea.

No matter; in place of gastronomy, you'll have a taste of what life was like for the trade caravans that roamed across this arid landscape for centuries before geopolitics placed arbitrary obstacles like international borders in their path.

■ PLAN IT

Prime time is September to March, when daytime temperatures are less oven-like. Nights can be chilly from December to February, but safari operators provide blankets and dinner is cooked on an open campfire. Fly to Delhi, then ride the rails west to Jodhpur and on to Jaisalmer. It's easy to arrange a safari on arrival with local agents so don't rush; there's plenty to see in the fortress city. Ganesh Travels, Sahara Travels, Trotters and Adventure Travel Agency are reliable operators.

■ DETOUR

Most visitors make a beeline for Jaisalmer, but the desert is dotted with historic outposts. About 160km to the south, Barmer was founded in the 13th century as a lookout where local Rajput rulers kept a careful watch for marauders. Eventually that long-feared invasion did come, reducing the ancient city of Juna Barmer to a scattering of stones and silent temples. For an adventurous camel safari, take a week to drift south from Jaisalmer to Barmer, then rattle back to Jodhpur on the railway.

OPENING SPREAD A camel train in the Thar Desert. **ABOVE** Jaisalmer is famous for its beautifully carved *havelis* (mansions); many are now hotels, some at the luxury end of the spectrum, others offering a basic, sleep-on-the-rooftop-and-watch-the-stars sort of experience.

DECKCHAIR

* **Rajasthan** (Pauline van Lynden) Lush coffee-table tome capturing the vivid colours of Rajasthan.

* **Octopussy** (1983) Get into the Rajasthan mood with this classic James Bond movie, partially filmed in the lavish surrounds of Udaipur's Lake Palace.

* **Trishna** (2011) The story of Tess of the d'Urbervilles, transplanted to modern-day Rajasthan by director Michael Winterbottom.

* **Sonar Kella** (1974) A rare children's film from Satyajit Ray, with Jaisalmer as an atmospheric backdrop.

* **Road, Movie** (2009) A mobile cinema rattles across Rajasthan in an art-house movie that bombed in India but earned respect overseas.

* **One Thousand & One Nights** (authors unknown) The original text of *Arabian Nights,* first published in English in 1706.

FAMILY

JOIN THE REVOLUTION IN BOSTON

TAKE THE FAMILY TO BOSTON TO DISCOVER THE DARING AND DEFIANCE OF AMERICA'S FIERY FOREBEARS. JUST DON'T BE SURPRISED IF YOUR CHILDREN START TO MAKE DEMANDS LIKE 'GIVE ME LIBERTY OR GIVE ME DEATH!'

'Dump the tea!' shouts the rabble-rousing patriot, as he storms down the gangway to Griffin's Wharf.

'Into the sea!' responds the frenzied crowd, following close on his heels.

The raving mob has come straight from the meeting house at the Boston Tea Party Museum, where Sam Adams and other Sons of Liberty have been stirring up trouble. Cries of 'Boo!' and 'Fie!' can be heard when the rebels remind the assembled townsfolk of the injustices they have suffered at the hands of the British Crown. 'Huzzah!' rings forth when the decision is made to take a stand against taxation without representation.

The Boston Tea Party Museum is one of many destinations in Boston where children can immerse themselves in events that led to the birth of a nation, but also to experience the peril and passion the early patriots knew. As the city where the American Revolution started, Boston is a living history museum. You can hardly walk a step on her cobblestone sidewalks without stumbling over a historic spot. Tour guides don colonial dress and share their 'personal' experiences, imbuing the stories with the energy and excitement of revolution.

It may give parents pause to think that a visit to Boston will encourage their children to be rebellious. But the take-away message is that principles like freedom and fairness are more important than order and obedience. As John Adams so eloquently put it, 'Let justice be done though the heavens may fall.'

With that sentiment in mind, the patriots on Griffin's Wharf hoist crates of tea high over their heads and hurl them into Boston Harbor. The crowd cheers and clicks of cameras are heard all around. Then the enthusiastic participants pull the crates out of the water by their tethers, and throw them overboard again. 'Boston Harbor, a teapot tonight! Huzzah!'

ESSENTIAL EXPERIENCES

* **Donning a Mohawk disguise and tossing crates of tea into the harbour at the Boston Tea Party Ships & Museum.**

* Investigating the bronze plaque that commemorates the Boston Massacre, the first violent encounter of the American Revolution.

* **Spotting the iconic grasshopper weathervane that tops Faneuil Hall.**

* Sampling the sweet colonial treat known as 'Indian pudding' at Durgin Park in Faneuil Hall.

* **Discovering the headstone of Captain Daniel Malcom in Copp's Hill Burying Ground – his epitaph apparently provoked British soldiers to use the headstone for target practice.**

* Getting the bird's-eye view of Boston from high atop the Bunker Hill Monument.

LOCATION BOSTON, MASSACHUSETTS, USA | **BEST TIME OF YEAR** APRIL TO OCTOBER | **TIME COMMITMENT** TWO DAYS
ESSENTIAL TIP MOST OF THE FREEDOM TRAIL SITES HAVE WEBSITES THAT OFFER GAMES, TRIVIA AND ACTIVITIES TO GET YOUR KIDS EXCITED ABOUT WHAT THEY WILL SEE | **BUDGET** $$ | **PACK** WALKING SHOES, RAIN GEAR AND SUNSCREEN

A TRUE SON OF LIBERTY

History has it that British soldiers in Boston
occasionally exhibited their aggression by taking aim
at headstones in local cemeteries. They were, perhaps,
particularly irked by one Daniel Malcom, whose final
resting place is in Copp's Hill Burying Ground. Malcom's
epitaph calls him 'A true son of Liberty...an Enemy to
oppression and one of the foremost in opposing the
Revenue Acts on America.' The headstone is marred
by pockmarks, apparently caused by muskets shot at
close range. Not much is known about this great patriot
Daniel Malcom, except that he was a local merchant
who was arrested for smuggling 60 kegs of wine and
brandy into Boston. True Son of Liberty, indeed.

INDEPENDENCE DAY

Encircled by cobblestones, the Boston Massacre site marks the spot where the first blood was shed for American Independence. On 5 March 1770, an angry mob of colonists swarmed the British soldiers guarding the State House. About 40 protesters hurled insults, snowballs and rocks. Thus provoked, the soldiers fired into the crowd and killed five townspeople. The incident sparked enormous anti-British sentiment; Paul Revere fanned the flames by widely disseminating an engraving that depicted the scene as an unmitigated slaughter. Interestingly, John Adams and Josiah Quincy defended the accused soldiers in court, and seven of the nine were acquitted.

THE PERFECT GETAWAY

Boston isn't called the Cradle of Liberty for nothing. To see where the action went down, follow the Freedom Trail. This 4km walking path winds around the city centre, connecting 16 of the most significant spots. Your children can download an activity-packed Junior Ranger Activity Book (or pick one up from the visitor centre in Faneuil Hall) before starting out. The Freedom Trail is a lot to take in, especially for the younger set, so stick to the highlights. And if things start to fall apart, the Boston Common – America's oldest public park – has a huge playscape, a spray pool and plenty of wide open spaces where kids can run free.

The Old South Meeting House is the location of the rally that led to the Boston Tea Party. Listen to a re-enactment and let your kids explore the building on a scavenger hunt. For years, Faneuil Hall and Quincy Market were the community's market place – and they still are, with shops, restaurants and street performers. Visiting them is less of a history lesson and more of a lunch break. Durgin Park is an atmospheric option for old-fashioned Boston fare, like roast beef or fish cakes.

After lunch, stroll to Long Wharf and catch the ferry to Charlestown, on the Charles River's north bank. It will drop you at Pier 3, near the USS *Constitution*. The country's oldest warship, it was launched during the War of 1812. Today, you can take a tour of its decks for a glimpse of life at sea. Your kids can try their hands at firing a cannon or furling a sail at the museum. If they still have energy, head to the Bunker Hill Monument. The young and spry can end their tour by climbing 294 steps to the top of the obelisk for a 360-degree vista of Boston.

PLAN IT

Boston is a straightforward escape. Logan International Airport is easy to reach by public transport. Accommodation tends to be pricey, but options are plentiful so it's often possible to score high-quality, centrally located hotels for a bargain online. Many companies offer guided tours of the Freedom Trail, some of which are designed for children: try National Park Service, Boston by Foot and Freedom Trail Foundation.

DETOUR

When your kids are historied out, explore Boston's connection to the sea. The New England Aquarium (NEAQ) is home to 600 species of sea creatures, from ethereal jellyfish to playful penguins. Highlights include an outdoor marine mammal exhibit, home to some charismatic fur seals, and the Shark & Ray Touch Tank, where your kids can dip a hand in and feel the silky-smooth skin of the sea creatures sliding past. NEAQ also takes whale-watching cruises out to Stellwagen Bank, a rich feeding ground for whales, dolphins and sea birds.

OPENING SPREAD The battle of Bunker Hill, part of the Siege of Boston, took place on 17 June, 1775; re-enactors commemorate the day. **ABOVE** Once polluted, the harbour is now clean enough for fishing and even swimming. **LEFT** The USS *Constitution*, nicknamed 'Old Ironsides', was built in Boston.

DECKCHAIR

* ***Make Way for Ducklings*** (Robert McCloskey) This classic describes the adventures of a mother duck and her ducklings in Boston.

* ***Willow's Walkabout*** (Sheila S Cunningham) An Australian wallaby escapes from the zoo and explores Boston.

* ***Paul Revere's Ride*** (Henry Wadsworth Longfellow, Ted Rand) Longfellow's famous poem is dramatised by Rand's vivid illustrations, making it a perfect introduction for children.

* ***Sam the Minuteman and George the Drummer Boy*** (Nathaniel Benchley) Chronicle of the Revolutionary War from the point of view of a colonial boy and a British boy, respectively.

* ***Johnny Tremain*** (Esther Hoskins Forbes) Follow a colonial-era teenager as he is swept up in the excitement of the Boston Tea Party.

* ***George vs George*** (Rosalyn Schanzer) Tells both sides of the story, with great illustrations and text.

GO WILD IN COSTA RICA

EXPLORE YOUR FAMILY'S WILD SIDE ON A COSTA RICAN ADVENTURE, WHERE IT'S POSSIBLE TO SEE A VOLCANO, HEAR HOWLER MONKEYS SCREECHING IN THE CLOUD FOREST, AND SURF WARM BLUE WATERS, ALL IN THE SAME DAY.

The sound of cicadas fills the forest like a screeching jet engine. You step over a dark trail of leafcutter ants carrying triangles of leaves over a snake-like tree root that's invaded the path. One of the many tall trees above your head rustles and you look up to see a troop of white-faced monkeys eating fruit. A monkey catches your gaze, then turns quickly to run up the branch, a baby clinging to her back. Your kid points at her, with an expression of pure awe.

Welcome to Costa Rica, arguably the easiest place to see wildlife in the Americas. But the nature-in-all-its-glory adventure doesn't end here. The same day you explore that forest you may have also visited a live volcano, and the Pacific coast with its sandy beaches and surfable waves could be steps away. As one of the safest and more developed countries in the region, Costa Rica is easy to get around; if you plan it right, you won't have any car trips longer than three hours. There are thrills for every age: soft beaches for tots, easy walks with lots of animals for kids, more-adventurous jaunts and surfing for tweens, and nightlife and adrenalin-charged activities (from rafting to zip-lining) for teenagers.

While almost anywhere in Costa Rica is good for family travel, the northwest part of the country and the central Pacific coast is easy to get to from the capital, San José, and offers tons of variety in a condensed space. In this exhilarating tropical playland you can explore Arenal's perfectly shaped volcanic cone and the surrounding Jurassic jungle before heading up to Monteverde for misty cloud forests filled with bright-coloured birds, outrageously large insects and weird animals, like nocturnal, prehensile-tailed porcupines. Then head to the coast for tall, humid jungles that hide sloths, snakes and coatis. Look down from river bridges to see colossal crocodiles bathing in the sun or spend a day at the beach learning to surf in gentle waves. And expect plenty more expressions of awe.

ESSENTIAL EXPERIENCES

* **Hearing the dinosaur-like call of scarlet macaws before watching them land in a flash of brilliant red on a tree branch at sunset.**

* Gliding on a gentle wave while warm ocean water lightly sprays your face.

* **Feeling the mist of a 40ft waterfall before seeing it post-descent from the Arenal Observatory Lodge and its volcano views.**

* Gaining exhilarating speed as you zip-line through the myriad greens of the rainforest canopy.

* **Searching for critters in the mists of Monteverde's Middle Earth-like cloud forests.**

* Getting a touch of vertigo from your very solid bridge, while watching gargantuan sunbathing crocodiles in the river below.

LOCATION COSTA RICA, CENTRAL AMERICA | **BEST TIME OF YEAR** NOVEMBER TO APRIL | **IDEAL TIME COMMITMENT** TEN DAYS
ESSENTIAL TIP YOU CAN USE US DOLLARS ALMOST EVERYWHERE IN COSTA RICA | **BUDGET** $$ | **PACK** SWEATERS FOR CHILLY NIGHTS, BINOCULARS FOR WILDLIFE-WATCHING, INSECT REPELLENT

COFFEE CULTURE

Cool, highland mountains run down Costa Rica's interior and hold the country's often vast arabica coffee plantations. Become a coffee savant on a plantation tour in the Tarrazú province near Jacó or around Monteverde. Start by exploring the plants themselves, from sprout to mature, when the red fruit is picked by hand and gathered in baskets. Then enjoy the aromas while watching the roasting process and learning about the industry's history. At the end it's time to learn how to taste the coffee's nuances – which are only heightened by a view over the rows of plants surrounded by mist-covered jungles.

HIGH IN THE CANOPY

Click into the harness, hang on and whoooooooop! Zip-lining through the forest canopy in Arenal and Monteverde is a real adrenalin rush, offering another angle on the forests (and open to ages four and over). If hanging from a wire 200m up isn't your thing, don't despair: there are also open-air trams and suspension bridges that let you enjoy the serenity of the treetops. Will you see wildlife up here? Not much, but it's said that 90% of living organisms in the rainforest exist at this level. The beauty is in the details.

■ THE PERFECT GETAWAY

Get out of San José – fast – and go straight to Parque Nacional Volcán Arenal. The volcano has recently stopped spouting lava and the views here look like something out of a dinosaur-meets-unicorn fantasy novel. Walk or horseback-ride to waterfalls, explore the dark grey rubble of old lava flows, or windsurf, boat or fish the 85-sq-km volcanic lake. Meanwhile, trees with massive root buttresses hold troops of monkey comedians that will keep you laughing. See some of the world's most dangerous snakes and colourful frogs up close at the Arenal Eco Zoo.

Next, go to Monteverde for higher, mistier, lichen-draped forests with more critters. Take a walk along the family-friendly Bajo del Tigre trail to spot toucans and agoutis by day or hairy tarantulas hiding in their ground lairs at twilight. There are specialist educational zoos here for butterflies, frogs, bats and snakes that allow you to see and learn about your favourite animals.

Then it's time to descend from the clouds to the sunny, humid coast. Jacó is touristy yes, but it's a beachside town with enough sleeping and eating options to keep any family happy. Days can be spent exploring the nearby macaw-filled Parque Nacional Carara. If you haven't had enough animal and beach action, then Parque Nacional Manuel Antonio, about an hour down the coast from Jacó, is sure to deliver. Here, vine-covered trees harbouring sloths give way to coconut palms and white sands where you can swim in warm blue water until an animal exciting enough (a spiny-tailed iguana, maybe?) draws you out. Again, this park is no secret but it merits its popularity through its beauty and density of animal life. Even at its most crowded it still feels like the monkeys outnumber people.

■ PLAN IT

Fly into the Costa Rican capital of San José and rent a 4WD. Book your lodging well in advance if you'll be travelling during the peak months of December and January or June and July. The driest (and most popular) time to visit is November to April. Humpback whales migrate along the coast in September and October. Monteverde gets packed for the annual Monteverde Music Festival (includes jazz, Latin and classical artists), held on variable dates from January to early April.

■ DETOUR

If you're travelling in December or January, visit the Playa Hermosa Wildlife Sanctuary to watch baby Olive Ridley turtles dig out of their nests and flail their way to the sea. From July to early December you may be able to visit the sanctuary at night to watch mama turtles come to shore to lay eggs. Any time of year you can visit the hatchery and see the efforts to protect the species. Tour companies can charge up to US$100 per person for day trips but it's perfectly fine to just show up on your own.

OPENING SPREAD Manuel Antonio is the most popular national park in Costa Rica; continue south to Corcovado National Park for true wilderness. **ABOVE** More than a volcano: there are 850 bird species in Arenal National Park. **LEFT** Here come the monkeys: a family of white-faced capuchins.

DECKCHAIR

* **The Wildlife of Costa Rica: A Field Guide** (Zona Tropical Publications) Packable illustrated fauna guide.

* **The Old Patagonian Express: By Train Through the Americas** (Paul Theroux) Late 1970s train voyage includes Limón and Puntarenas.

* **The Umbrella** (Jan Brett) Story and detailed art of the Costa Rican cloud forest. Ages four to eight.

* **Nancy Drew: The Scarlet Macaw Scandal** (Carolyn Keene) Nancy and friends volunteer in Costa Rica and find they have a mystery on their hands.

* **The Divide** (Elizabeth Kay) A 13-year-old boy falls into a world of legendary creatures while vacationing with his family in Costa Rica. .

* **Spy Kids 2: Island of Lost Dreams** (2002) Filmed on location in Arenal and Manuel Antonio.

SADDLE UP IN BARCELONA

BARCELONA IS EPIC ON TWO WHEELS. SOAR UP TO THE SAGRADA FAMILIA, SQUEEZE THROUGH THE ALLEYS IN THE GOTHIC QUARTER AND PARK AND CHILL AT THE SEASIDE - THERE'S NO BETTER WAY FOR FAMILIES TO PAY HOMAGE TO THE CATALONIAN PORT THAN IN A TEAM OF FRIENDLY BICYCLES.

210

Sitting in Parc Guell, on Gaudí's incredible serpentine mosaic bench, you'll look down at the panorama of Barcelona with the glittering Mediterranean beyond. Within 20 minutes, you're chewing pizza in the Barri Gótic (Gothic Quarter), and a short while later, eating ice cream on a baking beach.

And all of this can be done without stepping on a bus or a train, for Barcelona is becoming one of Europe's most cycle-friendly cities for families. Rent from one of its growing numbers of bicycle-hire shops and you'll soon be pedalling gingerly down those small, pedestrianised medieval streets, or in the summer sunshine of Barcelona's cycle-ways. Cycling in Barcelona particularly comes alive on Sundays, when a bike gives you and your children the freedom of the city. Fuel up on a chocolate croissant at a cafe in the hip El Born district, before pedalling across Ciutadela Park to Barcelona's old fishing quarter, Barceloneta, to witness one of Europe's great weekly *paseos*. On one side the area has urban beach; on the other, the dramatic architecture for which the city is renowned; in between, you'll find yourself part of an endless stream of walkers, roller-bladers and cyclists.

In recent years, Barcelona's administration has done much to promote cycling. Good news, as there's something about the city's pace, the sunshine, the slow traffic and child-friendly restaurants and museums that works well on wheels. Flanked by hills like Montjuïc (the fit are welcome to try), downtown Barcelona is mostly flat, an elegant mix of bisecting boulevards behind which run tangled medieval alleys. There's a coastline, a few beaches, myriad sights and museums, tapas bars everywhere and the most vivid street life in Europe.

By bike you can cover the sights more rapidly – and have a great time doing so. As Barcelona visitor Ernest Hemingway once put it, 'you have no such accurate remembrance of country you have driven through as you gain by riding a bicycle.'

ESSENTIAL EXPERIENCES

* **Witnessing some of Picasso's greatest paintings in an elegant palace.**

* Walking to Joan Miró's Foundation at Montjuïc hill, where great views join the modern master's work.

* **Browsing at La Boqueria, the colourful food market in the Laval district.**

* Posing as Lionel Messi at Camp Nou stadium & museum, Barça FC's stadium and museum.

* **Enjoying the cool, dark corners of La Seu Cathedral.**

* Strolling the white walkways at MACBA – the Musem of Contemporary Art of Barcelona – a dramatic, Richard Meier–designed building.

* **Cycling through Parc de la Ciutadella, Barcelona's most elegant park.**

* Soaring up the Sagrada Família. Gaudí's vertiginous masterpiece is scheduled to be completed in 2026. Finally.

LOCATION BARCELONA, SPAIN | **BEST TIME OF YEAR** HIGH SUMMER IS HOT BUT WITH LESS TRAFFIC | **IDEAL TIME COMMITMENT** ONE WEEK | **ESSENTIAL TIP** WATCH OUT FOR THIEVES; BARCELONA'S GREAT DRAWBACK IS ITS ROBBERY | **BUDGET** $$ **PACK** CLOTHES THAT ARE PICKPOCKET PROOF

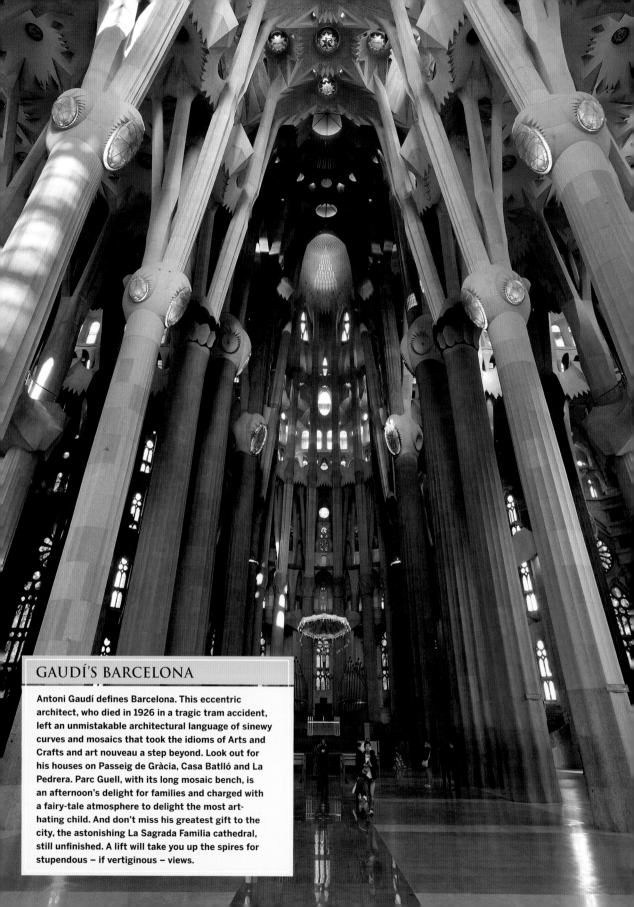

GAUDÍ'S BARCELONA

Antoni Gaudí defines Barcelona. This eccentric architect, who died in 1926 in a tragic tram accident, left an unmistakable architectural language of sinewy curves and mosaics that took the idioms of Arts and Crafts and art nouveau a step beyond. Look out for his houses on Passeig de Gràcia, Casa Batlló and La Pedrera. Parc Guell, with its long mosaic bench, is an afternoon's delight for families and charged with a fairy-tale atmosphere to delight the most art-hating child. And don't miss his greatest gift to the city, the astonishing La Sagrada Familia cathedral, still unfinished. A lift will take you up the spires for stupendous – if vertiginous – views.

■ THE PERFECT GETAWAY

Barcelona has increasing numbers of bicycle hire shops, as well as guided bike tours offering circuits that take in sights like La Sagrada Família, Barceloneta Beach and Gaudí's buildings. Most start on La Rambla, the heart of the old city. This broad pedestrian boulevard carves a slice from Plaça de Catalunya and the early 20th-century Eixample district to the steamy docks and then to the beaches. Or go the other way along Barcelona's Passeig de Gràcia boulevard – look out for Antoni Gaudí's Casa Batlló – leading to the elegant Gràcia district.

On La Rambla, stop at the Boqueria market, take a coffee at a bar, and then edge into El Raval, the district made infamous by Jean Genet in *A Thief's Journal* (1949). Although gentrifying with hip cafes, its picturesque alleys can be rough, but on a bike you'll sail past the city's saltier characters. Here, visit the Museum of Contemporary Art; while you muse over avant-garde artworks, the children will enjoy the views and walkways. Crossing to the other side of La Ramblas, cycle the Barri Gòtic towards the grand La Ribera district through a grid of medieval streets, taking in sights such as the Picasso Museum, an exquisite display in a rambling old palace. Break out into the Plaça Nova to see La Seu Cathedral, then stop at the El Born district for a hot chocolate and *churros* (Spanish doughnuts).

Freewheel down to Barceloneta to hit Passeig Marítim – the seafront promenade and Barcelona's best ride. Later, return to one of Barceloneta's earthy restaurants, for a *flauta* (tall glass) of beer and some fried octopus at Can Maño on Carrer del Baluard or La Bombeta on Calle de la Maquinista, where the speciality is *bombas*, deep-fried balls of mashed potato and minced meat. Rich, yes – but earned.

■ PLAN IT

Summer is hot; most locals leave in August so it's good for cycling. Spring and autumn are conducive but prone to showers. There are countless bike hire and tour providers. Most visitors enter via El Prat airport. Transfer is easy by train, which connects with the Metro at Barcelona Sants (Estacio Sants), Passeig de Gràcia and Clot stations. An Aerobus alights at Plaça Espanya or Plaça de Catalunya.

■ DETOUR

If the children liked Picasso and Gaudí, they'll love the Teatre Museu Dalí in Figueres, 1½ hours from Barcelona. This shrine to the moustache-sporting surrealist Salvador Dalí is noticeable for its vivid red walls and the eggs on its parapet. It'll make you smile as soon as you see it. The museum contains a huge collection of artworks, including Dalí's assemblage made to look like Mae West. To add to the unsettling effect, the artist himself is buried in a crypt in the basement. If you've got time, press on to see Dalí's coastal house in Portlligat and his castle in Púbol, in the countryside.

OPENING SPREAD Looking out from Park Güell; Gaudí's mosaic of a sea serpent will appeal to young and old. **ABOVE (L)** There are 420 Bicing stations. **ABOVE (R)** The aquarium has an 80m-long underwater tunnel. **LEFT** Gaudí worked out how tree-like columns could support the Sagrada Familia's roof.

DECKCHAIR

* **Barça: A People's Passion** (Jimmy Burns) This history of the Barça football team is a great accompaniment to a visit to the stadium.

* **Barcelona** (Robert Hughes) The late Hughes' pungent prose capivates in this romp through Barcelona's history.

* **Homage to Catalonia** (George Orwell) Eyewitness background about the city's role in the Spanish civil war, and part of Orwell's political journey.

* **Homage to Barcelona** (Colm Tóibín) More homage, from the Irish novelist who lived in the city and produced this literate guide.

* **Vicky Cristina Barcelona** (2008) An artist is at the centre of a love triangle in this Woody Allen Spanish romp.

* **Barcelona** (1994) A gentle piece from US director Whit Stillman, where US boys meets Barcelona girls with mixed results.

NORTHLAND: NATURE'S THEME PARK

WITH LAIDBACK VILLAGES, FRIENDLY LOCAL WILDLIFE AND BEACHES SO CLEAN YOU COULD EAT YOUR LUNCH OFF THEM, NEW ZEALAND'S NORTHERN TIP IS A PARADISE FOR FAMILIES.

214

With a rhythmic *psssh* an emerald-green sea laps at a beach of golden sand. Kids dive off a raft moored some 20m offshore. Others start another day in New Zealand by sliding down a huge sand dune towards warm Pacific waters. At the end of the beach people are fishing off the wharf. All is quiet except for birdsong. Sound like paradise? Sure – so long as you call this idyll 'Northland'.

Northland is the northern region of New Zealand's North Island. It separates the Pacific Ocean from the Tasman Sea – they crash together at its tip, Cape Reinga – and this narrow, fertile terrain is a natural wonderland. In Northland, locals say, there is no need for Hobbit villages or roller coasters or bungee jumping or whatever else gets pushed as 'tourist attractions' in more southern parts of New Zealand. That's because this magic land is a natural playground, one without height restrictions, queues or junk-food vendors. That makes it a magnet for outdoors-loving families, who come here to lose themselves – or perhaps rediscover themselves – among beaches and forests, up rivers and down sand dunes.

There are few rules. You could spend the morning beachcombing for washed-up treasure on beaches such as Tapeka, in the Bay of Islands, or learn to surf at a sheltered break. When you're hungry, amble along to a fish-and-chip shop serving the freshest catch of the day. If the weather's wet, explore local history in the tiny town of Russell, New Zealand's first capital, or climb to the historic Maori *pa* (fortified village) at Kororipo.

After hours of play, happy sandy kids with that sun-blushed glow will be ready for an early night, leaving you free to reflect on the day's thrills and spills. Yes, Northland may be a long way from the rest of the world, but who said that getting to paradise would be easy?

ESSENTIAL EXPERIENCES

* **Paying homage to the ancient kauri giants of the Waipoua Forest – nothing can prepare you for these mighty trees.**

* Exploring colonial treasures in sweetly historic Russell, the small town that was once, briefly, New Zealand's capital.

* **Enjoying the magnificent, peaceful beaches of Matauri Bay, home to the Rainbow Warrior Memorial.**

* Delving into history and culture at the Waitangi Treaty Grounds, where New Zealand's founding document was signed, before claiming your own island paradise in the Bay of Islands.

* **Driving along Ninety Mile Beach – paying careful attention to tides! – and up to Cape Reinga and Spirit's Bay at the country's top.**

LOCATION NORTHLAND, NEW ZEALAND | **BEST TIME OF YEAR** SUMMER (DECEMBER TO APRIL) | **IDEAL TIME COMMITMENT** SEVEN TO 10 DAYS | **ESSENTIAL TIP** BUY LOCAL ARTISANAL PRODUCTS FROM THE COTTAGE INDUSTRIES SURROUNDING KERIKERI **BUDGET** $$ | **PACK** SUNSCREEN, HAT AND BEACH GEAR

THE KAURI FORESTS

Much of the northern part of the North Island was once covered in mixed forest. The king of the forest was the kauri (Agathis australis), the world's second-largest tree after California's sequoias. The kauri produce a beautiful timber and were valued by the Maori for their height (to build huge canoes), while Europeans realised they were perfect for furniture and house building. Northland's Waipoua Forest – preserved in 1952 after much public pressure – is home to three-quarters of the country's surviving kauri and the best place to see the remaining giants. Today, efforts are being made to grow new generations of the nation's native tree.

HISTORIC NORTHLAND

The site of the earliest settlements of both Maori and Europeans, Northland is unquestionably the birthplace of the nation. Maori legend holds that the great Polynesian explorer Kupe discovered Hokianga Harbour and encouraged his people to settle there. The fertile lands and warm climate meant European settlers also embraced this land. This lead to early conflicts between the British and Maori, with the likes of the mighty Maori warrior Hone Heke outwitting the British in battle and cutting down the flagpole at Russell four times. Maori pa (fortified village) sites and British colonial buildings still exist across Northland.

THE PERFECT GETAWAY

A good place to start exploring Northland is Hokianga Harbour. At Omapere – one of several small settlements around the harbour – you can take a boat to some superb dunes, rolling hills of sand that are perfect for tumbling down. (Or, if tumbling is best left to the kids, you can view the majestic landscape.) Driving south of Hokianga Harbour leads to Waipoua Forest. Among this vast native kauri forest – thankfully saved from the timber mills that gobbled up so much Kiwi forest across the 19th and early 20th century – towers Tāne Mahuta (Lord of the Forest), New Zealand's mightiest tree. Yet the forest is not simply this single totem: there are many giant trees here alongside much younger native forest.

Puketi Forest, which is a more dense and winding wilderness than Waipoua, offers a great way of imagining Aotearoa before humans settled here. Puketi is close to the historic town of Kerikeri; stop for coffee and cake before heading up the coast. Here, Northland quickly gets rural, with small Maori communities living along the shore. While the beaches are magnificent, a special place to stop is Matauri Bay. Driving off the main highway, follow an inland ridge before dropping down into the bay. Owned by the local Maori – so developers have been held at bay – Matauri Bay has a campsite and store, golden beaches and, atop a short, steep hill, a huge stone rainbow. This is the *Rainbow Warrior Memorial,* by Kerikeri sculptor Chris Booth, and marks the resting place of the Greenpeace ship (now a dive site offshore). Look out for other works by Booth, who has built sculptures out of local stone across Northland, in addition to the *Gateway* sculpture at the entrance to Albert Park in central Auckland.

PLAN IT

International flights land at Auckland; Northland is four hour's drive north. Kerikeri and the Bay of Islands are the main hubs – buses and planes leave Auckland for Kerikeri every day. Note that the local Maori communities do not wish to be treated as tourist spectacles. Northland is open year-round; while it's warmer in winter than the rest of New Zealand, even summer can bring rain.

DETOUR

Kawakawa. south of Paihia, is just an ordinary Kiwi town, but its public toilets are anything but. They were designed by Austrian-born artist Friedensreich Hundertwasser, who lived nearby from 1973 until his death in 2000. The most photographed toilets in NZ are typical Hundertwasser – lots of wavy lines decorated with ceramic mosaics, and with plants on the roof. Kawakawa's other claim to fame is the railway line running through the centre of the main street, on which you can take a spin, pulled by Gabriel the steam engine.

217

OPENING SPREAD New Zealand's kauri trees, whose ancestors first appeared 190 million years ago, live in mixed forests. **ABOVE** Matai Bay on the Karikari peninsula. **LEFT** Let's go surfing: several surf schools operate in Northland, helping youngsters gain confidence in and out of the water.

DECKCHAIR

* ❋ *Sweet As: Journeys in a New Zealand Summer* (Garth Cartwright) The London-based Kiwi author returns home to wander New Zealand.

* ❋ *Woven Stone: The Sculpture of Chris Booth* (Edward Lucie-Smith) Beautifully illustrated and informative book on Kerikeri's most famous son.

* ❋ *The Penguin History of New Zealand* (Michael King) King was New Zealand's foremost historian and this highly readable book offers up much information on Northland as a major player in the nation's colonial history.

* ❋ *Kin of Place: Essays on Twenty New Zealand Writers* (CK Stead) Stead, one of the country's leading novelists and academics, meditates on leading Kiwi fiction writers.

* ❋ *The Scarecrow* (Ronald Hugh Morrieson) Set in a small town, this brilliant coming-of-age murder mystery is true Kiwi gothic.

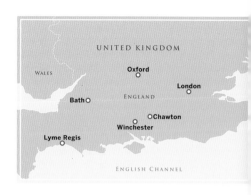

ON HAMPSHIRE'S JANE AUSTEN TRAIL

FOR FAMILIES WHO LOVE A GOOD COSTUME DRAMA, THIS ROMP AROUND SOUTHERN ENGLAND IN THE FOOTSTEPS OF JANE AUSTEN AND HER GENTEEL CHARACTERS WILL REVEAL QUAINT VILLAGES, STATELY HOUSES AND STEAM TRAINS – ALL WITHIN A CARRIAGE RIDE OF LONDON.

'The rooms were lofty and handsome, and their furniture suitable to the fortune of its proprietor; but Elizabeth saw, with admiration of his taste, that it was neither gaudy nor uselessly fine...' That's how novelist Jane Austen describes Elizabeth Bennet's first impressions of Pemberley, the ancestral home of Elizabeth's love-hate antagonist, Mr Darcy. The book, of course, is *Pride and Prejudice,* a story that is more inescapable now than it was 200 years ago. It has long exercised the talents of location scouts and set dressers, who scour Britain's stately homes in their quest for the perfect Georgian drawing room.

But Jane Austen inhabited only a small corner of the country. She was born and lived for a large part of her life in Hampshire, and the southern county's simple pleasures informed her own tastes and her writing. Her birthplace of Steventon is just a 30-minute drive along lanes from the village of Chawton, where she lived from 1809 to 1817; her red-brick house here is open to the public. Stroll down to the other end of the village to check out Chawton House, whose library has one of country's finest repositories of women's literature.

Austen died aged just 41 in Winchester, where she is buried – together with numerous kings of Wessex from a pre-Union England – in one of Britain's more beautiful cathedrals (from the inside, especially). Make a stop at Alresford on the 30-minute drive from Chawton to Winchester; from here steam trains on the Watercress Line puff their way back to Alton during the summer months.

When outdoor scenes are required, location scouts turn first to Lacock village, just across the county border in Wiltshire, which, with its higgledy-piggledy timbered houses and 13th-century abbey, looks as if it has been teleported here from the Middle Ages. Now conserved by the National Trust, here you can follow activity trails around Lacock's abbey and grounds or channel Elizabeth and Darcy for a photoshoot in period costume.

ESSENTIAL EXPERIENCES

* **Perfecting your 19th-century mannerisms.**
* Stopping for lunch at a country pub; check the website of the Campaign for Real Ale (CAMRA) for recommendations.
* **Going to the seaside and reading an Austen novel on the shingly shore.**
* Being pulled by steam locomotive along the Watercress Line from Alresford to Alton.
* **Seeing where scenes from movie and TV versions of Austen's stories were shot.**
* Walking or riding part of the South Downs Way; there are viewpoints from Harting Hill onwards to the south.

LOCATION HAMPSHIRE, ENGLAND | **BEST TIME OF YEAR** MAY TO OCTOBER | **IDEAL TIME COMMITMENT** TWO TO THREE DAYS
ESSENTIAL TIP PLAN SUMMER ACTIVITIES AT NATIONAL TRUST PROPERTIES ONLINE | **BUDGET** $$ | **PACK** A WINDPROOF JACKET

PRIDE AND PREJUDICE

In 2013, the 200th anniversary of Jane Austen's most famous novel was celebrated. Of all 18th- and 19th-century England's great wave of novels – this was the genesis of the genre, in English at least – *Pride and Prejudice* has inspired the most film and TV adaptations, fan-lit and even mash-ups with zombies. Austen herself described the work as 'rather too light, and bright, and sparkling'. But for all the formal balls at Netherfield, the mannered chit-chat in drawing rooms and the will-they-won't-they love story, perhaps the secret to the book's appeal is that it has a bit of bite: there are satirical barbs hidden in the froth.

UP ON THE SOUTH DOWNS

Britain's newest national park is an undulating chalk
ridge reaching 160km from Winchester to Eastbourne
on the south coast and covering 1600 sq km. With a
highest point of 270m, and a topography rounded by
millions of years of wind and rain, the South Downs may
not have the height of Britain's more northern national
parks. But what they lack in drama they make up for
with a beguiling beauty in the soft light of a summer
dawn. The sun shoos away the mist in the ridge's green
folds and glints off the sea, visible from around halfway
along the South Downs Way, a long-distance path for
walkers and riders running the park's length.

THE PERFECT GETAWAY

This is an England far removed from the tourist honeypots of the Cotswolds or the Dales. But there's an honest charm to the Hampshire landscape. Creases of the chalky land, wooded with beech trees, are known as 'hangers'; you can follow this line of hills on the Hangers Way footpath through a countryside that inspired Jane Austen. Local naturalist Gilbert White, who lived nearby in Selborne 200 years ago, described the wild appearance of the sunken lanes around Chawton as being five metres below the level of the fields, with tangled roots and icicles cascading down their sides. Such rugged scenes, he noted, 'affright the ladies when they peep down into them from the paths above, and make timid horsemen shudder while they ride along them'.

But to see where scenes from Austen's stories have been filmed, you will have to venture out of the county. In Wiltshire, to the west, privately-owned Wilton House starred as Pemberley in the 2005 film of *Pride and Prejudice,* with Keira Knightley and Matthew Macfadyen as the sparring couple. The property, home of the Earl and Countess of Pembroke, also appeared in Ang Lee's 1995 adaptation of *Sense and Sensibility.* North of Hampshire, in affluent Berkshire, Basildon Park played Netherfield Hall in the 2005 *Pride and Prejudice.* Now a National Trust property, like Lacock village, it was restored by Lord and Lady Iliffe in the 1950s. Both properties are open to the public.

If you have the time to continue on Austen's trail, venture west to the spa city of Bath, where two of her novels were set. This beautiful Georgian city has Regency tea rooms aplenty in which to wrap up your jaunt.

PLAN IT

All the Austen sites are just two hours by train or car from London. For Chawton, take a train from London Waterloo to Alton. Winchester is also on a direct line out of Waterloo. Gatwick or Heathrow will be the most convenient airports. Trains from Europe arrive at London's King's Cross St Pancras terminal. For accommodation, go money-no-object luxe at the Four Seasons Hotel near Basingtoke, or mid-range at the Hotel du Vin in Winchester; there are also many family-friendly B&Bs in the area. Wilton House is open from May to September.

DETOUR

It was to England's south coast and its louche seaside resorts that Austen's more wayward characters fled. Copy them by escaping to Lyme Regis in Dorset. Its harbour wall, the Cobb, plays a part in *Persuasion* and John Fowles' novel *The French Lieutenant's Woman.* And if you're into food, Dorset is the county for you: TV chef Hugh Fearnley-Whittingstall hosts cookery courses at River Cottage HQ, near Axminster.

OPENING SPREAD Scenes from a love story: the drawing room at Basildon Park. **ABOVE (L)** Lacock Abbey and its village host events and activities for families during the summer. **ABOVE (R)** The front entrance of Winchester Cathedral. **LEFT** The South Downs National Park remains a working landscape.

DECKCHAIR

* **Pride and Prejudice** (2005) Keira Knightley purses her lips and a fresh-faced Matthew Macfadyen glowers in perhaps the most successful movie adaptation of Austen's classic.

* **A Natural History of Selborne** (Gilbert White) Ground-breaking account published in 1789 of a year in the life of this Hampshire village's fauna and flora by one of the world's original naturalists.

* **Persuasion** (Jane Austen) Jane Austen's final novel, *Persuasion* was written entirely at her Chawton house and set partly in Bath.

* **Bleak House** (Charles Dickens) For some, the Hampshire-born writer's greatest work, turning on the Jarndyce v Jarndyce lawsuit.

* **Watership Down** (1978) An animated film about rabbits: the real Watership Down is north of Winchester. Lots of rabbits still live there.

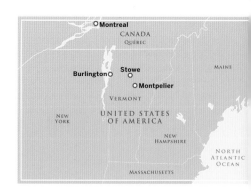

HIT THE SLOPES IN STOWE

HOME TO THE TALLEST PEAK IN VERMONT (MT MANSFIELD), SNOWY STOWE HAS A PICTURE-PERFECT VILLAGE WITH AN OLD-TIMEY GENERAL STORE AND A SURPRISING ARRAY OF GOOD PLACES TO EAT – CALL IT A SKI TOWN WITH BENEFITS.

222

A man sits on a stool playing a banjo and soulfully crooning American folk songs. Behind him, beyond a soaring glass wall, Mt Mansfield stands in all her snow-blanketed majesty. Families, couples and folks of all ages clomp around in ski boots, with red cheeks and beanie-mussed hair. Kids dart about, nibbling vegetable-topped flatbread and locally made cheeses while their parents sip wine by an oversized fireplace. Welcome to après-ski in the lobby of the grandiose Stowe Mountain Lodge, part of the Stowe Mountain Resort. It's quite the reward after a cold day's zooming downhill. The best part is that you don't have to be a hotel guest to indulge.

Lift tickets at Stowe are more expensive than at some nearby hills, but the seemingly endless array of terrain, from beginner runs to double black diamonds to backcountry trails, make for some of the best skiing and snowboarding in northeastern USA.

Stowe Mountain Resort first opened for business in 1934, making this one of the state's longest-running downhill ski operations. But Stowe village traces its roots back to the arrival of settlers in the late 18th century. Stowe is not one of those ski towns that proudly thumbs its nose at progress: here, among the '70s-style alpine inns and quaint B&Bs, you might find a new yoga studio or a wine shop specialising in Burgundy. And because of the diversity of things to see, do and eat, Stowe attracts folks looking for more than tons of white powder (though there is that). Some may not ski at all, preferring instead to loll about in one of the local resort spas, go snowshoeing or check out some contemporary art. Even the non-ski-bunnies in the family will never grow bored.

ESSENTIAL EXPERIENCES

* **Going (almost) vertical on a double black diamond trail at Stowe, Smugglers' Notch or Jay Peak for a hair-raising adrenalin rush.**

* Wandering quaint Stowe village for art, history and window-shopping.

* **Sipping a house-brewed beer and taking in the mountain views at the Trapp Family Lodge, founded in 1950 and still operated by the Von Trapp family of *Sound of Music* fame.**

* Strapping on snowshoes or cross-country skis and taking to the meandering Stowe Recreation Path or other local trail network.

* **Gorging on Vermont's bounty – be it artisanal cheese, maple-smoked bacon, organic apples or a full farm-to-table feast.**

LOCATION STOWE, VERMONT, USA | **BEST TIME OF YEAR** SKI SEASON IS NOVEMBER THROUGH APRIL, WITH IDEAL CONDITIONS DECEMBER THROUGH MARCH; LEAF-PEEPING IS MID-SEPTEMBER THROUGH LATE OCTOBER | **IDEAL TIME COMMITMENT** THREE TO FIVE DAYS | **ESSENTIAL TIP** FOR PRIME LEAF-PEEPING SEASON OR WINTER, BOOK HOTELS AND CAR RENTAL AS EARLY AS POSSIBLE **BUDGET** $$ | **PACK** CAMERA TO CAPTURE SNOWY VISTAS OR SPECTACULAR AUTUMN LEAVES

■ THE PERFECT GETAWAY

Pancakes: the perfect fuel for tackling a snow-covered mountain? The kids will say so. They'll delight in the thin, crêpe-like offerings at the wood-panelled Dutch Pancake Cafe, a Stowe institution inside the Grey Fox Inn. After breakfast, hit the slopes. Navigating the six distinct areas of Stowe Mountain Resort is a snap. Beginners and the littlest ones congregate on Toll House, the lowest bit of Mt Mansfield, which is flush with easy runs. Both Lower Spruce Peak, where the ski school is located, and Upper Spruce Peak are well suited to families. Steep Middle Mansfield has the goods for daredevils, while Mansfield Gondola and Mansfield Triple encompass trails for all levels. Those seeking more horizontal thrills can find them on the mountain's 45km of groomed cross-country trails; visit the information centre in Stowe village for maps of the area's many trail networks.

When not shredding moguls, set aside time to explore the area's bucolic surrounds. In the heart of Stowe village, check out the paraphernalia at the small-but-interesting Vermont Ski and Snowboard Museum, or stop into Shaw's General Store, opened in 1895, selling everything from thermal socks to books by local authors. Tucked away on the 2nd floor of the town library, which was built as a school in 1863, the serene Helen Day Art Center shows contemporary works by local and international artists.

Ice cream is the art form of local boys Ben Cohen and Jerry Greenfield, and in Vermont it's never too cold for the treat: the Ben & Jerry's factory in neighbouring Waterbury offers snowshoeing and ice-cream tours from late December to the end of March. Also in Waterbury, the Cold Hollow Cider Mill makes a fun pit stop. Watch the wooden 1920s press pulverise apples into cider, then pick up some jam and cider doughnuts for the road.

DECKCHAIR

❋ ***The Poetry of Robert Frost: The Collected Poems, Complete and Unabridged*** Four-time Pulitzer-winning Frost was the official poet laureate of Vermont.

❋ ***Ben and Jerry's Homemade Ice Cream and Dessert Book*** (Ben Cohen and Jerry Greenfield) The Vermont-based ice-cream barons offer up the secrets of their trade.

❋ ***Funny Farm*** (1988) A Chevy Chase comedy about what happens when a couple of New Yorkers move to country Vermont.

❋ ***The Secret History*** (Donna Tartt) This tale of murder at an elite Vermont liberal arts college is a dark and brooding page-turner.

❋ ***Phish: The Biography*** (Parke Puterbaugh) Follow Phish from humble beginnings at the University of Vermont to jam-band superstardom.

❋ ***The Trouble with Harry*** (1955) Alfred Hitchcock paints a loving portrait of quirky, small-town Vermont in this black comedy.

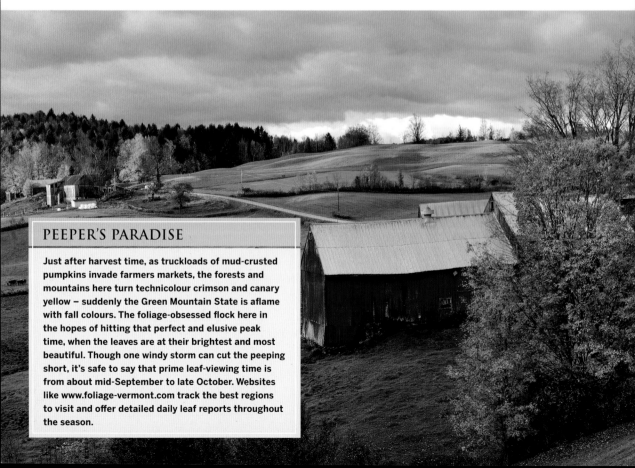

PEEPER'S PARADISE

Just after harvest time, as truckloads of mud-crusted pumpkins invade farmers markets, the forests and mountains here turn technicolour crimson and canary yellow – suddenly the Green Mountain State is aflame with fall colours. The foliage-obsessed flock here in the hopes of hitting that perfect and elusive peak time, when the leaves are at their brightest and most beautiful. Though one windy storm can cut the peeping short, it's safe to say that prime leaf-viewing time is from about mid-September to late October. Websites like www.foliage-vermont.com track the best regions to visit and offer detailed daily leaf reports throughout the season.

◼ PLAN IT

Stowe is a 40-minute drive from Burlington International Airport and a 2½-hour drive from Montreal. Driving the length of Vermont, the sixth-smallest state in the US, takes only 2½ hours, so you're never far from your next hill or hike. Book a rental car well in advance during peak times (autumn and ski season), and consider opting for a 4WD to handle hills and snow if you're going to be hopping between mountains.

◼ DETOUR

Jay Peak Resort, a one-hour drive north of Stowe, makes up for its lack of Stowe-style quaintness with its over-the-top, kid-tastic amenities, all part of the massive renovations the resort undertook in 2010–11. Kids of all ages go crazy for the Pump House indoor waterpark where, mercifully, parents have been granted a poolside bar. Had enough splashing about in your swimmers? Rent skates for the whole family and hit the Ice Haus rink. Or stick steadfastly to the hill, where 77 ski trails, tons of backcountry and metres of fresh powder await. And if the kiddies are too young or uninterested to be on the mountain all day, drop-off day care is free for children aged six months to seven years who are staying on-site.

TARA REECE | GETTY IMAGES ©

OPENING SPREAD Skiing the Perry Merrill trail: Stowe has seasonal programs for young skiers of all ages. **ABOVE** It's not all about the snow: summer fun at Vermont's lakes. **BELOW** Woodstock: when autumn leaves start to fall Vermont is the place to be.

FOLLOW GERMANY'S FAIRY-TALE ROAD

GET BEHIND THE WHEEL OF A CAR (THE NEXT BEST THING TO A PUMPKIN) TO RAMBLE ALONG THE GERMAN FAIRY-TALE ROUTE. ITS MYSTERIOUS OAK FORESTS, CASTLES FIT FOR A PRINCESS AND HALF-TIMBERED TOWNS ARE STRAIGHT FROM THE PAGES OF A STORYBOOK.

Once upon a time there was a very long road that led through enchanted forests of beech, spruce and ancient oak, beloved of woodcutters, wicked witches and industrious dwarves. On and on it went, through medieval towns home to wealthy merchants, passing hilltop castles with ivy-clad towers perfect for locking away maidens with flaxen hair and fair damsels that were a dab hand with a spinning wheel. It was the German Fairy-Tale Route, as seen through the happily-ever-after eyes of the Brothers Grimm in the 1800s.

Want to be whisked away to the faraway kingdom right now? *Kein Problem.* Why wait for a fairy godmother to wave her magic wand when you can hop on a plane to Frankfurt, minutes from the start of the 600km fairy tale route in Hanau? If you have kids in tow, there's at least a week's worth of myths, folklore and bedtime stories to fire little ones' imaginations and send them happily off to slumberland. If you don't, and can't borrow some, you can always act out a few fairy-tale fantasies of your own: losing the trail in misty woods of gnarled 1000-year-old oak and beech trees, cycling along the rivers Fulda and Weser, and cranking up the shining-armour romance with a night spent in a castle.

That the Brothers Grimm lived in and were inspired by this region is unquestionable, but many of the locations on the road are cloaked in a fine weft of fact and fiction. It matters not. This swath of the country is among the fairest of all: its towns and villages are storybook stuff with their timber-framed houses and cobblestones, its forests are a picture of sylvan loveliness, and there is a castle steeped in legend on almost every corner. Walk in the rat-catcher's footsteps in Hamelin and you might hear the distant strains of a flute; recline on a four-poster bed at Sleeping Beauty's comfortable castle in Sababurg and you might want to snooze for 100 years. Stranger things have happened...

ESSENTIAL EXPERIENCES

* **Eating flambéed 'rat tails' in the beamed tavern of Hamelin's step-gabled Renaissance Rattenfängerhaus (Pied Piper House).**
* Creating fairy tales of your own beneath millennia-old oak trees in the sylvan wonderland of Sababurg forest.
* **Meeting Bremen's motley Town Musicians: a rooster, cat, donkey and dog. Rub the donkey's nose for good luck.**
* Falling into a deep slumber in a four-poster bed in Sleeping Beauty castle in Sababurg. The bridal suite is reached by a spiral staircase.
* **Roaming the 13th-century ruins of Burg Polle, Cinderella's adopted castle.**
* Having your cake, then walking it off on trail after gorgeously wooded trail in the deep, dark and mysterious Black Forest.

LOCATION GERMANY | **BEST TIME OF YEAR** SPRING THROUGH AUTUMN (APRIL THROUGH NOVEMBER) IS MOST POPULAR; BOOK WELL AHEAD IN THE PEAK SUMMER SEASON | **IDEAL TIME COMMITMENT** ONE WEEK | **ESSENTIAL TIP** TRAVELLING BY CAR IS A DEFINITE BONUS | **BUDGET** $$ | **PACK** BREADCRUMBS TO MARK YOUR TRAIL

FAIRY-TALE EVENTS

Time your visit to catch one of the region's fairy-tale-themed plays, festivals or pageants. From Easter to October, Burg Sababurg stages courtyard plays of Sleeping Beauty, while Polle's medieval castle ruins are an evocative backdrop for the monthly rendition of Cinderella from May to September. The big deal in Hanau is the Märchenfest (Fairy Tale Festival), with Grimm fairy tales performed in an open-air amphitheatre from May to July. Burg Trendelburg hosts its own Märchenfest in May, where Grimm characters are mixed with medieval jousting, acrobatics, music and markets. The Märchenweihnachtsmarkt (Fairy Tale Christmas Market) brings festival sparkle and Grimm folklore to Kassel in December.

■ THE PERFECT GETAWAY

Little Red Riding Hood had no say in it, but her neck of the woods allegedly reaches north of Alsfeld, a town fit for a fairy tale with its ensemble of timber-framed houses, cobbled alleys and a silver-turreted town hall. In the 17th century Märchenhaus storytellers recounted the tale of Grandma and the greedy wolf. It's hard to lose the path in forested Wildpark Knüll, a 40-minute drive north, where kids can spot wolves, deer, beavers and lynx in near-to-natural surrounds.

To visit Snow White's fictional abode, head east to Bergfreiheit, perched in wooded hills above the spa town of Bad Wildungen. Her 'house' is a beautiful half-timbered affair, with seven little beds for her sidekicks. The real draw, however, is a tour of the Besucherbergwerk Bertsch, where you can walk hi-ho-style through the tunnels of a former copper mine, mined by hand for 450 years.

Two fabled beauties of the Grimm world are linked to the town of Trendelburg. The first is Rapunzel, who, lore has it, was locked in its whimsically turreted tower. Get here at 3pm on a Sunday to help Prince Charming find the girl of his dreams (she's hard of hearing) and watch her let down her lustrous tresses. Nearby is 14th-century Schloss Sababurg, every inch the Sleeping Beauty castle. There may be some truth in the legend: when the castle awoke from a century-long slumber in 1957, it was indeed overgrown with rose brambles.

Edging north, rats rule the streets of the picture-book town of Hamelin, just as they did in the Pied Piper's day. Rat symbols mark pavements and shops are stuffed with cute, furry rodents. For a historic twist on the story of the flute-playing rat-and-child-catcher, visit the recently revamped town museum.

■ PLAN IT

The German Fairy-Tale Route stretches 600km from Hanau, near Frankfurt, to Buxtehude, near Hamburg. Frankfurt Airport is a 30-minute drive west of the start. By train, Eurostar serves Cologne. Driving is easiest, though major towns along the route are connected by train. Spring to autumn is the best time. Book accommodation on www.deutsche-maerchenstrasse.com.

■ DETOUR

If you're a sucker for a fairy-tale setting, continue to the Black Forest, a swath of fir forest, lakes and low mountains in Germany's southwest. The region is set up for family outdoor activities, with back-to-nature farmstays giving kids free rein in beautiful surrounds; visit www.urlaub-bauernhof.de for details. Towns with a fairy-tale focus include Triberg, home to the world's biggest cuckoo clock; half-timbered Gengenbach, where a scene from *Charlie and the Chocolate Factory* was filmed; and Villingen-Schwenningen, where mythical giant Romäus guards one of the medieval gate towers.

OPENING SPREAD If you go down to the woods today: Harz National Park is a 2hr drive east from Hamelin **ABOVE (L)** Rapunzel lets down her long, golden hair (again!) at Trendelburg Castle. **ABOVE (R)** Bremen, setting for a Brothers Grimm tale about a group of four-legged musicians.

DECKCHAIR

* ✻ **Grimm's Complete Fairy Tales** (Jacob and Wilhelm Grimm) The definitive collection for fans of German folklore.

* ✻ **The Pied Piper of Hamelin** (Jacob and Wilhelm Grimm) Rats, flutes and rivers abound in this children's classic.

* ✻ **The Hard Facts of the Grimms' Fairy Tales** (Maria Tatar) Explores the dark side of the Grimm fairy tales, from murder to cannibalism. A book for grown-ups.

* ✻ **The Bremen Town Musicians** (Jacob and Wilhelm Grimm) An unwanted donkey, dog, cat and rooster become street musicians.

* ✻ **Romantic Fairy Tales: Goethe, Tieck, Fouque and Brentano** (Carol Tully) A different take on the German fairy tale, this time from the country's famous Romantics.

* ✻ **The Interpretation of Fairy Tales** (Marie-Louise von Franz) Delve into the psychology of fairy tales to find their deeper meanings.

WILD

✿

GREAT ESCAPES

EXPLORE COLOMBIA'S GHOST COAST

ONCE THE SOLE DOMAIN OF ESCAPED SLAVES AND DRUG RUNNERS, COLOMBIA'S LUSH PACIFIC COAST IS BECOMING A HAVEN FOR INTREPID BEACH LOVERS, SURFERS, WHALE-WATCHERS, AND ANYONE WITH A DESIRE TO GET FAR, FAR AWAY FROM IT ALL.

Nestor Tello is bucking waves like an aquatic rodeo cowboy. The local guide is standing on the bow of the *panga*, casually holding onto the bow line, trusting his compadre, Pozo Briceño, not to flip him out of the boat as Briceño guns the double outboards in the back. The two men, employees of El Cantil, a dreamy seven-casita ecolodge sitting on a half-moon bay on Colombia's Pacific coast, are racing toward a giant humpback whale. But out here, a mile off the coast, where sunlight shimmers on steely water, every giant wave looks like a whale. This particular crest, however, gracefully arcs its massive body 4.5m out of the sea, then thwaps its tail on the water, showering the camera-happy observers in a frothy spray before it disappears.

There are many elusive creatures along this 100km-long coastline, which runs south from Ensenada de Utría National Park to Cabo Corrientes. The steamy wetness from rivers, volcanic springs, mountain rain and sea infuses the humid air, creating a jungle so thick with trees such as La Palma Que Camina ('the palm that walks'), coconut palms and starfruit that you can almost see it breathe.

Hiding in the foliage are thousands of species, including an indigenous bird colloquially known as the Baja Tomo. It's so evasive that even the locals have never set eyes on one. The same goes for the drug runners who ply this empty stretch of coastline, transporting their wares north – they exist, but are practically invisible. And they prefer to keep it that way. The legend of their presence has been enough to keep this tangled coast of 21m-tall coconut palms and 5km-long volcanic black-sand beaches almost completely unexplored. But that's changing quickly. Urban Colombians and expat gringos alike – from surfing aid-workers to visiting university professors and mining executives – pilgrimage to El Cantil to play in their own private Eden. It's high time to join them.

ESSENTIAL EXPERIENCES

* **Renting a stand-up paddleboard and syncing up with the rolling Pacific in the half-moon bay in front of El Cantil.**

* Hiking 5km south on the sand to the village of Termales to meet the locals and soak in their jungle hot springs.

* **Surfing famous Pacific breaks like Pico de Loro, Pela-Pela and El Chorro with Guillermo Gomez, the owner-surfer of El Cantil.**

* Photographing arcing humpback whales from a *panga* in the Pacific.

* **Flopping in your hand-woven hammock to read *One Hundred Years of Solitude* and let the day fly by.**

* Eating pastries topped with *miel de panela*, a sweet syrup derived from sugarcane juice.

LOCATION EL CANTIL ECOLODGE, COLOMBIA | **BEST TIME OF YEAR** SUMMER MONTHS (JANUARY, FEBRUARY, MARCH) AND AUGUST | **IDEAL TIME COMMITMENT** THREE NIGHTS, FOUR DAYS | **ESSENTIAL TIP** EL CANTIL IS OFF THE GRID; THERE'S LIMITED MOBILE-PHONE SERVICE BUT DON'T EXPECT WI-FI | **BUDGET** $$ | **PACK** SWIMSUIT, LIGHTWEIGHT RAIN JACKET AND MOSQUITO REPELLENT

WET & WILD

The Chocó-Darien Rainforest, where El Cantil Ecolodge sits, stretches from Panama, in the north, down the Pacific coast of Colombia and into Ecuador. It covers 187,500 sq km and has the highest rainfall on earth. Some areas of this region, thankfully not where El Cantil is located, receive as much as 13m of rainfall per year. The Chocó-Darien has 8,000 plant species, 97 reptile species, 127 amphibian species, roughly 600 bird species and some of the highest numbers of endemic plants in South America. Roaming the jungle are jaguars, ocelots, giant anteaters, tapirs and cotton-top tamarins, one of the most endangered primates in Colombia. You'll know one when you see it: they have a crown of white fur pouffing from the top of their heads.

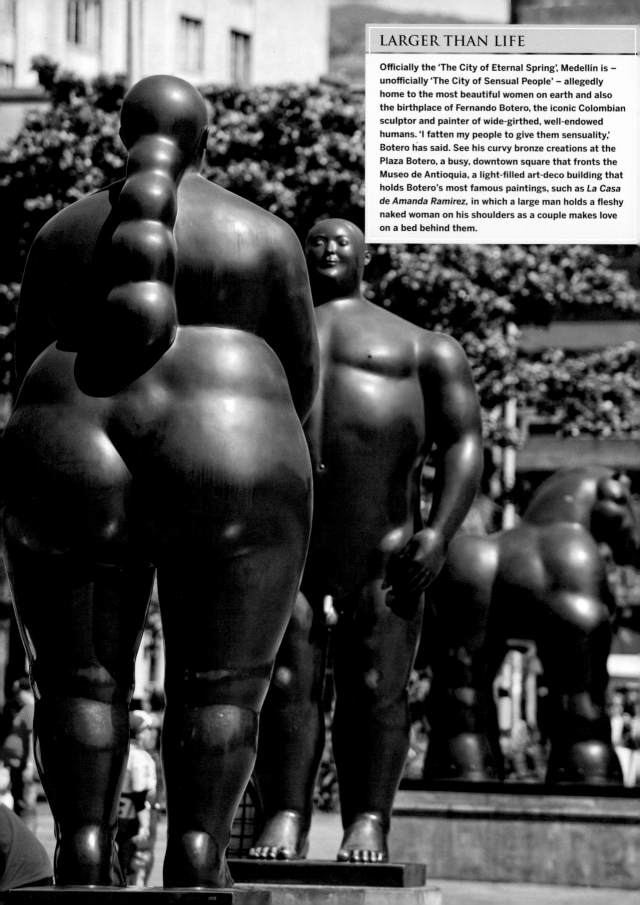

THE PERFECT GETAWAY

Backed by roadless jungle and facing a bay ringed by a black-sand beach, El Cantil Ecolodge is a far-out oasis, built by Guillermo 'Memo' Gomez and his family almost 20 years ago. At El Cantil, life beats at a barely perceptible pulse. The lodge's seven small *palafitos* – wood-framed, one-bedroom *casitas* with oil lamps, open-air windows, a bathroom and a deck strung with two hammocks – lead to El Cantil's open-air restaurant. Sound idyllic? It is.

The restaurant, which sits high in the canopy and has views of the Pacific, is where local women (who walk 5km every morning from the village of Termales) work their magic, producing family-style Chocoan meals like the *plato típico*: fish, coconut rice, fried plantains and fruit. They also serve frosty Aguila beers. It's easy to let lunch roll through to dinner and sit in the high breeze listening to the cacophony of crashing waves and squawking toucans, but save the second beer and the reverie for later. There's way too much to explore.

Surfers should enlist Memo for a dawn expedition, which requires a jungle hike or a boat ride, to one of the local breaks such as La Cascada del Amor. Or take a whale-watching ride in the lodge's *panga*: from July to September humpback whales, sometimes six at a time, rise out of the water. To meet the locals, walk to the village of Termales. The fishing community of a few hundred people, with its sand lanes and gardens sprouting oregano, chilli and onion, recently capitalised on its hottest asset – a sulphuric hot springs in its backyard jungle – by building a spa, complete with pebbled tubs and mud baths. Back at El Cantil, there's only time for a nap in the hammock before dinner and that second Aguila.

PLAN IT

There are direct flights to Medellín from some US cities, including New York (five hours). El Cantil is 193km from Medellín as the crow flies, but it requires an hour-long flight from Medellín's Enrique Olaya Herrera Airport on Satena Airlines to Nuquí. Someone from the lodge will be waiting to transfer you 40 minutes south by boat. All activities can be arranged at the lodge for an additional fee.

DETOUR

For a Caribbean equivalent, try Ecohabs, 35km north of the city of Santa Marta in Tayrona National Park. Its breezy, thatch-roofed cabanas sit on a high cliff overlooking Canaveral Beach. The 150-sq-km park rises from the sea to 900m peaks in the Sierra Nevada de Santa Marta. It's home to 300 species of bird; ruins from the Tayrona tribe, who roamed here long before the Spaniards came; and beaches lined with coconut palms. Hike stone-paved trails to indigenous settlements or take a 15-minute walk to Playa Grande, a white-sand beach at the head of a bay. (Surfers: beware the fierce riptides.)

OPENING SPREAD Sun seekers with a taste for adventure are making their way to Colombia's wild beaches, on both the Pacific and Caribbean coasts. **ABOVE** Where the Pacific weather systems meet the Andean *cordillera* valleys grow green. **LEFT** Full-bodied sculptures by Fernando Botero in Medellín.

DECKCHAIR

❋ **One Hundred Years of Solitude** (Gabriel García Márquez) Get lost in the creative genius of Colombia's Nobel Prize–winning novelist.

❋ **Love in the Time of Cholera** (Gabriel García Márquez) Follow the lifelong love affair between Florentino Ariza and Fermina Daza to its fitting conclusion.

❋ **Killing Pablo** (Mark Bowden) Gripping read about capturing and killing the world's most notorious drug lord.

❋ **Tropical Nature** (Adrian Forsyth and Ken Miyata) Fascinating primer on the ecosystems of Central and South America.

❋ **Even Silence Has An End** (Ingrid Betancourt) Frightening memoir by former Colombian presidential candidate about her six-year captivity by the FARC in the Amazon jungle.

❋ **Romancing the Stone** (1984) An entertaining romp through the Colombian jungle in search of buried treasure.

A POWDER PILGRIMAGE TO HOKKAIDŌ

THE ULTIMATE DREAM FOR SKIERS AND SNOWBOARDERS WHO LOVE RIDING DEEP-POWDER SNOW, JAPAN'S HOKKAIDŌ ISLAND PROVIDES A SERIOUS ADRENALIN FIX WITH AN EXTRA INJECTION OF QUIRKY CULTURE, EPIC SCENERY, INCREDIBLE FOOD AND FASCINATING TRADITIONS.

Put all those memories of icy slopes and rubbish ski holidays out of your mind. In Japan all your ski fantasies will come true. In Hokkaidō's finest resort, Niseko, the perfect volcanic peak of Mt Yōtei creates a dramatic backdrop to light, fluffy snow that is piled not just knee-deep, but usually waist-deep, and very often comes up to the armpits – an average 14m of snow falls each year. This makes for a stunning paradise playground where the efficient lift system zips skiers quickly to off-piste terrain that delivers that delicious floating sensation. A face full of powder is guaranteed – be prepared to end the day looking like the abominable snowman. More gnarly types might attempt to ski-tour up Mt Yōtei and ski down the side of a semi-dormant volcano.

Then it's après-ski time, so down to a traditional *izakaya* (drinking establishment serving food) for a steaming bowl of rāmen noodles or the freshest sushi, followed by a dip in an *onsen* (hot spring).

Even better is to visit one of the natural hot pools sometimes stumbled across in the forest, where you might hang your layers on a tree and bathe naked alongside snowboarders and old Japanese men in the 40°C water as snowflakes gently fall through the fog of steam. The undeveloped backcountry ski area of Tokachidake is a great place to do this, and has an excellent ryokan (traditional Japanese inn), where guests sleep on a tatami mat on the floor in a room with paper walls and sliding doors, like in a scene from a classic martial-arts film. It's as quintessentially Japanese an experience as the obligatory night out at a proper karaoke bar in Hokkaidō's second city, Asahikawa, where giggling Japanese teenagers pile into their own individual booths and take advantage of the popular 'all you can drink' deals. It's these kind of extracurricular activities that make a Hokkaidō ski trip more exciting than the average alpine escape.

ESSENTIAL EXPERIENCES

* **Carving up the slopes at Niseko and night-skiing in powder on the floodlit runs.**
* Charting a path through the wilderness in Daisetsuzan National Park.
* **Reviving your weary body after a day on the slopes as you steam in an onsen.**
* Singing karaoke in an authentic Japanese karaoke bar.
* **Exploring Tokyo's amazing Akihabara electronics district, which has morphed into the centre of the *otaku* (geek) universe.**
* Being happily bamboozled by the language and ordering a meal by just pointing at a picture.
* **Drinking the delicious liquid gold that is Sapporo beer, straight from the source.**

LOCATION HOKKAIDŌ, JAPAN | **BEST TIME OF YEAR** DECEMBER THROUGH MARCH | **IDEAL TIME COMMITMENT** TWO WEEKS | **ESSENTIAL TIP** HIRING A GUIDE TO GO OFF-PISTE IS ESSENTIAL IN MOST RESORTS | **BUDGET** $$$ | **PACK** GEAR THAT CAN HANDLE SERIOUS AMOUNTS OF DEEP SNOW

FIRST TRACKS AND LATE NIGHTS

On a typical European ski holiday, skiers at best catch the first lift at 8.30am and ski till 4.30pm. But in Niseko it's possible to ski from 7am until 8.30pm. Skiers who book a First Tracks trip from the purpose-built Niseko Village area can ride up on the piste-bashers that groom the slopes each morning before they open, so they get first tracks at 7am. You can ski Niseko's four areas all day, then go night-skiing in a vast floodlit area, open until 8.30pm, and so brightly lit it's possible to ski off-piste.

ICY FESTIVITIES

Hokkaidō hosts several snow festivals during February, featuring incredible snow and ice sculptures of anything from dragons to life-sized buildings. These include the Sapporo Yuki Matsuri (Sapporo Snow Festival), not far from Niseko, which usually draws over two million people; the Asahikawa Winter Festival, which has been going since 1947; and Otaru's charmingly named Snow Light Path Festival, during which the city is decorated with lights, candles, ice lanterns and small snow statues, and a long stretch of the canal is illuminated and turned into a winter wonderland. All were created to cheer up Japanese locals in the long, severe winters and are a stunning visual spectacle for guests.

■ THE PERFECT GETAWAY

Snow fiends hitting Hokkaidō make the premier resort of Niseko their main target, and for good reason: it's the most Western-style resort, so developed it's often dubbed the eastern Whistler, with fantastic runs, parks and slopes for all abilities, plus easily accessible backcountry to experience that famous powder.

Niseko town is a joy, full of great places to eat, drink and party, from Gyu, an ice bar in a fairylit ice palace accessed through a fridge door, to traditional izakayas serving spicy chicken-yakitori skewers and sake. Including a day in Sapporo, Hokkaidō's largest city, is also a good plan – it's packed with tiny bars and gyoza-dumpling places where salarymen slump into their sake. Factor in a few of the island's smaller resorts for a richer immersion into local life.

Furano is the second major resort, with a fun town, woodlands full of quirky cafes (run by rat-race escapees called 'slow-lifers') and some great runs through the trees (though off-piste riding is banned). Tomamu is a strange resort with tower-block hotels and a giant indoor wave pool, but slopes run through the wilderness, where you might spot deer. Rusutsu is also popular for its deep powder and tree skiing, while just outside Sapporo, Sapporo Tienne has one of the steepest slopes in Hokkaidō. A real adventure can be had by visiting Daisetsuzan National Park and skiing at Mt Asahi (2290m), Hokkaidō's highest mountain – and a live volcano that still smokes – where one big cable car leads to some exciting off-piste. Nearby, skiers can stay at Yumoto Yukomansou, a wonderful ryokan with its own onsen and meals served in a black lacquered case whose shelves are stuffed like a culinary jewellery box.

■ PLAN IT

Plan far ahead to get the cheapest package and flights. Most skiers fly to Tokyo for an onward connection to Hokkaidō, landing in Sapporo. From there, buses run to the main resorts; some travellers prefer the freedom of a hire car so they can visit smaller resorts and towns. It can be simpler to book with a specialist operator; Inside Japan is an expert tour provider that is very knowledgeable about skiing. The website www.snowjapan.com is an online guide with day-to-day snow reports.

■ DETOUR

Don't miss the spectacle of Japanese macaques – the famous 'snow monkeys' – taking an onsen in the natural hot pools of Jigokudani Yaen-kōen near Nagano. Their faces blush dark pink, their fur sticks up in spikes, they lie back with eyes half closed, and they even dunk each other under the water. The park, in the Yokoyu River valley, is home to a few hundred monkeys, whose species can survive temperatures of -15°C. But just like cold humans they relish the chance to warm up in a hot bath.

237

OPENING SPREAD It's a powder day at Niseko when Siberian weather systems dump snow on Hokkaidō. **ABOVE (L)** At a bar in Sappora, a couple prepare food. **ABOVE (R)** A crested kingfisher on Hokkaidō. **LEFT** From onsens to Afghanistan, macaques are the second-most widespread primates.

DECKCHAIR

* **Snow Search Japan** (Keith Stubbs) An in-depth guide to all the country's resorts, not just those in Hokkaidō.

* **Hokkaidō Highway Blues: Hitchhiking Japan** (Will Ferguson) A funny travelogue in which the author follows the Cherry Blossom Front.

* **Sushi and Beyond: What the Japanese Know about Cooking** (Michael Booth) Reveals delicious and bizarre cuisine, from cod sperm and whale penis to octopus ice cream.

* **Signatures** (2009) A ski and snowboard film by Sweetgrass Productions that follows a winter season in Hokkaidō, with endless powder footage and scenes with Taro Tamai, soulful maker of Gentemstick snowboards.

* **Who is Mr Satoshi?** (Jonathan Lee) An mystery novel set in Tokyo.

* **Tampopo** (1985) Director Juzo Itami's ebullient 'noodle western' will whet your appetite for the perfect bowl of noodles.

JORDAN'S DEAD SEA EXPERIENCE

BASE YOURSELF IN THE JORDANIAN CAPITAL OF AMMAN AND IMMERSE YOURSELF IN THE RICH HISTORY OF THE REGION – EXPLORING CRUMBLING CASTLES AND FORGOTTEN CITIES, WINDSWEPT LANDSCAPES AND HOLY PLACES.

238

Part space walk, part spa treatment, swimming in the Dead Sea counts as one of the strangest bathing experiences on earth. Name-dropped in the Old Testament and frequented by the likes of Cleopatra and King David, the Dead Sea has brought weary-limbed travellers to its shores for time immemorial – all seeking the sensation of floating light-as-a-feather on its mineral-rich waters.

Just as extraordinary is the country that hugs the Dead Sea's eastern shore. Though it may be small, Jordan has a story worthy of any Hollywood sword-and-sandals epic. Imagine giant armies of extras sweeping into shot; whole CGI empires rising and turning to dust; a cast of A-list characters – prophets, tyrants and freedom fighters – marching imperiously across the country's soil.

This might look like a big claim for a little country, but everywhere lies evidence of an eventful and stirring history. Even in Jordan's 21st-century capital Amman, you'll find a Roman theatre plonked obstinately in the heart of the downtown. Petra, in the country's south, is considered the trump card among Jordan's ancient attractions, but you don't have to stray far from Amman to meet larger-than-life characters from the past. Within an easy day-trip's reach of the city, you could be following in the footsteps of Emperor Hadrian (of wall fame) down Roman streets or exploring castles haunted by the ghost of Lawrence of Arabia.

The region's greatest stories, however, are set around the shores of the Dead Sea. Few experiences can be more spiritual than floating on its surface, reflecting on the biblical dramas said to have unfurled around it: Sodom and Gomorrah's destruction, the beheading of John the Baptist by King Herod, or the wanderings of Moses along the arid canyons of Wadi Mujib. And a short distance upstream, along the River Jordan, is Bethany, where Jesus Christ himself was thought to have been baptised, and where another famous story began.

ESSENTIAL EXPERIENCES

* **Climbing Mt Nebo for sweeping views across the Dead Sea and the Holy Land.**
* Smothering yourself with the Dead Sea's mineral-rich mud, then washing it all off with a swim.
* **Trying to get your bearings on Madaba's extraordinary mosaic map.**
* Following in the footsteps of Moses in Jordan's answer to the Grand Canyon – Wadi Mujib.
* **Trying to heave open the heavy stone door at Qasr al-Azraq – Lawrence of Arabia's castle in the deserts east of Amman.**
* People-watching while feasting on felafel and sipping mint tea in an Amman restaurant.
* **Swaggering through Jerash's ornate Triumphal Arch.**

LOCATION JORDAN, MIDDLE EAST | **BEST TIME OF YEAR** SEPTEMBER TO APRIL | **IDEAL TIME COMMITMENT** THREE DAYS
ESSENTIAL TIP DON'T GO INTO THE DEAD SEA WITH CUTS, UNLESS YOU QUITE LITERALLY WANT TO RUB SALT IN YOUR WOUNDS
BUDGET $$ | **PACK** A GOOD TOWEL TO SCRUB OFF DEAD SEA MUD

THE DYING SEA

The Dead Sea isn't actually a sea – it's a lake. It is, however, most definitely dead: little aquatic life can exist in its condition of extreme saltiness, caused by its high evaporation rate. This makes the water very dense, so visitors can bob about on its surface with ease. Unfortunately, the Dead Sea is dying – with waters from its source, the River Jordan, being diverted for agriculture, water levels are dropping by as much as 1m per year. There are various plans afoot to rescue the Dead Sea, including channelling water from the Red Sea, but in the meantime, make the most of it while it's there.

MAPPING THE PAST IN MADABA

Long before the days of satnav, those seeking to get directions in the Middle East would have been well advised to visit Madaba – home to perhaps the oldest existing map of the Holy Land. Dating back to the 6th century and discovered during chance excavations in 1884, the map takes the form of a multimillion-piece mosaic spread across the floor of a Byzantine church. Like many jigsaws, some pieces have been lost, but colourful details remain: look out for leaping fish in the River Jordan, multicoloured mountains and a lion chasing a gazelle at Bethany-beyond-the-Jordan.

■ THE PERFECT GETAWAY

Put politely, Amman isn't the most beautiful city in the Middle East, but what it lacks in looks it compensates for with boisterous charm, and it's an excellent base for exploring the Dead Sea and beyond. Get your bearings in town by scrambling to the top of the Roman theatre before joining locals on an evening stroll along the winding streets below and dining at Hashem on Al-Amir Mohammed St. Said to be Amman's oldest restaurant, it serves up exemplary Jordanian fare with few airs and graces – expect crunchy felafel, hummus, sweet tea and plastic chairs.

The next day, hail a cab and make a pilgrimage to Bethany-beyond-the-Jordan, the place where Jesus was believed to have been baptised. From spiritual elation, it's only a short drive to the lowest dry point on earth, the Dead Sea. Resist the temptation to take a dip at the first opportunity; its salinity means skin will sting if you can't shower afterwards, so make use of the Amman Beach complex nearby.

Having emerged reinvigorated from the Dead Sea, head to the town of Madaba to marvel at an ancient mosaic map of the Holy Land before catching the sunset from Mt Nebo – the summit from which Moses saw the Promised Land at the end of his life. A few thousand years on, it's still a view that takes some beating, with a panorama across the shimmering mass of the Dead Sea and the hazy outline of the Judean Hills – on a clear day you'll even see as far as Jerusalem.

There's plenty else deserving your attention around Amman. An hour east is Qasr al-Azraq, a Crusader-era castle where Lawrence of Arabia made his home. A short drive to the north is Jerash, a Roman town that was unearthed in the 19th century; like everywhere else in Jordan, the deeper you dig the more you'll find.

■ PLAN IT

A number of airlines connect Jordan to the rest of the Middle East; Royal Jordanian also offer flights from America, Europe and Asia. Jordan can be visited overland from Israel and the West Bank; the King Hussein Bridge (aka Allenby Bridge) border is the quickest route from Jerusalem. Public buses are cheap and plentiful – JETT runs services between major destinations. One budget accommodation option in Amman is the Jordan Tower Hotel.

■ DETOUR

To classicists it's the millennia-old capital of the Nabateans – to everyone else it's where the Holy Grail is kept in *Indiana Jones and the Last Crusade*. Either way, Petra is Jordan's showpiece attraction: a city of tombs carved into a valley a three-hour drive south from Amman. The approach to Petra is as dramatic as Hollywood would have you believe, with visitors treading down a narrow canyon to be confronted by the city's most famous monument, the Treasury. You can find out more about Petra in the Jordan Archaeological Museum in Amman.

241

OPENING SPREAD Too salty to sustain life, a dip in the Dead Sea has long been prescribed for health reasons; King Herod was an early advocate.
ABOVE Sunrise at Wadi Rum in southern Jordan. **LEFT** Watching the sun set at the Monastery, Petra's largest monument.

DECKCHAIR

* **Lawrence of Arabia** (1962) David Lean's classic was filmed in Wadi Rum, in the south of Jordan.

* **TE Lawrence: An Arab View** (Suleiman Mousa) A critical view of Lawrence by one of Jordan's most acclaimed historians.

* **Lion of Jordan: The Life of King Hussein** (Avi Shlaim) A biography of the late King Hussein of Jordan, who remains a celebrated figure in the country.

* **A Line in the Sand** (James Barr) A masterly account of Britain and France's tussle for control of the Middle East after WWI.

* **The New Book of Middle Eastern Food** (Claudia Roden) Roden's book is the definitive manual for Levantine cuisine.

* **Modern Arabic Fiction: An Anthology** (Salma Jayyusi) A collection of contemporary writing edited by Jordanian poet Salma Jayyusi.

PLANE-HOPPING ACROSS THE KIMBERLEY

Forget the Great Northern Highway, the best way to access the colossal Kimberley region is on the new Aerial Highway. Fly into the remote bush camps and coastal settlements pioneered by pearl luggers, diamond miners and the hardiest Aboriginal tribes.

242

'The Big Wet' is a huge preoccupation in the Kimberley. Even during the six dry months of the year, when red dust rises from the region's scant roads like mist and heat haze makes the always-distant horizon wobble like a hallucination, the wet season's storms and cyclones loom large in the Kimberley's consciousness. Beneath the beehive domes of the Bungle Bungles, aboriginal guides show hikers arid holes where fish miraculously appear when the rains arrive. In the north, where the Indian Ocean meets the Kimberley's red cliffs, pearlers weave legends around cyclones that sent ships crashing to shore. This is a place of extremes.

The Kimberley is one of the world's last great wildernesses. Here geology and meteorological might shape 1.3 million sq km of sunburnt deserts, surreally domed mountains, deep river gorges and palm-fringed oases. With a population barely that of a small city (40,000) spread across an area bigger than Germany, Australia's northwest is one of the most remote, least populated places on the planet. In its coastal hub of Broome you'll be closer to Bali than Brisbane.

Drive the Gibb River Road and Great Northern Highway, both major outback arteries, and you'll be carving mere scratches across the Kimberley's undulating map. And then, only when the Big Wet doesn't render the region inaccessible. But take to the skies and the Kimberley's remotest corners are yours, following a network of bush airstrips and floatplane landings known as the Aerial Highway.

Hop aboard an eight- or 12-seat Cessna to buzz above landscapes that desiccated early pioneers. Then put down in remote bush camps with fine dining and flushing loos: islands of comfort amid thorny oceans of acacia. Don't overindulge, though. The highway's hardy bush planes cope with most seasonal extremes but carry limited cargo, with passengers, luggage and emergency water supplies carefully weighed onto each flight.

ESSENTIAL EXPERIENCES

* **Marvelling at the mind-boggling beehive mountains of the Unesco World Heritage–listed Bungle Bungle Range.**

* Exploring a million acres of deep river gorges, rainforest pockets, waterfalls, hot springs and rugged red ranges in El Questro Wilderness Park.

* **Looking for the Kimberley's rare black grasswrens at Mitchell Falls' remote tiered waterfalls.**

* Sailing the partially uncharted Buccaneer Archipelago, a far-flung northwesterly string of islands, on a yachting or fishing trip.

* **Taking a seaplane over Horizontal Waterfalls, the world's only sideways-flowing falls.**

* Dipping a toe into the blue water of Cape Leveque and seeing the pristine coastline's white-sand beaches and red cliffs on an Aboriginal tour.

LOCATION THE KIMBERLEY, WESTERN AUSTRALIA | **BEST TIME OF YEAR** APRIL TO OCTOBER (DRY SEASON) | **IDEAL TIME COMMITMENT** TEN DAYS | **ESSENTIAL TIP** PACK A FLEECE; IN DRY SEASON, NIGHTS CAN BE CHILLY
BUDGET $$$ | **PACK** SUN HAT, SUNSCREEN AND BUG SPRAY

DIAMONDS & PEARLS

The silver-lipped shell of the indigenous Pinctada maxima oyster first put the Kimberley on the map in the 1800s, when it was sold to make buttons for the world's tightly fastened upper classes. By the 1900s, the market for the oyster's jewelled contents was booming and Broome's pearl masters, the wealthiest men in Australia, were ordering furniture from Paris and shipping their white linens to Singapore for laundering. Today, the South Sea pearls produced by the oysters are still among the most sought after pearls in the world, although nothing beats the glittering reign of the region's prized pink Argyle diamonds. This vast Kimberley deposit, discovered 25 years ago, now supplies 90% of the world's pink diamonds.

RANCH DRESSING

Brush the trail dust off your shoulders and stamp your boots clean: it's time to dress for dinner. El Questro Homestead may be set within a million-acre wilderness park but pleasures here are distinctly civilised: fine dining and plush suites, cliffside Retreats whose interiors wouldn't look out of place in Sydney or New York. Frills like alfresco tubs and feather-topped beds keep the big names booking. But take a horse out into El Questro's red gorges, seeking scant shade from gnarly baobabs, or stop at hot springs to laze under livistona palms, and you'll see it's the easy, pioneer-era charm that draws people back.

THE PERFECT GETAWAY

From the Indian Ocean to the outback is a day's drive or 1½ hours by plane. From the air, the white beaches of Broome are barely out of sight before the diamond-mining town of Kununurra rises up out of the scrub. This travel hub for Aerial Highway travellers offers onwards connections to bush camps, and is the dusty gateway to the 4047-sq-km El Questro Wilderness Park.

Kylie Minogue, Nicole Kidman and other A-listers land at El Questro's airstrip to check into the Homestead's nine cliffside suites, set above the Pentecost River. An hour's drive brings you to the park's affordable bungalows and campgrounds, surrounded by riding trails, hot springs, red canyons and croc-rich rivers.

South from Kununurra, where the walls of the Osmand Ranges give way to Purnululu National Park and the Kimberley's Bungle Bungle Range, a new crop of bush camps is popping up around. Standout stays include the Bungle Wilderness Lodge, which has impeccable eco-credentials, and the Kurrajong Camp, whose location in the north of the park comes with perfect Bungles panoramas and comfortable, safari-style tents.

Days here start early with sunrise hikes, and end around campfires under canopies of stars, bellies heavy with roast lamb and Australian wine. Walking tours are led by Aboriginal guides, who reveal the gorges and geological strata that inform the Bungles' Dreamtime stories. These fables only go some way to reconciling awestruck tourists with the weirdness of it all. The Bungles were only brought to international attention in 1983, which shows just how uncharted the area is. But if your highway is aerial, it's an increasingly accessible wilderness.

PLAN IT

Kununurra and Broome are the Kimberley Aerial Highway hubs, serving some 20 regional landing strips and lodges. The network's airlines offer fixed-wing, floatplane and helicopter flights. Most flights and accommodation can be booked independently, but reservations at select camps (especially those in Purnululu) are made exclusively as part of tours with companies such as APT (Australian Pacific Touring) and Kimberley Wild Expeditions.

DETOUR

Most of the Kimberley's outback camps have road access, but its coastal lodges demand passage by air or sea. Kimberley Coastal Camp, Faraway Bay and Berkeley River, along the region's north coast, offer an Australian castaway experience, with the chance to explore places that few but pearl luggers have seen. Humans are rare but dugongs, turtles, sharks and saltwater crocodiles are numerous, as are rainbow bee-eaters, blue-winged kookaburras and tiny double-barred finches. Camp guides can reveal ice-age rock art and incredible star-gazing shows.

245

OPENING SPREAD Around the Kimberley's islands dugongs graze on seagrass meadows. **ABOVE** Watch for crocs: the wet season brings tempting torrents to the Kimberley. **LEFT** Cowandyne Creek in the Mornington Wildlife Sanctuary, which is home to 200 species of bird, including the vivid Gouldian finch.

DECKCHAIR

* **The Voice of the North** (Jim Kelly) Classic poems from Western Australia's cattle camps in the 1930s and '40s.

* **The Kimberley: Australia's Unique North-West** (Jocelyn Burt) Armchair travel at its best: glossy photos, personal stories and lyrical description, including poetry from Neroli Roberts.

* **Australia** (2008) Baz Luhrmann's overblown epic features Kununurra, El Questro Wilderness Park and the Kimberley Range.

* **The White Divers of Broome** (John Bailey) Based on fact, this history of 19th-century pearling reads as riveting fiction.

* **Rhythms of the Kimberley: A Seasonal Journey Through Australia's North** (Russell Gueho) A glossy guide detailing the region's delicate, cyclical ecology.

* **Dirt Music** (Tim Winton) The 2001 Booker Prize–shortlisted story of love in remote coastal Kimberley.

WHERE RHINOS STILL REIGN

THE LAST STRONGHOLD OF THE ENDANGERED BLACK RHINO, NAMIBIA'S DAMARALAND IS SO VAST THAT CHANCES ARE YOU'VE NEVER HEARD SILENCE LIKE THIS BEFORE. SHARE ITS HORIZONS ON A SAFARI WITH GROWING NUMBERS OF RHINO AND THE MOST CHEETAHS IN THE WORLD.

246

Fly over Damaraland in northwest Namibia and the mountains below look like naked bodies – brown, curvaceous and bare. This 500-million-year-old shale, limestone and volcanic basalt landscape, known as 'the Place of Empty', is so wide open that it seemingly swallows black rhinos whole. The uncanny ability of megafauna to blend in here is perhaps one reason Namibia is the only country in Africa where the population of elephants, lions, giraffes and rhinos is growing.

On the ground, however, the animals make their presence known – especially if you have a guide like Anthony Dawids, who grew up here and can tell you how hard the wind is blowing based on whether an ostrich is sitting or standing. He also knows where the elephants, who roam up to 70km per day, will most likely be feeding, sucking up acacia pods like giant vacuum cleaners. Today a family of seven is dining on the banks of the waterless Huab River. They're so engrossed in their eating that Dawids is able to manoeuvre his 4WD close enough to see the musth secretions streaming from one male's glands. The elephants have Namibia's conservation-minded government to thank for their peaceful feast. Namibia was the first country in the world to incorporate environmental protection into its constitution when it won independence from South Africa in 1990. Today, 42% of the country is under protection management.

There are other reasons to be thankful: the water's clean, the roads are easy to navigate and the lodging is roughly two-thirds the cost of Botswana's. Fourteen indigenous groups, including the nomadic San people and the famously remote Himba, still have room to roam. Then there's the 1609km-long Skeleton Coast, the shape-shifting Sossusvlei Dunes, and Etosha National Park, one of southern Africa's most accessible game-viewing venues. It may require more work to see animals in Damaraland, but visit once and the place will get under your skin.

ESSENTIAL EXPERIENCES

* **Embarking at dawn on a rhino-tracking expedition in an unnamed valley, an hour from Damaraland Camp, that's rich with poisonous euphorbia bushes, a favourite rhino delicacy.**

* Watching the perfectly framed sun rise from the rectangular window in your luxurious shower.

* **Hiking to the top of a 100m sand dune to launch a front flip and gain so much momentum that you land at the bottom with sand in every orifice.**

* Getting so close to an elephant immersed in eating acacia pods that you can see the musth secretions dripping down the side of his face.

* **Watching 'Bush TV', local parlance for the 180-degree view from Damaraland Camp's open-air bar.**

LOCATION DAMARALAND, NAMIBIA | **BEST TIME OF YEAR** JUNE TO NOVEMBER | **IDEAL TIME COMMITMENT** THREE NIGHTS, FOUR DAYS | **ESSENTIAL TIP** BRING HIGH-POWERED BINOCULARS | **BUDGET** $$$ | **PACK** GOOD HIKING BOOTS AND LAYERS OF LIGHTWEIGHT, LIGHT-COLOURED SAFARI CLOTHES

BLACK GOLD

Wildlife poaching is now the third-largest criminal industry in the world. In Africa, rhino poaching has reached epidemic proportions. A recent report released by the South African government states that a record 668 rhinos were killed in that country alone in 2012, a staggering increase from 2007, when 13 were killed. The poached horn is sold to the Asian black market for as much as US$200,000 per pair, where traditional folk medicine practitioners grind up the keratin-filled horn. The good news: in Namibia the black rhino population is growing at an average of 5% per year and is currently up to 1,750. Unfortunately, it is still considered 'critically endangered'.

■ THE PERFECT GETAWAY

Watch the full moon rise while sipping a glass of South African sauvignon blanc on a high ridge behind Damaraland Camp. These impromptu celebrations – a picnic breakfast on a mesa overlooking Brandberg Mountain (2606m), the tallest in Namibia, or a full 'Boma' dinner under the stars – are part of the magic at the ecofriendly camp. The 10 luxurious safari tents sit on a mountainside and surround an open-air lounge with a bar, a swimming pool and plush chaises where you can soak up views of the Martian-like landscape.

To experience country like this is not only thrilling, it's historical. In the 1990s Damaraland Camp became Namibia's first joint venture between a local conservancy and a private tourism business. The 1,200 Torra Conservancy members have a 40% share; the other 60% is owned by South Africa–based Wilderness Safaris. In return, Wilderness Safaris has a promise that poaching on Torra land will stop. The partnership has been an unprecedented success: game counts of cheetahs, lions and elephants have increased, and Namibian

black rhinos have bounced back to become the largest free-roaming population in the world.

But that doesn't mean that the animals are easy to find. There's no guarantee a black rhino will lumber up on cue in its favourite grazing valley (a place that will go unnamed because poachers are still a serious threat). But that's the excitement of Damaraland Camp – you never know when the chomping megafauna will make an appearance. If you still need proof that there's something lurking beyond the silence, grab a pair of binoculars, point them toward the Huab River Valley and find a plain teeming with hartebeest, secretary birds, ostrich, kudu and zebra. And be comforted that, in Namibia, the wild kingdom still exists.

DECKCHAIR

* ***Soul of a Lion: One Woman's Quest to Rescue Africa's Wildlife Refugees*** (Barbara Bennett) A story about Sam the 'AIDS' lion and Marieta van der Merwe, the woman behind the Harnas Wildlife Foundation.

* ***An Arid Eden*** (Garth Owen-Smith) The father of Namibian conservation writes about his 40 years living in the Kaokoveld.

* ***The Living Deserts of Southern Africa*** (Barry Lovegrove) A comprehensive look at the region's flora, fauna, geology and ecology.

* ***Green Hills of Africa*** (Ernest Hemingway) Hemingway kills a rhino in Tanzania. Not so cool.

* ***Skeleton Coast*** (Clive Cussler) A gripping read about pirates, romance and a shipwreck full of diamonds off Namibia's wild coast.

* ***A History of Namibia*** (Marion Wallace) The definitive, in-depth history of Namibia.

■ PLAN IT

South African Airways has flights to Windhoek, the capital of Namibia, from major international cities like London, Washington, DC, and Sydney, with a connection through Johannesburg. From Windhoek, Damaraland Camp is 470km northwest. It's possible to rent your own 4WD and drive, but it's a lot faster to fly. Wilderness Safaris has a fleet of small planes and the 1¾-hour flight allows for stunning views of the arid landscape. Damaraland Camp is a year-round destination; the best time to visit is from June to November, when the animals seek waterholes. Expect cool nights and hot days.

■ DETOURS

The possibilities for further exploration are endless; Wilderness Safaris operates a number of lodges around Namibia and provides flight service to all of them. Additionally, a top priority should be a flight-seeing safari over the Skeleton Coast, where shipwrecks rust in the sea, whalebones bleach in the sun and the sand stretches on forever. Skeleton Coast Safaris, owned by the Schoeman family since 1977, offers a tour of the 1931km-long coastline that begins and ends in Windhoek. Be sure to enquire about a stop at Sossusvlei Dunes, the eternally shifting, second-highest sand piles in the world.

COURTESY OF WILDERNESS SAFARIS ©

OPENING SPREAD You can tell black rhinos from white by their pointed top lip, if you look closely. **ABOVE** Sundown at the plunge pool: there's no need to rough it at Damaraland Camp. **BELOW** The widescreen wonder of Namibia, complete with a kudu on the move.

FORCED MIGRATION

Damaraland may be a beautiful haven for big animals, but it's a harsh landscape for humans. Most of the 1,200 local residents, who live in Bergsig, Torra Conservancy's largest town, were placed on the back of a cattle truck and forcibly removed from Riemvasmaak, South Africa, in the early 1970s to make room for a military base. To eat, the new migrants farmed cattle, sheep, and goats, but stampeding elephants and hungry lions often interfered. After 40 years of struggle, Torra Conservancy now has its own game guards that not only protect the animals from poachers, but also reimburse farmers for damages caused by wildlife. It's a precarious harmony.

FIND YOURSELF ON THE LOST COAST

A TRIP TO CALIFORNIA'S LOST COAST BRINGS VISITORS TO THE RUGGED, REMOTE AND UTTERLY UNTAMED EDGE OF THE CONTINENT, WITH SCANT TRACES OF HUMAN IMPACT. WHEN THE FOG LIFTS, THE COASTAL EPIC REVEALS BEACHES OF GNARLED DRIFTWOOD, RUSTING SHIPWRECKS AND WILD SURF.

250

If you find yourself on a trail penetrating California's Lost Coast, congratulate yourself. As one of the superlative hiking and backpacking destinations in Northern California, the Lost Coast is a rugged, mystifying stretch of coastline where narrow trails ascend imposing coastal jags, cross empty volcanic beaches and traverse forests of mist-shrouded redwood. It's the provenance of majestic Roosevelt elk, lording redwood giants and ethereal banks of fog. During the three-day hike along its length, the scale of your surroundings might just spark an existential crisis, set to the powerful heartbeat of pounding waves: visitors tend to feel like an infinitesimal speck in a great big universe as they inch along between the 1200m peaks of the Kings Range and the icy rage of the Pacific. The coast became 'lost' when state highway surveyors deemed it impassable in the early 20th century and cut the highways inland, where the terrain was more manageable.

The three-day hike is a chance to connect with Northern California's flora and fauna – including some 300 species of birds, sea lions, seals, elk, river otter and migrating whales. It's also the perfect chance for Silicon Valley execs and the rest of us to unplug from the frantic pace of modern life: mobile-phone reception around these parts is virtually non-existent.

After cutting ties to the outside world, your experience on the Lost Coast will be one of rich rewards, filled with days of meditative hiking and cool nights where you'll zip into your sleeping bag and drift off to the rhythm of the waves. The hike encounters some challenging terrain, with boulder-hopping, stretches that need to be timed with the tide, and a fair bit of slow-going sand. But when you set up camp to enjoy the spoils of your effort, it's more than worth it: a beachfront view of a deep-orange sunset and a brilliant display of stars.

ESSENTIAL EXPERIENCES

✷ **Wandering around the Punta Gorda Lighthouse, a retired relic of the early 20th-century California coast, and scanning the horizon for migrating whales.**

✷ Climbing Kings Peak, a detour that takes some effort but rewards with a 360-degree view.

✷ **Scouring the beaches for treasures of all sizes – from tiny shells to the rusting hulks of abandoned fishing vessels.**

✷ Devouring a basket of fish and chips at Shelter Cove's Airport Deli, a place with 'World Famous' fried goodies that taste like heaven after the hike.

✷ **Finding one of the area's 'drive-thru' trees, mid-century roadside attractions that allow drivers to navigate through the carved-out belly of a living redwood.**

LOCATION CALIFORNIA, USA | **BEST TIME OF YEAR** JUNE, OR LATE AUGUST THROUGH EARLY OCTOBER | **IDEAL TIME COMMITMENT** FIVE DAYS | **ESSENTIAL TIP** REFER TO A TIDE TABLE FOR CROSSING CREEKS | **BUDGET** $ | **PACK** A DECENT TOPOGRAPHICAL MAP IS A MUST FOR KNOWING WHICH SIDE TRAILS TO NAVIGATE

THE SHELTER COVE SWINDLE

The only community found along the Lost Coast is
Shelter Cove, a sleepy seaside burg that includes an
airstrip, a few lodges and some humble restaurants.
In the mid-20th century, Southern California
developers built the airstrip, cut a system of roads and
constructed a nine-hole golf course. Then they flew
in potential investors, fast-talking them into buying
seaside lots where they could enjoy their retirement.
What they didn't tell them was that only one route went
in and out – a ruddy, steep, one-lane bone-rattler – and
that their investments were eroding into the sea.

THE LOST COAST'S SHIPWRECKS

With lots of thick fog and churning tides, the waters off the Lost Coast were fearsome during California's settlement. A state database lists 350 ships along this stretch that were wrecked, stranded or severely damaged between the 1850s and the 1950s. Many of them were shipping lumber up and down the coast, but the most notorious was the SS *Brother Jonathan*. Carrying 244 passengers and a full load of gold – payments to honour local treaties with Native American tribes – the ship ploughed into a rock near Crescent City. Divers didn't find the wreck until 1993, 125 years after it sank.

THE PERFECT GETAWAY

This getaway starts with the leisurely drive north from San Francisco to the trailhead. Passing larger and larger stands of redwood, the drive is dotted by historic logging towns. A favourite among these is tiny Garberville, the last town with any real services in the area. It's a place where the longstanding rivalry between loggers, tree-huggers and cannabis farmers is palpable. It also has a couple of excellent restaurants and a string of comfortable family-run motels.

After stocking up in Garberville, find your way to the start of the hike at the Mattole Campground, 1½ hours northwest at the mouth of the Mattole River. It's at the ocean end of Lighthouse Rd, 6.5km from Mattole Rd (which is sometimes marked as Hwy 211), south and east of a speck of a town called Petrolia. Locals know the area and often point Patagonia-clad greenhorns in the right direction.

It's best to get to the trailhead as early as possible on the first day. The Lost Coast Trail – the main thoroughfare for foot traffic – follows 40km of coastline from Mattole Campground in the north to Black Sands Beach at Shelter Cove in the south; the best way to tackle this hike is from north to south, which takes advantage of the prevailing winds. Given the conditions of the trail, you'll want weatherproof boots with lots of foot support.

If you're not up to the three-day hike, you can get a taste of the Lost Coast on a day hike that starts from the campground at Lighthouse Rd, following a 4WD trail out to the Punta Gorda Lighthouse. Alternatively, you can use Shelter Cove, the isolated town that is the southern point of the hike, as a hub, and get your fill of the North Coast's dramatic scenery without the need for fancy outdoor gear.

PLAN IT

From San Francisco, the trailhead is a long (and lovely) five-hour drive north. Two shuttle companies are licensed to operate within the federally protected land: Lost Coast Trail Transport Service and Lost Coast Shuttle; if you don't use them you'll have to take two vehicles and stash one at the end of the hike. For supplies and insider information, hit Garberville's sporting goods stores. No camping fees or overnight permits are required, but you'll need a campfire permit, available at trailheads.

DETOUR

Want to be gobsmacked by Northern California's natural splendour without breaking a sweat? Cruise the 50km Avenue of the Giants to see the region's redwood groves. The route passes through the Humboldt Redwoods State Park, which has the largest stand of virgin redwoods in the world. The more ambitious can navigate the well-marked network of short trails. Hungry? Good: the Avenue features roadside restaurants, several places to taste wine and lots of options for an unforgettable picnic.

OPENING SPREAD Found: an end-to-end hike tailormade for a long weekend camping trip. **ABOVE** Seeking the mythical break at Ghost Point: cold-water surfing doesn't get more adventurous than this. **LEFT** Humboldt Redwoods State Park has 250 camp sites if you want to continue the canvas theme.

DECKCHAIR

* ***The Wild Trees: A Story of Passion and Daring*** (Richard Preston) A must-read for those interested in the astounding magical life of the world's tallest trees.

* ***California's Lost Coast*** (Wilderness Press Maps) An excellent, waterproof map that covers King Range National Conservation Area and Sinkyone Wilderness State Park. It also has great day hikes.

* ***If a Tree Falls: A Story of the Earth Liberation Front*** (2011)

Although mostly set above the Northern California border, this documentary provides gripping insight into the radical environmental movement.

* ***Return of the Jedi*** (1983) Adorable Ewoks live in the canopy of the redwoods in this *Star Wars* sequel.

* ***The Big Trees*** (1952) Kirk Douglas plays an unscrupulous timber baron who meets resistance from a band of plucky Quaker homesteaders.

253

BOSNIA–
HERCEGOVINA

SERBIA

CROATIA

MONTENEGRO

KOSOVO

Kotor Podgorica

ADRIATIC
SEA

ALBANIA

VENTURE INTO THE BAY OF KOTOR

MOTHER NATURE WAS, QUITE FRANKLY, SHOWING OFF IN COMPOSING THE BAY OF KOTOR. THE CASUAL JUXTAPOSITION OF DRAMATIC, SCREE-COVERED MOUNTAINS THAT PLUNGE TO OPAL-AZURE INLETS AND COVES CREATES A STRIKING LANDSCAPE THAT WILL AROUSE YOUR INSTINCTS FOR EXPLORATION.

254

Your heart is pounding. Step by step, facing the mountain, you've been ascending – for ages, it seems. But as you near the fortress of Sveti Ivan you begin to appreciate the pleasing sturdiness of the path under your feet. At altitude now, a breeze ruffles your hair, bringing a scent of pine and wild aniseed. Then you turn to survey your domain and immediately realise your exertions were entirely worthwhile. The vista is exhilarating: 1200m beneath you the terracotta roofs and domes of the walled city of Kotor front the bottle-green waters of the bay, and beyond the elephantine bulk of merciless mountains are haloed with wisps of cloud.

Known to locals as the Boka Kotorska, or simply 'the Boka' (from the Italian *bocca,* literally 'mouth'), the bay rambles in a cluster of inlets, hemmed by the limestone mass of the Dinaric Alps. Sometimes described as the Mediterranean's only fjord – though geological purists would dispute this – it is a landscape that has captivated and been captured by a variety of visitors, from Illyrian queens to Romantic poets. Lord Byron enthused that all of Montenegro was strewn with the 'Pearls of Nature', while Shakespeare waxed lyrical about this 'Illyrian shore', even though he never came here. The human hand has only enhanced what Mother Nature already wrought. Handsome stone-built villages face the bay and the town of Kotor itself has won Unesco World Heritage status.

Kotor, with its medieval walls and vibrant nightlife, is the focal point for many travellers, but the various corners of the bay offer attractions for history buffs, art and architecture for culture vultures, and activities aplenty for those who want to embrace the outdoors. From the vantage point of the fortress of Sveti Ivan, it is not uncommon after the exhilaration of the climb to feel the lord of all you survey – and downright weird not to feel impelled to explore.

ESSENTIAL EXPERIENCES

* **Island-hopping: visiting church-topped Our Lady of the Rocks in a taxi boat from Perast or kayaking out to diminutive Mamula from Herceg Novi.**

* Getting lost in the labyrinthine streets of Kotor. It's pretty small so you'll never be truly lost, but random wandering, discovering churches, cobbled squares and cafes, is great fun.

* **Circuiting the bay by car – a winding 43km from Herceg Novi to Kotor – or cycling a shorter stretch along the waterfront between Igalo and Kamenari.**

* Tucking into freshly grilled squid with garlic and olive oil at Konoba Feral near the waterfront in Herceg Novi.

LOCATION BAY OF KOTOR, MONTENEGRO | **BEST TIME OF YEAR** MAY AND JUNE OR SEPTEMBER AND OCTOBER – EITHER SIDE OF THE HIGH SEASON | **IDEAL TIME COMMITMENT** ONE WEEK | **ESSENTIAL TIP** MONTENEGRINS LOVE TO PROMENADE EVERY EVENING, A PHENOMENON KNOWN AS THE CORSO | **BUDGET** $ | **PACK** STURDY SHOES FOR ADVENTURES, SOMETHING SMART FOR THE CORSO

MARTIAL MONTENEGRINS

After holding out against the Ottoman Turks, overlords of the Balkans from the 15th century until the late 19th century, the Montenegrins were characterised by Western observers as a noble race of warriors, akin to Homeric heroes. Their chief concerns, it was alleged, were poetry and war. The Montenegrins themselves revelled in – and perhaps played up to – their martial reputations. Until the early 20th century, weaponry was *de rigueur* for any self-respecting male, and so inclined to poetry were they that a government minister once delivered a budget entirely in verse. These days you won't see locals packing weapons, but the landscape is known to provoke lyrical outbursts.

ROCK OF AGES

According to Montenegrin folklore, when God had finished making the world he realised that something was missing: rocks. So he set off shouldering a large sack of boulders with the intention of scattering them evenly across the surface of the globe. As he reached Montenegro, however, the sack split, with the rocks tumbling out and coming to rest in splendid profusion. There the rocks have remained ever since. The rugged landscape was said to have allowed the Montenegrins to forge their distinct identity in unspoiled seclusion, but also to have prevented the advance of civilisation. These days it means boundless opportunities for outdoor enthusiasts.

THE PERFECT GETAWAY

Montenegrins have a reputation among the peoples of the former Yugoslavia as being lazy, a stereotype that some revel in. But living in such beautiful surrounds, perhaps it's more a case of taking life at a gentle pace, the better to appreciate its charms. Travellers to the Bay of Kotor are well advised to do the same: a leisurely ramble rewards many times over.

At the western end of the bay, closest to the Croatian border, is Herceg Novi. Between the waterfront Fortemare bastion and the hillside Španjola fortress, this centuries-old town is an appealing conglomeration of flag-stoned squares and churches linked to the beach by some steep *stepenište* (staircases). It's also a great base for the active traveller, with an array of outfitters.

Risan, the bay's oldest settlement, was once the seat of Illyrian queen Teuta. She attracted the attention of expansionary Romans, who inevitably took over and built mansions with water views, including Villa Urbana, which dates to the 2nd century AD. The villa's claim to fame is its mosaic floors – the dining room floor is adorned with flowers and vines, while in the bedroom sprawls Hypnos, the god of sleep. Nearby Perast, with the elegance and architecture of a Venetian outpost, distils the bay's history. Its museums display relics of the town's seafaring past: exhibits of charts, weapons, costumes and nautical miscellany will have you imagining yourself a corsair.

To the south, on the Luštica Peninsula, the abandoned settlement of Gornji Stoliv stands sentinel above the water, while elsewhere are remote beaches and bucolic olive groves, galleries, churches and monasteries to explore.

PLAN IT

The Bay of Kotor is reached by bus or taxi from Dubrovnik (which has plenty of international flights). The walled town can get noisy during summer. Dobrota, within walking distance, is quieter and has good accommodation options. Herceg Novi, at the western end of the bay, is more peaceful than Kotor – and boasts better beaches and an array of adventure sports operators.

DETOUR

If you're feeling vigorous, set out on the Ladder of Cattaro, a centuries-old caravan trail from Kotor that ascends to meet the Coastal Mountain Traversal on Mt Lovćen. This is the eponymous 'black mountain' that gives the country its name and is the site of the Njegoš Mausoleum, final resting place of Petar II Petrović Njegoš, spiritual father of modern Montenegro. For the less energetic, the trip can be taken by car, a switchback journey with breathtaking vistas and white-knuckle moments. Beyond Lovćen the road continues to Cetinje, home to an array of stately mansions and museums.

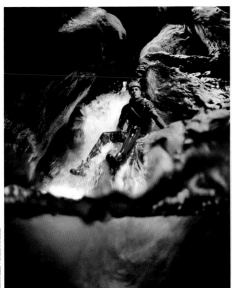

OPENING SPREAD Mediterranean cultures clashed in the now-flourishing Bay of Kotor. **ABOVE (L)** Montenegro is a mecca for caving and canyoning. **ABOVE (R)** Hiking the Tara River gorge, Europe's deepest. **LEFT** A short drive down the Adriatic coast is the town of Budva.

DECKCHAIR

※ **Black Lamb and Grey Falcon** (Rebecca West) Seventy years old but still the pre-eminent Balkan travelogue, brimming with wry observations and historical insights.

※ **Montenegro: A Novel** (Starling Lawrence) This ripping yarn set in the early 20th century mixes romance, bloodshed and intrigue.

※ **Realm of the Black Mountain** (Elizabeth Roberts) Montenegrin history, from the ancient Greeks to independence in 2006.

※ **Wild Europe** (Božidar Jezernik) An anthropologist's compilation of quirky observations and cultural curios from across the Balkans.

※ **Life and Death in the Balkans: A Family Saga in a Century of Conflict** (Bato Tomašević) The subtitle says it all; this account of Montenegro's troubled recent history is ultimately life-affirming.

※ **The Mountains of Montenegro** (Rudolf Abraham) Practical information for walkers and trekkers.

DO THE SAN JUAN ISLAND-HOP

KAYAKING BLUE COVES AND SCANNING THE HORIZON FOR ORCAS, CYCLING COUNTRY ROADS PAST BUCOLIC FARMS AND BREATHING AIR SCENTED WITH SALT AND CEDAR. THE SAN JUAN ISLANDS OFFERS TIMELESS ADVENTURES AT A LAID-BACK PACE IN THE US NORTHWEST.

The escape begins as soon as the ferry pushes away from the dock. As it starts to parade between the scattered emerald-green islands off the northwest tip of the United States, move out onto the deck and take a deep breath. In that air – cool, humid, strangely fresh – you'll be introduced to the San Juan Islands. This trip is a chance to leave behind day-to-day concerns, sink into the easygoing pace of the Pacific Northwest and recharge. But there's something else in the air here that inspires people to get outdoors. With a plethora of options for cycling, hiking, birding and kayaking, the escape is ideal for people who like relaxing adventures.

Situated within sight of Canadian land, the islands were the subject of some dispute throughout the 1850s, when both countries wanted to claim them. This brought about the colourfully named but casualty-free Pig War in 1859, the remnants of which are still visible in two historic sights on San Juan Island, English Camp and American Camp.

Four of the 172 named islands off the Washington coast – San Juan, Orcas, Lopez and Shaw Islands – are served by ferries. Spend an afternoon cruising around San Juan Island, the second-largest and most populated of the islands, and it's easy to see what all the fuss was about. By car or by bike, you'll roll past gentle green hills dotted with sheep, cattle and alpaca, tidy rows of grape vines or lavender plants, sun-dappled forests and sparkling ocean views. Bring binoculars for the visit to the island's pair of historic lighthouses to search for the resident pods of orca whales. Better yet, rent a kayak to join them on the water. After you've paddled the last stroke and the bikes are put away, make for the adorable downtown of Friday Harbor for a nightcap. By the time you retreat back to your B&B for some shut-eye, you might just dream of staying here forever.

ESSENTIAL EXPERIENCES

* **Hugging the adorable and inquisitive creatures at Krystal Acres Alpaca Farm.**
* Visiting the lighthouse at Lime Kiln Point State Park, a great place to spot orcas.
* **Breathing deeply at Pelindaba Lavender Farm, where all manner of lavender products are made on-site.**
* Hunting for antiques in the island's excellent antique shops, galleries and boutiques – most are found in downtown Friday Harbor.
* **Cruising the country on a rental bike and pedalling out to the ocean for a picnic.**
* Paddling out through one of the protected harbours to join the local orcas.

LOCATION BETWEEN MAINLAND WASHINGTON, USA, AND VANCOUVER ISLAND, BRITISH COLUMBIA, CANADA | **BEST TIME OF YEAR** SUMMER (JULY AND AUGUST) | **IDEAL TIME COMMITMENT** FOUR DAYS | **ESSENTIAL TIP** DOUBLE-CHECK THE FERRY SCHEDULE FOR SEASONAL VARIATIONS | **BUDGET** $$ | **PACK** BINOCULARS, PLUS APPROPRIATE CLOTHES AND SUN PROTECTION IF YOU PLAN ON CYCLING AND KAYAKING

THE PIG WAR

On a midsummer day in 1859, the serenity of San Juan Island was interrupted by a gunshot. Thirteen years after the Oregon Treaty was signed, ambiguous borders between the US and Canada had created a tense environment on the islands. When Lyman Cutlar, a salty American homesteader, saw a black pig uprooting his potatoes, diplomacy was no option. He pulled the trigger and started the so-called Pig War. Aside from the swine, no lives were lost, and the land dispute was settled peacefully, but its legacy lives on in the pair of historic military camps – American Camp and English Camp – on the island.

ORCAS AROUND THE ISLANDS

Three pods of orcas live around the San Juan Islands and are frequently sighted during the warmer months, usually between mid-April and October. The families are named J, K and L Pods and have a population that hovers around 80 whales. Each whale is individually identified by the unique patterns of black and white patches on their saddle patch, behind their large dorsal fin. Lime Kiln Point State Park is an excellent place to learn more about these magnificent creatures, as it has ranger-led programs and informative placards set up right on the water.

THE PERFECT GETAWAY

Want an idyllic visit to San Juan Island? Book your trip in the late spring or early summer, when you'll miss the peak-season crowds but still enjoy clear skies and warm days. A large spectrum of accommodations can be booked in Friday Harbor, including a couple of very swish hotels and an affordable youth hostel, but the serenity and charm of a B&B further out on the island can't be beat. Many of them even have bikes to borrow if you want to get around by pedalling.

Over the next three days you'll be exploring the island, so start with a cruise around the perimeter to get acquainted with your surroundings. History buffs will enjoy stopping at American Camp and English Camp, but the best park on the island is Lime Kiln Point State Park, where you can spend a few hours wandering the bluffs, scanning the skies for bald eagles and the ocean for orcas before unpacking a picnic overlooking the water. This is home to a lighthouse, and the rangers on hand will give you tips on spotting whales. Other day trips include a jaunt to the Krystal Acres Alpaca Farm or San Juan Vineyards for a taste of their award-winning siegerrebe. In the evening, head into town for the catch of the day at one of Friday Harbor's restaurants, then watch a flick at the little movie house or a performance by the island's local theatre community.

If you extend your trip by a couple of days, the possibilities grow exponentially. Consider a side trip to one of the other islands: you can hike to the top of the modest Mt Constitution on Orcas Island for a view of the archipelago and distant snowcap of Mt Rainier, or you can circumnavigate Lopez Island by bike, a breezy trip that can be made in a leisurely afternoon.

PLAN IT

The islands' small airport receives charter flights, but most visitors arrive via the Washington State Ferry from Anacortes, which accommodates cars. If you're flying into Seattle-Tacoma International Airport, it's a two-hour drive to the dock. The ferry weaves through the San Juan Archipelago before arriving at Friday Harbor; transfer to other islands via inter-island ferries. Island Bicycles in Friday Harbor rents a variety of bikes. For kayak rentals, try Sea Quest Expeditions.

DETOUR

Many lookouts from the islands offer views of the Olympic Mountains. For naturalists, they are an essential detour; no other place in North America can match the biodiversity in such a compact area. A two-day detour will follow the string of little towns around the edge of the Olympic Peninsula, and offer a chance to visit Olympic National Park. You can walk through one of the only temperate rainforests in the northern hemisphere, and visit the location for the blockbuster *Twilight* films.

261

OPENING SPREAD Limekiln lighthouse, on the west coast of San Juan Island, dates from 1919. **ABOVE AND LEFT** Though it's illegal to deliberately approach orcas by boat or kayak in the state of Washington, the local whale pods have been known to check out paddlers very closely.

DECKCHAIR

* ***Time Shadows and Tall Tales: San Juan Island in Earlier Years*** (Jack J Crawford) A colourful local history.

* ***Your Sister's Sister*** (2011) Shot on the islands in only 12 days on a shoestring budget, this indie film has a number of marquee stars.

* ***Free Willy*** (1993) This family drama about a young boy who befriends a captive orca was filmed in the area.

* ***Snow Falling on Cedars*** (1999) A beautifully shot adaptation of David Guterson's award-winning tale of prejudice in a San Juan Island fishing community during the mid-20th century.

* ***Short Nights of the Shadow Catcher*** (Timothy Egan) A riveting biography about Edward Curtis, a photographer who worked to document and preserve local native customs during westward expansion.

CHINA

TIBET

Taktsang
Goemba   ○ Punakha
Paro   ○ Thimphu

BHUTAN

INDIA

BANGLADESH

GET A SPIRITUAL HIGH IN BHUTAN

The Himalayan kingdom of Bhutan offers natural highs, with a mesmerising mix of devout Buddhism, pristine peaks and valleys, and ancient culture. Cast off your daily cares and find inner peace in the Land of the Thunder Dragon...

262

Famous for pursuing Gross National Happiness, rather than purely financial GDP, the long-isolated nation of Bhutan definitely has something to teach jaded materialists. The mental gear-shift starts as you fly in to Paro Airport: weaving its way between patchwork-green valleys, the Druk Air flight is a buzz in itself.

Spirituality is never far away in this mystical Buddhist nation, dotted with *dzongs* (fortress-monasteries), practising monks and religious art. And there's no better way to tap into a bit of soul-searching than tackling the day-trek up to Tiger's Nest (Taktshang Goemba), Bhutan's most magical mountaintop monastery, clinging to a cliff-face high above the Paro Valley. Eerie white tree moss, like strands of Gandalf's beard, drapes branches along the two-hour hike. The journey feels like a physical experience of the Buddhist dharma, or 'path of righteousness', with each breath-snatching step clearing the mind of clutter. As you walk up the winding trail, you'll pass sure-footed horses, saffron-robed monks (clutching digital cameras!) and prayer wheels you can spin by hand.

Halfway up, chill out with a cuppa in a teahouse with neck-cricking views of Tiger's Nest. Then push on up to the top, where prayer flags frame the mist-shrouded monastery and the only sounds are the whistling wind, tumbling waterfalls and chanting. You can peek into the dark inner rooms, populated by praying monks honouring Guru Rinpoche, where medieval tradition, intense devotion and mystery rule. Guru Rinpoche is believed to have flown to this spot on the back of a tigress to subdue a local demon, bringing Buddhism to Bhutan from Tibet. Afterwards, he meditated in a cave, now designated a holy place and home to the current monastery. It's not an easy hike, given the altitude, but if you're fairly fit you should manage it – remember: no pain, no spiritual gain.

ESSENTIAL EXPERIENCES

* **Trying your hand at archery, Bhutan's national sport; you'll see local tournaments everywhere.**
* Picking up a dandy *gho* to go – the stylish, knee-high, belted robe still popular as the male national costume. (The female *kira*, a full-length dress, can also be found at shops in Paro or Thimphu.)
* **Tackling Tiger's Nest, the ultimate day-trek.**
* Visiting a fortress-monastery; those at Paro and Punakha are particularly striking.
* **Catching a traditional dance festival, for powerful, spiritually inspired performances.**
* Chilling out (or should we say warming up?) with a hot-stone bath treatment.

LOCATION BHUTAN IS IN THE HIMALAYAS, TUCKED BETWEEN INDIA, TIBET AND CHINA | **BEST TIME OF YEAR** AUTUMN (SEPTEMBER TO NOVEMBER) BRINGS THE BEST TREKKING WEATHER, CLOSELY FOLLOWED BY SPRING (MARCH TO MAY) | **IDEAL TIME COMMITMENT** SEVEN TO 10 DAYS | **ESSENTIAL TIP** TAKE TIME TO ACCLIMATISE, AS THE HIGH ALTITUDE CAN BE TAXING **BUDGET** $$$ | **PACK** WORN-IN TREKKING BOOTS, WALKING POLES, HAT, SUNSCREEN AND SHADES; PERSONAL MANTRA

BIKING BHUTAN

Walking uphill not your bag? Then how about freewheeling downhill on a mountain bike for 35km? The ride from Cheli La Pass – at 3810m, the country's highest motorable road pass – down to Paro is an adrenalin-fuelled, wind-in-your-hair thrill, but suits riders of all levels. Bikes, helmets and even a lift to the top can be arranged; from there, you can whizz past stray dogs, chickens, kids, meandering monks and the occasional motor vehicle, before sweeping past the airport into town. You'll scarcely need to pedal, although you may want to apply the brakes...

HOT-BATH HEAVEN

No time to meditate? Let the spa take the strain with
a traditional Bhutanese *dotsho* (hot-stone bath),
guaranteed to soothe trek-weary muscles. Stones
are heated over hot coals then dropped into a deep
wooden tub, warming the water up to deliciously toasty
temperatures. (Don't worry, a handy grill stops them
from sizzling your skin.) Even smaller hotels often
sport one of these must-visit bathing marvels. At Uma
by COMO in Paro, floating mountain flowers dot the
bath and tranquil valley views provide a backdrop to
your secluded treatment room. After sipping tea as you
soak, continue the pampering with a massage.

■ THE PERFECT GETAWAY

Fancy starting the day with yoga, gazing out over the Himalayas? At boutique hotel Uma by COMO, perched high above Paro town, it's easy to get in touch with your spiritual side. Set amid pine forests, this lofty retreat is a contemporary take on traditional Bhutanese architecture, with 20 airy lodge-rooms arranged around a sunny courtyard and nine stand-alone villas. Spend a day acclimatising to the altitude (you'll feel yourself puffing); take a dip in the stone-lined pool or enjoy a soothing bath at the spa.

Just here for a few days? Descend to Paro town, to tour its fortress-monastery; wander the courtyards surrounding the central tower to see murals and carvings. A conch-shaped watchtower nearby houses the National Museum, displaying an eclectic mix of weapons, teapots, stuffed animals, stamps and *thangkas* (religious paintings). Devote a day to climbing to Tiger's Nest, stopping for a tiffin-box picnic, or trekking to ancient nunnery Kila Goemba, near Cheli La Pass.

Buzzy capital Thimphu, a winding two-hour drive from Paro, boasts a dzong, a reconstructed farmhouse at the Folk Heritage Museum, and the National Institute for Zorig Chusum, where young artists and crafts trainees work. Wildlife fans can also take in the Motithang Takin Preserve, home to Bhutan's national animal, the moose-like takin. Straddling the Wang Chhu River, the Weekend Market is full of food, clothing and Buddhist curios. Multiday camping treks are up for grabs, such as the six-day Druk Path or Dagala Thousand Lakes hikes, or the nine-day Jhomolhari trek. Bhutan's accommodation options range from budget guesthouses to luxe retreats Amankora and the Taj Tashi in Thimphu.

■ PLAN IT

National carrier Druk Air offers flights to Paro Airport from Bangkok, Delhi, Kolkata, Kathmandu and Singapore; book early. Visas must be arranged in advance. The government's commitment to preserving Bhutan's cultural identity means you're required to spend a minimum of US$250 each day. Book through an approved tour operator (some hotels can sort out the red tape for you).

■ DETOUR

Punakha, a five-hour drive east of Paro, is an ideal spot for acclimatising at lower altitude and in a verdant landscape. Once the country's capital, the town makes a blissful base for trekking, rafting, biking or visits to Bhutan's most jaw-dropping dzong, straddling the confluence of two rivers. You can also ogle the nearby Temple of the Divine Madman (Chimi Lhakhang) for more Buddhist insights. COMO has a serene sister lodge here, with just nine valley-view rooms and two villas nestled on a bend of the Mo Chu River. February's Punakha Festival is an action-packed time to visit.

OPENING SPREAD Bringing firewood supplies to a guest's villa at the hotel Uma by COMO in Paro. **ABOVE** Fire and water: hot-stone baths and fire-side dining at Uma will soothe aching limbs after a hike up to the Tiger's Nest monastery. **LEFT** The Tiger's Nest temple complex dates from the 17th century.

DECKCHAIR

* ***The Cup*** (1999) This Bhutanese-directed film tells the tale of two young, soccer-mad Tibetan refugees at a monastery, desperate to watch the World Cup.

* ***An Open Heart: Practising Compassion in Everyday Life*** (the Dalai Lama) A basic Buddhist primer by neighbouring Tibet's spiritual leader.

* ***The Miracle of Mindfulness*** (Thich Nhat Hanh) A guide to meditation by a Vietnamese Zen master.

* ***Beyond the Sky and the Earth*** (Jamie Zeppa) The memoir of a Canadian teacher's years in remote Bhutan.

* ***Travellers and Magicians*** (2003) In this Bhutanese-language film, a frustrated civil servant dreams of leaving Bhutan, but a road trip persuades him happiness can be found at home.

* ***Bhutanese Tales of the Yeti*** (Kunzang Choden) Enchanting stories about the *migoi* (yeti).

MOUNT UP IN MONTANA

FANCY LEARNING HORSERIDING SKILLS, HERDING CATTLE ACROSS PLAINS WITH BONA FIDE COWBOYS AND SLEEPING IN CENTURY-OLD HOMESTEAD CABINS? THE AMERICAN WEST IS NO MERE MYTHOLOGY AT J BAR L, A WORKING CATTLE RANCH IN SOUTHWESTERN MONTANA'S REMOTE CENTENNIAL VALLEY.

266

Guests who make the long drive to J Bar L can look forward to being welcomed by a latter-day Marlboro Man, an honest-to-goodness cowboy who doffs his hat and greets female visitors as 'ma'am'. It's a scene out of a John Wayne film, minus the shootouts but full of possibility and adventure.

J Bar L is first and foremost in the beef business: it looks after some 400 head of cattle, which are eventually sold as grass-fed steaks to restaurants and retailers. The hospitality component came second, in order to support the ranching operation. But it's no afterthought: the tricked-out, rustic-luxe solar-powered houses and cabins have plush beds and stylish frontier furnishings.

During J Bar L's weeklong working-ranch vacations, up to eight guests get to accompany the cowhands on their daily rounds, herding cattle, administering medication, fixing fences and whatever other chores need to be done. Then they eat a hearty, home-cooked dinner together, sharing stories with people who lead a completely different way of life. The peace that comes from sauntering across limitless prairies with snow-speckled mountains in the distance is a tonic for desk jockeys who wonder if their information-age jobs serve any actual purpose. Cowboying is good old-fashioned work: the animals depend on you. And at the end of the day, your hunger is well earned and your tiredness well deserved.

Sleep comes easily here, both because of the outdoor exertions and because the ranch is impossibly quiet – it's 35km from pavement, and two hours from a city of any size. The cabins might be 6km from the dining hall. It's just you and the lonesome prairie – you're more likely to spot a wolf or an elk than another human being. It's rugged and difficult, and it forces you to contemplate what it was like for pioneers a century ago, before Gore-Tex and gas stoves. It all has quite a way of putting things into perspective.

ESSENTIAL EXPERIENCES

* **Mounting a spirited steed for horsemanship training with the ranch hands before heading out onto the plains, taking in unfathomably vast prairies and mountain ranges.**

* Dining with ranch staff: Montana cowboys break bread with city-slicker guests, and conversations can go in any number of fascinating directions.

* **Eating grass-fed steak straight from the ranch – the epitome of farm-to-table and undeniably delicious (as well as healthier than most beef).**

* Sleeping in the middle of nowhere – and remembering the pioneers who did it not for a vacation but because it was their only choice.

LOCATION MONTANA, USA | **BEST TIME OF YEAR** JUNE THROUGH SEPTEMBER | **IDEAL TIME COMMITMENT** WORKING-RANCH WEEKS ARE HELD ON SPECIFIC DATES, AND MUST BE BOOKED FOR A FULL WEEK | **ESSENTIAL TIP** BE PREPARED FOR VARIED WEATHER CONDITIONS | **BUDGET** $$$ | **PACK** A COWBOY HAT: THE SUN IS FORMIDABLE AT THIS ALTITUDE; YOU'LL FEEL SILLY IN A BASEBALL CAP

BEYOND PLAYING COWGIRL

In addition to the working-ranch weeks, J Bar L opens its cabins and historic homes to visitors throughout the summer. During non-working weeks, guests use the lodging as a base for pursuits like fly-fishing, bird-watching – there are more than 230 species in the nearby Red Rock Lakes National Wildlife Refuge, considered one of the United States' most beautiful reserves – hiking, mountain biking and horse riding, or making day trips to nearby Yellowstone or Grand Teton National Parks. And don't underestimate the pleasure of sitting on the porch and watching the sun crest the mountains on a clear, crisp morning.

GRASS-FED BEEF

J Bar L has encouraged more than a few vegetarians to sample its ranch-raised beef; when the animals are treated this well, many of the objections to eating meat disappear. Their cattle are raised without hormones or antibiotics on thousands of hectares of pristine pasture and they eat grass their entire lives. This makes their meat high in healthy omega-3 fatty acids and low in potentially harmful omega-6s. Because they're moved on horseback, rather than mustered with vehicles, and they're slaughtered in the most humane way possible, they score zero on beef-cattle stress tests, which improves the taste of the meat.

THE PERFECT GETAWAY

There's not much planning that goes into a stay here. The biggest task is to surrender to the slower pace and old-fashioned work ethic and values. Centennial Valley hasn't changed much in the past 100 years: you can still see 80km from one end of the valley to the other – taking in the ridges of five mountain chains.

The ranch welcomes riders of all experience levels, but before you're allowed on the ranch's working horses you must complete some rigorous horse training. Expect to saddle your own horse and if you need a step to mount, you won't be riding. Once guests are deemed saddle-worthy, they'll head out to pasture. You may be on the plains for six or seven hours, and it's tiring in the best possible way. That's why it feels like such a blessing to come back to your room at the homestead, where the historic houses and cabins have been restored and updated to include 21st-century comforts like gas stoves and (for better or worse) wifi.

The kitchens are stocked with breakfast fixings. Lunch is usually a simple sack affair, eaten outside quickly between chores. Dinner is more festive, and shared with staff who have been in Montana for years and have ranching in their blood. Guests are genuinely welcomed, and not seen as big-city poseurs – a real exchange of perspectives and ideas often occurs. One issue that has everyone on pretty much the same side is the stunning, wide-open nature. The owner put all 3642 hectares of the ranch under conservation easement, meaning none of it can be developed. She also co-founded the Centennial Valley Association, which helps ranchers and environmentalists find common ground. A stay here makes it easy to see how much they have to agree on.

PLAN IT

The easy way to reach J Bar L is to fly to Idaho Falls Regional Airport in Idaho, then drive 2½ hours north to Montana's Centennial Valley. Rent a 4WD, as part of the drive is on unpaved roads; buy a can of Fix-A-Flat. The ranch offers four working-ranch weeks each summer: it books up far in advance. The beginning and end of the season are the best times: the heifers are calving and the river is full in June, and the leaves are turning in September.

DETOUR

Mountain Sky Guest Ranch (a 1¼-hour drive northwest of Bozeman, Montana) is a family-friendly version of the rugged American West. Guests – most of whom have kids in tow – arrive Sunday and depart the following Saturday, and in between they enjoy old-time activities such as hayrides, cowboy cookout breakfasts and talent shows. Staff refer to one another as 'counsellors', communal meals are announced when someone (usually a youngster) rings the dinner bell, and the vibe is very much like the summer camp you wish you'd gone to.

269

OPENING SPREAD Follow the leader: you'll need to be confident on a horse to get the most from a stay at the J Bar L ranch. **ABOVE (L)** Horses remain the best way to cover this frontier state. **ABOVE (R)** Centennial Valley is an important wetland ecosystem. **LEFT** Roping steers at the J Bar L.

DECKCHAIR

* **Riding the White Horse Home: A Western Family Album** (Teresa Jordan) A rich family chronicle of four generations on a ranch.

* **Trails Plowed Under: Stories of the Old West** (Charles M Russell) Written in Old West vernacular, this book is alive with hilarious stories.

* **This House of Sky: Landscapes of a Western Mind** (Ivan Doig) A beautifully rendered story of growing up in western Montana.

* **Gardeners of Eden: Rediscovering Our Importance to Nature**

(Dan Dagget) Many of Dagget's philosophies on land conservation have been implemented at J Bar L.

* **Another Turn of the Crank** (Wendell Berry) Essays on country communities by Kentucky's inspirational farmer-philosopher-poet.

* **Centennial Valley 1820–1930 Vol 1: A Journey Through Time** (Centennial Valley Historical Society) An entertaining and informative collection of historic articles written by local folk.

A TWO-WHEELED TRIP IN CENTRAL OTAGO

PEDAL ACROSS MAJESTIC PLAINS AND THROUGH TUNNELS IN TOWERING MOUNTAINS ON A LEISURELY CYCLE TOUR OF THE CENTRAL OTAGO VALLEYS ON NEW ZEALAND'S SOUTH ISLAND, STOPPING FOR SUSTENANCE AT INVITING COUNTRY PUBS AND WARM B&BS.

270

If New Zealand's South island is typically a place of harsh landscapes and hard adventures, you wouldn't know it here. In these Central Otago valleys the land has a softer finish. The hills shimmer with grasses that are brushed like velvet by the wind, and the waterways are lined with willows. They're scenes suitably matched to this most gentle of rides.

Still, there's still something fantastic about the scenery, a cinematic immensity to the open country. These are the plains of Rohan, after all, as shown to the world, big and bold, in the *Lord of the Rings* trilogy. The low ranges around you are quilled with rock but the valleys have been ironed blessedly flat by time. In the rivers, gold once flowed as freely as water – the original railway on which the trail runs was built to cart the precious metal out to Dunedin – and even today the willows and the grape vines electrify into autumn shades, making the land look as though it's been papered in gold leaf.

The gold rush is long gone and today there's no rush of any sort. Though the cycling is easy, the distractions are many. The trail is punctuated with pubs – a dozen hotels in about 150km – making this a ride as civilised (and ciderised) as any in the world. It's the Central Otago way: laid-back, laconic, unhurried – the trail seems to have acquired these characteristic as much as the locals.

Even the climbs can't seem to be bothered being climbs. In this most mountainous of islands, there's only Tiger Hill, and as you crest it you can't help but wonder if it's really over. Was it that easy, this hill that's all meow and no bite? It may be the longest and steepest climb on the Otago Rail Trail, but it's as gentle as the lands that encase it.

ESSENTIAL EXPERIENCES

* **Pub-hopping as you ride through the small towns that dot the Otago valleys – sometimes at pubs that have outlived their towns.**

* Tunnelling through cliff faces inside the Poolburn and Taieri Gorges.

* **Delivering a stone and sweeping the ice at the curling rink in Naseby.**

* Watching the willows turn as golden as Central Otago's history during an autumn ride.

* **Stamping your rail-trail passport at each former railway station along the route.**

* Changing from the rail trail to the running rail as you return to Dunedin on the Taieri Gorge Railway.

LOCATION CENTRAL OTAGO, SOUTH ISLAND, NEW ZEALAND | **BEST TIME OF YEAR** OCTOBER TO MAY | **IDEAL TIME COMMITMENT** THREE TO FOUR DAYS | **ESSENTIAL TIP** THE SURFACE IS GRAVEL, SO RIDE A MOUNTAIN BIKE OR HYBRID | **BUDGET** $$ **PACK** PADDED CYCLING SHORTS, SUNSCREEN, MAP

KEEP ON PEDALLING

Following the success of the Otago Rail Trail – which 200,000 people cycle each year – the New Zealand government made the decision in 2008 to invest NZ$50 million in building 18 new cycleways across the country. A number of them are now open while others remain works in progress. Flagship rides are likely to include the 300km Alps 2 Ocean, descending from Mt Cook Village, at the foot of the country's highest mountain, to the coast at Oamaru; and the 175km Around the Mountains ride out of Queenstown. See the New Zealand Cycle Trail website for the latest updates.

■ THE PERFECT GETAWAY

Tiger Hill is, if nothing else, a ready excuse for a refreshment stop. At its foot, only 25km from the rail trail's beginning in Clyde, is the Chatto Creek Tavern. You could just ride past – the tiny Tiger barely warrants a stop – but what's the hurry? There are hammocks strung out the back of the pub, and it's a chance to try the end-product of those Central Otago pinot noirs you will have seen growing by the trail near Alexandra.

If one wine or beer isn't enough, Omakau's Commercial Hotel is just 12km ahead. Then the pub at Lauder another 7km from there. And then...well, then, there are more pubs, but not before one of the rail trail's most scenic sections.

Out of Lauder, the trail turns with the Manuherikia River, burrowing through Poolburn Gorge, travelling over a viaduct and then almost balanced on the edge of the gorge's rock walls. These steep cliffs were such a puzzle to the railway builders, they resorted to blasting through a couple of tunnels – little patches of darkness that now briefly turn day into night for cyclists.

Across the Ida Valley, it's about time for another pub stop, and if you're at the Oturehua Railway Hotel early enough, the freshly baked scones may just be coming out of the oven. Otherwise, you can always try the Big Bike Burger before scratching about in the eclectic collection of goods across the road at Gilchrist's Oturehua Store, the oldest continually operating general store in New Zealand.

At the trail's high point – 618m above sea level – just past Oturehua, a sign promises that 'it's all downhill from here', the great cycling catch-cry that will propel you across the Maniototo Plain, through the Taieri Gorge, along the edge of the Rock and Pillar Range and into Middlemarch. Now that you've finished, it's definitely time for a thirst-quencher...

DECKCHAIR

* ***Otago Rail Trail Guide Book*** (Peter Andrews) Offers exactly what the name on the tin suggests.
* ***Classic New Zealand Cycle Trails*** (Kennett Brothers) Guide to 46 rides around the country – including the Otago Rail Trail – by New Zealand's most prolific and noted cycling writers.
* ***Over the Garden Wall: The Story of the Otago Central Railway*** (J Dangerfield & G Emerson) History of the trail's raison d'être: the railway.
* ***The Hut Builder*** (Laurence Fearnley) This coming-of-age novel takes the reader from the grassy expanses of Mackenzie Country to the heights of Mt Cook.
* ***Lord of the Rings*** **film trilogy** (2001–03) It's about fantasy and quest, but really it's about New Zealand landscapes.
* ***The Hobbit*** (2012) For the prequel to Tolkien's epic (above) Peter Jackson returns to New Zealand and conjures a CGI dragon.

WINE ON WHEELS

As you ride into Alexandra, you'll notice the vineyards beside the rail trail – you're skirting the edge of the world's southernmost wine region: Central Otago. Straddling the 45th latitude, it's a cool-climate wine region, famed for its pinot noir. It's worth parking your bike for a tipple, or even detouring away onto the Central Otago Wine Trail, which features more than 30 wineries. In Alexandra you'll find Hinton Estate and Shaky Bridge Wines, both open to the public. Venture just off the trail in Clyde and you never know who you might bump into – actor Sam Neill owns the Two Paddocks vineyard.

PLAN IT

Dunedin is the nearest city to the rail trail and its airport provides the best access point for travellers. InterCity runs buses from Dunedin to Clyde that stop at the trailhead outside of town. The trail has a fantastic support infrastructure: you can hire bikes and organise pack transfers, transport from Dunedin and accommodation through the official trail website. There are a number of private operators who can facilitate trips – Adventure South is a good starting point, operating a range of guided rides.

DETOUR

From the trail's end at Middlemarch, it's a scenic journey on the Taieri Gorge Railway (part of the original railway that forms the basis of the rail trail) into increasingly urbane Dunedin. The city has some grand Victorian architecture, built with the gold-rush wealth from Central Otago, including the gorgeous basalt train station. Be sure to head out from the city onto the wild Otago Peninsula. Taiaroa Head, the eastern tip of the peninsula, is the site of the world's only mainland albatross colony, while yellow-eyed penguins – said to be the world's rarest variety – shuffle ashore at several peninsula beaches.

ANDREW BAIN | GETTY IMAGES ©

OPENING SPREAD Mt Cook: the Alps 2 Ocean route descends eastward to the coast and is New Zealand's longest unbroken cycle trail. **ABOVE** Riding the Central Otago Rail Trail. **BELOW** You'll pass near wineries, such as the Wooing Tree Vineyard, along the way.

MOTORCYCLING IN NORTH THAILAND

SURE, YOU'VE BEEN TO THAILAND. BUT HAVE YOU REALLY EXPERIENCED THAILAND? WE'RE TALKING 360-DEGREE VIEWS FROM MOUNTAINTOPS, MIXING WITH THE LOCALS, THE FREEDOM TO STOP WHENEVER AND WHEREVER YOU LIKE AND, MOST IMPORTANTLY, THE WIND IN YOUR HAIR.

274

Specifically, we're talking about experiencing Thailand from the saddle of a hired motorcycle. And there's no better place to do this than in Mae Hong Son, a remote and mountainous province in the country's north. The area is the setting for the popular self-guided motorcycle circuit known as the Mae Hong Son Loop, an up-to-600km ride that begins in Chiang Mai and heads northwest, taking in Rte 1095's curves (all 1864 of them) before following the Burmese border south and circling back to Chiang Mai.

Half-forgotten in Thailand's northwest corner, Mae Hong Son is custom-made for motorcycle touring. The province's main artery is a ribbon of hairpin turns that brings together limestone cliffs, mountain valleys, hilltribe villages and some of the country's most astonishing viewpoints. This ride means sweeping through cool valleys bordered by tiered rice fields one minute, and in the next, inching by pine trees at the top of a sunburned peak. Fuel stations are often little more than oil drums, and rest stops are made of bamboo – this isn't a Sunday drive at home.

Stops include Pai, the valley town that is one of Thailand's buzziest tourist spots; the rugged, cave-riddled Pangmapha district; Mae Hong Son city, one of Thailand's more attractive provincial capitals; and Mae Sariang, a sleepy town surrounded by virgin teak forest that is also home to a trekking scene. The province is populated by a mix of Shan, Karen and northern Thais, and home to a unique local cuisine. Simply put, experiencing this corner of the country by motorcycle offers both an exciting journey and a unique destination.

Yet the best thing about the loop is that anybody can do it. Renting a motorcycle in Chiang Mai is cheap and easy; Mae Hong Son's roads are well maintained and unchallenging, with relatively few other vehicles; and there's ample and conveniently spaced accommodation and food along the entire route.

ESSENTIAL EXPERIENCES

* **Embarking upon a classic road trip – Thai-style – and in the process, mastering the art of making a hairpin turn on a motorcycle.**

* Partying with backpackers, rocking to live music and taking advantage of the international cuisine restaurants in Pai.

* **The literal highs and lows: photographing some of Thailand's most impressive mountaintop viewpoints, and slogging through caverns in Pangmapha district.**

* Staying in some of northern Thailand's best guesthouses and hotels, or if you're keen to get off the beaten track, diverging from the loop to visit hill-tribe villages and remote border areas.

* **Sampling the earthy, savoury and often meaty flavours of authentic northern Thai cuisine.**

LOCATION CHIANG MAI AND MAE HONG SON, THAILAND | **BEST TIME OF YEAR** NOVEMBER TO JANUARY | **IDEAL TIME COMMITMENT** ONE WEEK | **ESSENTIAL TIP** WEAR STURDY PROTECTIVE CLOTHING | **BUDGET** $ | **PACK** THE GOLDEN TRIANGLE RIDER'S EXCELLENT MAP/GUIDE, *MAE HONG SON: THE LOOP*

CHOOSING YOUR RIDE

Shelve those Enduro fantasies. Unless you are intending to go off-road or plan on crossing unpaved roads during the wet season, it's highly unlikely you'll need one of the large dirt bikes you'll see for rent in Chiang Mai. Despite their rather emasculating names – Spacy i, Fino, Spark, Click – the automatic-transmission, 110cc-to-150cc, scooter-like motorcycles found across Thailand are fast and powerful enough for the Mae Hong Son Loop. Recommended and longstanding Chiang Mai motorcycle hire shops include Mr Beer and Mr Mechanic; hire prices range from about 150B per day for a 125cc Honda Wave/Dream to 1200B per day for a Honda CB1000.

■ THE PERFECT GETAWAY

The loop begins in Chiang Mai, northern Thailand's largest urban centre, where you'll also take care of essential logistics: hiring a motorcycle and buying supplies. Your first overnight stop is the backpacker mecca of Pai, situated in a mountain valley approximately 150km (about three hours' drive) from Chiang Mai. Heaps of accommodation, cafes and restaurants and a fun live-music scene may have you staying here longer than the obligatory single night.

From Pai, it's 40km to your next stop, Soppong (also known as Pangmapha). Along the way you'll encounter numerous ascending hairpin turns culminating at Kiew Lom viewpoint (1500m), the highest point on the loop. From here it's a brief, twisty downhill run to Soppong, a rural market town surrounded by jutting limestone mountains. Despite its tiny stature, Soppong is home to a handful of great places to stay, including Soppong River Inn and the rustic Cave Lodge.

Your next destination is Mae Hong Son's eponymous provincial capital, and this 65km stretch – taking in both soaring viewpoints and mountain valleys – is arguably the loop's most picturesque. Mae Hong Son city is quiet, but offers great accommodation – Fern Resort, 7km from town, is one of Thailand's best rural retreats – as well as the potential for some side trips. At this point in the trip you can choose your own adventure. At Khun Yuam, 65km south of Mae Hong Son, it's possible to head east and circle back to Chiang Mai via mountainous and remote Rte 1263, with a possible overnight in the tiny but pretty valley town of Mae Chaem. Or continue 160km south to overnight in Mae Sariang; afterwards, Rte 108 offers a longer but more beaten-track route back to Chiang Mai.

■ PLAN IT

Chiang Mai is the logical base. The ideal time to tackle the loop is during Thailand's brief winter, from November to January. During these months, the weather is cool (it can be cold at night) and the countryside is at its most beautiful. Avoid the wet season (June to October), although it should be noted that it generally only pours once a day. The best source of information on motorcycle travelling in the north – and publishers of terrific motorcycle touring-based maps – is Golden Triangle Rider.

■ DETOUR

If you've never ridden a motorcycle before, an easy introduction to motorcycle touring is the Mae Sa Valley/Samoeng Loop, a 100km ride that can be tackled in half a day. The route extends north from Chiang Mai and follows Rtes 107, 1096 and 1269, taking in jungle scenery, moderate climbs and ample bends, providing a taste of what a longer ride will be like. Details on the route and the area's attractions can be found in *Mae Sa Valley: The Samoeng Loop*, a map/guide published by Golden Triangle Rider.

OPENING SPREAD Wat Thaton is a Chinese pagoda in Chiang Mai that looks out towards Myanmar. **ABOVE (L)** Thailand's Loy Krathong floating lantern festival usually takes place in November. **ABOVE (R)** Always wear a motorcycle helmet; riding in northern Thailand can be an unpredictable experience.

DECKCHAIR

* *Caves of Northern Thailand* (Pindar Sidisunthorn, Simon Gardner) A guide to the sacred and secular caverns of Thailand's north.

* *Khon Muang: People and Principalities of North Thailand* (Andrew Forbes and David Henley) An illustrated history of the people who inhabit northern Thailand.

* *Lanna Renaissance* (Joe Cummings) The art, history and culture of northern Thailand's former kingdom.

* *Lanna: Thailand's Northern Kingdom* (Michael Freeman) A cultural encyclopedia of northern Thailand.

* *Very Thai* (Philip Cornwell-Smith) Colourful photos and essays on Thailand's quirks.

* *Wild Times* (John Spies) Self-published book chronicling the author's 30-plus years in the region; available at Cave Lodge in Soppong.

PARTY

GREAT ESCAPES

SUMMER IN STOCKHOLM'S ARCHIPELAGO

GET BACK TO NATURE WITH SUN-LOVING SWEDES FOR A MIDSUMMER NIGHT'S DREAM IN STOCKHOLM'S ARCHIPELAGO. MUSIC, FLOWERS AND STRANGE MYTHS COLLIDE ON THE SHORTEST NIGHT OF THE YEAR.

278

With wildflowers garlanded in their hair, a group of people – young and old – are singing and dancing in circles around a maypole that has been entwined in greenery. The fiddle players change tempo and a new dance begins, one that involves everybody hopping like frogs. Soon, the dancers collapse in laughter and the music changes again.

Summer is a fleeting experience in Sweden and it's seized with both hands. For a few weeks, when daylight dims for just a couple of hours at night, the country exists in a heightened state of anticipation. The season peaks for the Midsummer Eve festival, close to the summer solstice in June. This is a nationwide party that sees Swedes shed their sensible side to down *nubbe* (shots of snaps or aquavit), feast from a smorgasbord of pickled herring, new potatoes, and salmon with sour cream and dill – and dance like little frogs.

The festival's pagan origins are barely concealed: the day is about being connected to nature, about celebrating the harvest to come and another winter survived. It's when you see another side to the typically strait-laced Swedes.

There is no more magical place to let your flower-decked hair down than in Stockholm's archipelago – all 30,000 islands of it. This is where the capital city decamps for the summer. Some islands, such as Vaxholm and Sandhamn, are well-established destinations with guesthouses and jetties for ferries. For smaller, more distant islands you'll need a boat.

After the maypole has been raised, drinks drunk and dances danced, it's time for sack races, tug-of-war contests and apple bobbing. A golden light filters through birch trees, shimmering over the flaxen-haired revellers. But even Midsummer's Day can't last forever. Later, much later, as the sun briefly slips below the horizon, you'll wish for more time: more time here, more summertime – more everything.

ESSENTIAL EXPERIENCES

* **Sailing or kayaking between the archipelago's islands, weather permitting.**
* Meeting people and making friends at a Midsummer Eve party; every town will have a public event.
* **Eating enough pickled herring and potato salad in a day to last a lifetime.**
* Dancing like a little frog.
* **Watching the sun come up, just a few hours after it set, and continuing the party.**
* Exploring Gamla Stan, Stockholm's beautiful, water-bound old town when you return to the Swedish capital.

LOCATION SWEDEN | **BEST TIME OF YEAR** LATE JUNE | **IDEAL TIME COMMITMENT** ONE WEEK | **ESSENTIAL TIP** YOU CAN BRING DUTY-FREE ALCOHOL INTO SWEDEN | **BUDGET** $$ | **PACK** SWIMMING GEAR AND WATERPROOFS FOR UNPREDICTABLE WEATHER

MIDSUMMER MADNESS

Sweden's Midsummer Festival (Midsommarfirande) takes place on the penultimate Friday in June. It's celebrated with the enthusiasm you'd expect from a nation that spends half the year in the dark and the cold. Entwined with pagan symbolism, the solstice layers a very Swedish appreciation of the outdoors with old myths, such as the one that says that putting seven different flowers under your pillow will cause you to dream of your love-to-be, and traditional dances such as Smä Grodorna (Little Frogs), the gist of which is that tiny frogs look funny without ears or tails. Learn more at Stockholm's Skansen, the world's first open-air museum (founded 1891) on the island of Djurgården, reached by ferry from Gamla Stan.

WINTER WONDERLAND

Not for nothing is Stockholm nicknamed the Ice Queen. In winter, as the waterways lacing the city freeze, commuters swap bicycles for ice skates. Some years, the sea around the archipelago also turns to ice. But more usually inland lakes, such as Vättern, southwest of Stockholm, are where Swedes go to glide on the glassy ice. Long-distance ice skating is a national passion; it's demanding and potentially dangerous but endlessly exhilarating, swooshing past pine forests and beaches for 50km (or 200km for racers), beyond the reach of roads. As Bengt Kull of local tour operator 30.000 Öar says: 'Every day on the ice is an adventure.'

■ THE PERFECT GETAWAY

Stockholm empties faster than a bottle of Swedish snaps in the days leading up to Midsummer. Families and friends will have booked their favourite holiday spots long in advance (tip: cultivate any Scandinavian contacts for an invite) and accommodation in the archipelago fills up quickly. Spend a day seeing the city, including the remarkably preserved 17th-century ship at the Vasa Museum, before getting out of the ghost town. The day before the Midsummer Eve festival, Swedes stock up on herring, potatoes and sour cream. Don't forget to buy a bottle from a state liquor store if you're a guest at a party.

The archipelago is divided into northern (around Arholma island), southern (around Utö) and central (around Svartsö) sections. What the islands have in common – at least those inhabited by people rather than seals and seabirds – is a charming beauty. The clapboard cottages and boathouses are painted red with white window frames and doors. The modern world is left at the port; most people get around by boat and bicycle.

Even in autumn and winter there is a meditative beauty to the archipelago, as sea, sky and stone merge in a thousand shades of grey. Adventurous types charter sailing boats or explore beyond the bigger islands in a sea kayak, pitching up at beaches hidden among the tumble of rocks and trees. Camping is permitted on some islands and others have cabins; take local advice before setting out.

Nature is believed to assume supernatural powers for this one day (on islands such as Blidö watch for wild deer as you pick flowers). What is indisputable, however, is the annual baby boom that occurs around March.

■ PLAN IT

International airlines fly into Stockholm's Arlanda airport, from where an express shuttle train takes 20 minutes to reach the city centre. Some islands in Stockholm's archipelago are connected to the mainland by causeways and bridges. Those that are slightly further out, such as Vaxholm, are reached by a host of small ferry operators, the largest of which is Waxholmsbolaget. To visit islands in the outer archipelago you may need a private vessel. Book accommodation at www.visitsweden.se.

■ DETOUR

With its red-painted cottages, lakes and forests, Dalarna's sylvan landscape is a Swedish archetype. Four hours northwest of Stockholm, in central Sweden, the region is a popular destination for holidaying Swedes at Midsummer. At the southern tip of Lake Siljan, the town of Leksand – and its 25m maypole – is the focus for festivities, with 20,000 Swedes letting their hair down. Dalarna can be reached by plane (to Borlänge) or train (to the regional capital Falun) from Stockholm.

OPENING SPREAD Swedes weave garlands of flowers for Midsummer Eve festival. **ABOVE** Here comes the sun: it's time eat, drink, dance and celebrate the summer. **LEFT** Stockholmers head to their holiday homes or cabins in the Swedish archipelago.

DECKCHAIR

* ***Fanny and Alexander*** (1983) Ingmar Bergman's Oscar-winning film of a family falling apart is set in Uppsala.

* ***Let The Right One In*** (2008) A romantic-horror film set in Stockholm, about a boy who befriends a vampire.

* ***The Girl With The Dragon Tattoo*** (Stieg Larsson) Author Stieg Larsson was a frequent visitor to Stockholm's archipelago and his fictional detective Mikael Blomkvist has a summer house there.

* ***Bright Lights, Dark Shadows: The Real Story of ABBA*** (Carl Magnus Palm) A super-fan's biography of the Swedish supergroup.

* ***Wallander*** There are British and Swedish TV series following the eponymous detective, created by crime writer Henning Mankell over 12 novels. Both versions are excellent.

* ***Behind Blue Skies*** (2010) A satirical coming-of-age film set in the archipelago, from director Hannes Holm.

PARTY HARD IN THE BIG EASY

NEW ORLEANS IS ONE OF THE GREATEST MUSIC CITIES ON EARTH. AND EVERY FEBRUARY THE WHOLE CITY SHUTS DOWN TO CELEBRATE MARDI GRAS – THE WILDEST PARTY FESTIVITIES IN ALL OF NORTH AMERICA.

282

Here they come! All feathers and finery, dancing and chanting and surrounded by their followers. Hey, hey, it's the Mardi Gras Indians. 'Iko! Iko!' they chant while dancing in the street, surrounded by revellers, everyone caught up in the joy and excitement of Fat Tuesday, the final day of the craziness that is Mardi Gras in the city of New Orleans.

The Mardi Gras Indians are African American men who every year sew strikingly original, outrageously colourful 'suits' – suits that make Lady Gaga's stage costumes look conservative – then come out and parade in their 'tribes' on Fat Tuesday, Mardi Gras's climax. Also taking to the streets on Fat Tuesday is the Zulu Parade, when black New Orleans comes out to strut and celebrate. This parade starts early – be out on the streets by 8am to catch it – and moves across the central city. It is a feast of brass bands, marching girls and elaborate floats as 'krewes' toss beads and gifts (try and catch a painted coconut – exclusive to Zulu!) and huge fun. Follow the parade as it moves across downtown and you will get a real feeling for the city celebrating its survival.

Great live music can be heard year-round in this humid, sensual city. There are bars and clubs and the best buskers on earth around the French Quarter, from funky brass bands and jazz musicians to crusty young folkies and blues singers and rockers – and a myriad music festivals.

But Mardi Gras is when the whole city comes out to play. It precedes the Catholic celebration of Lent: Louisiana was, firstly, a Spanish and then a French colony (until 1803). The French allowed their slaves a degree of freedom to dance and perform music – providing the foundations for New Orleans as a hotbed of music-making. These days, Fat Tuesday's party is about witnessing a city that's survived hard times get up and shake its tail feathers.

ESSENTIAL EXPERIENCES

* **Riding the streetcar through the Garden District – a glorious way of experiencing New Orleans' architectural glory.**

* Wandering around lively Frenchmen St: dive bars, superb clubs, buskers, beggars, eccentrics and a very fine bookshop. Never a dull moment.

* **Following a street parade with brass band and dancers during Mardi Gras – part of black New Orleans tradition.**

* Attending concerts by local artists: Dr John, Irma Thomas, Allen Toussaint, Jon Cleary, The Wild Magnolias, Hurray for the Riff Raff, Little Freddie King, Aaron Neville, Chuck Perkins, Walter 'Wolfman' Washington, Kermit Ruffins, George Porter Jr and others.

* **Sinking happily into a Cajun-Creole food-induced coma.**

LOCATION NEW ORLEANS, LOUISIANA, USA | **BEST TIME OF YEAR** SEPTEMBER TO NOVEMBER; MARDI GRAS TAKES PLACE ACROSS FEBRUARY OR EARLY MARCH | **IDEAL TIME COMMITMENT** ONE WEEK | **ESSENTIAL TIP** TO CATCH THE MARDI GRAS INDIANS HEAD TO TREMÉ ON FAT TUESDAY AFTERNOON | **BUDGET** $$ | **PACK** GOOD SHOES (YOU'LL BE ON YOUR FEET ALL DAY)

THE MARDI GRAS INDIANS

The Mardi Gras Indians' historic tradition dates back to the late 19th century and is thought to possibly reflect the kinship of recently freed African slaves and Native Americans. For decades they were an underground movement who often fought pitched battles (between the tribes) on the street. But in recent decades several of the Mardi Gras Indian tribes (The Wild Tchoupitoulas, The Wild Magnolias) have embraced the wider world, making seminal albums and joining the likes of Dr John and Willy DeVille on stage while also becoming a popular part of New Orleans folklore.

BRASS BANDS

New Orleans is full of funky black brass bands: the Treme Brass Band play old-school style; the Dirty Dozen Brass Band bring fine jazz flavours in, and the Stooges Brass Band are young and tough. The most well known of these brass blasters is the Hot 8 Brass Band, who bring a swaggering, rap-influenced groove to their music. The Hot 8 have released two fine albums and often play concerts and parades across the city (find them at their Sunday night residency at the Howlin' Wolf). This is party music with funky chops. Watch the locals dance!

▣ THE PERFECT GETAWAY

While Mardi Gras may be when New Orleans becomes one big party, the city is open for those wanting a good time all year round. From when jazz first flowered in the city's brothels a century ago, through New Orleans' finest blues and soul, R&B and funk, rap and rock, it is *the* US music metropolis, a city rich with talent. The French Quarter, with its historic buildings, faded grandeur and wrought-iron balconies, is what visitors initially discover. In the Quarter there is Bourbon St, home to bars and clubs, fast-food joints and strip joints, the place where every weekend young Americans head to party and get very drunk. But beyond such hedonism the French Quarter does offer more refined experiences, including Preservation Hall, a venue dedicated to trad Dixieland jazz.

The city spreads beyond the French Quarter's narrow warren of streets. On Frenchmen St in the 7th Ward – a good 15-minute walk from the French Quarter – there are considerable music venues. This is where the young and hip come out to party. Legendary music venues such as the Howlin' Wolf, Tipitina's and the Maple Leaf Bar are spread across the city and require a car to get to.

Let your tastebuds join the fun: alongside Louisiana's gumbo and jambalaya, there's superb *beignets* (doughnuts) and coffee. The city also has excellent museums, while its gothic cemeteries are fascinating to explore. Take a streetcar (tram) out to the Garden District, where huge antebellum-era mansions offer a vision of an old South, one of luxury and servitude. New Orleans gave the world jazz and blues, gumbo and voodoo, Louis Armstrong and Lil' Wayne. This is where music, magic and an ever-present hint of madness come together to party.

▣ PLAN IT

Louis Armstrong Airport receives few international flights: it's likely you will change planes in Atlanta, Georgia, or Houston, Texas. Amtrak trains provide a pleasant overnight journey from Chicago. New Orleans is popular year-round (although it is hot and sticky in summer), but Mardi Gras is when the city swells in size – you should book at least two months in advance. A car is not necessary – street cars, buses and taxis are plentiful and should be used (after dark the city can be dangerous).

▣ DETOUR

Had enough of the Crescent City? Drive 90 minutes north to Lafayette, the capital of 'Cajun Country' – a good place to learn about Cajun history and praised as a top food destination in the South. Here, French is still widely spoken and violins and accordions get everyone dancing. Restaurants serve great gumbo while dance halls host rocking Cajun and zydeco bands. Swamp tours allow you to observe bird life and feed alligators. After being in New Orleans, you'll find Lafayette laid-back.

285

OPENING SPREAD Rivalries between Mardi Gras' Indian krewes are conducted via costume today. **ABOVE (L)** Behind the French Quarter's balconies are music venues such as Preservation Hall. **ABOVE (R)** and **LEFT** Preservation Hall's role, says its mission statement, is to protect and honour jazz.

DECKCHAIR

* **Treme** (2010–13) This HBO TV series by David Simon is about the renewal of New Orleans after Hurricane Katrina.

* **Mister Jelly Roll** (Alan Lomax) Brilliant oral autobiography of jazz piano pioneer Jelly Roll Morton, rich with detail on New Orleans in the early 20th century.

* **All On A Mardi Gras Day** (2003) Royce Osborn's fascinating documentary on black New Orleans' Mardi Gras traditions.

* **Heaven Before I Die: A Journey to the Heart of New Orleans** (Michael Oliver-Goodwin) This collection of journalism covers local music-making in all its facets.

* **Mardi Gras Indians** (Michael P Smith) The late Smith was the great photographer of New Orleans vernacular culture.

* **A Streetcar Named Desire** (1951) Film version of Tennessee Williams' classic New Orleans drama, starring Marlon Brando and Vivien Leigh.

CULTURE-CLUBBING IN PUNTA DEL ESTE

URUGUAY'S PUNTA DEL ESTE IS NOTORIOUS FOR ITS JET-SET REVELRY, BUT BEYOND THE NONSTOP PARTY MORE SUBTLE PLEASURES AWAIT, FROM CONTEMPORARY ART TO ROLLING WINE COUNTRY.

286

Bronzed, bikini-clad sylphs sip cocktails while their well-fed sugar-daddies convene over cigars, and a shirtless DJ in mirrored aviators spins thumping disco house under a makeshift canopied booth in the sand. It's just another afternoon on the beach in 'Punta', as regulars call it. By turns referred to as the St-Tropez or Hamptons of South America, Punta del Este is exactly what you'd expect from those comparisons: a high-end festival of flesh and flash. Attracting Brazilian millionaires and high Buenos Aires society, the area explodes into one continuous beach bash from December through to the end of February. Outside of this frenzied high season, when hotel prices skyrocket and traffic jams are commonplace, many local businesses are shuttered and holiday homes sit empty.

As in Spain and Argentina, the dinner rush starts at 10pm and the clubs likely won't be bumping until well after 2am. Punta del Este proper, a built-up small peninsula of hotels, low-lying residential and commercial buildings and a small marina, isn't entirely where it's at anymore. The party has shifted east to the surf town of La Barra, with its scene-y Bikini Beach, and the formerly sleepy fishing village of José Ignacio, where a small number of modernist inns and the odd seafood restaurant now exist. Beyond the sand and socialising, Punta del Este has cultural cachet that the average merrymaker is blissfully unaware of. One need only head inland a few minutes to hit up a sculpture park, working cattle ranch or winery.

Punta's quieter side is just as compelling, from the natural splendour of the windswept coves, dunes and cliffs along the coast to the green pastureland and sun-dappled, canopied country roads that snake through it – a refreshing respite from that thumping house beat.

ESSENTIAL EXPERIENCES

* Lingering over a sunset dinner at a beachside *parador* (restaurant) and sampling freshly caught *brótola* (a local white fish) or grilled octopus.

* Visiting the kitschy, colourful Museo del Mar for the weird and wonderful sea creatures preserved in bottles, the shells and the vintage beach paraphernalia.

* Splashing about, then sprawling and gaping at the eye-candy on the beaches in La Barra, Punta and José Ignacio.

* Shaking a tail feather till the sun comes up in a downtown Punta club or at a La Barra beach party.

* Exploring Casapueblo, a rambling, gleaming-white Gaudí-esque villa housing a hotel and art gallery built on the water in Punta Ballena.

LOCATION PUNTA DEL ESTE, URUGUAY | BEST TIME OF YEAR IF YOU WANT TO PARTY: HIGH SEASON (DECEMBER TO FEBRUARY)
IDEAL TIME COMMITMENT FOUR TO SEVEN DAYS | ESSENTIAL TIP BOOK WELL IN ADVANCE DURING HIGH SEASON, INCLUDING ANY FLIGHTS OR THE FERRY FROM BUENOS AIRES | BUDGET $$$ | PACK SUNSCREEN, TEENY BIKINI, CAMERA, CASH

SANDWICH OF CHAMPIONS

The chivito's story of origin involves an Argentine woman vacationing in Punta del Este in the 1960s who ordered a 'chivito' (baby goat) sandwich. The chef didn't have any baby goat on hand so he improvised this dazzlingly extreme sandwich instead, which quickly rose to unofficial national sandwich status. Make sure that you don't have anything to do after eating one – you will need to lie down for a while once you've ingested the lethal combination of fried meats (steak, ham, bacon), mayo, egg and sundry fried and grilled toppings such as olives and peppers, squashed into an oil-sodden bun.

THE PERFECT GETAWAY

Punta del Este's South Beach–esque condos and nightclubs are just a part of this resort town, but start your explorations here. Climb the giant concrete fingers emerging from the sand on Playa Brava, sample the *asado* (charcoal-grilled beef) at a traditional *parrilla* (grill) restaurant and check out the yachts in the marina. Listen out for the summer's happening club, then make a game of getting past the ever-humourless bouncer.

To the east, the striking Museo-Taller Casapueblo, perched on Punta Ballena, is artist Carlos Páez Vilaró's workshop, gallery and hotel. Now head west for youthful La Barra, where a mix of art galleries, surf emporiums and ice-cream shops attract glitterati, backpackers and families alike. Go inland to discover the delightful Museo del Mar, a treasure trove of whalebones, sea-creature taxidermy and thousands of neat-o collectibles.

In José Ignacio, lunch at beachfront hot spot La Huella may entail a long wait, but the people-watching and impossibly fresh seafood, like the white-fish *brótola*, make up for it. The serene Pablo Atchugarry sculpture park is 5km inland from here and includes local sculptor Atchugarry's studio. Venture further west and you'll hit sleepy Garzon, a tiny town in *gaucho* (cowboy) country now best known as the home of Argentine celebrity-chef Francis Mallman's eponymous restaurant.

There are also places with a feral beauty to them, like the hippie-magnet village of Cabo Polonio, which has no roads into it, just 7km of dunes from Hwy 10 (walk or hitch a ride on the open-air dune-rider bus to get there). Other things Cabo Polonio does not have: electricity; running water. And not a beefy bouncer in sight.

PLAN IT

Fly into Montevideo (the capital of Uruguay) or Buenos Aires (the capital of Argentina). From Montevideo, take a bus or rental car to Punta. From Buenos Aires, take a quick direct flight (less than an hour) or ferry across to Uruguay. The ferry will either take you to Colonia or Montevideo, then take a rental car or bus to Punta. Book accommodation well in advance in high season (December to February); avoid the crowds by going in the shoulder season (November and March).

DETOUR

Though overshadowed by grape-growing giants like Argentina and Chile, Uruguay is South America's fourth-largest producer of wine. The closest winery to Punta del Este is the award-winning Alto de la Ballena, which has eight hectares of vineyards at the foothills of the Sierra de la Ballena. Here, owners Paula and Alvaro Lorenzo grow merlot, tannat, cabernet franc, syrah and viognier. Visit their incredibly scenic estate – by appointment only.

289

OPENING SPREAD With murals and sculptures, Casapueblo is as quirky on the inside as it on the outside. ABOVE (L) Cabo Polonio: off the beaten track. ABOVE (R) Classic American cars: more show than go. LEFT Partying in Punta del Este.

DECKCHAIR

※ *Open Veins of Latin America: Five Centuries of the Pillage of a Continent* (Eduardo Galeano) A famously scathing indictment of American and European exploitation of Latin America.

※ *Seven Fires: Grilling the Argentine Way* (Francis Mallmann) Experience Mallmann's fiery magic first-hand at his restaurant-hotel in the village of Garzon.

※ *The Rest is Jungle and Other Stories* (Mario Benedetti) This cross-section of tales spans five decades of work by the late respected Uruguayan journalist, poet and author.

※ *Montevideo, God Bless You!* (2010) A Belgrade soccer team that travels to Montevideo to participate in the first FIFA cup in 1930.

※ *Miracle in the Andes: 72 Days on the Mountain and My Long Trek Home* (Nando Parrado) Parrado tells of surviving the crash that killed most of his Uruguayan college rugby team in 1972.

CELEBRATE LOST SOULS IN OAXACA

CEMETERIES COME ALIVE IN CENTRAL MEXICO AS LOCALS MAKE A MIDNIGHT PILGRIMAGE TO THE GRAVES OF THE DEPARTED DURING DÍA DE LOS MUERTOS (DAY OF THE DEAD) – A PARTY LIKE NO OTHER.

290

It's midnight. Among the crumbling headstones and the ruins of an old church there are shadows shuffling, swaying. Dark figures move in the moonlight, their voices rising into the air.

They're singing, these people. Some are even dancing, stepping through candles that throw flickering light across the busy cemetery. There's a mariachi band playing just outside the walls, where a crowd is dancing in the streets. Inside people are sitting on graves, some drinking and chatting, others passing the night sedately with hands clasped in silent vigil.

Even stranger still, there's a small girl perched on one of the stones, dressed in a bridal gown and veil. She's sitting there stony-faced, flanked by two other young girls draped in the dark robes and black lace worn by widows in mourning. Peer a little closer and you can see their faces are caked in white, with scarlet gashes painted on their cheeks.

Death is all around. It's in the costumes and the painted faces of the revellers in the cemetery. It's in the fake skeletons and skull decorations that bedeck the town. Most of all, it's buried 6ft beneath the earth at everyone's feet.

Here, death isn't feared. It's not even the cause for sadness. At least, not today. It's a time for Mexicans to get back in touch with loved ones, friends and relatives, who have passed to the other side. For many people that means a couple of long, silent nights perched on the end of a grave, waiting to meet up with lost souls. For others it's a celebration of those who will never return, a time to indulge in their favourite activities – dancing, singing, drinking – in the presence of their spirits.

It's both a party and a pilgrimage, haunting and glorious.

ESSENTIAL EXPERIENCES

* **Spending a ghoulish night at Xoxo cemetery, with its gravestones, church ruins and mariachi band.**

* Painting your face like it's Halloween and joining a parade in Oaxaca City.

* **Checking out Day of the Dead–themed sand sculptures near Oaxaca's cathedral.**

* Settling back with a drink and taking in all of the action – from markets to parades – at the Zócalo (Oaxaca's main square).

* **Trying mole, Oaxaca's famously dark, complex sauce that's served with meats and vegetables year-round.**

* Enjoying the warmth of the people of Oaxaca, among the most hospitable in Mexico.

LOCATION OAXACA CITY, MEXICO | **BEST TIME OF YEAR** DAY OF THE DEAD IS CELEBRATED ON 1 AND 2 NOVEMBER | **IDEAL TIME COMMITMENT** FIVE DAYS | **ESSENTIAL TIP** BOOK ACCOMMODATION IN ADVANCE; OAXACA CITY IS THE MOST POPULAR PLACE TO CELEBRATE THE DAY OF THE DEAD | **BUDGET** $ | **PACK** YOUR FAVOURITE HALLOWEEN COSTUME AND SOME SCARY MAKE-UP

WHO'S THAT SKELETON?

One of the most striking and frequently seen images
associated with the Day of the Dead is Catrina, the
skeleton of an upper-class woman in a hat and a dress.
It was originally sketched by Mexican printmaker José
Guadalupe Posada in the early 1900s, and became part
of Day of the Dead celebrations in the 1920s. Now 'La
Catrina' images form a huge part of the festival, from
the paintings and sculptures displayed throughout
Oaxaca City to the costumes worn by festival-goers
around town. The artist Diego Rivera even incorporated
Catrina into one of his murals, *Dream of a Sunday
Afternoon in Alameda Park,* in the 1940s.

WHY THE DAY OF THE DEAD?

As with many festivals in Latin America, the Day of the Dead is a blend of Catholicism and ancient Aztec and pagan rituals. While the Aztecs dedicated an entire month to remembering their dead ancestors, the modern form of the celebration takes place on All Saints and All Souls Days at the beginning of November: 1 November is dedicated to deceased children and infants, while 2 November is dedicated to remembering adults. It's typical for Mexicans to celebrate those lives by practising the things their loved ones held dear, including music and dancing, and visiting their graves to be closer to their souls. It's also become something of an artistic festival, where local artisans' Day of the Dead–themed works can be seen throughout cities.

■ THE PERFECT GETAWAY

Oaxaca City buzzes with life during the Day of the Dead, when the streets are constantly filled with people during the day, and the cemeteries are packed at night. The daylight hours are the perfect time to wander through town looking at the art displays: huge skulls are painted by local artists, while sand sculptures of skeletons dominate the space in front of Oaxaca's cathedral.

As evening sets in there's no better place to be than the Zócalo, Oaxaca's main square and home to the markets and Day of the Dead parades. There's also room for an occasional political protest, in the form of more sculptures and posters – a reminder that all is not completely well in this sometimes turbulent country. Still, it's mostly a good-natured celebration, as cafes place 'Catrina' skeletons at their tables, and bags of bones laugh from balconies overlooking the square.

When night falls there are two cemeteries worth checking out, which visitors can split across the two days of the festival. Oaxaca's main cemetery, the Panteón General, is the easiest to get to (it's walking distance from the Zócalo), and the busiest. There's a full fairground outside it, and plenty of dark, costumed figures spending the night inside. It's an amazing experience to simply sit or stand by the walls of candlelit tombs and watch the festival's living celebrants pass by.

Out in Xoxo, a few kilometres south, it's even spookier. There's hardly any light here bar the flickering of tea-light candles placed on graves. Some groups of people sing songs in the ruins of an old church, while others sit on graves and chat, and others still choose to wait out the night in solo vigil. It will take a trip by bus or car to get here from Oaxaca, but it's well worth the effort.

■ PLAN IT

The Day of the Dead is celebrated throughout Mexico and some parts of Central America on 1 and 2 November. To get to Oaxaca City, fly to Mexico City and catch a six-hour bus transfer south. There are also flights between the two cities. Most Day of the Dead activities happen in Oaxaca itself; Xoxo cemetery is a short drive out of town. Plenty of tourist shops run bus trips out to Xoxo each night. It's a good idea to spend one night out at Xoxo, and another soaking up the atmosphere in Oaxaca itself.

■ DETOUR

Those needing a change of scenery after all that ghoulishness should head west to the coast. The most popular destination is Puerto Escondido, a town with a relaxed vibe and plenty of empty sand. Off the beaten track (and about an hour south of Puerto Escondido), the former hippie haunt of Zipolite is as laid-back as it comes, with people doing yoga on the beach in between munching on shrimp tacos from the local restaurants. (There's nothing else to do in Zipolite, and that's the point.)

OPENING SPREAD Expect to see plenty of stylised skeletons for sale. **ABOVE** In Xoxo cemetery, Oaxacans remember friends and relatives. **LEFT** They might look ghoulish, but the Day of the Dead is about honour not horror.

DECKCHAIR

* ***Ask a Mexican*** (Gustavo Arellano) A tongue-in-cheek book for those with questions about some of Mexico's more interesting quirks.

* ***Y Tu Mamá También*** (2001) Entertaining coming-of-age tale about two privileged Mexico City teenagers.

* ***The Power and the Glory*** (Graham Greene) This classic, about a priest on the run at a time when Catholicism was outlawed in Mexico, provides excellent background to a fascinating country.

* ***The Old Gringo*** (Carlos Fuentes) The story of an American journalist living among the soldiers of famous revolutionary Pancho Villa.

* ***Amores Perros*** (2000) It's not often a film about fighting dogs and disfigured supermodels makes it so big on the world scene, but this is gripping, occasionally brutal cinema.

* ***Frida*** (2002) One of Mexico's most famous artists, Frida Kahlo, is immortalised in this biopic.

PARTY ON THE BEACH AT HVAR

COME HIGH SUMMER, THERE'S NO COOLER ISLE IN CROATIA FOR GETTING YOUR GROOVE ON THAN HVAR. THINK ROUND-THE-CLOCK FUN – APRÈS-BEACH PARTIES AS THE SUN DIPS BELOW THE ADRIATIC, FULL-MOON SHINDIGS AND DESIGNER COCKTAILS SIPPED SEASIDE TO FRESH, DJ-SPUN TUNES.

294

Violet lavender terraces, ancient olive groves and sun-kissed vineyards greet you as the boat approaches Hvar. Zoom in on Hvar Town and what appears is a hideaway with many a nuance. Bass-infused beachside parties dotting the coastline merge with eight centuries of architecture. Riva, the seafront harbour lined with palms and Venetian palaces, contrasts with a line-up of extravagant yachts. And there's the sunshine: capturing more than 2718 hours of sunshine per year, this marvel in the azure Adriatic Sea is a sunbather's party paradise.

Hvar's got celeb cred, too: Beyoncé was so mesmerised by the island that she named her daughter Blue Ivy after discovering an old tree wrapped in this beautiful flower. In Veneranda Club, within the walls of a 16th-century Spanish fortress overlooking Hvar Town, Prince Harry made quite the impression in summer 2011 when he partied it up with a pool plunge.

Stepping off the gangway onto the ancient quayside you enter straight into the après-beach party zone at Carpe Diem, the pioneer of seafront clubs that pinned Hvar on the party map. Mojito in hand, take centre stage under the weathered palace arches and absorb the island vibe as the shimmering sun sinks into the sea. Pick up the pace and groove to the music beneath the pink sky, setting the mood for the rest of your Hvar holiday.

The clock strikes 2am and the party shifts to Hvar's backyard, Pakleni Otoci, an archipelago of uninhabited islands a quick boat-hop from town. The skipper navigates by the stars to Carpe Diem Beach club in Stipanska Bay on the isle of Marinkovac. Here, in a secluded seaside venue, deep house mixes with the song of crickets. You rave till sunrise on this flyspeck with a barren beach and neon rays lighting up five vibrant bars. On the boat back in the early hours you're already plotting your return for some refreshing dips in the crystal-clear bay.

ESSENTIAL EXPERIENCES

* **Hanging about on the Pjaca, Hvar's main square and the heart of town.**
* Enjoying local wines in the laid-back 3Pršuta wine bar, down a narrow alley behind the Pjaca.
* **Savouring delicious cakes at Nonica, a hole-in-the-wall bakery owned by a local who studied at the Cordon Bleu Culinary School as a pastry chef.**
* Taking a two-hour heritage walking tour with Secret Hvar and discovering the town's history.
* **Stumbling across 'budget bars', such as the ever-popular Kiva, Nautica and Sidro, and enjoying cheap beers and grappa shots.**
* Treating your hangover at boho beach hang-out Falko, a 20-minute walk west of Hvar's centre.

LOCATION HVAR, CROATIA | **IDEAL TIME COMMITMENT** FOUR TO SEVEN DAYS | **BEST TIME OF YEAR** JULY TO SEPTEMBER | **ESSENTIAL TIP** MOST BARS ONLY ACCEPT CASH AND DOWNTOWN CLUBS CLOSE AT 2AM | **BUDGET** $$ | **PACK** SHOES TO BATTLE THE ROCKY BEACH SURFACES AND SEA URCHINS

FOODIE HVAR

In between the partying, don't miss exploring Hvar's varied culinary showcase. Climb the 'stairs to heaven' to artsy Luna Restaurant for seafood pasta under the stars, or pop into upscale Giaxa next door for lamb *pašticada* (stew) in a late-Gothic palace. Book a table at Gariful on Riva, a seafood hot spot known for its pricey crustaceans. Neighbouring DiVino provides an exclusive retreat with modern French-Adriatic fusion and fab sunset vistas. To sample local, down-home specialities, lean back in the rustic and affordable Konoba Menego, found up the ancient stairs towards the hilltop fortress. Pair your dishes with Dalmatia's favourite red grape, *plavac mali*, or take a wine tour to taste '2718 hours of sun in a bottle' at the boutique Duboković Winery, in the town of Jelsa on the island's northern coast.

ADVENTURE HVAR

After a few days of hitting it hard with bass-matched seaside bevvies, it's time for a change of pace. Next up, discover the wild beauty of Hvar – with a sprinkle of adventure on the side. Strap into your harness with Hvar Adventure for an exhilarating rock climb in Milna, or bike through mysterious abandoned villages, such as Malo Grablje. For water-based fun, kayak to the Pakleni islands or hire a sailing boat for the day to search for secluded bays. Don't miss Secret Hvar's thrilling off-road tour, which shows you Hvar's hidden charms, such as verdant inland valleys, ghost hamlets and fields of lavender.

THE PERFECT ESCAPE

Wake up to a breakfast buffet at the Hotel Riva on the palm-dotted wharf as you observe the nouveau riche do the same aboard their Azimut yachts. Grab a detox Jack Sparrow juice (with ginger, carrot and apple) at Mama Leone and you're set for a day at Hula-Hula beach club, just past the glitzy Amfora Hotel.

Pre-book one of Hula-Hula's sunbeds mounted along the jagged shore and snooze under the sun, with a sporadic dive into the refreshing sea. Squint to take in the sunny Pakleni islands on the horizon, as an iced bucket of Veuve Clicquot poised between you and your sidekick cools your thigh. The DJ's lounge tunes gradually develop into an uplifting house session and tanned quarter-lifers start dancing in their swimwear at the edge of the sea.

When Hula-Hula winds down at 9pm, dress up and head to Carpe Diem for the famed après-beach party, where you boogie and chit-chat over cocktails till 2am, when time's up. The crowds then head up to Veneranda Club, a hilltop mega-discotheque housed in a medieval fortress. This open-air venue surrounded by 16th-century defence walls unites hardcore clubbers for a techno mosh pit with flaring mixologists, a VIP section, laser shows and neon water features. As the sun rises, a sobering hike downtown to your digs is just what the doctor ordered.

The next day pack your beach gear and head to Riva, where taxi boats can bear you to any of the Pakleni islands for a day in nature. Drift to Jerolim, a figure-eight-shaped isle known as one of the world's best nudist hideaways, and skinny-dip to your heart's content. For a sun-infused party, lounge on AMO Beach Club's beanbags, scattered across a pebble beach, as chill-out tunes linger in the air.

PLAN IT

Fly into Split Airport on the mainland and grab a shuttle to Split's port. A one-hour trip by catamaran (Jadrolinija or Krilo) takes you to Hvar Town; buy tickets from the booth on the harbour. Or, take a two-hour car ferry to Hvar's town of Stari Grad and a 30-minute bus ride to Hvar Town. Sunčani Hvar Hotels group has the island's most luxe accommodation. A few hostels have sprung up, such as Hostel Marinero and Luka's Lodge.

DETOUR

Don't skip an opportunity to explore Dalmatia's capital of Split before or after your island getaway. Venture into the city's nucleus, the 1700-year-old Diocletian's Palace, for a walking tour that starts on Peristil. Grab a hearty chicken *tingul* (stew) at Grego Levante before hitting the bars along Dosud for cheap *rakija* (local grappa) shots and neon cocktails. An early wake-up the next morning calls for a stop in the Tradicija patisserie on Bosanska, to keep your coffee company on the Riva harbourfront as you while away the time people-watching.

OPENING SPREAD From Hvar's harbour you can see the archipelago's islands, venues for secret beach parties. **ABOVE (L)** Enjoy fresh, Mediterranean seafood. **ABOVE (R)** Boat partying. **LEFT** For a different sort of buzz, some go deepwater soloing (climbing without ropes) over the surrounding sea.

DECKCHAIR

✳ **Hvar: An Insider's Guide to Croatia's Premier Island** (Paul Bradbury) A comprehensive guide about Hvar Island written by an expat who has lived on the island for 10 years.

✳ **The Konoba** (Miki Bratanić) Poetry and stories about the importance of the Croatian 'tavern', with photography of the author's family *konoba* in Vrbanj, Hvar.

✳ **Altered State: The Story of Ecstasy Culture and Acid House**

(Matthew Collin) If you've ever danced all night, this is a must-read account of club culture's impact on society.

✳ **A Guide to the Wines of Croatia** (Saša Špiranec) Comprehensive tasting notes on the best wines of Croatia by the country's leading wine writer.

✳ **Black Lamb and Grey Falcon** (Rebecca West) A tour-de-force travelogue through the Balkans, from Croatia to Montenegro.

PARIS, AFTER SUNSET

LIVE IT UP AFTER DARK IN PARIS' MOST BUZZING NEIGHBOURHOODS, STARTING WITH A LAID-BACK APERITIF ON A CAFE TERRACE AS THE SUN SETS AND THEN GOING ON TO CLANDESTINE COCKTAILS AND LATE-NIGHT DANCING AT THE CAPITAL'S MOST HAPPENING BARS AND CLUBS.

298

As the sun starts its descent towards the horizon, squeeze in at a crowded cafe terrace on a street corner in the Northern Marais, Canal St-Martin or South Pigalle – Paris' animated up-and-coming neighbourhoods – and witness a quintessentially French evening ritual start to unfold: the aperitif.

Locals swoop to take over tiny tables as they become free, cramming around them in a microclimate thick with cigarette smoke and the hum of chatter as the *apéro* hour begins. Sporting casual ensembles that appear to be serendipitously thrown together, each of these Parisian *bobos* (bourgeois bohemians) is actually styled with meticulous care and attention, most likely with the latest threads from one of the independent boutiques in the Northern Marais.

No menus are given; each person just knows what they want and gives their order without hesitation to the bumptious waiter. And over an ice-cold rosé or a refreshing beer – fancy cocktails come later – clusters of Parisians nonchalantly put in place plans for this evening's activities: relaxed dinner, hip drinks, and then onto a bit of dancing.

As darkness falls, these attractive groups meander to their dinner reservations, to share a small-plate supper of delicious bits of charcuterie, pâté and cheese at wine bars that appear as laid-back as their patrons but, like them, are – behind the scenes – just as judiciously put together. And then it's on through an unmarked door to cocktails at a hidden bar that only the initiated know about – then dancing past the midnight hour at a subterranean or riverside club.

Tonight's adventures will be retold tomorrow over a restorative brunch. But first, we'll warm up with the quintessential Parisian pastime of apéro-drinking, people-watching and terrace-hogging, and then we'll be ready to let our hair down in Paris after midnight – because that's when the fun really starts.

ESSENTIAL EXPERIENCES

* **Joining in on the essential French apéro-hour ritual with an early-evening drink.**
* Sitting outside on a cafe terrace on a balmy summer night with a cool beer in hand.
* **Sneaking past an unmarked door and into a hidden, speakeasy-style cocktail bar.**
* Looking out for the Eiffel Tower twinkling on the horizon, when it lights up every hour, on the hour, once darkness falls.
* **Channelling Toulouse-Lautrec and sipping on an Absinthe-based cocktail in Pigalle – try those at trendy bars Glass or Le Mansart.**
* Getting a strong dose of coffee and a hearty yet healthy brunch in the Northern Marais the morning after.

LOCATION PARIS, FRANCE | **BEST TIME OF YEAR** YEAR-ROUND, BUT SUMMER (MAY TO JULY) IS A PARTICULARLY LIVELY TIME TO VISIT | **IDEAL TIME COMMITMENT** A WEEKEND | **ESSENTIAL TIP** DON'T LET ANY STEELY-EYED DOORMEN INTIMIDATE YOU: HOLD YOUR HEAD HIGH, WALK WITH PURPOSE AND GO STRAIGHT IN | **BUDGET** $$ | **PACK** SUBTLY COOL CLOTHES

LATE-NIGHT CULTURE

There are several annual nocturnal events organised by the City of Paris that are suitable for all ages. Nuit des Musees sees museums across the capital open their doors for free until midnight on one night in spring, with many putting on special exhibits for the occasion. Nuit Blanche is a cultural event that takes place from dusk until dawn on one night in autumn, featuring art, dance, music and even special activities for children. Its name may be the French way of describing an all-nighter, but rather than being aimed at fluorescent teenagers, Nuit Blanche is there for everyone from kids to grannies to stay up until dawn and see something different during the moonlit hours.

MOONLIT MOVIES

A quintessential Parisian nocturnal summer activity is the outdoor cinema festival at the park at La Villette. The annual Cinema en Plein Air event lasts for around a month from mid-July to mid-August, and has a different theme each year, reuniting films from around the world and from a variety of genres and eras. Get there early to secure a good spot, and bring a picnic and something warm, as even on the hottest nights it gets a bit chilly once the night draws in. Films begin after sunset and entry is free, although deckchairs and blankets are available to hire for a small fee also.

CLASSIC COCHES

A popular pastime in Uruguay is lovingly restoring and maintaining classic cars from the 1960s through to the 1920s. Keeping cars running as long as possible has also been a necessity in the country: import taxes and sky-high insurance rates keep new cars prohibitively expensive. Founded in 1996, the Punta del Este Sport and Classic Car Club holds rallies and races in the summer so people can parade their treasures and admire each other's workmanship. It's also not uncommon to find an abandoned, rusted-out shell of a 1940s Ford pick-up adding visual interest to a roadside field.

THE PERFECT GETAWAY

Paris' hip neighbourhoods come to life after dark, with the early-evening apéro hour going strong, and the new trends of small-plate dining and low-key cocktail bars attracting the stylish set. Base yourself in the Northern Marais, Canal St-Martin or South Pigalle – moving between each of these quarters is easy.

After shopping for your perfect Paris outfit in the Northern Marais at boutiques such as Surface to Air and Isabel Marant, start the evening with an aperitif at Northern Marais stalwart La Perle or newer hangout Le Mansart in South Pigalle. Go on to share tapas-sized portions of modern French food at Rem Koolhaas–designed Le Dauphin or former workmen's cafe Au Passage – a short walk from the Northern Marais or Canal St-Martin – before heading off for cocktails at one of the capital's hyped bars. Candelaria, in the Northern Marais, has a speakeasy-style cocktail bar hidden behind its taco canteen – push the unmarked door at the back of the cafe to go through to a dimly lit den of fashionable fun. Or, go to the sublimely decadent Le Carmen, just steps away from the red-light district in Pigalle, with its original baroque features (it was formerly the residence of composer Bizet) and rock-and-roll vibe. Afterwards, head to the trendy after-hours dive bar L'Embuscade, also in South Pigalle, for rum-based cocktails and a spot of dancing. Or, for some serious music, make your way to the 2nd arrondissement for Silencio – the subterranean members' club designed by David Lynch that opens to the public after midnight. Alternatively, head across town to the Seine-side club Wanderlust, which has the largest outdoor terrace in Paris – perfect for shaking your tail feather on balmy nights.

PLAN IT

A weekend – preferably in May to July – is ideal for this getaway. Avoid August: the city dies down as Parisians go on holiday. The Eurostar takes you straight from London to Paris, or you can fly from other points of departure to Charles de Gaulle or Orly airports. From there take the overground RER train or the shuttle bus into Paris. On your night out, transport is straightforward: the metro runs until around 1.30am on weekends, and after that you can hail a taxi or take a Vélib public-hire bike.

DETOUR

There is also plenty of fun and frolics to be had in Paris during the day. The multifaceted venue Wanderlust hosts events around the clock in its restaurant, club and outdoor space overlooking the Seine, from yoga, children's workshops and brunch in the daytime to alfresco partying late into the night. To the north of Paris, the vast park at La Villette hosts an array of daytime events throughout the warmer months, including the free electro music festival La Villette Sonique in May.

OPENING SPREAD Young Parisians graze from bar to bar at the weekend. **ABOVE** The perfect start to the morning after the night before: pick up a warm *pain au chocolat* from a bakery. **LEFT** Each season of the open-air cinema has a theme that unites a diverse selection of films, old and new.

DECKCHAIR

* **Before Sunset** (2004) The sequel to the film *Before Sunrise* takes Ethan Hawke and Julie Delpy's characters around Paris in the afternoon as their romantic narrative unfolds.

* **La Haine** (1995) Night-time escapades in this cult movie starring Vincent Cassel as a young delinquent in Paris and its suburbs.

* **Mégalopolis** (2005) A short film showing an alternative side to Paris' dance and music scene, by painfully cool director Romain Gavras.

* **Midnight in Paris** (2011) Woody Allen's nostalgic take on a Jazz Age Paris after dark.

* **A Moveable Feast** (Ernest Hemingway) Hemingway recounts the exuberance of Paris in his autobiographical memoirs of his time in the capital.

* **Clair de Femme** (Romain Gary) A novel about love and death set over the space of one night in Paris.

LEAVING LAS VEGAS' STRIP

THERE'S PLENTY TO DO IN SIN CITY AWAY FROM THE FAMOUS CASINO STRIP, FROM PLAYING AROUND WITH HEAVY MACHINERY TO WINERY VISITS, GO-KART RACES AND 3D DODGEBALL.

302

You know you want to. Anyone who had a sandbox as a kid would want to; anyone who's driven past a building site and peered inside would want to. And now here you are perched up in the cabin of a proper bulldozer, about to push some dirt around. Serious dirt, too – tonnes of it. Press a few buttons, pull a few levers. The big engine revs, the caterpillar tracks start moving, the shovel digs into the earth...

They say you can do just about anything in Las Vegas, although when they say that they're probably thinking more along the lines of gambling and strippers than building a big mound of dirt and then driving over it. But it takes all kinds in this place, and it's only once you get away from that famous neon-lit Strip that you realise just how much there is to do in Vegas. Forget the gambling and postpone the Elton John show. There's work to be done.

The bulldozer is part of Dig This, which has to be about the most bizarrely great attraction in Vegas. The idea is simple: drive a real bulldozer or excavator, and do all the work those big machines normally do. Dig trenches, move huge tyres around, and drive over large mounds of dirt. It's brilliant in its simplicity, and the perfect salt-of-the-earth antidote to the glitzy fakery of the Strip.

It's also just the beginning. Once you're done playing in your giant sandbox there's plenty of amusement awaiting in Vegas that doesn't involve cards and chips. Take a helicopter ride over the Grand Canyon and combine it with dinner and wine-tasting at a vineyard. Fire guns at a rifle range. Play 3D dodgeball on trampolines. Race go-karts. Eat at Michelin-starred restaurants. Party in a pool. Drink at a dive bar.

And don't gamble a cent.

ESSENTIAL EXPERIENCES

* **Visiting the Las Vegas Boneyard and seeing where neon cowboys go to die.**

* Knocking back a few drinks with the locals at Double Down Saloon, Vegas' dingiest and best dive bar.

* **Jumping behind the controls of a bulldozer at Dig This and living your childhood sandbox dreams in full size.**

* Taking a helicopter joy flight over the Grand Canyon – or just getting dropped off at a winery.

* **Enjoying the sun, the water, the DJs, the cocktails and the cabanas at one of Las Vegas' famous pool parties.**

* Indulging your inner child with a game of 3D dodgeball at Sky Zone Indoor Trampoline Park.

LOCATION LAS VEGAS, NEVADA, USA | **BEST TIME OF YEAR** THERE'S NO BAD TIME TO VISIT; POOL-PARTY SEASON RUNS FROM MARCH TO SEPTEMBER | **IDEAL TIME COMMITMENT** FOUR DAYS | **ESSENTIAL TIP** MAKE USE OF YOUR CONCIERGE | **BUDGET** $$ **PACK** CLOTHES TO GO OUT IN, AND CLOTHES TO GET DIRTY IN

MR LAS VEGAS

Elvis has been there. Elton John has done plenty of
shows there. Celine Dion never seems to leave. But
none of them can claim the title of Las Vegas' most
frequent performer – that would be Wayne Newton, or
'Mr Las Vegas', who has done more than 30,000 shows
in Sin City. Newton, a singer and entertainer most
famous for the single 'Danke Schoen', has done cameos
in his fair share of Vegas-based films as well, including
The Hangover, *Ocean's Eleven* and *Smokin' Aces*. The
road to the airport is even named after him: Wayne
Newton Boulevard.

BIGGER IS BETTER

The first casino on the Las Vegas Strip was a Spanish-style place called El Rancho Vegas, which had 110 rooms and a gambling floor consisting of two blackjack tables, one roulette wheel and a craps table. That was back in 1941 – how things have changed. The biggest building on the Strip now, by size, is the Palazzo, which has 3068 rooms and 9800 sq metres of gambling floor – it topples the Pentagon as being the largest building in the USA. For pure punting, however, the biggest is the MGM Grand, which has 139 gaming tables and more than 2500 slot machines spread out over almost 16,000 sq metres of casino space.

■ THE PERFECT GETAWAY

Away from the Strip, away from the lure of all those neon lights and singing slot machines, there's plenty to keep visitors to Las Vegas occupied. Dig This, the earthmoving theme park, is one of the more inventive attractions, but the fun doesn't stop there. Sky Zone Indoor Trampoline Park is another place popular with overgrown children, where you can bounce around doing somersaults and trying to avoid being hit with squishy balls. Makes a change from blackjack.

Meanwhile, those who've hit the jackpot should get high with a helicopter joy flight – some tours soar over the Grand Canyon, others take in the Hoover Dam, and still others go further afield, taking guests out to Pahrump Valley Winery, near the California state line. Have a meal, some wine, and then fly back to Vegas.

Take in a little of the town's history at the Boneyard. The Las Vegas Neon Museum's huge yard is strewn with old neon signs and billboards dating back as far as the 1930s, a monument to a city that outgrew itself several times over.

Another Vegas institution and a must-visit for anyone jaded by all the glitz is Double Down Saloon, a dive bar that's proud to call itself such. The bar is dark and dingy, it's patronised by Vegas' more interesting characters and the live music borders on 'experimental', but the drinks are cheap.

Want to slow down? Pay a visit to the Mob Museum to learn about Vegas' past. Want to speed things up? Leap into a go-kart at Pole Position Raceway. Finally, don't miss Vegas' famous pool parties. Be it Wet Republic, Encore or Rehab, the formula is basically the same: get thousands of party-goers in the pool, add a DJ, some drinks, and see what happens. You've probably got a fair idea of the results.

■ PLAN IT

Summer is when Vegas is busiest, but attractions are open year-round. Access is by plane from almost anywhere in the US and some Canadian centres; alternatively, hire a car in Los Angeles and take a drive made by many before you. Accommodation in Las Vegas is relatively cheap; the casinos know they'll recoup those losses. How much you decide to give back is up to you.

■ DETOUR

There's no way you'll stay out of Vegas' gambling dens forever. So where to go, and what to do? Top of the list has to be watching the fountains at the Bellagio, which is spectacular, crowded, and doesn't cost a cent. Next up, wander the canals of Venice – or, at least, the canals of the Venetian Casino. Then step back a little further into fake Italian history with a stroll through the Roman-themed Caesars Palace. It's all tropical island dreaming over at the Mirage, while the Wynn is just pure luxury. Finish up with drinks at New York New York, the casino that never sleeps (actually, that goes for all of them).

305

OPENING SPREAD Pool parties, Vegas-style: just your mates – and 7000 other half-dressed people; this is Rehab at the Hard Rock Hotel. **ABOVE (L)** The South Rim of the Grand Canyon. **ABOVE (R)** Better to burn out than fade away: the Boneyard. **LEFT** Be a five-year-old for the day at Dig This.

DECKCHAIR

* ***Fear and Loathing in Las Vegas*** (Hunter S Thompson) Don't try this at home, kids. Hunter S Thompson goes on his now-famous drug-spiked rampage through Sin City, changing journalism in the process.

* ***The Hangover*** (2009) Four guys, one bachelor party, one baby, one guy in a car boot, one tiger, and one former heavyweight champion of the world. It'll seem unlikely until you experience Vegas for yourself.

* ***Ocean's Eleven*** (2001) Attempting to steal from a Las Vegas casino is a really, really bad idea. Unless, of course, you've got George Clooney, Brad Pitt and Matt Damon on board.

* ***Casino*** (1995) Wait, there's a dark side to Las Vegas? Involving the Mob? Of course there is, and Robert De Niro and Joe Pesci portray it perfectly in Martin Scorsese's classic of the genre.

* ***Leaving Las Vegas*** (John O'Brien) Man leaves wife and job, goes to Vegas to drink himself into oblivion and... Well, that would spoil it.

ONE NIGHT IN TOKYO

FROM TINY WHISKY DENS TO TRADITIONAL BACK-ALLEY IZAKAYAS, DRUNK SALARYMEN TO GIRLS IN FETISH GEAR, TRIPS TO JAIL TO GAMES OF MARIO BROS, THERE'S NEVER A DULL MOMENT ON A NIGHT OUT IN TOKYO.

Click, click. The handcuffs go on. This would normally be the sign of a night gone horribly wrong, but not in Tokyo. Things tend to be a little different here.

Prisoners scream in the distance as you're led into the jail, past rows and rows of iron bars, before finally arriving at your cell. The cuffs come off. The warden slams the door. You sit and ponder your fate. There's only one thing to do: order a drink.

This is the Lockup, one of Tokyo's more eccentric theme bars. Cocktails can be chosen according to what you think you did wrong to end up here, from 'Bad Loan' to 'Drug Addiction'. They'll arrive in beakers, test tubes and syringes, as if you've been doomed to a life of internment as a science experiment. They're highly alcoholic, too – maybe prison life isn't so bad after all.

Sound strange? This is but a taste of the outlandishness that a night out in Tokyo can deliver, a mere nibble at the edges of a city that specialises in the fetishist and the fascinating. It's going to be a surreal, bizarre evening, and it's already in full swing.

Remember earlier in the night? You were being served milkshakes by a manga character and screamed at by a maid. Then there was time for some karaoke, which, naturally, you sang from a bathtub. After that you decided to play Nintendo games with a Power Glove while slugging back beers. Later this evening you'll step into a bar with room for six people and drink whisky cocktails with rich salarymen clientele. And much, much later you might call past a 'love hotel', where rooms are hired by the half-hour and Hello Kitty-styled props are as prominent as whips and chains.

It's just a standard night. For now, however, you're not in a bar – you're behind bars. And the drinks have arrived.

ESSENTIAL EXPERIENCES

* **Having one of the strangest experiences of your life by visiting a maid cafe in Akihabara.**
* Calling past a Shinjuku love hotel – even if you're not in the mood it's worth the price for sightseeing alone.
* **Gorging yourself at Tokyo's drunken pit stop of choice: a rāmen noodle bar.**
* Izakaya-hopping in Asakusa – it's the joy of discovery that counts.
* **Grabbing an expertly made cocktail at one of Shinjuku's almost ridiculously tiny bars.**
* Getting sent to jail at the Lockup.
* **Slicing into an ice-cream-topped loaf of crispy bread while belting out your favourite tunes in a karaoke palace.**

LOCATION TOKYO, JAPAN | **BEST TIME OF YEAR** YEAR-ROUND; APRIL FOR CHERRY BLOSSOMS | **IDEAL TIME COMMITMENT** FIVE DAYS | **ESSENTIAL TIP** DON'T BE AFRAID TO EXPLORE: MOST SMALL BARS AND IZAKAYAS WON'T HAVE ANY ENGLISH SIGNAGE | **BUDGET** $$ | **PACK** FANCY CLOTHES: BETTER TO BE OVERDRESSED THAN KNOCKED BACK FROM A BAR FOR NOT LOOKING SMART

KNOW YOUR SAKE

The tipple of choice for boozing salarymen the country over, sake is a rice-based spirit that's as Japanese as sumo and sushi. For an indication of how your sake may taste, check for a number on the label (or on the drinks menu). Anything listed in the positives from one upwards will have a dry taste, while anything with a negative number will be progressively sweeter. Asking for premium sake to be served warm is a serious faux pas – only cheap or old sake is served hot, and usually only in winter. Do as the Japanese do, and go cold.

■ THE PERFECT GETAWAY

Most of Tokyo's best places are unsigned, or only signed in kanji, which makes finding them a serious task; identify a popular area and then explore on your own. In the traditional suburb of Asakusa, wander the back alleys until you spy the telltale red lanterns that signify izakayas (traditional Japanese bars), then step inside and see what you find. Sake is served hot or cold here, and the different variations are numbered according to their degree of sweetness. Beer is always good, and always cold. Food is served in tapas-style portions and, like most things in Japan, created with meticulous care.

Now it's time to get weird. A metro ride will take you to Akihabara, an area rich with 'maid cafes' – Tokyo institutions that have to be seen to be believed. The waitresses dress like manga cartoon characters – some will be cutesy and sweet, others brash and rude. Try Mai Dreamin' to get you started.

Enjoy geek culture? Then head to the 8bit Cafe in Shinjuku, where customers get the chance to play old-school Sega and Nintendo games while downing cold beers. *Sonic the Hedgehog* and a Sapporo: the perfect combination. Next it's time for some karaoke action in the foreigner-friendly Roppongi district, though fans of the movie *Lost in Translation* will want to go to Karaoke Kan in Shibuya, which is where Bill Murray famously hit the microphone.

While you're in Shibuya call into the Lockup for handcuffs and cocktails. Then return to Shinjuku to explore alleyway after alleyway filled with the tiniest and classiest of whisky bars. Cocktails are approached in the same way food is here: as an art. It's not just a drink, it's a show. Sit back and watch the masters at work.

■ PLAN IT

Getting to Tokyo is easy: fly into Narita airport and take a bus transfer into the city. Base yourself in either Shibuya or Asakusa. Shibuya is the city's main nightlife hub; Asakusa is older, quieter and more traditional, providing a nice contrast to the bustling city centre. Tokyo is generally very safe at night. Just be aware that some clubs with strict door policies may not let foreigners inside.

■ DETOUR

Tokyo by night is an eye-opener, but there are still surprises in the daylight hours. On a Sunday, head to the district of Harajuku and the area around Jingu Bridge. This is where the 'Harajuku girls' in their over-the-top outfits hang out. Their costumes defy description – from manga-inspired gothic dolls to artistic pieces that Lady Gaga would be proud to call her own, it's a feast of the creative and bizarre. A word of warning: as if to add to the contradiction of all this outlandishness in a conservative country, the girls who are dressed to impress will be less than impressed if you try to take a photo of them.

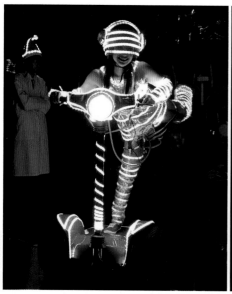

OPENING SPREAD Some antique porcelain sake bottles can fetch tens of thousands of dollars at auction; more recent bottles aren't quite so precious. **ABOVE** Behind bars: a night out in Tokyo could see you surrounded by people dressed as robots or locked up with your partners in crime.

DECKCHAIR

* *Lost in Translation* (2003) Sofia Coppola's Oscar-winning film provides some great snapshots of Tokyo by night.

* *Gai-Jin* (Foreigner; James Clavell) This historical novel charts Japanese politics and anti-Western sentiment in 19th-century Japan.

* *Lights Out in Wonderland* (DBC Pierre) Only one section of this novel takes place in Tokyo, but it so brilliantly captures the potential for the absurd on a night out here it's well worth a read.

* *After Dark* (Haruki Murakami) Taking in wrestlers, prostitutes, computer geeks and jazz aficionados, this seminal novel about a dreamlike night in Tokyo should have readers prepared for anything.

* *Godzilla* (1954) This all-time classic spawned monster film after monster film, but this is the original and best.

* *Tokyo Vice* (Jake Edelstein) An American journalist's account of his time immersed in Tokyo's mobster underbelly.

INDEX

❦

INDEX

INDEX

INDEX

INDEX

INDEX

GREAT ESCAPES

ENJOY THE WORLD AT YOUR LEISURE

1ST EDITION
Published August 2015

Managing Director, Publishing Piers Pickard
Commissioning Editor Robin Barton
Written by Ann Abel, Kate Armstrong, Brett, Atkinson, Andrew Bain, Sarah Barrell, Robin Barton, Sarah Baxter, Oliver Bennett, Joe Bindloss. Abigail Blasi, Catherine Bodry, Gemma Bowes, Celeste Brash, Cameron Bruhn, Austin Bush, Garth Cartwright, Nate Cavalieri, Kerry Christiani, Sophie Davies, Emilie Filou, Drew Gardam, Will Gourlay, Ben Groundwater, Roz Hopkins, Juliet Kinsman, Kim Laidlaw, Sarah Lewis, Emily Matchar, Lindsey Millar, Anja Mutic, Genevieve Paiement, Stephanie Pearson, Helen Ranger, Tim Richards, Sophy Roberts, Brendan Sainsbury, Daniel Savary Raz, Andrea Schulte-Peevers, Oliver Smith, Matt Swaine, Nick Trend, Mara Vorhees, Luke Waterson, Penny Watson
Editors Elizabeth Jones, Ali Lemer, Gabrielle Stefanos
Series Designer Mark Adams
Layout Designers Laura Jane, Katherine Marsh, Joseph Spanti
Pre-Press Production Ryan Evans
Mapping Wayne Murphy

PUBLISHED BY
Lonely Planet Publications Pty Ltd ABN 36 005 607 983
90 Maribyrnong St, Footscray, Victoria 3011, Australia
ISBN 978 1 74360 751 0
Text & maps © Lonely Planet Pty Ltd 2015
Photos © as indicated 2015

Printed in China
10 9 8 7 6 5 4 3 2 1

AUSTRALIA (HEAD OFFICE)
90 Maribyrnong St, Footscray, Victoria, 3011
Phone 03 8379 8000 **Fax** 03 8379 8111

USA
150 Linden St, Oakland, CA 94607
Phone 510 250 6400 **Toll free** 800 275 8555

UNITED KINGDOM
240 Blackfriars Road, London, SE1 8NW
Phone 020 3771 5100

FRONT & BACK COVER IMAGES **Front** (top) Rome, Italy (fotoVoyager/Getty Images); (bottom) British Virgin Islands (M. Dillon/Corbis); **Back** Québec City, Canada (Alan Copson/Corbis); prayer wheels, Bhutan (Kurt Werby/Corbis); lei, Hawaii (NJOSEPHPHOTO/Alamy) FRONT AND BACK MATTER IMAGES **Pages 2–3** The Bahamas (Alberto Pomares/ Getty Images) **Page 4** Interior, Paris (Oric1/Getty Images) **Page 6** Andalucia, Spain (Stephen Morris/Getty Images) **Page 7** Masai Mara, Kenya (Mike Hill/Getty Images) **Page 8** New York City (Michael Spry/Getty Images) **Page 310** Uluwatu beach, Bali (Kimberley Coole/Getty Images) **Page 315** Doorframe, City Palace, Jaipur (Shanna Baker/Getty Images) **Pages 318-19** Floating market, Bangkok (Mint Images/Art Wolfe/Getty Images)